War, Armed Force, and the People

War, Armed Force, and the People

State Formation and Transformation in Historical Perspective

Walter C. Opello Jr.

ROWMAN & LITTLEFIELD
Lanham • Boulder • New York • London

Published by Rowman & Littlefield
A wholly owned subsidiary of The Rowman & Littlefield Publishing Group, Inc.
4501 Forbes Boulevard, Suite 200, Lanham, Maryland 20706
www.rowman.com

Unit A, Whitacre Mews, 26-34 Stannary Street, London SE11 4AB

British Library Cataloguing in Publication Information Available

Library of Congress Cataloging-in-Publication Data

Names: Opello, Walter C.
Title: War, armed force, and the people : state formation and transformation in historical perspective / Walter C. Opello Jr.
Description: Lanham : Rowman & Littlefield Publishers, 2016. | Includes bibliographical references and index.
Identifiers: LCCN 2016027269 (print) | LCCN 2016033946 (ebook) | ISBN 9781442268791 (cloth : alk. paper) | ISBN 9781442268807 (pbk. : alk. paper) | ISBN 9781442268814 (electronic)
Subjects: LCSH: State, The--Origin. | State, The--History. | Sociology, Military.
Classification: LCC JC11 .O633 2016 (print) | LCC JC11 (ebook) | DDC 320.1/1--dc23

Printed in the United States of America

For my grandson Alec,
and
to the memory of my college roommate,
Captain William N. Payne, USAF,
killed when the B-52G on which he was copilot crashed on takeoff,
Loring AFB, Limestone, Maine, September 4, 1969.

"War is the father of all things." —Heraclitus

"War is the living fountain from which flows the entire society." —J. P. Oliveira Martins

"Without war, there would be no state." —Heinrich von Treitschke

"War made the state and the state made war." —Charles Tilly

"War is the locomotive of history." —Leon Trotsky

"War creates the people." —Jean Bethke Elshtain

Contents

Preface

This book derives from lecture notes for a course I developed and taught called "War, Technology, and the State" during the ten years preceding my retirement at the end of the fall semester 2014, from the State University of New York at Oswego. I decided to expand my notes into a book because I saw a need for a text on the interplay between war, military technology, and state formation, and the relations between the armed forces and the people in the contemporary global order. Although it was written primarily for advanced undergraduates and beginning graduate students studying political science and international relations who are uninitiated in the sub-fields of war studies and studies of the state, I believe that students all over the world who can read English, and academics not specialized in war studies and studies of the state, will find it useful as a primer to those subjects.

The book's primary theoretical argument derives from a tradition of scholarship known as the "bellicist" school of state formation. This approach is not interested in the causes of war, in general or in particular. It challenges the commonly held idea that war is *abnormal*, a disruption in the normal course of events, and accepts that war has been a *normal* part of human existence since time immemorial.[1] The bellicist approach argues that war has been good for something: It has brought into being large, organized states with strong, capable governments that have provided peace and prosperity for their peoples, brought into being citizenship and democratic forms of government, and created social welfare programs that have bettered the lives of their citizens.[2]

The book synthesizes and compresses a vast body of literature to make three related arguments regarding the interplay among war, military technology, state formation, and the relationship between the armed forces of the state and the people. First, it argues that war by powerful, predatory neighboring states has been, until relatively recently, the prime mover of state formation on the planet. Second, it argues that war no longer is the prime mover that it once was and explains why this is the case. Third, it argues that change in military technology has changed the conduct of war, which, in turn, has profoundly changed the relationship between the state, armed force, and the people.

The book is organized historically because these changes can only be discerned if they are studied over a very long span of time. It foregrounds the way that these transformations have occurred in the *West* (that is, among the Judeo-Christian peoples of Europe and states not actually in Europe but created by those peoples, such as the United States, Australia, and New Zealand) for the following reasons:

First, much more detailed knowledge is readily available about how the threat of war by predatory neighbors brought into being the states of Europe than in non-European regions of the world despite the recent advances made in the knowledge of how war formed and transformed states among various peoples of the world provided by the "new military history."[3]

Second, the book's intended primary readership, American college students, suffers from an acute case of historical ignorance with regard to the role of war in the formation of the states of the West. They do not realize that the so-called "Western Way of Warfare" and the particular form of politico-military rule (i.e., the territorial state) that it brought into being are as much a part of Western Civilization as are its great works of art, literature, music, and poetry.

Third, its primary readership is also ignorant of the fact that war *continues* to shape the relationship between states and their peoples in the West and the rest of the world. There being neither a draft nor an ongoing major inter-state war, the majority of undergraduate students do not think that war and the military have anything to do with them, their lives, and their politics. As the Russian Marxist, revolutionary, intellectual, and founder of the Soviet (Red) Army, Leon Trotsky (1879–1940), is purported to have remarked apropos of this mistaken belief, "You may not be interested in war, but war is interested in you."

Fourth, and most important, *war among states in Europe was distinctive* and is, therefore, deserving of close study. Like nowhere else on Earth, centuries of incessant warring among states of roughly the same size, the heavy use of gunpowder technology, massive military spending by their rulers, and the regular adoption of new military technologies, even from enemies,[4] gradually pushed the development of European military technologies far ahead of the development of such technologies in other regions of the world.[5] Over the centuries, European states continuously made strenuous exertions to build up their armed forces, advance their lethal military technologies, and build up the bureaucratic and fiscal infrastructures necessary to sustain them. Military competition as intense as that of Europe did not take place anywhere else on the planet.

Fifth, the lethal military technologies produced by this intense military competition, especially the gunboat and the machine gun,[6] made it possible for European states to make "war on the world," conquer and subjugate vast numbers of non-European peoples, and create a Western-dominated global order of overseas empires and spheres of influence that encompassed about 90 percent of the planet's land area.[7] The European conquest of the world *profoundly transformed the politico-military landscape of the planet* in the following ways: First, it reversed the political-military-technological dominance of certain non-European peoples who had organized the first true armies and states on the planet[8] and created a large politico-military disequilibrium in favor of the West against the Rest; that is, the non-Western world. Second, it drew boundaries and created "territorial" politico-military spaces in the form of colonies and League of Nations mandates across the planet where none had existed before. Third, it permeated these new territories with European political, economic, and social institutions, greatly modified, to exploit their human and nonhuman resources. Fourth, it curtailed war-driven state-making among non-Europeans by suppressing wars and other forms of deadly force between conquered peoples. Fifth, it made the Western armed forces the model for all armed forces and the European national state the global benchmark of the successful state. Finally, it forced already-formed non-European states, such as China and Japan, to emulate Western politico-military institutions and practices by adopting and adapting Western science and technology; building Western-style armed forces; and Westernizing their societies, economies, and governments in order to survive as sovereign states in the emerging European-created global order.[9]

The sixth reason to look at the European experience in detail is that knowing how war formed and transformed states in Europe provokes new thinking about the subject of non-European state formation, or lack thereof, in the contemporary global order.[10] Knowing that centuries of incessant war built and strengthened European states challenges the standard explanations (the disjunctures of colonialism, stresses of modernization, and economic dependency, for example) of non-European state weakness and failure. It leads one to ask: Does the "obsolescence"[11] of inter-state war in the current global order deny states the state-building benefits of incessant war against other states? This is not an unreasonable question to ask (and I am not the first to ask it)[12] in light of the overwhelming historical evidence showing that military rivalry and incessant war with neighboring states was a major factor in the production of strong states in Europe and, here and there, outside of Europe.

I have concluded from this history that the absence of inter-state war *does* keep weak states weak because they are being denied the incentives provided by predatory inter-state war to build up their administrative capabilities and give sharpness to the boundaries of their national communities. Moreover, I have concluded that the obsolescence of inter-state war debilitates and weakens strong states. And, I have concluded that a return to old-fashioned inter-state war would strengthen the capabilities of *all* states and make them less indifferent to the plight of their peoples. Some readers may think that my conclusions are those of a warmonger because they give the impression that I am arguing for more, not less, war. Readers should understand them not as arguments for war but simply as conclusions based on the knowledge of that which has gone before.

I believe that knowing how changes in military technology changed war, and how changes in modes of war changed the state, especially with regard to the relationship between the armed forces and the people, will encourage students *to think critically* about (1) the real *nature* and primary purpose of contemporary war, (2) the real *meaning* of contemporary war for states and the people who live within them, (3) the real *prospects* for successful state- and nation-building given the prohibition against war in the contemporary global order, and (4) the real *causes* of the increasing debilitation and deformation of many older, well-formed states.

Thinking critically about these matters will, I hope, encourage students to be wary about the explanations, rationales, and predictions of success given by those in the American political class who, at the drop of a hat, want to put "boots on the ground" and use air power to settle or find a solution to armed conflicts around the world. I also hope that critical thinking will encourage students to become cognizant of the great psychological, emotional, and physical costs that American interventionism in the age of the all-volunteer military has placed on that wafer-thin segment of the American people who serve in the armed forces.

Some readers may find that the book overemphasizes the role of war and does not consider other ways that states have been built and transformed, such as by the gradual expansion of their political economies.[13] Two things need to be said about this complaint. First, the historical record, which shows that war has been the essential factor in the creation and maintenance of states, cannot be refuted. Second, other factors that contributed to state-building, such as industrialization and the rise of nationalism, are *secondary* not primary phenomena that occurred alongside, or parallel to, war.

Other readers may find that the book's argument is overly simple because it draws a direct line between changes in military technology, changes in war, and changes in the form of the state without considering so-called "intervening variables" or other factors in a more "nuanced analysis." Two things need to be said about this possible complaint. First, the strong emphasis on military technology is my way of focusing the reader's attention on that which has been ignored by the discipline of political science for too long: *the role of military technology in political development and change.* Second, since the mechanization of war in the nineteenth century, technology has become an even more important factor in the transformation of war and the state than hitherto. Increasingly, technology has eliminated human beings from the so-called "battlefield" and replaced them with remotely controlled, robotic machines of war. Some scholars of war even argue that, in the Robotic Age, soldiers are *becoming* their technology.[14]

Finally, some readers may not be very happy with the book's focus on the state as an organizing concept instead of alternative concepts, such as "political system"[15] and "polity."[16] I realize that the concept of the "state" has many problems; nonetheless, I believe it is worth keeping as the book's main organizing concept. The state is a socially constructed territorial form of politico-military rule that has a certain history and relationship to the people who live within it that *sets it apart from all other forms of politico-military rule that have ever existed on planet Earth.* It has become the dominant form of politico-military rule on Earth, the land surface of which is organized into 200-plus discrete territorial units called states. The state has the power and the legitimate right to do things within its territory and to its people that no other form of rule is permitted to do. It literally has the *power of life and death* over the people who live within it. The role of war in the creation of this form of rule and the way that the contemporary norms regarding war within the current states system restrict opportunities for building strong states and weaken states already formed by war are the main threads, the leitmotif as it were, that bind the chapters of the book together.

I believe that gaining the knowledge to think more critically about the nature of war, armed force, and the relationship between the state and the people in the current world can only be achieved by pulling back from the present, because a long historical perspective allows one to discern broad patterns that make the particularity of the present easier to understand. A long historical perspective will help students comprehend our present dilemmas with regard to war and state formation, transformation, and deformation as well as the relationship between the state, armed force, and the people. Therefore, the book proceeds chronologically after the initial chapter, which presents the bellicist approach to state formation and transformation.

Chapter 1 is followed by seven chapters that present the historical transformations of war that have altered the connection between the state, armed force, and the people. In keeping with the *longue durée* approach taken to the subject, chapter 2 begins the discussion by examining the transformation of public war and the idea of armed civic virtue of the Roman imperial state to the private war of the feudal "state" in which the people had no military function. Chapter 3 shows how new weapons that utilized gunpowder encouraged the development of the centralized, coherent kingly state, which increasingly monopolized armed force by bracketing and institutionalizing

war and suppressing private armed force, beginning to change the relationship between war and the people. Chapter 4 discusses how the rise of the
twined ideas of the "nation-at-arms" and of the "citizen-soldier," as well as
certain evolutionary changes in military technology at the time of the French
Revolution, profoundly transformed the relationship between war and the
people such that the state, army, and the people were tightly bound together
into a powerful politico-military entity, the national state. Chapter 5 discusses how the techno-scientific advances in weaponry from the Industrial
Revolution onward made war a *total* struggle of national states against one
another and, consequently, made the state more managerial and increasingly
concerned with the health and well-being of its people. Chapter 6 shows how
the development of atomic weapons changed war such that the strong connection between the state, army, and the people made in the previous two
centuries became unnecessary for deterrent air-atomic war. Chapter 7 shows
how the revolution in information technology and the development of unmanned robotic weapons during the last thirty years have almost completely
eliminated the state's need of its people *en masse* to make war effectively.
Chapter 8 shifts the focus of the book to a discussion of the problem of war
and state formation, transformation, and deformation in the non-Western
regions of the world. It shows that the non-Western war/state-formation dynamic is profoundly different from that of the West, which has implications
for the weakness of many of those states. Chapter 9 concludes the book with
a discussion of the ways that the two principal modes of war in today's world
(global-policing war and internal wars) are increasingly networked, resourced, privatized, and "disconnected" from the state and people.

Included in chapters 2 through 8 are one or more concrete cases of state
formation, transformation, and deformation at different times and different
places around the world. Two things need to be said about the case studies.
First, they are deeply historical. They begin at the beginning of each state in
order to provide the long historical perspective needed to show that states
that were formed by what I call "indigenous war-driven state-making" are
more viable and less likely to weaken and collapse than "artificial" states that
have no such history because they were created by Europeans as they dominated the planet. Second, the use of a particular state to show how war
brought forth a certain form of the state does not mean that the same case
could not be used to show how another mode of war formed another type of
state. The case of the United States, for example, which is used in chapter 6
to show how nuclear weapons and deterrent air-atomic war produced the
American "national security state," could have also been used to show how
unmanned robotic weapons (i.e., drones) uncoupled the people from the
armed forces and influenced the transformation of the American managerial
welfare state into its current "neoliberal" form. The choice of cases for each
chapter was influenced by my familiarity with their histories, their relevance

for the book's theoretical arguments, and their relevance for American students because of American involvement in their formation and transformation.

NOTES

1. Azar Gat, *War in Human Civilization* (Oxford: Oxford University Press, 2006).

2. See Ian Morris, *War! What Is It Good For? Conflict and the Progress of Civilization from Primates to Robots* (New York: Farrar, Straus and Giroux, 2014). See also, Benjamin Ginsberg, *The Worth of War* (Amherst, NY: Prometheus Books, 2014). This positive view of war and the state is not shared by libertarians who see the state as a form of organized robbery and exploitation created and upheld by conquest. For a libertarian view see: Franz Oppenheimer, *The State: Its History & Development Viewed Sociologically*, trans. John Milton Gitterman (B. W. Huebsch, 1922).

3. Jeremy Black, *War and the World: Military Power and the Fate of Continents, 1450–2000* (New Haven, CT: Yale University Press, 1998).

4. Philip T. Hoffman, *Why Did Europe Conquer the World?* (Princeton, NJ, and Oxford: Princeton University Press, 2015).

5. Jeremy Black, *War and Technology* (Bloomington and Indianapolis, IN: Indiana University Press, 2013).

6. Daniel R. Headrick, *The Tools of Empire: Technology and European Imperialism in the Nineteenth Century* (New York: Oxford University Press, 1981). See also, John Ellis, *The Social History of the Machine Gun* (Baltimore, MD: The Johns Hopkins University Press, 1975).

7. Morris, *op. cit.*

8. Doyne Dawson, *The First Armies* (London: Cassell & Co., 2001).

9. Walter C. Opello Jr. and Stephen J. Rosow, *The Nation-State and Global Order: A Historical Introduction to Contemporary Politics*, Second Edition (Boulder, CO: Lynne Rienner, 2004).

10. This was the purpose of Charles Tilly (ed.) in *The Formation of National States in Western Europe* (Princeton, NJ: Princeton University Press, 1975).

11. John Mueller, *Retreat from Doomsday: The Obsolescence of Major War* (New York: Basic Books, 1989).

12. See, for example, Anna Leander, "Wars and the Unmaking of States: Taking Tilly Seriously in the Contemporary World" in Stefano Guzzini and Dietrich Jung (eds.) *Contemporary Security Analysis and Copenhagen Peace Research* (London and New York: Routledge, 2004), pp. 69–80, and Mohammed Ayoob, *The Third World Security Predicament: State Making and Regional Conflict in the International System* (Boulder, CO, and London: Lynne Rienner, 1995).

13. For example, Robert H. Bates, *Prosperity and Violence* (New York: W. W. Norton & Co., 2001) and Margaret Levi, *Of Rule and Revenue* (Berkeley, Los Angeles, London: University of California Press, 1998).

14. See, for example, Christopher Coker, *The Future of War: The Re-enchantment of War in the Twenty-First Century* (Oxford: Blackwell Publishers, 2004) and *Waging War without Warriors? The Changing Culture of Military Conflict* (Boulder and London: Lynne Rienner, Publishers, 2002).

15. David Easton, *The Political System: An Inquiry into the State of Political Science* (New York: Knopf, 1953).

16. Yale H. Ferguson and Richard W. Mansbach, *Polities: Authority, Identities, and Change* (Columbia: University of South Carolina Press, 1996).

Acknowledgments

I have profited enormously from the counsel and advice of my good friend and former colleague Stephen J. Rosow, who read an earlier draft of the manuscript and offered invaluable comments and suggestions. I am also grateful for the comments made on the manuscript by three anonymous readers whose suggestions I have worked into the final version. I especially wish to thank Marie-Claire Antoine, acquisitions editor at Rowman & Littlefield, for going the extra mile to get the manuscript approved by the editorial board. Finally, I wish to acknowledge my wife, Olivia, for proofreading the final version, and for her support and companionship throughout the nearly fifty years of our marriage. I am, of course, entirely responsible for any errors of fact that knowledgeable readers may discover.

Chapter 1

Introduction: War, State Formation, and Transformation

There is no shortage of books about war. Novels of war; scholarly works on the history of warfare; books on the sociology of the military; books on the causes of war, in general and in particular; books on decisive battles that changed the course of history; writing on strategy and tactics; memoirs of soldiers of all ranks; and works opposing war and arguing for peace fill library shelves.

Courses in American colleges and universities about war invariably focus on the causes of war or the causes of particular wars, such as the First World War, the Second World War, and America's Vietnam War. The fervent hope of those who teach these courses is that by studying the causes of particular wars, their students, when they leave the university and become full-fledged citizens, will be able to avoid the mistakes that led to them and avert future wars.[1]

Despite the existence of a huge volume of literature on the subject of war, political science in general has not seriously examined the problem of war, although there are exceptions to this rule to be mentioned below. This is surprising given the fact that war has been ubiquitous in human history.[2] It can be said that political science (and the other social sciences) have "side stepped the phenomenon of war either completely or to a great extent."[3] There are several reasons for this lack of "war studies" in American institutions of higher learning. First, and foremost, is the fact that the American academy has been strongly shaped by the pacific and rational principles of the Enlightenment. Many Enlightenment thinkers saw violence and war as pathologies of unenlightened peoples and saw rational inquiry and debate as the chief instruments of progress to civilization.[4] According to Joas and Knöbl, a "substantial number of social scientists are still caught up in the peaceful utopian mood of the European Enlightenment and continue to dream the dream of non-violent modernity."[5] Wars are dismissed as "extreme exceptions, as temporary disturbances in the civilizational equilibrium."[6] Thus, the tendency of academics has been to marginalize the study of war and treat it as an aberration, an anomaly in the normal peaceful course of history.

A second reason is the fact that war has never been a central topic within the social science disciplines. During the formative years of economics, sociology, and anthropology, far more attention was paid to "economic, social, and political inequalities than to the phenomenon of violence in general and war in particular."[7] Much attention was devoted to *individual* violence rather than *collective* or *state* violence. Violence was seen as a collapse of the social order or the loss of normative individual rationality.

A third reason for marginalizing the study of war is the strong attachment of Western social sciences to the ideology of liberalism. The liberal worldview regards war as a relic of the pre-liberal era. The philosophers who formulated the classical liberal interpretation of war (Immanuel Kant [1724–1804], Charles-Louis de Secondat Montesquieu [1689–1755], Marquis de Condorcet [1743–1794], Adam Smith [1723–1790], and Thomas Paine [1737–1809]) believed that war was caused by the martial spirit of the aristocracy and mercantilism of European monarchy, which "interfered with people's ability to pursue their natural inclination to peaceful intercourse."[8] Liberal government and free trade were seen as the solutions to the problem of war. This view of the causes of war still prevails among the vast majority of American academics who view globalized free trade and democratization as promoting global peace.

A fourth reason for the sidestepping of war as an object of study was the entry into many American and European universities of a generation of Vietnam War–era activists who brought with them strong anti-war sentiments garnered from the nuclear disarmament (Ban the Bomb) movement and protests against the American war in Vietnam that sprang up during the 1950s and 1960s. Many of this generation were critical of the participation of American universities in clandestine activities during the Cold War and the fact that certain academic disciplines, such as international relations, political science, sociology, psychology, anthropology, and sociology, were receiving government funding to do studies that helped what were seen as unjust colonial wars.[9] They were also highly critical of cooperation between the academy and conservative think tanks and foundations that were funding research aimed at perpetuating the "military-industrial complex."[10]

One does find many works by American military sociologists and military historians, however, who have studied the ethnic or class compositions of armed forces,[11] the personal characteristics that make good generals,[12] civil-military relations,[13] or landmark battles.[14] One also finds "security studies" programs at certain universities (the Olin Institute for Strategic Studies at Harvard, International Security Studies at Yale, and the Merrill Center for Strategic Studies at Johns Hopkins, for example), which are not concerned with war "per se but how to prevail in it, or more broadly, how to use military and other instrumentalities to attain or secure interests and other valued ends."[15] Therefore, none of these exceptions is sensitive to war as a social/political/technological phenomenon that deserves concentrated study as a normal, unexceptional aspect of politics; that is, a "social activity related to the whole complex of social life and organization."[16]

This book has been inspired by what has come to be called the "bellicist" approach to the study of war and the state. The bellicist approach is not interested in the causes of war but, rather, how perpetual war has acted as a general social force, especially with regard to the way that it has impacted and changed political organization. It also argues that the reciprocal impact of war on the development of political organization and political organization on the development of war can be seen only if both are studied in parallel over a very long period of time.

The history of *Homo sapiens* on planet Earth shows that social and political organization have been deeply affected by war and, in turn, war has been deeply affected by social and political organization. As Vivienne Jabri has written, "War is hence not some extra-social element that takes place outside society, but is rather both its product and implicated in its formation and transformation."[17] Essentially, "[w]ar and society stand in a dynamic interrelationship with one another. Changes in warfare affect society, while changes in society affect warfare."[18] The book accepts that the war vs. peace dichotomy is a philosophical construct. Peace is a fiction because war is always present in one mode or another.

This book is concerned with the dialectics of one of these effects: the complex interplay between war and political development. It will show how, over time, war and political organization have been mutually constitutive and reinforcing. It will show how war built the modern state and contemporary state system and how the modern state and contemporary state system have transformed and are transforming modes of war. It will reveal the extent to which war "has been a meaningful and dynamic activity, in its own right, exerting profound and complex effects on politics and culture."[19] In doing so, it will make clear the extent to which war "lurks at the heart of . . . [all] modern state[s]."[20] It argues against the prevailing liberal view that war is "an aberration, a virus that afflicts societies" in favor of the view that it is embedded in society and "is part of [political] development."[21]

WHAT IS WAR?

War is fighting.[22] There are many ways that fighting has changed over time in terms of weapons, combatants, purpose, and justification. In his classic study of war, Quincy Wright (1890–1970) defined three types of war: animal, primitive human, and modern.[23] The military historian John Keegan (1943–2012) identified two types of "warrior traditions," a primitive and a modern tradition.[24] Recently, a third type of war, variously called "new war,"[25] "wars of the third kind,"[26] "wars amongst the people,"[27] "composite wars,"[28] and "wars of national debilitation,"[29] has been identified by different scholars. The characteristics of these forms of war are discussed in turn.

Scholars of war argue that *primitive war* is as old as humankind itself. It was used to settle disputes with people outside the community, to deter external enemies, and to promote internal solidarity. According to Doyne Dawson,

> Primitive people who belong to the same descent group and form a community have sanctions against intragroup violence; neighboring communities with kinship ties usually settle disputes through arbitration; but if a man is wronged by someone from an unrelated community, there is no nonviolent recourse so he has to call on his kinsmen and start a "war." Any insult or injury will do as a reason. . . . A woman has been seduced or abducted, or a bride price has been paid and not delivered, or vice versa. . . . Other disputes may involve accusations of malicious magic, for primitive people tend to attribute all misfortunes, including natural death, to the witchcraft of the enemy. Then again, retribution may be demanded for deaths in earlier wars generating a long series of wars that go on until all blood debts have been paid.[30]

Azar Gat says that raids on other tribes were the most common mode of primitive war. Raids were started by chiefs who brought the wrong done before a warrior assembly. All males were potential warriors and an "army" consisted of the warriors who chose to join in. These warriors were usually from the chief's clan or related clans. Military leadership exercised by the chief was minimal and tactical control rudimentary. Warriors joined the raid for a variety of reasons: revenge, the capture of booty and women, or to enhance their reputations as warriors. Head taking and scalping were indications of a warrior's fighting prowess and enhanced the reputation of the individual warrior. Chiefs vied for status by staking their cause on single combat with their counterparts from the enemy tribe. Weapons were owned by each warrior and consisted of spears, axes, clubs, knives, bows and arrows, and shields. Warriors often painted their bodies and fought naked or half-naked. Chiefs led by example, in heroic fashion, alongside their companions. Battle consisted of individuals and small groups engaging in melee-style hand-to-hand fighting.[31] According to Keegan, this kind of fighting was "an act of self expression by which a man displayed not only his courage but also his individuality."[32]

According to Gat, the transition from primitive war to modern war began when tribes gained a degree of centralized political organization, a formal leadership hierarchy, and a specialized warrior class. In such societies war increasingly became an instrument for the acquisition of chiefly wealth and power. Booty (cattle, precious metals, slaves, land, etc.) taken in war became a major way that chiefs accumulated wealth and prestige among their tribesmen. Chiefs and the tribal warriors formed a more or less permanent "war band," which required frequent war fighting to stay intact. Essentially, permanent raiding for booty transformed unstratified tribal societies into stratified ones and their chiefs and their war bands into a nascent aristocracy. A successful warrior career became one of the main avenues for social advancement; consequently, young warriors were eager to join a famous warband leader in order to make their fortunes and establish themselves in the society. Together, they "formed 'retinues' or hosts of 'companion' warriors . . . making warfare their occupation, with predatory existence as its rationale. They lived and dined together."[33] Permanent war bands transformed tribal societies. Power was no longer connected solely to kinship. According to Gat,

> a new element was introduced. Chiefs and "big men" could now make use of armed retainers, dependents, and clients to throw their weight around in social dealings. These hosts [of warriors] largely came from their own clan or related clans, but also from other clans and even from outside the tribe altogether, and were bound to their patron [chief] by the supra-kin ties of economic and social benefits and obligations.[34]

The status of chiefs was determined by the size of their entourages of companion warriors. The larger the entourage, the more powerful the chief.

The primitive mode of war used stealth, ambushes, and hit-and-run-attacks. Warrior bands looted, raped, burned, killed, and extorted, which drove people to defend themselves by building and taking refuge in fortified settlements. Gradually, chiefs secured authority and control over their tribes. Chiefly power became more centralized, and more formal. The chief's warrior companions supervised the chief's domain. Chiefdoms were more hierarchical than the more egalitarian tribal societies whence they evolved. Power was no longer connected to kinship and societies became increasingly stratified. A gap appeared and gradually widened between the chief and his retinue of warrior companions (from the Latin, *com pani,* meaning, literally, those with whom he ate bread, and figuratively, those with whom he dined) on the one hand and ordinary people on the other. Incessant warring and raiding between chiefdoms caused politico-military power to become increasingly centralized, hierarchical, and formal.

As will be shown in subsequent chapters, war transformed tribal chiefdoms in a number of different places on Earth into kingdoms with rudimentary centralized administrative structures that supported the king's armies. Increasingly, war became political; that is, a way of settling conflicts and disputes between centralized, stratified, and territorial societies by force of arms.

True war, or modern war, is distinguished from primitive war by the advent of what the Prussian army officer and military theorist Carl von Clausewitz (1780–1831) called the "remarkable trinity": the "historically contingent and constantly transforming structure of people, government, and military."[35] *Modern war* involves reciprocal fighting between states to achieve a specific public/political objective through the deployment of a formally organized armed force consisting of land, sea, and air forces under the command and control of political leadership. Fighting is institutionalized and carried out by a permanent, hierarchically organized body of military professionals recruited, trained, equipped, paid, fed, supplied, and armed by the state. In modern war, killing, which is an instrumental and unavoidable cost of war, begins when war is declared and ceases once the political objectives of the war have been achieved and a truce arranged.

Over time, the armed forces of states came to have hyper-masculine subcultures clearly distinguishable from civilian society. Soldiers lived together in barracks on military bases, had their own quotidian routines, ceremonies, dress (uniforms), music, language (mostly obscene), and social function (defense of the state). Many, but not all, military subcultures instilled a code of ethical combat in their soldiers that included distinguishing "between combatant and non-combatants, legitimate and illegitimate targets, moral and immoral weaponry, and between civilized and barbarous treatment of prisoners and wounded."[36]

Before the French Revolution, there was no separation of the "military" from the "civilian." For the Greeks, war was inevitable, even an essential part of life, and therefore the Greek city-state was a community of warriors. For the Romans, armed civic virtue was expected of all male citizens and valor in war was virtue (*virtus*) itself.[37] According to David Bell, "the men who dominated Old Regime [i.e., pre–French Revolutionary] societies did not draw sharp lines between their professional role as military officers and their social identity as aristocrats."[38] In other words, before the French Revolution, for men at least, there was no distinction between being a civilian and a soldier.

After the French Revolution and the rise of the national state, a hard and fast distinction between civilian and military life came into being. The French Revolutionaries, especially Maximilien Robespierre (1758–1794), strongly absorbed the thinking of Jean-Jacques Rousseau (1712–1778), who believed that all males must defend *la nation une et indivisible* by force of arms when under siege by enemies from within and without. Therefore, male citizens were subjected to conscription (*levée en masse*) and expected to serve in the nation's armed forces during times of military crisis. It is important to note that in Rousseau's notion of armed civic virtue there remains a distinction between the *public* and the *private* such that the male citizen remains a private individual/citizen but "should stand prepared to give up 'civilian' life in times of national emergency and cross the boundary into the *distinct realm* of the 'military'"[39] and become *soldiers* (from the Latin, *soldi,* meaning those who fight for pay); that is, individuals recruited, trained, and licensed to use weapons and fight on behalf of the state. War became a public function that may be waged only for reasons of state (*raisons d'état*). Soldiers are permitted to fight and kill for the state only when in uniform and under the command of officers who can be held accountable for their actions to higher state authority. Thus, according to the anthropologist Harry Turney-High (1899–1982), the transition from primitive war to modern war is marked by the "rise of an army with officers."[40]

Modern war gradually came to be highly institutionalized and seen by European states as the last resort when other means, such as diplomacy and sanctions, failed to gain compliance. After war is declared it must be waged by the state within certain "laws of war," such as the 1863 Instructions for the Government of Armies of the United States in the Field (General Order No. 100), also known as the Leiber Code; the Hague Conventions of 1899, 1907, and 1922; the Geneva Conventions of 1864, 1906, and 1929; and the Geneva Protocols of 1949 and 1977, that have been agreed upon and signed by many, but not necessarily all, states. The purpose of these conventions and protocols was to limit and restrain the conduct of war by "(1) identifying legitimate and illegitimate targets, (2) specifying rules of conduct with regard to prisoners, civilians, and the wounded, (3) outlawing the use of certain weapons, (4) prohibiting the deliberate killing of distinct civilian groups, and (5) defining the legal status of belligerents, that is, identifying parties to be bound by the laws of war."[41]

It should be noted that European states ignored the laws of war, especially when engaged in extra-state wars of conquest outside of the European continent against non-European peoples, but also against one another, as, for example, when the Germans used chlorine gas against British and Commonwealth troops in the Second Battle of Ypres (April 22, 1915) during the First World War in clear violation of the First Hague Convention's prohibition of poisonous and asphyxiating gases.

European states also ignored the laws of war when war became total, the most extreme form of modern war. *Total war* is indiscriminate in the application of force. States waging total war ignore the distinction between the military personnel of the armed forces and the civilian population, and do not distinguish civilian places, such as cities, towns, seats of government, and factories, from the military forces and facilities of the enemy state. In total war, the warring states *abandon all restraint* in the conduct of war. They mobilize all of their human, economic, industrial, and technological resources in order to annihilate the enemy's armed forces, occupy its territory, and transform the enemy's society and government. In total war, the distinction between combatant and noncombatant is ignored and civilians are deliberately targeted by air forces in an attempt to break the enemy's will to fight. In total war, unconditional surrender is demanded. According to Jeremy Black, the Age of Total War began with the American Civil War in 1860 and ended upon the completion of the Second World War in 1945. During this period, "the range (geographical and/or chronological) of conflict, the nature of the goals, and the extent to which civil society was involved in war . . . was, at once, more intense and more extensive than hitherto."[42]

Many scholars of war have observed that wars between states with organized armed forces that clash on designated battlefields have become very rare since the end of the Second World War. Keegan believed that war was "ceasing to commend itself to human beings as a desirable or productive, let alone rational, means of reconciling their discontents."[43] Steven Pinker has amassed a vast quantity of statistical evidence that demonstrates the declining trajectory of inter-state war, especially since 1945.[44] Nonetheless, certain regions of planet Earth are still wracked by fighting that resembles war that is variously called "new war," "wars of the third kind," "wars amongst the people," "composite wars," and "wars of national debilitation." Essentially, fighting since 1945 has been transformed from "pitched battles between organized forces [of states] into more fragmented, uncontrolled, and indeterminate series of military events."[45] In this book these wars will be known collectively as "post-modern war."

According to John Mueller, there are two basic types of *post-modern war*: low-intensity localized wars *within* poor non-Western states and "militarized efforts by developed countries to bring order to [such] civil conflicts."[46] Of Mueller's first type, which can be called *"internal war,"* Holsti says that the purpose of the fighting is usually one of the following: (1) to create a new state by ending what is seen as illegitimate rule by outsiders; (2) to reunify a real or imagined political community; or (3) to secede from a political community to form a new state.[47] Internal wars can also entail fighting among "all types of 'militias,' gangs of thugs, professional racketeers, drug runners, and hopped up, testosterone toxic children"[48] that resembles war. It can also include wars waged by the state against certain categories of its people defined racially, linguistically, religiously, and/or ethnically that the state seeks to eliminate from the body politic.[49]

Mueller calls the second basic type of post-modern war "policing war." *Policing wars* are fought by advanced Western states for the following reasons: (1) to put an end to internal wars; (2) to end the killing of civilians; (3)

to reconstruct state institutions in so-called "failed states"; and (4) to establish liberal political and economic institutions.[50] In such wars there are no enemy states to be defeated in modern war fashion, only "bad guys" (usually identified as terrorists, crime bosses, drug lords, pirates, warlords, and tyrants) who must be apprehended, tried, sent to prison, or executed for war crimes or crimes against humanity.

It should not be assumed that Mueller's two types of post-modern fighting are disconnected phenomena. They are, in fact, intertwined. As will be shown in chapters 8 and 9, both internal wars and policing wars intersect most commonly in non-Western states. Mark Duffield has suggested that internal wars and policing wars are "networked"; that is, "instead of conventional armies [engaging one another on a defined battlefield] the post-modern wars typically oppose and ally the trans-border resources networks of state incumbents, social groups, diasporas, strongmen, and so on."[51] In post-modern internal war, "[t]he political and . . . economic support of the masses becomes superfluous; [because] the resources vital to waging war can be requisitioned without mass support, resulting in an endless spiral of violence."[52] Since 1945 there has been a dramatic increase in the number and duration of post-modern internal wars.[53]

It should be noted that earlier modes of war are never completely replaced by later modes. Primitive war is still being fought in places on the planet where tribal ties are strong and state control is weak to nonexistent, such as in Somalia and Papua New Guinea. Gang wars in American cities and other cities around the world are not unlike primitive war.[54] Post-modern war is not a fundamental rupture with modern war with respect to goals, methods, and combat financing. Many of its elements were present in the period of modern war, especially in the wars of European colonial conquest and expansion in which private economic interests, private capital, and actors were heavily involved in military activity. Post-modern internal wars are also connected to modern war through the

> large stocks of surplus weapons built up during the Cold War that became available as the competitive engagement of the superpowers in the Third World wound down; the selling off in the 1990s by former Warsaw Pact countries of non-NATO standard equipment[;] . . . the creation of semi-official and secret arms pipelines that have continued to fuel war in the aftermath of the Cold War; [and] the privatization of Cold War security services and intelligence outfits, some of whose members have found new work as "conflict entrepreneurs" and "violence specialists" on the African continent and elsewhere.[55]

Even the savagery, brutality, and atrocities of today's internal wars (e.g., beheadings, ethnic cleansing, sexual violence, local massacres, indiscriminate bombardment of urban areas, etc.) have precedence in modern war.

Colonial wars of pacification and imperial control waged by European states against non-European peoples resulted in their extermination, and, during the Second World War, fourteen million civilians were systematically murdered by German and Soviet armies in the "bloodlands" of Eastern Europe.[56] The Japanese Imperial Army abducted thousands of women and girls from their homes in occupied territories and forced them into sexual slavery. The United States Army Air Corps and the British Royal Air Force immolated and asphyxiated hundreds of thousands of civilians in firestorms created when they dropped incendiary devices on Japanese and German cities.

WHAT IS THE STATE?

This is a difficult question to answer easily, because the word "state" conjures multiple meanings and associations and because in the English language the words "state," "nation," and "country" are used interchangeably. This problem is compounded for Americans because they believe that the United States does not constitute a "state." This misconception exists, in part, because the Founding Fathers never used the word when speaking or writing about the new politico-military entity they were creating in Philadelphia during the summer of 1787. Instead, they called it a "republic," or a "union." When they used the word "state" they were referring to one of the thirteen constituent parts of the new entity (New York, Virginia, Connecticut, etc.) or to Britain or France. Most Americans do not realize that the Founders came from states that had won their independence separately from Britain and had been brought together as a league of friendship under the Articles of Confederation. Thus, today, the word "state" to an American means one of the several constituent parts of the union, such as New York State, or the State of California. Americans tend to use the words "nation" or "country" to refer to what is meant by the word "state" in this book.

Another reason the concept of the "state" is difficult to impart is because the "state," like war, is no longer an object of study by political scientists and rarely the subject of courses in political science. Throughout the nineteenth century and the early twentieth century, the state received much scholarly attention. It needed to be explained and understood by political scientists who were at that time professors of law, history, and philosophy. These scholars focused their attention on the formal-legal aspects of the state; that is, its constitution and governmental institutions, especially those of the major European powers, which were seen as the epitome of the well-developed state.

After the Second World War, especially among American political scientists, scholarly attention shifted away from the formal-legal institutions of the state to the "informal" politics within society because it was thought that formal-legal studies were too narrow and missed the "real" politics that lay hidden behind state institutions. This new theory of politics, which came to be called "pluralism,"[57] studied the ways in which social classes and civil associations of the people, organized into political parties and interest groups, pressured the institutions of government to produce certain public policy outcomes. Pluralists assumed that "society" was separate from and prior to the state. The state, understood as "the government," was seen as less important than the other groups in society, such as labor unions and civic associations, and was seen as simply responding passively to what these groups wanted or pressured it to do. In short, politics was to be explained by what happened in society and the state, *cum* government, was reduced to being little more than a subordinate institution that responded to the pressures put upon it by outside political and economic forces. An unfortunate result of this paradigm shift was that "many of the important insights of our forebears [who studied the state were] . . . erased from memory."[58] The state was replaced by the "political system."[59]

The paradigm shift in political science away from the state to the political system was reinforced by the decolonizations after the Second World War that brought forth a plethora of so-called "new," "emerging," "developing" states in what came to be known as the "Third World," and now called by some scholars the "global south." A new paradigm called "modernization theory" came into being. Modernization theory, like pluralism, moved away from the state in an effort to extend the range of political science beyond the developed states of the West and into the Third World by separating out analytically the structures that perform the essential political functions in all societies no matter their geographical location or level of development.

The paradigm shift away from the state to the political system was unfortunate because the rise of the modern state was, without a doubt, the most important development in human history on the planet. The modern state, which has eclipsed all other types of politico-military rule that have existed on Earth, is, and will continue to be for the foreseeable future, the basic building block of the global order. Every square kilometer of the planet, except Antarctica, falls within the exclusive domain of one state or another.

The following attributes are generally recognized as the common currency of the modern state: First, it has a distinctive, *geographically demarcated territory* over which it claims exclusive authority. Its territory is represented by lines on a map and demarcated on the ground by entry and exit points, and, in some cases, fences patrolled by border guards and armies. Second, it has *sovereignty* over its territory, which is, theoretically, absolute, indivisible, and unlimited. This means that the state's jurisdiction is exclusive of all outside interference by other states or international organizations, such as the United Nations. Third, it has *institutions of governance* made up of the public offices and officials (elected and appointed) who rule and administer the territory and people within the state's jurisdiction. Fourth, it has, to a greater or lesser degree, a *monopoly on the legitimate use of the means of physical coercion* (i.e., the police and the armed forces) over its territory and people. The greater the degree of this monopoly the stronger the state, the lesser the degree the weaker the state. Fifth, it has a *nation*; that is, it contains a people who believe themselves united by some set of characteristics (language, culture, religion, etc.) that differentiate them from outsiders, which coincides, more or less, with the state's territory, and who are prepared to take up arms to defend it.[60]

It should be noted that the modern state is an abstraction, an idea that exists in the minds of its people and its officials above and beyond the formal institutions of governance, and cannot be seen or touched. A state is much like a corporation, university, church, or trade union in that it "possesses a legal *persona* of its own, which means that it has rights and duties and may engage in activities *as if* it were a real, flesh-and-blood, living individual."[61]

It should also be noted that the modern state is not imbedded within a pre-existing society and, therefore, simply one "polity" among many competing polities, as some scholars contend, that make it undeserving of its special status.[62] In fact, the state has special rights and duties under international law that set it apart from other polities that may exist on the globe, such as families, clans, tribes, and cities. One of the most important of these rights is the right to make war when warranted. Only states are allowed by the international community of states to arm themselves in order to preserve their sovereignty, avoid dismemberment, and defend their people. Only states can decide to go to war, legally demand military service of their people, and require that they unhesitatingly kill designated enemies of the state, and, possibly, be killed by those enemies. International law and the agreement among the global community of states prohibits non-state forms of politico-military rule from doing these things.[63] Non-state entities that make war operate outside of the laws of war and individuals who participate in such war are "unlawful combatants" and may be detained and prosecuted by state authorities.

It should also be noted that no modern state, not even the oldest and most developed, manifests all the characteristics of the state given above fully and completely. There is always a degree of "contestation" between individuals and groups, sometimes armed, within the state's jurisdiction and the state itself.[64] Many states in the Third World contain within them a multiplicity of competing non-state entities (clans, tribes, sectarian groups, etc.) that challenge the state's territorial integrity and its monopoly over the means of physical coercion. In some cases, such as Somalia, Libya, and Iraq, the state manifests almost none of these characteristics of the modern state and can be said to be hollow shells with governments that do not have a monopoly of the means of legitimate physical coercion and face a high degree of contentiousness by the clans and tribes within their legally recognized jurisdictions. In the United States, the contestation between the state and its people usually involves fulminations by individuals and groups, such as the Tea Party faction of the Republican Party, against "big government" and filibusters in the Senate to stop the enactment into law of "another big government program."[65] It has also been manifested in the United States by violent means from time to time, such as the New York City draft riots of 1863 and the anti–Vietnam War protests of the late 1960s and early 1970s.

Finally, it should be noted that transformations of the state system from one historical epoch to another are never "clean" and "neat." A certain number of previously existing forms of politico-military rule survive into subsequent periods despite the fact that they were less efficient makers of war and should have disappeared from the system and despite the fact that they have a form of governance at variance with the form that is accepted as legitimate in that period. Vatican City, for example, the world's smallest (109 acres/44 hectares) juridically sovereign state, is the remnant of the once powerful and legitimate Papal States that transversed the midsection of the Italian Peninsula during the Middle Ages. It exists not because of the superior war-making abilities of its popes, who had armies at one time, but, rather, because powerful states within the current states system recognize its sovereignty and permit it to exist, especially the Italian state within which it is entirely enclosed.

The fact that no state manifests without fault all the attributes of the state presented above does not mean that the concept of the state should be abandoned in favor of a new conception of politico-military space, such as "nested polities."[66] It should always be kept in mind that the "interstate system and the states that make it up are constantly being renegotiated and the modern state is as much a product of the *agreements among states* as it is agreements between governments and the populations they govern."[67] The state remains a powerful form of territorial politico-military rule and the focus of the collective identity for millions and millions of people on Earth. The real question is, why do some states manifest most of the characteristics of the state given above and others do not? This book suggests an answer that is little considered today: war.

WHENCE CAME THE STATE?

Theories about how the state came into being are generally of two types: consensus theories and conflict theories. *Consensus* theories of state formation hold that "at some point in their histories, certain peoples *spontaneously, rationally, and voluntarily* gave up their individual sovereignties and united with other communities to form a larger political unit deserving to be called a state."[68] The best known of such theories is that of Thomas Hobbes

(1588–1679), who hypothesized that without a state, people lived in a "state of nature" plagued by war "where every man is Enemy to every man," which made the "life of man, solitary, poore, nasty, brutish, and short."[69] According to Hobbes people living in a state of nature *agree among themselves to create a state*, which he called "a sovereign power," to defend themselves from "the invasion of Forraigners, and the injuries of one another, and thereby to secure them in such sort, as that by their owne industrie, and by the fruites of the Earth, they may nourish themselves and live contentedly."[70]

Another well-known consensus theory of early state formation is the "hydraulic hypothesis" of Karl Wittfogel (1896–1988), who argued that the early state came into being when "an experimenting community of farmers, or protofarmers, finds large sources of moisture in a dry but potentially fertile area, a number of farmers eager to conquer [agriculturally] arid lowlands and plains are forced to invoke the organizational devices of *premachine* technology—offer the one chance of success: they must work in cooperation with their fellows and [voluntarily] subordinate themselves to a directing authority."[71]

Conflict theory, on the other hand, argues that *conquest* brought the state into being. The first conflict theories were articulated by European academics and jurists, such as the Pole Ludwig Gumplowicz (1838–1909), the Austrian Gustav Ratzenhofer (1842–1904), and the German Franz Oppenheimer (1864–1943). Oppenheimer, for example, wrote that the early European state emerged when the productive capacity of settled agriculturalists combined with the energy of pastoral nomads through the conquest of the former by the latter.[72]

According to Robert Carneiro, the problem with consensus theories of early state formation is that no "social contract," as described by Hobbes, was ever subscribed to by human groups, and archaeological evidence has shown that in the areas that Wittfogel cites as exemplifying his hydraulic hypothesis (Mesopotamia, China, and Mexico), full-fledged states developed well before large-scale irrigation projects (i.e., the building of canals) were undertaken.[73] He also argues that the problem with the conquest theories of Gumplowicz, Ratzenhofer, and Oppenheimer is that pastoral nomadism arose in Europe after the earliest states had emerged, and was unknown in aboriginal America where states arose in Mesoamerica.

Despite the deficiencies noted, Carneiro believes that only a coercive theory can account for the rise of the early state:

> There is little question that, in one way or another, war played a decisive role in the rise of the state. Historical or archaeological evidence of war is found in the early stages of state formation in Mesopotamia, Egypt, India, China, Japan, Greece, Rome, northern Europe, central Africa, Polynesia, Middle America, Peru, and Columbia, to name only the most prominent examples.[74]

He cites approvingly the British professor of law Edward Jenks (1861–1939), who wrote in his book *History of Politics*[75] that "historically speaking, there is not the slightest difficulty in proving that all political communities of the modern type [that is, states] owe their existence to successful warfare."[76]

What of the modern state? Does conflict and war account for its rise and proliferation across the globe? This question was not even thought about, much less asked, by American political science until the 1970s for two reasons. First, the state had become so ubiquitous on the planet by that time that its existence was taken for granted by political scientists and was rarely noticed, even by scholars of international relations.[77] Second, the discipline was enthralled by "modernization theory," which focused on the development of societies, not states.

Modernization theory posited stages, sequences, paths, or problems in the formation of modern societies. Cyril Black (1915–1989), for example, defined four critical problems: the challenge of modernity, the consolidation of modernizing leadership, economic and social transformation, and the integration of society.[78] A. F. K. Organski (1923–1998) saw societal modernization taking place in four stages: the politics of primitive unification, the politics of industrialization, the politics of national welfare, and the politics of abundance.[79] Leonard Binder (1927–) and others proposed a scheme that enumerated a series of challenges or crises faced by any society undergoing political development: penetration, integration, participation, identity, legitimacy, and distribution. The idea was that the accumulation of crises results in a high degree of societal strain and, therefore, a greater likelihood of intense social conflict and change.[80] Samuel Huntington (1927–2008) sought to show how democratic stability depends on the symmetry between the process of mobilization and the process of institutionalization. "Political modernization involves the rationalization of authority, the differentiation of structures, and the expansion of political participation."[81]

Alternatives to sequence theories posited strong relationships among different types of changes without suggesting a particular developmental path. Sociologists showed that urbanization and industrialization frequently occur together and reinforce one another but did not specify which occurs first.[82] Political scientists argued that complexity in one sphere of society, such as the economy, is followed by complexity in another, but did not specify which occurred first. The sociologist Talcott Parsons (1902–1979) saw the formation of modern governments as the inevitable accompaniment of complexity in other social realms, such as the economic realm, but did not specify which occurred first.[83]

There were two major problems with these modernization theories. First, they contained "absolutely no discussion of the organizational structure of states."[84] Second, like pluralist theory, they were "particularly neglectful of the topic of violence . . . [and] clung to the Enlightenment faith in progress."[85] Consequently, coercion, violence, and war were completely ignored as factors in the modernization of societies.

These shortcomings began to be overcome in the 1970s when modernization theory finally came under intellectual scrutiny by political scientists who began to focus explicitly on the state as an object of study. These scholars examined how the state had functioned historically both as an organization of domination and as a promoter of the public good. The scholars who sought to "bring the state back in"[86] to the study of politics argued that the state was not just one institution among the many within a certain territorial space but could be understood as an independent entity that was superior to and transcended all other groups and associations within its territory, and which could take independent action, even against the wishes of the groups and associations within it.

The avoidance of the role of war and armed force in social and political development was eventually challenged by scholars who saw development as being violent in nature and believed that power and coercion were part of the process of modernization. The first such challenge came from Reinhard Bendix (1916–1991), who saw that modernization theory was ahistorical and was skeptical about its assumption of linearity of the process and the idea of equilibrium between the "political system" and other social systems. For Bendix, the use or threat of violence always plays a central role in politics. He showed that political development was by no means linear and demonstrated how different uses of force will induce different forms of the state.[87]

Bendix's work caused some scholars to wonder if the history of the origins and development of the modern European state would shed light on the problems and prospects of political development in the new states of the Third World. In 1975, Charles Tilly (1929–2008), who had become one of the leading American scholars of protest, edited a volume (the ninth and last book of a series of works produced by the Social Science Research Council [SSRC] on the subject of political development) that examined the European history of state formation. This volume challenged the conventional picture painted by modernization theory by showing that European states were the "unintended outcomes of the efforts of European state-makers to build their armies, keep taxes coming in, form effective coalitions against their rivals, hold their nominal subordinates and allies in line, and fend off the threat of rebellion on the part of ordinary people."[88] The European state, he said, came about because of the intimate connection between the conduct of war, the building of armies, the extension of regular taxation to support those armies, and the growth of a state apparatus to administer them.

The Tilly volume did more than any other to make the connection between war, the building of armed forces, and the making of modern states. In Europe, at least, Tilly concluded, "[p]reparations for war has been the great state-building activity. The process has been going on more or less constantly for at least five hundred years."[89]

WAR AND MODERN STATE FORMATION

The idea that war is a major cause in the formation and strengthening of the state is not new, however. It has been around for a long time. In his classic study of the causes of war, Kenneth Waltz (1924–2013) wrote that the Greek philosopher Aristotle (365–322 BCE) "argued that the political structure of the state may be greatly affected by its military organization and that the type of military organization necessary may in turn be determined by such extra-political factors as geographic location."[90] He also said that the sixteenth-century French lawyer, political philosopher, and member of the Parlement of Paris, Jean Bodin (1530–1596), believed that war promoted the internal unity of the state. For Bodin, a state plagued by internal strife, such as sedition, rebellion, and civil war, might start a war in order to "keep the subjects in amity one with the other."[91] The English historian Edward Gibbon (1737–1794), the author of *The History of the Decline and Fall of the Roman Empire*, believed that the pressure of military competition within a network of rival states affected the nature of those states.[92]

At the end of the nineteenth century and the beginning of the twentieth century the relationship between war and state-making was formalized in a law-like way by two European scholars, the Cambridge historian John Robert Seeley (1834–1895) and the German constitutional historian Otto Hintze (1861–1940). Seeley and Hintze argued that political development cannot be conceived of as a dynamic completely internal to the state. Seeley wrote that one should "[n]ever be content with looking at states purely from within; always remember that they have another aspect which is wholly different; their relations with foreign states."[93]

Hintze wrote more than fifty monographs and articles attacking the work of scholars of his day who sought to understand political development purely in terms of internal factors. He argued that his contemporaries had failed to understand the importance of external factors in the political development of states, especially the threat of war by powerful neighbors. Political development cannot be understood, he wrote, by examining single states in isolation "from the context in which it was formed . . . exclusive in itself, without raising the question whether its particular character is co-determined by its relation to its surroundings."[94]

The connection between the internal political development of a state and its external threat environment was formalized by Seeley and Hintze as follows: "The degree of government will be directly proportional, and that means that the degree of liberty will be inversely proportional, to the degree of [external] pressure." And, "Intense government is the reaction against intense pressure, and on the other hand liberty, or relaxed government, is the effect of relaxed pressure."[95] The evidence for their proposition was the intensity of government in France and Prussia in contrast to the slackness of government in Britain and the United States.

Drawing on Seeley's observation, Hintze wrote two essays in 1913 and 1914 in which he showed how the constant threat of war affected the political development of European states with respect to three major aspects of the state: its armed forces, its government, and its parliament. He pointed out in these essays that Europe had two basic types of states, the British and the Continental European. He noted that by the seventeenth century states on the continent were becoming increasingly centralized, bureaucratic, and absolutist while in Britain the monarchy was being weakened and Parliament strengthened. Hintze argued that the cause of this difference in political development was the different *threat environments* in which the states existed. The British monarchy was isolated from the monarchies on the continent by the English Channel; therefore, it did not have to build a large standing army, a powerful bureaucracy, and an absolute monarchy to control them because it did not have powerful threatening neighbors immediately adjacent. In contrast, the monarchies on the continent were in immediate proximity to one another; consequently, the environment in which they existed was highly threatening, in military terms, which required them to develop large and expensive standing armies, powerful and efficient bureaucracies to maintain them, and absolute monarchies to control them.[96]

Tilly, like Seeley and Hintze, realized that the key factor in the development of Europe's states was military rivalry and incessant warfare, which produced a state-forming dynamic, to wit:

> Taxation was the chief means by which the builders of states in the sixteenth century and later supported their expanding armies, which were in turn their principle instrument in establishing control of their frontiers, pushing them out, defending them against external incursions, and assuming their own priority in the use of force within those frontiers. . . . So turned the tight circle connecting state-making, military institutions, and the extraction of scarce resources from a reluctant population.[97]

In the years following the publication of the final volume of the SSRC series, Tilly elaborated the conflict theory of European state formation. In several subsequent books he showed in great detail how the "organizational and technological innovations in warfare of the fifteenth and sixteenth century" gave European monarchies with "access to large volumes of men and capital a clear advantage" and gave them the ability "to draw mass armies from their citizens" and give them the means "to defeat smaller units."[98]

A number of scholars followed Tilly's lead. For example, Rodney Hall showed that the units that were able to construct a coherent collective identity within territorially segmented units that overrode regional, class, and religious loyalties mobilized "entire societies and transformed entire economies for war."[99] Hendrik Spruyt showed how Europe's threatening environment encouraged monarchs to use their territorial authority to build uniform, centrally administered, territorially wide systems of law, taxation, weights and measures, coinage, and tariffs, which regularized the realm and made the extraction of men, money, and matériel to make war more efficiently and effectively.[100] Basing his work on that of Seeley and Hintze, Brian Downing showed how war influenced the development of both democratic and autocratic government in Europe. He argued that late medieval Europe had certain "constitutional arrangements" that "if combined with light amounts of domestic mobilization of human and economic resources for war, provided the basis for democracy in ensuing centuries."[101] Conversely, he argued monarchies confronted by a highly threatening environment that required extensive resource mobilization produced military-bureaucratic absolutism in subsequent centuries.

Bruce Porter has summarized the way that war has acted as a powerful force for change within states: When they wage war, political leaders are able to undertake a whole range of activities that would be difficult, if not impossible, in peace time. Porter points out that many of the great reforms in European and American history, such as granting the right to vote to the working class and to women, and, in the United States, to eighteen-year-olds, occurred either during or immediately after major wars. War encourages the territorial consolidation of weak states into fewer, larger, stronger ones. War promotes internal integration by uniting the state's people behind the war effort. Political cooperation (bipartisanship in the United States) increases and agreement reigns during wartime. Full citizenship rights denied certain groups, such as immigrants, are granted with military service. War encourages the centralization of the state's governing institutions so that the government can mobilize the men, money, and matériel to wage war successfully. War concentrates power in the executive. It rationalizes the administrative apparatus of the state in order to improve the ability of the state to extract more of what it needs to fight war successfully. War increases popular demands for social reform. This results in the improvement and expansion of domestic welfare programs as a reward to the population for making great sacrifices during the war. War contributes to the growth of the state's taxing and spending. War has a socializing effect as mass conscription brings large numbers of young men into the armed forces where they learn that they are part of a single nation and trained to defend it. In other words, military service welds individuals from diverse walks of life, races, and ethnic groups into a unified nation. At the same time, military service erodes class, racial, religious, and ethnic differences because individuals from all categories of the state's people are recruited, trained, and deployed in defense of the nation. Finally, Porter writes that war helps create a sense of national identity by connecting the fate of the people to that of the state.[102]

The above works, when taken together, constitute what has come to be called the the *"bellicist" theory of state formation*, which can be summarized as follows:

> First, states survived, defeated other states and incorporated their territory, grew and prospered by mobilizing the resources, weaponry, and men to fight wars. The institutional apparatus of the modern state grew out of this war-making function, as cycles of extraction and coercion succeeded one another. Second, in order to mobilize the resources and men for war, the rulers of states had to offer inducements to subjects who gradually acquired the rights of modern citizenship, including those of equality before the law, universal suffrage, and parliamentary representation, as well as (in some cases) universal education and the social rights of the welfare state. Third, in developing its "warfighting" capacity, the state gradually developed a near monopoly on legitimate violence, disarming its civilian population and gradually accumulating an overwhelming superiority of force vis-à-vis social actors. Fourth, military power was gradually "caged" by civilian institutions, and the state's coercive forces came to be divided between specialists in fighting external war (the military) and uniformed but civilian forces responsible for domestic order (the police).[103]

The developmental success of the state as a form of politico-military rule is not due to war and the "logic of territoriality" alone, however. According to Carneiro, "warfare is surely the prime mover in the origin of the state, [but] it cannot be the only factor."[104] While war is the *mechanism* of state formation, the *conditions* under which it gave rise to the state must be specified.

For early states, Carneiro specifies "circumscribed agricultural land," which sharply delimited the area that simple farming peoples could occupy and cultivate as their numbers grew. Hence, they could not flee and had to fight in order to gain more arable land to feed a growing number of people.[105] For modern states, the most significant condition is the gradual and simultaneous construction of a *system of similarly organized states* from which emanate pressures and demands that states *within* the system conform to the emerging idea of what constitutes legitimate politico-military rule by the dominant states in the system. States that violate the dominant organizational logic come to be viewed as illegitimate by the "system" and are forced to adapt themselves to it or be eliminated from it. As Hendrik Spruyt has written, "Sovereign actors only recognize particular types of actors as legitimate players in the international system."[106] Such pressure has gradually resulted in a global system of states that is increasingly similar in terms of the internal economic, political, and social organization of the states that make it up. In Cerney's words:

> A state's relations with other states have historically had a mutually reinforc-
> ing effect on state structures. States may be in competition and conflict with
> each other, but their very character as states was born out of, has been nurtured
> by, and is reinforced through the fact that their external environment has been
> increasingly dominated by other states. State structures have tended to repro-
> duce themselves—both internally and externally—and to expand their scope
> and range. [107]

Moreover, Cynthia Weber has shown that the increasing alignment around a common organizational format involves violations of sovereignty by the interventions of some states into the internal affairs of other states, which are justified by reference to the state's violation of the accepted norms that regulate the legitimate organizational structure of states. In other words, a system of states forms an "interpretive community" that judges violations of sovereignty in terms of the extant norms of the state system. When a state's internal organization does not "fit the intersubjective understandings of what a sovereign state must be, then interference by a sovereign state into the affairs of an 'aberrant' state is [seen as] legitimate."[108] As will be demon-strated in subsequent chapters, what constitutes legitimate sovereign state-hood has different meanings in different historical eras. Weber has shown that powerful hegemonic states seek to reproduce equivalent forms of politi-co-military rule by disciplining and regulating the sovereignty of non-con-forming so-called "aberrant," "deviant," or "rogue," states. The power to discipline and regulate the states in the system is usually claimed by one or more "correcting states," such as the United States, the European Union, or the African Union, which act on behalf of the extant norms and organizing principles of the system and sub-systems of states.[109]

In effect, as Andreas Osiander has pointed out, the biggest and most powerful states in the system act as a kind of "management committee," or in Weber's words, "a community of judgment," which takes it upon itself to maintain the system according to the prevalent conception of legitimate state organizational practices. Thus, the existence and survival of a state depends on both "internal" and "external" factors. A state's sovereignty is codeter-mined by actions at the state and state-system levels simultaneously. It can be shown historically that if less-powerful rival forms of politico-military rule hoped to survive in a particular era, they had to mimic the dominant/legiti-mate forms of politico-military rule by reforming their internal governing, economic, and social structures to mirror those of the dominant forms. Those forms of politico-military rule that refused to conform were forced to do so by the dominant states, which form a "community of judgment" through various means of intervention, which range from "external scrutiny" to "imposition" by force.[110] The ultimate price for refusal to adopt the dominant forms and principles was elimination from the system.

The extent to which the relationship between war and state formation still obtains in the current global order will be discussed in chapter 8.

THE ROLE OF MILITARY TECHNOLOGY

Martin van Creveld maintains that

> war is completely permeated by technology and governed by it. The causes that lead to wars . . . the blows with which campaigns open . . . the relationship between the armed forces and the societies that they serve . . . even the very conceptual frameworks employed . . . in order to think about war and its conduct—not one of these is immune to the impact that technology has had.[111]

Despite its importance, the impact of military technology on war and state formation has been mostly ignored by those who have employed the bellicist theory of state formation. This will not be the case in this book. Innovations in military technology and the way they have impacted war and the state are foregrounded in the following chapters.

The pattern that the history of changes in military technology reveals is the same pattern one can see for *all* technology, to wit: change to achieve greater and greater *efficiency* and *effectiveness* in the intended use of the technology.[112] In the case of military technologies, achieving greater efficiency and effectiveness means finding the "one best way" to kill the enemy while sustaining the fewest casualties possible to one's own armed forces. In general, this search has led to the invention, refinement, and production of weapons capable of *actualizing violence at greater and greater distances and with greater and greater lethality.* Historically, close combat with primitive slashing and piercing weapons was replaced by the distant combat and the greater lethality of gunpowder weapons, which in turn was replaced by even more distant combat and the greater lethality of machine weapons, which was replaced by the extreme distant combat of super-lethal atomic and unmanned robotic weapons. The search for the one best way to kill the enemy with the fewest casualties to one's own forces resulted in the marriage of science and technology to warfare, especially since the beginning of the sixteenth century, and has brought into being a "scientific way of warfare."[113]

The distinction between *innovations* and *revolutionary changes* in the scientific way of war needs to be made. Technological modifications that give greater firepower to certain types of weapons, such as the shift from the matchlock to the flintlock musket and the shift from finely ground to "corned" gunpowder, are innovations, not revolutionary changes. Several times in the history of warfare, the discovery and application of certain techno-scientific principles have changed weapons, changed the character of war, changed the organization of armed force, and changed the form of the state. These innovations can be regarded as "revolutionary." Keith Krause has argued that there are only four technological innovations that can be considered revolutionary:

> [First,] the cannon/gunpowder revolution of the fifteenth and sixteenth centu-
> ry; [second,] the application of steel and steam to warfare associated with the
> Industrial Revolution of the nineteenth century; [third,] the mobility revolution
> characterized by the marriage of the internal combustion engine and modern
> electronics of the twentieth century; and [fourth,] nuclear weapons. [114]

It should be noted that some of these technologies originated outside of the West (gunpowder, military rockets, and cannon, for example, originated in China). It should also be noted that there is never a complete supplanting of one military technology by another.[115] Even in the current age of high-tech war, soldiers very occasionally use their bayonets in close hand-to-hand combat. Finally, it should be noted that, until relatively recently, the officer corps of most armed forces were opposed to any new technology that challenged their conception of proper war, which led them to oppose its adoption. Resistance to and contempt for new military technologies was strongest among European aristocratic officers who "believed in the glorious cavalry charge and, above all, the supremacy of man as opposed to machines."[116] This resistance ended with the First World War during which new machines of war (machine guns, tanks, and aircraft) that were the very antithesis of their faith in individual endeavor and courage appeared in great numbers and forced the officer corps of European armies to acknowledge the changing face of war. They came to realize that "the quality of a country's weaponry and the capacity of its industrial output became the determinants of success [in war], rather than any will to win born of idealism, faith or personal self-respect."[117]

   In the chapters that follow, the ways that these technological revolutions changed war and subsequently formed and transformed states and formed and transformed the relationship of the state, the people, and war are studied. The general pattern of weapons technology changing warfare, then changing the form of the state, is interrupted only one time with the advent of the national state, which, as will be shown in chapter 4, was brought into being not by the development of a new military technology but rather by the articulation of a new ideology that legitimized the assertion of state power through the people and brought into being the nation-at-arms and the citizen soldier.

NOTES

1. See, for example, Geoffrey Blainey, *The Causes of War*, 3rd Edition (New York: Free Press, 1988); Jack S. Levy, *The Causes of War* (New York: John Wiley & Sons, 2010); David Sobeck, *The Causes of War* (Cambridge: Polity Press, 2009); John G. Stoessinger, *Why Nations Go to War*, Tenth Edition (Belmont, CA: Thompson-Wadsworth, 2008); and John A. Vasquez, *The War Puzzle Revisited* (Cambridge: Cambridge University Press, 2009).

2. Azar Gat, *War in Human Civilization* (Oxford: Oxford University Press, 2006), *passim*.

3. Hans Joas and Wolfgang Knöbl, *War in Social Thought: Hobbes to the Present* (Princeton, NJ: Princeton University Press, 2013), p. 1.

4. Tarak Barkawi and Shane Brighton, "Powers of War: Fighting, Knowledge, and Critique," *International Political Sociology*, 5 (No. 2), June 2011, pp. 127–31.

5. Joas and Knöbl, *op. cit.*, p. 2.

6. *Ibid.*

7. *Ibid.*

8. Christopher Cramer, *Violence in Developing Countries: War, Memory, Progress* (Bloomington: Indiana University Press, 2006), p. 280.

9. For example, the University of Michigan's involvement in the infamous Phoenix Program.

10. I am indebted to my former colleague Steve Rosow for this observation.

11. Morris Janowitz, *The Professional Soldier: A Social and Political Portrait* (New York: Free Press, 1960).

12. Thomas E. Ricks, *The Generals: American Military Command from World War II to Today* (New York: Penguin, 2012).

13. Samuel P. Huntington, *The Soldier and the State: The Theory and Politics of Civil-Military Relations* (Cambridge, MA: Harvard University Press, 1957).

14. Victor Davis Hanson, *Carnage and Culture: Landmark Battles in the Rise of Western Power* (New York: Anchor Books, 2001).

15. Tarak Barkawi and Shane Brighton, "Conclusion: Absent War Studies? War, Knowledge, and Critique," in Hew Strachan and Sibylle Scheipers (eds.) *The Changing Character of War* (Oxford: Oxford University Press, 2011), p. 528.

16. Martin Shaw, *Dialectics of War: An Essay in the Social Theory of Total War and Peace* (London: Pluto, 1988), p. 11.

17. Vivienne Jabri, *War and the Transformation of Global Politics* (New York: Palgrave Macmillan, 2007), p. 23.

18. Tarak Barkawi, *Globalization and War* (Lanham, MD: Rowman & Littlefield, 2006), p. 29.

19. David A. Bell, *The First Total War: Napoleon's Europe and the Birth of Warfare as We Know It* (Boston/New York: Houghton Mifflin, 2007), p. 10.

20. Shaw, *op. cit.*, p. 14.

21. Cramer, *op. cit.*, p. 229.

22. Hew Strachan and Sibylle Scheipers, "Introduction: The Changing Character of War," in Hew Strachan and Sibylle Scheipers (eds.) *op. cit.*, p. 6.

23. Quincy Wright, *A Study of War*, Abridged (Chicago and London: University of Chicago Press, 1964).

24. John Keegan, *A History of Warfare* (New York: Vintage Books, 1994).

25. Mary Kaldor, *New & Old Wars* Second Edition (Stanford, CA: Stanford University Press, 2007).

26. Kalevi J. Holsti, *The State, War, and the State of War* (Cambridge: Cambridge University Press, 1996).

27. Rupert Smith, *The Utility of Force: The Art of War in the Modern World* (New York: Random House, 2008).

28. Sidney Tarrow, *War, States, and Contention: A Comparative Historical Study* (Ithaca, NY: Cornell University Press, 2015), p. 19.

29. Kalevi J. Holsti, "Reversing Rousseau: The Medieval and Modern in Contemporary Wars," in William Bain (ed.) *The Empire of Security and the Safety of the People* (London: Routledge, 2006), p. 43.

30. Doyne Dawson, *The Origins of Western Warfare: Militarism and Morality in the Ancient World* (Boulder, CO: Westview Press, 1996), p. 16.

31. Gat, *op. cit.,* pp. 183–89.

32. Keegan, *op. cit.,* p. 10.

33. Gat, *op. cit.,* p. 211.

34. *Ibid.*

35. Barkawi and Brighton, *op. cit.,* p. 534.

36. Holsti, "Reversing Rousseau," p. 39.

37. Jean Bethke Elshtain, *Women and War with a New Epilogue* (Chicago: University of Chicago Press, 1995), pp. 47–56.

38. Bell, *op. cit.,* p. 11.

39. *Ibid.,* p. 12.

40. Quoted in Keegan, *op. cit.,* p. 91.

41. Holsti, "Reversing Rousseau," p. 40.

42. Jeremy Black, *The Age of Total War, 1860–1945* (Lanham, MD: Rowman & Littlefield, 2006), pp. 1–2.

43. Keegan, *op. cit.,* p. 59.

44. Steven Pinker, *The Better Angels of Our Nature: Why Violence Has Declined* (New York: Penguin Books, 2011). See also Jack S. Levy, *War and the Great Power System: 1495–1975* (Lexington, KY: University of Kentucky Press, 1983).

45. Raimo Väyrynen, "Introduction: Contending Views," in Raimo Väyrynen, *The Waning of Major War: Theories and Debates* (London and New York: Routledge, 2013), p. 1

46. John Mueller, "Accounting for the Waning of Major War," in Väyrynen, *Ibid.*, 74.

47. Holsti, *The State, War, and the State of War*, p. 21.

48. Holsti, "Reversing Rousseau," p. 43.

49. Daniel Jonah Goldenhagen, *Worse Than War: Genocide, Eliminationism, and the Ongoing Assault on Humanity* (New York: Public Affairs, 2009).

50. John Mueller, *The Remnants of War* (Ithaca, NY: Cornell University Press, 2004).

51. Mark Duffield, *Global Governance and the New Wars: The Merging of Development and Security* (London/New York: Zed Books, 2014), p. 14.

52. Joas and Knöbl, *op. cit.,* p. 32.

53. Ann Hironaka, *Neverending War: The International Community, Weak States, and the Perpetuation of Civil War* (Cambridge: MA: Harvard University Press, 2005), p. 7.

54. Jared Diamond, "Vengeance Is Ours," *The New Yorker*, April 21, 2008, pp. 74–86.

55. Mats Berdal, "The 'New Wars' Thesis Revisited," in Hew Strachan and Sibylle Scheipers (eds.), *op. cit.,* p. 112.

56. Timothy Snyder, *Bloodlands: Europe Between Hitler and Stalin* (New York: Basic Books, 2010), p. viii.

57. Brian C. Schmidt, *The Political Discourse of Anarchy: A Disciplinary History of International Relations* (Albany: State University of New York Press, 1998), p. 4.

58. *Ibid.,* p. 5.

59. David Easton, *The Political System: An Inquiry into the State of Political Science* (New York: Knopf, 1953).

60. Andrew Vincent, *Theories of the State* (Oxford: Basil Blackwell, 1987), pp. 19–21.

61. Martin van Creveld, *The Rise and Decline of the State* (Cambridge: Cambridge University Press, 1999), p. 1.

62. Yale H. Ferguson and Richard W. Mansbach, *Polities, Authority, Identities, and Change* (Columbia: University of South Carolina Press, 1996).

63. Carl Schmitt, *The Concept of the Political,* Expanded Edition (Chicago: University of Chicago Press, 1996).

64. Tarrow, *op. cit.,* p. 13.

65. *Ibid.*

66. Ferguson and Mansbach, *op. cit.,* pp. 393–404.

67. Harrison Wagner, *War and the State: The Theory of International Relations* (Ann Arbor: University of Michigan Press, 2007), p. 125. Emphasis added.

68. Robert L. Carneiro, "A Theory of the Origin of the State," *Studies in Social Theory No. 3*, Institute for Humane Studies, 1977, p. 4.

69. Thomas Hobbes, *Leviathan*, ed. Richard Tuck (Cambridge: Cambridge University Press, 1991), p. 89.

70. *Ibid.*, p. 120.

71. Karl Wittfogel, *Oriental Despotism: A Comparative Study of Total Power* (New Haven, CT: Yale University Press, 1957), p. 18.

72. Franz Oppenheimer, *The State: Its History and Development Viewed Sociologically* (Indianapolis, IN: Bobbs-Merrill Co., 1914).

73. Carneiro, *op. cit.*, p. 4.

74. *Ibid.*, p. 6.

75. Edward Jenks, *History of Politics* (London: Macmillan, 1900).

76. Carneiro, *op. cit.*, p. 7.

77. Alexander B. Murphy, "The Sovereign State System as Political Territorial Ideal: Historical and Contemporary Considerations," in Thomas J. Biersteker and Cynthia Weber (eds.) *State Sovereignty as Social Construct* (Cambridge: Cambridge University Press, 1996), pp. 81–120.

78. Cyril Black, *The Dynamics of Modernization* (New York: Harper & Row, 1966), p. 7.

79. A. F. K. Organski, *The Stages of Political Development* (New York: Knopf, 1965).

80. Leonard Binder, *et al.*, *Crises and Sequences in Political Development* (Princeton, NJ: Princeton University Press, 1997).

81. Samuel P. Huntington, *Political Order in Changing Societies* (New Haven, CT: Yale University Press, 1968), p. 93.

82. Phillips Cutright, "Political Structures, Economic Development, and National Social Security Programs," *American Journal of Sociology*, 70, pp. 537–48.

83. Talcott Parsons, *The System of Modern Societies* (Englewood Cliffs, NJ: Prentice-Hall, 1971).

84. Charles Tilly, "Western State-Making and Theories of Political Transformation," in Charles Tilly (ed.) *The Formation of National States in Western Europe* (Princeton, NJ: Princeton University Press, 1975), p. 617.

85. Joas and Knöbl, *op. cit.*, p. 192.

86. Theda Skocpol, "Bringing the State Back In: Strategies and Analysis in Current Research," in Peter B. Evans, Dietrich Rueschemeyer, and Theda Skocpol (eds.), *Bringing the State Back In* (Cambridge: Cambridge University Press, 1985).

87. Reinhard Bendix, *Kings or People: Power and the Mandate to Rule* (Berkeley, CA: University of California Press, 1980).

88. Tilly, *op. cit.*, p. 633.

89. *Ibid.*, p. 74.

90. Kenneth N. Waltz, *Man, the State and War: A Theoretical Analysis* (New York: Columbia University Press, 1954), p. 124.

91. *Ibid.*, p. 81.

92. Jeremy Black, *War and the World: Military Power and the Fate of Continents, 1450–2000* (New Haven, CT: Yale University Press, 1998), pp. 4–5.

93. Quoted in Gabriel A. Almond, *A Discipline Divided: Schools and Sects in Political Science* (Newbury Park/London/New Delhi: Sage Publications, 1990), p. 265.

94. Quoted in *Ibid.*, p. 266.

95. *Ibid.*, p. 268.

96. *Ibid.*, p. 269.

97. Quoted in Joas and Knöbl, *op. cit.*, pp. 197–98.

98. Charles Tilly, "Entanglements of European Cities and States," in Charles Tilly and Wim P. Blockmans (eds.) *Cities and the Rise of States in Europe: AD 1000 to 1800* (Boulder, CO: Westview Press, 1994), p. 25. See also Tilly, *Coercion, Capital, and European States, AD 990–1990* (Cambridge, MA: Basil Blackwell, 1990).

99. Rodney Bruce Hall, *National Collective Identity: Social Constructs and International Systems* (New York: Columbia University Press, 1995), p. 20.

100. Hendrik Spruyt, *The Sovereign State and Its Competitors: An Analysis of Systems Change* (Princeton, NJ: Princeton University Press, 1994).

101. Brian M. Downing, *The Military Revolution and Political Change: Origins of Democracy and Autocracy in Early Modern Europe* (Princeton, NJ: Princeton University Press, 1992).

102. Bruce D. Porter, *War and the Rise of the State: The Military Foundations of Modern Politics* (New York: Free Press, 1994), pp. 11–15.

103. Anthony W. Pereira, "Armed Forces, Coercive Monopolies, and Changing Patterns of State Formation and Violence," in Diane E. Davis and Anthony W. Pereira, eds., *Irregular Armed Forces and Their Role in Politics and State Formation* (Cambridge: Cambridge University Press, 2003), pp. 387–88

104. Carneiro, *op. cit.*, pp. 7–10.

105. *Ibid.*

106. Spruyt, *op. cit.*, p. 178.

107. Philip G. Cerney, *The Changing Architecture of Politics: Structure, Agency, and the Future of the State* (London/Newbury Park/New Delhi: Sage, 1990), p. 86.

108. Cynthia Weber, *Simulating Sovereignty: Intervention, the State and Symbolic Exchange* (Cambridge: Cambridge University Press, 1995), p. 4.

109. *Ibid.*, p. 28.

110. Andreas Osiander, *The States System of Europe, 1640-1990: Peacemaking and the Internal Conditions of Society* (Oxford: Clarendon Press, 1994), p. 332.

111. Martin van Creveld, *Technology and War* (New York: Free Press, 1989), p. 1.

112. Jacques Ellul, *The Technological Society*, trans. by John Wilkinson (New York: Vintage Books, 1964), *passim*.

113. Antoine Bousquet, *The Scientific Way of Warfare: Order and Chaos on the Battlefields of Modernity* (New York: Columbia University Press, 2009).

114. Keith Krause, *Arms and the State: Patterns of Military Production and Trade* (Cambridge: Cambridge University Press, 1992), p. 22. Note that Bousquet, *ibid*, identifies four regimes of the scientific way of warfare: mechanistic warfare, thermodynamic warfare, cybernetic warfare, and chaoplexic warfare.

115. Jeremy Black, *War and Technology* (Bloomington: Indiana University Press, 2013), pp. 20 and 27.

116. John Ellis, *The Social History of the Machine Gun* (Baltimore, MD: The Johns Hopkins University Press, 1975), p. 49.

117. *Ibid.*, p. 180.

Chapter 2

Private War and the Feudal "State"

This chapter will show how, following the collapse of Roman imperial rule, Europe disintegrated into a welter of weak, internally fragmented forms of territorial rule with no one form being dominant over another and no agreement existing among European peoples about what constituted legitimate government. The result was incessant war over the centuries between 500 and 1500 CE "between emperor and pope, between the principal monarchs, between city states and territorial princes, between barons, between rival cities, and between peasants and lord."[1] The violent competition among these different forms of politico-military rule created a serious threat environment for them all. Even the pope had an army and on occasion donned armor and personally commanded troops in battle against enemies of the Catholic Church. Julius II (1503–1513) did this so often that he was known as the "Warrior Pope."[2]

Why was Europe fragmented into warring forms of territorial rule for a millennium after the fall of Rome? The standard answer that has been given by most scholars is Europe's physical geography, which, being broken up by mountain ranges, having scattered population concentrations, and having considerable climate variation from north to south, was difficult terrain upon which a single, centralized form of territorial rule, even by the most determined consolidator, could be raised. One scholar of this mind has written that Europe's

> variegated landscape encouraged the growth, and continued existence, of decentralized power, with local kingdoms and marcher lordships and highland clans and lowland town confederations making the political map of Europe drawn anytime after the fall of Rome look like a patch-work quilt. The patterns might vary from century to century, but no single color could ever be used to denote a unified empire.[3]

The explanation of Europe's territorial fragmentation by reference to the continent's physical geography has been challenged by Philip Hoffman, who argues that Europe's *"peculiar political history"* itself is the cause of European territorial fragmentation, not its physical geography. He writes that Europe was set on its peculiar political path after the fall of the Roman Empire, which reinforced itself over a long period of time:

> In particular, the centuries of war fought after the collapse of the Roman Empire, when western Europe had warriors and military leaders, but nothing that would qualify as a strong state—in other words nothing like a state with permanent taxation and a durable fiscal system able to raise appreciable amounts of revenue over the long haul . . . [kept Europe splintered into a multiplicity of] hostile groups dominated by warlords and devoted to fighting [which stamped] the region with many of its distinctive features: the high value that rulers and elites (particularly the nobility) attached to victory in war . . . and—even more important—the enduring enmities between peoples that made it difficult for anyone to unify . . . Europe. [4]

These distinctive political, military, and cultural practices were called "feudalism," about which more will be said below.

Europe's very long history of political fragmentation was exceptional. In China, Ying Zheng (259–210 BCE), the king of the state of Qin, defeated the other warring states and unified China in 221 BCE. Ying Zheng became Qin Shi Huang, the first emperor of China. The following Han dynasty created a centralized bureaucracy that consolidated the empire by drawing local elites into paid imperial service, which loosened their ties to their locales and made them loyal to the central government. In Japan, the Japanese warlord Tokugawa Ieyasu (1542–1616) managed to seize power in 1600 CE, establish central rule, and end the continuous fighting among the samurai families and clans that had ravaged Japan for several centuries. [5] Thus, in China and Japan hegemonic power was established fairly early and ended the warring-states phase of their political histories. Europe's political history was different: no single enduring hegemonic power *has ever emerged* in Europe despite determined efforts by the likes of Charlemagne (742–814), who built the short-lived Carolingian Empire (800–814); Napoleon Bonaparte (1769–1821), who sought to unite Europe under French leadership from 1800 to 1815; and Adolf Hitler (1889–1945), who dreamed of a united Europe under German domination.

Hoffman also says that the Europe's church-state relationship was exceptional. In Europe the Catholic Church was centralized, politically autonomous, and consisted of an organized clergy. This encouraged fragmentation because it could and did prevent secular rulers from becoming too strong by applying the terrifying (for people of that age) spiritual weapons of *excommunication* (official censure to deprive an individual or groups membership in the Church) and *interdict* (official censure to deprive individuals or groups certain rites and sacraments without ceasing to be members of the Church). These weapons were used effectively by the Church in its struggles with secular rulers beginning in the eleventh and twelfth centuries over the appointment of bishops, the so-called Investiture Controversy. According to Hoffman, "the rest of Eurasia lacked the autonomous religious force that kept western European rulers from unifying their corner of the world."[6] In China and Japan, for example, religion was not politically autonomous and staffed with an organized clergy that could keep rulers from becoming too strong.

Finally, Hoffman says that Europe's politico-military fragmentation was never overcome because rulers continually sought to improve their military technology and faced few obstacles to their procuring, even from opponents, the latest advances in military hardware. He writes:

> Embargoes could not block the diffusion of the latest weapons, skill, and tactical innovations, since enforcement was difficult in early modern Europe. In the sixteenth century, for instance, the Holy Roman Emperor Charles V could not stop gunsmiths from Nürenberg from peddling firearms to his enemy, the king of France; his ban on sales proved ineffective. The major obstacle to diffusion was therefore distance, but the western European states were close enough to eliminate it as an impediment. Markets for military goods and services . . . helped spread the latest advances.[7]

For these reasons, then, the many kingdoms that came into existence in Europe after the fall of the Roman Empire had neither *internal hierarchy* nor *external autonomy*. They were territorial spaces over which "[the Catholic] Church, lords, kings, emperor, and towns often exercised simultaneous claims to jurisdiction."[8] In order to construct internal hierarchy kings had to bring the warring dukes, counts, and knights and religious orders within their realms under their direct control by stripping them of their armed retinues, castles, and lands. In order to construct external autonomy, kings had to free themselves from their religious obligations to the pope, and their feudal obligations to more powerful neighboring monarchs. These actions resulted in many conflicts between the king and his barons and the king and the Catholic Church, as well as wars against other kings who claimed rights of inheritance. Gradually, over several centuries, certain kings in Europe were able to consolidate their politico-military rule by subordinating their nobles, gaining control over the appointment of bishops within their realms, breaking their feudal obligations to their sovereigns (the pope and the emperor), denying rights of inheritance to royal claimants outside of the realm, and defeating neighboring kings in battle. In other words, they gained a monopoly over the means of coercive force within their kingdoms and recognition by other kingdoms as legitimate rulers.

The construction of a system of similar units of exclusive territorial rule also came about by the imposition of a particular structure of politico-military rule on other competitive forms during the Feudal Age. As feudal "states" were gradually transformed into kingly states, they began to form a system of similar entities. As the system became increasingly composed of the same form of politico-military rule (i.e., kingly states), the states in it began to be "recognized or denied certain forms of [politico-military] organization as legitimate . . . actors."[9] Thus, the state system *and* the dominant form of the state in the system recognize or deny certain forms of politico-military rule as legitimate or not. In the words of one scholar: "When a particular type of unit comes to dominate the international system, it transforms the deep structures of the system."[10] Transformation occurs in one of two ways: first, by eliminating the aberrant form from the system, and second by coercing the aberrant form to transform itself into the legitimate form.

It is necessary to present a brief discussion of the rise and fall of the Roman Empire, because it was the collapse of the Roman imperial state that allowed Europe's peculiar political history to unfold.

THE ROMAN IMPERIAL STATE

Roman politico-military rule can be divided into three forms: monarchical, republican, and imperial. Monarchical rule dates from the founding of Rome, the "Eternal City," in 753 BCE by Romulus and Remus, the orphaned twins supposedly suckled by a female wolf, to the expulsion of the last of seven kings in 510 BCE. Republican rule began in 509 BCE with the election of the first ruling consuls by the Senate and ended in 31 BCE when the first imperial dynasty was established by Caesar Augustus (63 BCE–14 CE). Imperial rule lasted until the collapse of the western portion of the empire in the fifth century CE, and the eastern portion in 1453 CE with the fall of Constantinople to the Turks. The Romans were able to build and sustain their empire for many centuries because they had a genius for military organization, administration, and civil engineering.[11]

War built the Roman state and the Roman state made war because war was seen by the Romans as natural, honorable, and glorious, an important arena where Roman men could distinguish themselves in the eyes of their fellow citizens by acts of physical courage in battle. Therefore, the Roman republic was a "society [in which] citizenship was synonymous with military service."[12] Every male citizen who owned property was required to serve in the army, if called to duty, and "from their teens, war was their whole way of life. Volunteering for service, decorated for bravery, breeding children for the next generation's army, [Roman men] were willing to serve as long as they could pass the physical."[13] Serving in the army and extending Roman rule by participating in the conquest of so-called barbarians (i.e., Germanic and Slavic tribal peoples) was the way that Roman men made their civic contribution. In sum, war was for Roman men a single-minded search for glory and noble self-sacrifice for the Republic, adversity endured, and victory by the republic over increasingly formidable enemies. Almost every year, Rome's army marched out, fought, and humbled an enemy. According to Azar Gat, the fact that about 700,000 male citizens could be mobilized for war and kept under arms for years, gave the Roman army a tenacity in battle unmatched by its enemies.[14] By 275 BCE the Roman army had conquered the Italian peninsula, defeated the Carthaginians in a campaign known as the Punic Wars (264–202 BCE), and between 201 and 146 BCE, conquered the Greeks and the Macedonians.

Rome's army was the finest military organization of its day. It was highly trained, extremely disciplined (desertion was punished by death), and very mobile, the Romans having built a vast network of roads throughout the empire on which to march troops rapidly from place to place to defend the empire from external invasion and from internal rebellion. The army was positioned along the empire's *limes* (frontiers) which were demarcated by defensive walls and watch towers built of stone.[15] In effect, Rome was *militarized* and had Europe's first *standing army*; that is, a permanent military force recruited, trained, armed, equipped, fed, and paid by the state.

It should be noted that while women were neither citizens nor soldiers, they played an important role in Rome's militarized society as "Spartan mothers [of citizens-to-be and mothers-to-be of citizens] and civic cheerleaders, urging men to behave like men, praising the heroes, lamenting the destruction of the war although the most horrendous possibility of all is defeat of the city [of Rome], not the deaths of particular individuals including their own husbands and sons."[16]

The victories of Rome's legions gradually transformed the republic into an empire. As the institutions of the Republic were unable to administer the empire efficiently, many of them, such as the Senate, declined in power and importance. The durability of the empire was bolstered by the transformation of the primitive customary law of the Roman tribes into a rationally codified system of civil, criminal, and public law that was applied uniformly throughout the empire. It was also bolstered by a uniform system of territorial administration. The empire was divided into provinces ruled by proconsuls, who were usually proven generals appointed by the emperor. The proconsuls were assisted by a small band of administrators who were drawn from Rome's wealthy class. The purpose of this legal-administrative-military apparatus was to collect taxes, maintain Roman peace (*Pax Romana*), and adjudicate disputes according to Roman law. The official language of administration and government was Latin, but Greek was widely spoken and used as a *lingua franca* in the eastern provinces.

In sum, the Roman Empire constituted a very large territorial politico-military state extending across eastern and western Europe that through its official language, its laws and courts, its governing institutions, its concept of citizenship, and its army provided a sense of belonging to a unified world, a single civilization within which Roman peace and order prevailed, despite regional variations in local languages and cultures.

The disintegration and collapse of the Roman imperial state was gradual, extending over several centuries. It was caused not by classical imperial "overextension"[17] but, rather, by what might be called imperial "under-extension." First, the empire ceased expanding during the reign of the emperor Hadrian (76–138 CE), which meant that booty and tribute from newly conquered peoples stopped flowing into the imperial treasury. Therefore, taxes had to be raised, eventually to confiscatory levels, to pay for the army, bureaucracy, and public works. Second, agricultural production, which relied heavily on slave labor, began to stagnate because no new peoples were being conquered to provide slaves. Third, the "Romanity" of the army was compromised by the emperor Theodosius (347–395 CE) who accepted "under his command large units of barbarian 'federates' who served, not as the auxiliaries of old had done in units raised and officered by imperial officials, but as allies under their own leaders."[18] Gradually Roman armies became increasingly "Teutonic in composition, carried Teutonic weapons, lost all semblance of legionary drill, and even adopted the German war cry, the *baritus*."[19] Slowly, the Roman army ceased to exist as an instrument of the Roman state controlled by the emperor. The central government's monopoly over the means of physical coercion gradually dissipated from the city of Rome and the Italian peninsula to the outer provinces, where provincial generals began to rival one another for power, glory, and wealth, which diverted them from frontier defense.[20]

In an attempt to reverse disintegration, the emperor Diocletian (244–311 CE) divided the empire in 285 CE into eastern and western portions along a line extending north and south through the Adriatic Sea. He devised the *"tetarchy,"* a scheme that gave the empire four rulers: Two *augusti,* or co-emperors, exercised supreme authority, one in the western portion and one in the eastern portion. Each co-emperor was assisted by a *caesar,* the second in command, who was intended to succeed him. The areas for which the co-emperors were responsible were called prefectures, which were subdivided into dioceses under a vicar. The dioceses, of which there were one hundred, were subdivided into small units of equal taxing capacity.[21] Civil administration was reformed and the army revitalized. Diocletian also enlisted the gods in his struggle to save the imperial state from collapse by declaring that the empire rested on its special relationship to the Roman pantheon of gods, not on the Senate and the people.[22]

The special relationship between religion and the imperial state requires extended discussion because it eventually led to the establishment of Christianity as the official religion of Rome, challenged the Roman understanding of virtuous war, and gave rise to Europe's uniquely powerful religious institution, the Catholic (meaning universal) Church.

The Romans worshipped the gods of the Greco-Roman pantheon as well as deified deceased emperors. They believed that they were especially loved by their gods, and Roman imperial success was seen as having been produced by their divine favor. Therefore, according to one historian, Roman religion "had nothing to do with salvation and not much with individual behavior; it was above all a public matter. It was part of the *res publica,* a series of rituals whose maintenance was good for the state, whose neglect would bring retribution."[23]

Despite Diocletian's efforts to reinforce the connection between the state and its official pantheon of gods, many Romans began worshiping foreign gods, such as Isis, the Egyptian goddess of motherhood; ancient fertility gods from pre-Roman times, such as the goddess Cybele; and various so-called "mystery cults" from the eastern provinces of the empire. Initially, the Roman state allowed people to follow these unofficial religions, as long as they continued to publicly recognize the official gods of Rome and the cult of the deified emperors.

One of the mystery cults founded by an itinerant Jewish preacher and holy man, Jesus of Nazareth (c. 2 BCE–c. 33 CE), developed rapidly into a revolutionary movement that spread among Rome's town-dwelling poor social classes, as well as among aristocratic women. It spread quickly because its theology carried great hope for Rome's long-suffering lower classes and because the "physical conditions in the Roman Empire . . . were ideally suited for the spread of Christianity. The establishment of *Pax Romana* made it possible for missionaries to travel in perfect safety from one end of the empire to the other, and the strategic Roman roads provided an ideal means of communication. The common languages of Greek and Latin could be understood everywhere."[24]

Jesus presented himself as the "Prince of Peace" and challenged the central role of the warrior in the Old Testament. He redefined the Old Testament God of Revenge as the merciful Father, and his followers as the "children of God." Jesus refused to countenance the use of violence to bring the Kingdom of Heaven and he blessed the peacemaker and chastised the war maker. He enjoined his disciple, Peter (?–64 CE), to sheathe his sword and told his followers to go as sheep among wolves offering their lives for their religious beliefs, if need be, but never to use violence or take the lives of others in its cause. Jesus asked his followers to examine their actions in light of his injunction against violence in word and deed. Thus, Jesus "held up a concept of peace at odds with the notion that peace and unruffled order maintained by [Roman] armies of occupation were one and the same."[25]

Initially, the Roman state tolerated Christianity. However, because Christians practiced their rites in secret, refused to acknowledge the Roman pantheon of gods and the cult of the deified emperors, and refused to participate in the public worship of Rome's official gods, they were declared enemies of the Roman imperial state. In effect, Christianity's monotheism and the idea that all people, no matter their social class, were equal in the eyes of its one god, as well as its pacifism and its emphasis on kindness, humility, charity, mercy, love for one's neighbor, and individual salvation offered an alternative to the Roman understanding of virtue, which, as was shown above, was connected to manliness, valor in battle, and the maintenance of the imperial state. Christian teaching conflated wartime killing with murder and labeled war as evil. Christian virtue was manifested in acts of love, piety, and charity rather than acts of courage and honor on the battlefield.[26] Christianity stripped the citizen-soldier of his honored place within Roman society.

Therefore, great efforts were made by the Roman state to destroy Christianity by persecuting Christians unmercifully. During Diocletian's reign, thousands of Christians were tortured and put to death in the arena because they refused to worship the Roman emperor as a divinity and the gods of the Roman pantheon. Despite these efforts to suppress Christianity, the numbers of Christians increased and the Roman state was forced to issue an edict of toleration of all religions in 311 CE. Christians were allowed to resume their own worship and the authorities enlisted the Christian god by encouraging Christians to pray for (not worship) the emperor and for the good of the Roman imperial state.[27]

In 312 CE, just before a battle against his rivals for the imperial throne, the general Flavius Valerius Aurelius Constantinius (272–337 CE) had a vision in which he saw a flaming cross in the sky and ordered his soldiers to put a cross on their shields in order to show respect for the Christian god and to enlist his help in battle. Constantinius won the battle and became emperor, after which he let it be known that he owed his victory to the god of the Christians. In 313, he granted freedom of worship to all Christians and chose the Christian god to be one of the protectors of Rome. Constantinius restored the property of Christians confiscated during the persecutions, educated his children in the Christian religion, and was himself baptized a Christian on his deathbed in 337. The emperor Theodosius (347–395 CE) outlawed paganism in 380 CE. He prohibited blood sacrifices, closed pagan temples, and sanctioned the use of coercion to gain the acceptance among the Roman population for Christianity. Now pagans were persecuted by the Roman state and military service was restricted to Christians. In 381 Christianity became the official—that is, *established*—religion of the Roman Empire. Roman politico-military power was gradually disconnected from paganism and joined to Christianity. Christian dogma became binding on all citizens of the empire, and the empire's survival came to be seen as depending upon its conversion to Christianity. By the fifth century, Christianity's pacifism had been adumbrated, and arms bearing, with restrictions, made a comeback, especially after Christian theologians "accepted the Old Testament as a divinely inspired portion of Holy Scripture."[28] Thereafter, emperors took on the responsibility of caring for the faith of Romans and increasingly used the coercive power of the Roman state to spread Christianity throughout the empire and to ensure the rightness of Christian belief.[29]

In order to achieve the conversion of Rome, Constantinius believed that he needed a new capital city free from all pagan traditions. Therefore, he founded and built a new capital city on the site of the small town of Byzantium on the Bosphorus in 330. The city's name was eventually changed from Roma Nova (New Rome) to Constantinople in honor of its founder.

The conversion of Rome to Christianity fused Christianity's *pacifism* (kindness, humility, patience, purity, and chastity) with Rome's *militarism* (order, patriarchy, law, hierarchy, heroism in battle, and conquest). Despite the efforts of Christian emperors after Constantinius to completely eliminate the "old religion," paganism also fused with Christianity. In the words of one scholar, the Christian church "took on the vestments of pagan priests, use of incense and holy water in purification, burning of candles before the altar, worship of saints, the architecture of the basilica, Roman law as the basis of Canon law, the title of Pontifex Maximus for the pope, the Latin language, and the vast framework of the government of the Empire."[30] In addition, the church also fused its episcopal organization with the administrative structure of the empire devised by Diocletian. Essentially, the Roman Empire stayed alive by morphing into the Roman Catholic Church, which provided Europe with a universal religious institution that for many centuries provided a substitute for secular political unification.

GERMANIC KINGDOMS

At the time the Roman republic was expanding northwestward, Germanic tribal peoples (Franks, Lombards, Frisians, Burgundians, Alemmani, Jutes, Angles, and Saxons) were experiencing population explosions that caused them to expand southwestward from the Baltic region and overrun the indigenous Celtic inhabitants of Europe. By 200 BCE they had reached the Rhine River, and by 100 BCE the Danube. The Rhine and Danube rivers became the frontier between these semi-nomadic Germanic peoples and the Roman Empire.

In about 375 CE the Huns, a nomadic warrior people from the steppe lands of central Asia, swept westward. To escape the Huns, the German tribes began to flee across the Danube and Rhine into the Roman Empire, where they settled on uninhabited border territory as federates (self-governing allies) of Rome in exchange for land, money, and service in the Roman army. Eventually, the infiltration of Germanic peoples into the empire became a full-scale invasion. From 407 to 429 CE the Roman provinces of Italia, Galicia, and Hispania were invaded. In 410 the Visigoth chieftain, Alaric (370–410 CE), invaded the Italian peninsula and sacked Rome. Rome was sacked a second time in 455 by Vandals. The frontier provinces were also overrun: Jutes, Angles, and Saxons invaded Britannia between 441 and 442. Galicia fell to the Franks and Burgundians, Alemmani, and Visigoths. Hispania fell to the Suevi, Vandals, and Visigoths. In 476, the last Roman emperor was deposed and replaced by the German chieftain, Odoacer (435–493 CE), who ruled as a king.

The Germanic invaders of the western empire were *stateless* peoples. Except for an occasional temporary federation of tribes during wartime, formal-legal territorial structures of politico-military rule did not exist among the Germanic peoples. The basic unit of the tribe was the clan, which was composed of a small number of related families living in close proximity to one another. The Germans practiced animal husbandry (cattle, horses, swine) and hunted game in order to survive. They were polytheists who worshiped the gods of the Norse pantheon. Since they lacked the territorial formal-legal structures of politico-military rule (i.e., a state), decisions affecting the tribe were made by a chieftain called "king," selected from a certain clan. Kings were *war-band leaders* who, in consultation with an assembly of the tribe's leading warriors, were expected to lead the tribe in battle, settle disputes among the tribe's members, and act as intercessors with the gods through the performance of religious rituals, such as making sacrifices for successful hunting, good grazing, or victory in battle. A king's successor was chosen from among his direct male offspring, usually the eldest, and confirmed by an act of acclamation by an assembly of the tribe's leading warriors.[31]

As was explained above, the Romans exercised politico-military power through a set of formal-legal institutions and offices. The emperor was an official of the Roman imperial state who ruled its territory by means of a hierarchically organized bureaucracy and the army according to Roman law. His power derived from these institutions and the law. In contrast, Germanic kings whose kingdoms filled the void left by the Roman collapse

> could not conceive of political relationships on any basis other than one of *personal* loyalty. They had no notion that authority could be exercised other than by one man over another. Therefore, the effectiveness of a particular king depended on his military strength alone and the personal loyalty that he engen-

dered among his followers, who swore to serve him with absolute fidelity and
who considered it a disgrace to survive him in battle. In exchange for such
loyalty, the king provided his followers with food and weapons, as well as a
share of the booty taken from defeated enemies.[32]

In the Germanic kingdoms, the realm was seen as the *patrimony* (property) of
the king who could divide it among his heirs, mortgage it, and will portions
of it to the Catholic Church as he saw fit. In other words, Germanic kings
"considered their new kingdoms as their property, and the [Roman] distinction between public and private would have baffled them."[33] Therefore, the
successor Germanic kingdoms did not have a standing army, formal-legal
administrative structures, and regular taxation as did imperial Rome. An
alternative method of exercising politico-military rule had to be devised.

As the Germanic kingdoms were viewed as the property of their king,
they were ruled with the help of the members of the king's household: the
king's brothers, his sons, his sons-in-law, as well as his trusted companions.
Ruling the kingdom in this way was not too difficult as long as the kingdom
was small. As kingdoms grew in size through marriage, inheritance, and
conquest, a new method had to be found for ruling an extensive territory
without the help of a formal-legal administrative structure staffed by officials
of the state. The method devised was to subdivide the kingdoms into smaller
territorial units called "counties" and place in each a loyal follower, usually a
kinsman, called a "count," who represented kingly authority and governed in
his name. Counts were expected to rule their counties as the king ruled the
kingdom; therefore, they were granted the same military, judicial, and financial powers exercised by the king. They were assisted in these duties by their
household companions. Thus, the solution found during the Feudal Age to
the problem of administering a large territory without the benefit of a formal
administrative structure was to break it down into parcels small enough to be
ruled personally by a few individuals.[34]

Ruling a large territory in this way had a significant drawback, however:
it allowed counts to become independent of the king and gave them the
wherewithal to challenge kingly authority. Kings tried to prevent counts from
becoming too independent by requiring them to pay homage and render
military service. They also established powerful, unswervingly loyal companions in counties scattered throughout the kingdom on whom they could
rely to bring a too-independent count to heel.[35]

Despite these efforts to maintain control from the center, the successor
Germanic kingdoms, already fragmented into counties, became even more
fragmented into a bewildering array of smaller quasi-independent principalities, duchies, and counties, each possessing its own military, governing,
financial, and judicial powers. This fragmentation of territory and politico-

military power was exacerbated by the Germanic practice of dividing the kingdom among the king's male heirs when he died.[36]

The decentralization of politico-military power was also the result of military threats to Europe by (1) Muslim armies from North Africa, known as *Saracens*, in the eighth century; (2) tribes from Scandinavia, known as Norsemen (*Norse,* meaning "North," thus, "Norsemen"), in the ninth century; and (3) in the tenth century by the *Magyars* (Hungarians), a nomadic horse people from the steppes of central Asia who were being displaced westward by the rise of the Ottoman Turks. The brunt of these assaults was borne by local counts and their retainers because kings could not raise armies quickly enough to confront bands of swiftly moving Muslim, Norse, and Magyar raiders. Therefore, counts had to defend their counties themselves. Gradually, this led them to believe that the counties they defended were their personal property, not the king's. The people that the count defended also came to believe that the count was their ruler, not the distant king. Thus, the necessities of military defense against swiftly moving raiders gradually undermined the king's ability to govern the realm through his counts. Territory became increasingly fragmented, and politico-military rule became increasingly indirect and local.[37]

PRIVATE WAR

The decentralized, fragmented, indirect way of exercising politico-military rule in the Germanic kingdoms that filled the void left by the collapsed western Roman Empire came to be known as feudalism, the word coming from the medieval Latin, *feodum,* itself a derivative of the German word *fee,* meaning "cattle" or "property."[38] *Feudalism* was a method of exercising politico-military rule by means of *private arrangements among individuals* rather than by a formal-legal administrative structure and a standing army, as had been the case in the Roman Empire.

The feudal society of Europe was organized into "estates," to which different rights, duties, and privileges were attached. This way of organizing society was based on the medieval understanding that humankind, since the beginning of time, had been divided into three hierarchically ranked *categories* of people based on three complementary but unequal *social functions*: the first estate, the clergy, who *pray* for all; the second estate, the nobility, who *fight* for all; and the third estate, the peasants, who *work* for all.[39] Of these social categories, the most important for the present discussion is the second estate, those who devoted themselves to a lifetime of fighting and among whom there was no schism between war-making and social life. It should be noted that the "vast majority of the population was uninvolved [in

war, which] was an unexceptional fact of life, chronic but limited, the voca-
tion of an aristocratic minority"[40] —that is, the second estate.

The *second estate* consisted of all members of the nobility, whose social
function was the exercise of secular politico-military power. When the Roman Empire collapsed, its large standing army was replaced with small private retinues of mounted, aristocratic warriors called knights in English,
cabalarii in Italian, *cavalheiros* in Portuguese, *chevaliers* in French, *Rittern*
in German, and *szlachta* in Polish. As Michael Howard has written, "During
the eighth and ninth centuries the only fighting man of any consequence . . .
was the mounted warrior, the knight."[41] Thus, the organized state-supported
mode of war of the Romans reverted to a kind of semi-primitive private war
that was heavily influenced by the "distinctive military culture of the Teutonic tribes, which encouraged face-to-face fighting with edged weapons"[42] as
well as the fragmented, indirect politico-military rule of the age. Not unlike
the Germanic war bands, retinues of heavily armored knights mounted on
large warhorses, "especially bred for their carrying and staying power and
the momentum they could engender in the charge,"[43] became the principal
military formation of the Feudal Age. The merging of the Germanic warrior
culture with the horse was made possible by advances in horse breeding and
the development of the *solid seat saddle* with attached *stirrups*. Thus, "from
the eighth century onward, the mounted warrior bestrode his horse from a
high saddle, lodged his feet in stirrups, and in consequence could manage
weapons and wear equipment hitherto associated exclusively with the foot
soldier."[44] European war changed from skirmishes between light cavalry
units into the *massed charge of heavy cavalry*. Foot soldiers were of little use
in such fighting because they could not stand up to the head-on charge of the
cavalry.[45] The aristocracy also forbade "the horseless from carrying arms,
since they might thereby . . . defend and even claim rights to which the
warriors did not concede their entitlement."[46]

An army during the Feudal Age, known as a *host*, was a temporary
coalescence of many private retinues of mounted armored knights called into
temporary war service by the king. By Roman standards, feudal armies were
small, between 10,000 and 15,000 knights and their attendants. In addition to
the knights, a feudal army contained the knights' *esquires* (shield bearers),
grooms for their horses, and their *sergeants* (servants). Individual knights
were responsible for procuring their own military equipment, which included
several especially bred stallions of exceptional size and stamina trained to
bite, kick, and butt; packhorses to carry food and equipment; a *broadsword*,
shield, mace, helmet, and *lance*; and a very expensive, chain-mail *surcoat*
reaching from neck to knee, made of 25,000 or more handmade, interlinked
iron rings. Knights were granted parcels of land called *fiefs* from which they
could derive sufficient wealth to purchase and maintain their equipment and
horses, as well as feed and clothe themselves and their family members, and,

if their fiefs were large enough, a number of retainers who formed the knights' retinues of fighting companions. Knights were granted by their lords the power to collect taxes and tolls and to dispense justice within their fiefs according to local customary law. It was from such taxes and fees that knights derived the wealth to pay for their military equipment and that of their retainers. In exchange for their fiefs, knights were expected to appear fully armed and prepared to render war service for forty days in peacetime and eighty days in wartime when summoned by their lords. The practice of granting land to knights as recompense for their military service encouraged localism and indirect rule even more. Over several centuries Europe became a welter of quasi-independent fiefs of various sizes, which supported a "land-owning warrior class . . . free of all duties save that of rendering mounted service to their lord for a given number of days during the year."[47]

To ensure the possession of their fiefs, knights built high, stone-walled castles "normally sited so as to command access roads, with a 'donjon' or keep in which their families could live, outbuildings for their retainers, the whole surrounded by a high curtain [stone] wall rendered proof by battlements against escalade and protected by a moat."[48] This resulted in the encastlellation of Europe, especially in the west, where feudalism originated and was deeply rooted. Across western Europe the impregnable stone-walled castle built on a strategic crag or hilltop provided the peasants living on and working the fief's land with a place of refuge in case of attack. The garrison of knights living in the castle sallied forth each day to maintain order within the fief during times of peace and to meet the enemy in times of war. Gradually, the knights who lived in these castles defied the king's commands and their castles became points of defiant local politico-military rule and obstacles to the king's kingdom-wide authority.[49]

War during the Feudal Age was about inheritance and ownership of lands, castles, and cities or wars of conquest against non-Christian peoples, pagans, and Muslims. Most often they involved the siege of a castle, strong points in a landscape, or a fortified town or city. Mechanical, counter-weight and torsion-powered siege engines, *trebuchets* and *mangonels*, respectively, inherited from the Romans, were used to heave at castle walls heavy rounded stones to breach them, or rotting animal carcasses and, occasionally, plague-ridden human corpses over them to spread disease among the defenders. Movable *siege towers* and *battering rams* were also used by attackers to gain entrance into the castle or fortified town. Those defending the castle, strong point, or town poured rocks, pots of quicklime, scalding water, and burning pitch on the attackers as they scaled the walls on ladders.[50]

As no king, duke, prince, or count had the administrative wherewithal to mobilize sufficient men, money, and matériel to make war over a long period of time, wars tended to be short and war-making episodic. The Hundred Years' War (1338–1453), for example, was not a sustained hundred-year-long conflict, but, rather, a series of battles and skirmishes to retain the ownership of English lands, towns, and castles situated in the Kingdom of France against the desire of French kings to take possession of those lands and make them an integral part of the French kingdom. The Christian *Reconquista* (Reconquest) of the Iberian Peninsula from the Muslims was not a sustained five-hundred-year war but numerous short wars fought by rival Christian kings, often decades apart.

The *martial culture* of feudalism placed a high value on the physical strength and fighting prowess of the individual knight; that is, on his horsemanship; dexterity with sword, lance, and mace; and ferocity in combat.[51] Knights valued close hand-to-hand combat because it was through such combat that a knight could demonstrate his fighting prowess, bravery, and honor. Kings donned armor and led their hosts in battle. Skill in mounted close hand-to-hand combat with sword, mace, and shield could only be acquired by individuals if they trained for it from early youth, usually in the castle of an uncle who taught the apprentice knight the manly arts of combat. Only after completing his apprenticeship would a young nobleman *"win his spurs"* and be proclaimed a knight by *accolade* in a ceremony blessed by the Catholic Church.

The holding of the warrior in high esteem in western Christendom and the blessing of the knight by the Catholic Church, despite the fact that the Church taught that war was evil, came about not because the Church renounced its prohibition against war, but rather because the Church shifted from its strict pacifism to the conditional acceptance of collective violence. In order to rectify war with Christian teaching against war, the Church developed a theory of *just war*: "Christian theologians agreed that certain wars were 'just'; broadly speaking, those waged on the authority of a lawful superior in a righteous cause."[52] One historian attributes this change from pacifistic Christianity to militaristic Christianity in western Christendom to the infusion of Germanic tribal traditions, such as the war band, prowess in battle, the joy of plunder, and the duty of revenge, into western Christian society.[53]

At the beginning of the Feudal Age, recruits for knighthood came from among young men who had the strength and skill to wield from horseback sword, lance, and mace. Knighthood was open to all those with the physical strength and dexterity to fight with such weapons. By the twelfth century, however, all members of the second estate, from the pettiest knight to the greatest duke, came to believe that they belonged to the same social group based on their ownership of territory and politico-military power, not prowess on the battlefield. Thus, an *aristocracy* came into being that believed that its sole reason for being was to fight and govern. It lived apart from the rest of feudal society according to a personal code of conduct called *"chivalry."* According to the chivalric ideal, all male members of the aristocracy were "gentlemen" (from the French *gentilhomme,* or man of good lineage) who were expected to comport themselves according to the chivalric cult of honor that required knights to be brave, strong, good horsemen, dexterous with weapons, and ferocious in combat. In addition, they were expected to have polished manners, a high moral sense, and skill and knowledge in the social arts of courtly life. Knights were expected to protect the Catholic Church, give aid to the weak, respect women, obey their lords, fight infidels, be truthful, be just, and keep their word.[54] Medieval aristocratic women were not combatants but spectators and witnesses to the bravery and prowess of knights on the field of battle and in the mock battle of the tournament.

The notion that knights were socially superior because of their martial skills, bravery, and devotion to duty, honor, and morality eventually gave rise to the idea that such status could be acquired only by being born to it. The right to be a knight became hereditary and the aristocracy became subject to its own legally recognized rights, duties, and obligations. Certain activities, such as trade and manual labor, were deemed incompatible with noble standing and were legally forbidden to the aristocracy. Such activities were considered mundane and dirty and contrary to the honor and good breeding of the nobility. Eventually, the aristocracy came to be subdivided into legally recognized ranks based on wealth and power, to which specific rights and duties were attached. The most powerful and prestigious were kings and dukes, followed by counts and knights.[55] The second estate dominated European political and military affairs until the end of the nineteenth century.

The practice that connected the territorial fragments of feudal politico-military rule together was *"vassalage,"* a formal set of personal dependencies within which all men were the "men of other men" to whom they owed obedience and loyalty and from whom they expected unwavering protection, assistance, and beneficence. The system was a blend of the idea of personal loyalty to the leader of the war band (*comitatus*) inherited from the Germanic tribes with the medieval ideal of faithfulness and reciprocal obligation.[56] By the ninth century the personal relationship between lords and vassals was entered into in a ceremony presided over by a cardinal or bishop of the Catholic Church. It involved the taking of an oath of fealty sworn by the vassal on the Bible, or a sacred relic, and an act of homage sealed with a kiss. Ties of vassalage, theoretically, lasted during the entire lives of both lord and vassal.[57]

By the tenth century, vassalage and other feudal politico-military practices had spread, in varying degrees, to most of western Europe in one form or another. The king was considered to be the *suzerain,* or overlord, of the entire kingdom. Below the king were several dukes who held huge tracts of land and were the king's direct vassals. Dukes, in turn, retained a number of counts who held the counties within their dukedoms and were their direct vassals. Counts, in turn, retained a number of knights who had been granted fiefs within their counties and were the direct vassals of their counts. Knights retained a number of companions to whom they granted manors within their fiefs. Kings were considered vassals of the emperor of the Holy Roman Empire and the pope, who was God's vassal on Earth.

Although vassalage created a reciprocal pyramid of politico-military obligations and personal service between superiors and inferiors, which ran from the king down through his direct vassals (dukes) and his indirect vassals (counts), the reality in most kingdoms was, according to one historian, a "confused mass of conflicting dependencies and loyalties, riddled with exceptions and exemptions, where the once clear lines of service were fouled up by generations of contested privileges, disputed rights, and half-forgotten obligations."[58] This fact gave rise to endless disputes over the ownership of lands and castles that, more often than not, were settled by war.

It was common practice for a lord at stated intervals or for special purposes to summon his vassals to his court, at which time problems common to the realm would be discussed. Vassals were obligated to attend their lord's court and give counsel and consent to the lord's requests for money and military support. Gradually, the court became a council, usually convened around a major holy day (holiday), such as Christmas or Easter, and attended by the upper nobility, the higher clergy of the Catholic Church, and representatives of the realm's largest towns. These individuals did not represent individuals in a particular geographical portion of the realm but, rather, the estates to which they belonged; that is, the category of people everywhere within the realm having the same social function (praying, fighting, or working) to which bundles of rights, privileges, and obligations were attached.

These councils of the three estates, which came to be called the Parliament in England, États-Généraux in France, the Riksdag in Sweden, the Sejm in Poland, the Cortes in Spain and Portugal, the Reichstag in German-speaking realms, and the Duma in Russia, voiced protest, restated to the king the rights of the estates, gave the king advice, helped him adjudicate disputes, and agreed to his requests for money, usually to cover extraordinary expenses, such as making war. As kings were often in want of money to make war and needed the consent of their great councils to levy the taxes to get the money they wanted, the relationship between kings and their councils was one of constant tension. Kings needed money, especially in time of war, and councils were reluctant to give it and expected justification.[59] As will be shown in the next chapter, the tension between crown and estates evolved in two main directions in Europe: one was in favor of the king to the detriment of the council and the other was in favor of the council to the detriment of the king.

In addition to the great council, the exercise of direct politico-military power by feudal kings over their realms was also curtailed by the Catholic

Church, the Church's military orders, such as the Templars and Hospitallers, as well as the nobility, especially dukes, all of whom owned large tracts of land within the kingdom. Many feudal kings also faced threats from neighboring monarchs who had rights of inheritance or predatory designs on their thrones.

VARIETIES OF FEUDAL "STATES"

The purpose of this section is to show how war and conquest brought into being two different types of European "states" during the Feudal Age. The first case shows how the politico-military practices of feudalism (rule by private arrangement among individuals, usually family members; personal obligation and service, especially in war; vassalage; inheritance as a legitimate reason for war) brought forth the Kingdom of Portugal. It also chronicles the struggles, often violent, of early Portuguese kings against the nobility, the neighboring Kingdom of Castile, and the Catholic Church in order to establish internal hierarchy and external autonomy for the new kingdom.

The second of these two cases of the feudal "state" is the ecclesiastical order-state of the Catholic Church. Although ignored or treated as an exotic politico-military organization of a bygone era by students of the state and warfare, the order states of the Catholic Church were powerful and legitimate forms of politico-military rule that competed effectively with secular kingdoms during the Feudal Age. A discussion of one of them, that of the Teutonic Knights, shows how the emerging European system of secular kingdoms began to see them as aberrant forms of politico-military rule and eliminated them from the system.

Portugal: From Galician County to Feudal Kingdom

Portugal emerged as a feudal kingdom during the Christian *Reconquista* (wars of reconquest) against Muslim peoples who had invaded the Iberian Peninsula from North Africa in 711. The *Reconquista* began from Asturias, a redoubt of Christian nobles in the extreme north of the peninsula, which was never conquered by the Muslims and incorporated into Muslim Spain. Asturias was declared a Christian kingdom in 722 and, in the tenth century, after the conquest and incorporation of the town of León, the Kingdom of León.

When Ferdinand I (1017–1065), king of León and count of Castile, died he willed his kingdom to his five children. The eldest son, Sancho (1036–1072), received Castile; the middle son, Alfonso (1043–1109), received León; and the youngest son, Garcia (1042–1090), received Galicia, which had been carved out from León. He gave his eldest daughter, Urraca (1033–1101), the town of Zamora and his youngest, Elvira (1038–1101), the town of Toro. In 1068, his oldest son, Sancho, resolved to reconsolidate his father's kingdom and rule it in its entirety. In order to do so he had to make war on his siblings. After defeating Garcia in 1071, he turned against Alfonso and Urraca. Alfonso was defeated in 1072 and Sancho reunited his father's territories as the Kingdom of León and Castile. In the same year, while besieging his sister Urraca in her fortified town of Zamora, Sancho was assassinated by a Zamoran nobleman who had infiltrated his encampment on a pretext. With Sancho's death, Alfonso, who had gone into exile to the Muslim vassal town of Toledo after his defeat, inherited his father's property, reunited the kingdom, and ruled as Alfonso VI from 1072 to 1109. The threat from Garcia was eliminated by enticing him to return from exile and then imprisoning him for life.

Henri (1066–1112), the youngest son of the duke of Burgundy, who had little chance of acquiring lands and titles by inheritance, joined Alfonso VI, his uncle by marriage, on a campaign against the Muslims. In reward for his loyal military service he was given in marriage the king's favorite but illegitimate daughter, Theresa (1080–1130), and the County of Portugal, then a fiefdom of the Kingdom of Galicia. Count Henri (Henriques in Portuguese) built an impressive high stone-walled castle at Guimarães. Henri was bound to Alfonso VI by the usual ties of vassalage: he was expected to be personally faithful and loyal to the king and to render him military service when required. Henri dutifully carried out his feudal obligations by attending royal councils and giving the king military aid by joining his campaigns against the Muslims.

Before Alfonso died in 1109 he designated his eldest illegitimate son Sancho as his successor. However, Sancho died in battle at Uclés in 1108, which made Alfonso's eldest legitimate daughter, Urraca, queen upon her father's death the following year. Before he died, Alfonso had arranged a marriage between Urraca and the king of Aragon, whom she reluctantly married to honor her father's wishes. This ignited a rebellion of Galician barons and scheming by her illegitimate half sister, Theresa, and her brother-in-law, Henri, countess and count of Portugal. In 1110, Urraca separated from her husband, whom she accused of abuse. Their estrangement escalated into a war and the marriage was annulled in 1112. Urraca ruled the kingdom until her death in 1126. She was followed on the throne by her son, who ruled as Alfonso VII (1105–1157).[60]

In order to consolidate control over his possessions, Alfonso VII decided to assert his suzerainty over Castile, which had fallen under the control of the king of Aragon and Navarre, as well as over his aunt, Theresa, countess of Portugal, who had inherited the county when Henri died in 1112. She refused to pay him homage. Alfonso forced her into submission in a six-week war in 1127. The barons in the County of Portugal blamed Theresa for the loss of their independence and abandoned her in favor of her son and heir, Afonso Henriques (1109–1185). Supported by the barons, Afonso Henriques rebelled against his mother's rule. In 1128 Theresa's host attacked Afonso Henriques and his barons at São Mamede near Guimarães. Theresa's host was defeated and she was forced to flee to Galicia. Afonso Henriques took possession of the county and called himself "Prince of Portugal."[61]

In 1135, Alfonso VII, finally secure in his control over León and Castile, proclaimed himself to be "Emperor of All Spain" and convoked a great council so that the kings and princes of northern Spain could pay him homage. Afonso Henriques, supported by his barons, refused to attend and even marched on Galicia to regain territory lost to Alfonso five years earlier. The emperor ordered the Galician barons to make war on Afonso. War was averted, however, when Afonso and Alfonso opened negotiations in 1137. A permanent peace was agreed in 1143. By the terms of the peace, Afonso Henriques was recognized by Alfonso as king of Portugal, although he was required to pay homage to the emperor and render him military service.[62] In order to solidify his legitimacy as king, Afonso Henriques declared himself to be a vassal of the pope and paid tribute to the Holy See in exchange for recognition. The Holy See did not immediately respond to this request because papal policy was to unify the Iberian peninsula under one crown in order to better carry out the *Reconquista*. Finally, in 1179, a papal bull issued by Pope Alexander III (c. 1100–1181) recognized Afonso Henriques as king of Portugal, granted him legal possession of all his conquests, and recognized the right of his successors to the throne of the kingdom.

At the time of Afonso Henriques's recognition as king, about one-half of the Iberian peninsula was still under Muslim control. Like other Christian kings on the peninsula, Afonso Henriques saw the *Reconquista* not only as his religious duty but an opportunity to expand the territory of his kingdom. In 1135, he built a castle at present-day Leiria, south of Guimarães, whence he and his host could sally forth against the Muslims to the south. In 1139 he achieved his most famous victory by conducting a daring campaign across the Tajo River deep into Muslim territory.[63] Almost ten years later, in 1147, assisted by crusaders sailing for the Latin East, he captured the Muslim castle at Olissipo, present-day Lisbon. He advanced across the Tagus (Tejo in Portuguese) River into the heartland of Muslim Iberia, Al-Andalus. Beja fell in 1162. In 1165, Geraldo Geraldes (?–1173), a local freebooter and adventurer, considered by some the Portuguese Cid, attacked Évora. He captured Serpa in 1166, and Badajoz, still Muslim, but under Leonese protection. This attack, which was not authorized by Afonso Henriques, brought the intervention of Ferdinand II of León (1137–1188). As Ferdinand was approaching Badajoz with his host to oust the Portuguese from his lands, Afonso Henriques, who had arrived to take command of the Portuguese host, was knocked from his horse, broke his leg, and was captured while fleeing on foot. After two months of captivity, he was ransomed in return for assurances that he would abandon all territorial claims in Galicia and Castile. At Afonso

Henriques's death in 1185, his domain extended from the Minho in the north well into the Alentejo in the south, and had been granted papal recognition and protection.[64]

Although Afonso Henriques's son and heir, Sancho I (1154–1211), continued the *Reconquista*, he devoted most of his energy to consolidating his kingdom by repopulating captured Muslim territory with Christian settlers and founding new towns. His son and heir, Afonso II (1185–1223), was little interested in conquest, but continued his father's policy of consolidation. His son and heir, Sancho II (1209–1248), was the least successful of Portugal's feudal kings. He was a competent military commander but a poor administrator; consequently, his reign was marked by much internecine fighting among his barons over lands and castles and towns and he was deposed with the blessing of the pope in 1247. He was succeeded by his younger brother, Afonso III (1210–1279), who, with the help of passing crusaders, besieged an isolated enclave of Muslims in Faro in the Algarve, the extreme south, in 1249. This campaign extended the Kingdom of Portugal to the Atlantic Ocean west of the Straits of Gibraltar. Afonso III was the first Portuguese king to use the title "King of Portugal and the Algarve."[65]

Early Portuguese kings did not have a politico-military monopoly over the kingdom but ruled indirectly through the aristocracy, the Catholic Church, and the ecclesiastical military-religious orders. To the north of the Tejo River, Portugal was divided into many *terras* (fiefs) governed by noblemen confirmed by the king. The Church divided the Portuguese kingdom into dioceses each under a bishop appointed by the pope. In the southern part of the kingdom, beyond the Tejo River, the military-religious orders (Templars, Calatravans, etc.) and monastic orders (Cistercians, Benedictines, etc.) had been granted huge tracts of land as payment for taking part in the wars against the Muslims and cultivating the land. The towns, which belonged to the king, were self-governing but were overseen by an agent of the crown, the *alacide,* who was empowered to intervene in local matters on the king's behalf when necessary.[66]

Thus, the king had little direct politico-military control over the realm. It was curtailed in the north by the prevailing feudal system over which the crown retained the last word only in matters of high justice but little else. In the south, the monastic orders were integrated into the hierarchy of the Catholic Church and the religious-military orders were self-governing and answerable only to the pope. In the north, the aristocracy ruled their fiefs themselves with little interference from the king. As the principal source of the king's revenue was taxes on the lands of the king's vassals as well as tithes on lands directly owned by him, the maintenance of the royal patrimony intact was imperative.

When Afonso II ascended the throne in 1212 he discovered that his father had willed large portions of the royal patrimony to the Church. After a lengthy legal battle with Rome over the provisions of his father's will, the Holy See recognized the king's right to maintain the royal patrimony intact.[67] From then on, the crown gradually won the right to revise all grants of lands and donations to the Church and inheritances of the nobility. Subsequently, Portuguese kings began the practice of sending forth royal commissions to investigate land ownership to ensure that crown lands were not being expropriated by the aristocracy or the Church. These inquiries (*inquerições*), which gathered evidence independently of the bishops of the dioceses, usually revealed illegal extensions of land boundaries by the bishops. The head of the Catholic Church in the Kingdom of Portugal, the archbishop of Braga, angered by the investigations of the king's commissioners, excommunicated Afonso II in 1219. The king responded by seizing Church property and deposing the archbishop, who fled to Rome. In 1220, the pope confirmed the king's excommunication and relieved him of his oath of fealty to the Holy See. The conflict between Afonso and the Church ended when he died excommunicate in 1223. His chancellor arranged an ecclesiastical burial in exchange for the return of property taken from the Church and a promise that future inquires would respect canon law.[68]

The struggle between the crown and the Church resurfaced when, in 1258, Afonso III revived the *inquerições.* Once again the Church was found to be the biggest expropriator of the king's lands. In 1267, Portugal's bishops revolted and the archbishop and four bishops went to Rome where they accused the king of illegally confiscating Church lands. Afonso placated the pope by launching a new campaign against the Muslims. He appointed a new archbishop and bishops in the four abandoned bishoprics and retained the confiscated Church property. The pope answered by excommunicating Afonso, who remained defiant and did not pledge obedience to the Holy See until just before his death in 1279.

The struggle between the Church and the crown finally ended during the reign of King Dinis (1261–1325), who, like his predecessor, launched *inquerições* and forbade the Church and the monastic orders from purchasing land and required them to sell land purchased since the beginning of his reign. For this, Dinis, like his father and grandfather before him, was excommunicated. This time the king refused to pledge obedience to the Holy See and died an excommunicate. No attempt was made to have the Holy See lift the excommunication order after his death. It could be said that King Dinis risked the fate of his immortal soul to establish the crown's right against the Church to regulate the royal patrimony.[69]

During the reign of Afonso IV (1291–1357) various disputes and fighting occurred with the Kingdom of Castile to whom some ties of vassalage still existed. After the relatively peaceful interlude during the reign of his son and heir, Pedro I (1320–1367), the conflict with Castile resurfaced when, in 1383, Fernando I (1345–1383) died leaving no son to inherit the throne. His only child was a girl, Princess Beatriz (1373–1420), who was married to Juan I (1358–1390) of Castile. The prenuptial agreement said that the throne of Portugal would be the property of the male offspring of their union. When Fernando died, his queen, Eleanor Teles (1350–1386), became regent from 1372 until 1383, during which time she avidly supported her daughter Beatriz's claim to the throne. The nobility was unwilling to support Beatriz because she would merge the Portuguese kingdom with the Kingdom of Castile. Queen Teles's main rival was her husband's bastard son, João, the master of the Order of Avis, the Portuguese branch of the Knights of Calatrava. A revolt by João and his supporters drove Teles from Portugal. The Castilian king chose not to relinquish his wife's claims to the Portuguese throne and invaded the kingdom in 1384, but was defeated at Atoleiros by Nuno Álvares Pereira (1360–1431), later constable of Portugal. The next year, on the anniversary of that battle, the Portuguese cortes proclaimed João (1357–1433) king of Portugal. After his accession, João annexed the towns and cities that had supported Beatriz.

Juan of Castile was enraged by this turn of events and assembled a host of 30,000 Castilian and French knights to invade the Portuguese kingdom, depose João, and install Beatriz on the throne. The Castilians were met by a much smaller Portuguese host, again led by Nuno Álvares Pereira, at São Jorge near Aljubarrota on August 14, 1385. Supported by a contingent of English longbowmen, veterans of the Hundred Years' War, the Portuguese host, which had the advantage of the high ground, the longbowmen, and a prepared system of ditches and obstacles, inflicted a crushing defeat on the Castilians. The battle turned into a rout of the Castilian host and King Juan fled the field of battle on foot in order to avoid being captured. Scattered skirmishes continued between Portuguese and Castilian forces until the death of Juan I in 1390. Eventually, Castile recognized the independence of the Portuguese kingdom in 1411. The victory assured João of Avis accession to the throne and the founding of a new ruling dynasty, the House of Avis. He ruled from 1385 to 1433.[70]

During the lax reign of Afonso V (1432–1481), the nobility in the north had accrued enormous wealth and power by overstepping their rights and privileges; usurping large parcels of land from the king's patrimony; involving themselves in the affairs of the king's towns; and administering their own justice. When João II (1455–1495) came to the throne, he found the royal patrimony to be so reduced that he is purported to have said that he was little more than "king of the roads" of Portugal, and resolved to gain control of the nobility.[71] Most of the king's property had been usurped by about a dozen noble families, the most powerful being the Duke of Bragança and Guimarães, who was also the Marquis of Vila Viçosa and Count of Barçelos, Ourém, Arraiolos, and Neiva. The duke had a private retinue of 15,000 knights and squires.[72] João required the nobility to take an oath of allegiance and show title to their lands. The Duke of Bragança and other great nobles refused. A search of the duke's papers by agents of the king revealed correspondence between the duke and King Ferdinand (1452–1516) and Queen Isabella (1451–1504) of Spain concerning the marriage of a Bragança to an illegitimate daughter of the Spanish king. João used this correspondence as a pretext to arrest and try the duke for treason. In June 1484, he was found guilty and beheaded in Évora. This act caused the nobles to conspire to assassinate the king and put one of their own, the Duke of Viseu, on the throne. There being a large number of conspirators, João learned the exact day of the assassination attempt and surprised the conspirators with armed force. The king himself stabbed to death the leader of the conspiracy and imprisoned the rest. Three were later tried, found guilty, and beheaded.[73]

João's successor, Manuel I (1469–1521), completed the process of subduing the aristocracy by turning it into a dependent court nobility appointed by the crown and given annual stipends on which to live. He also completed the takeover and secularization of the military-religious orders in the south of the kingdom. With the pope's permission, he absorbed the lands and castles of the Order of Christ (formerly the Templars) into his patrimony. The land holdings of the Cistercian and Benedictine monasteries were sold.

During the reigns of João and Manuel, the struggle between the crown and the Church, the military-religious orders, the nobility, and Castile was finally won by the crown. Over the next two centuries, the crown managed to put in place the administrative structures necessary to bypass the nobility and the Church and rule the kingdom directly.

The Teutonic Knights: From Ecclesiastical Order-State to Two Secular Duchies

The religious-military order-states emerged during the Crusades, the "succession of military expeditions from western Christendom to Syria and Palestine in the twelfth and thirteenth centuries whose aim was to recover the Holy Places of [Christianity] from their Islamic rulers."[74] At the end of the eleventh century, the Byzantine emperor, besieged by the Seljuk Turks, appealed for military assistance from the pope, the spiritual leader of western Christendom. The pope responded in November 1095 by convening a council of high churchmen at Claremont, after which he preached a sermon calling on "Frankish knights to vow to march to the East with the aims of freeing Christians from Islamic rule and liberating the tomb of Christ, the Holy Sepulcher in Jerusalem, from Muslim control."[75] By the following spring, a vast army of Crusaders was assembled and marched to the Levant to relieve Constantinople and to recover Jerusalem, which had been occupied by Muslims since 638 CE. Those who took part in these military expeditions were assured by the pope that they were fighting a holy war and were guaranteed certain spiritual benefits: Crusader souls would spend less time in Purgatory, and, if killed battling the infidel, they would be martyrs for the faith and their souls would go directly to Heaven.[76]

There were five official Crusades: the first in 1096, the second in 1146, the third in 1189, the fourth in 1204, and the fifth in 1217. In between these papally sanctioned military expeditions there was a more or less continuous flow of smaller expeditions led by individual barons, clerics, and even children.[77] The first three Crusades succeeded in establishing four Christian secular feudal states in Syria and Palestine: the Kingdom of Jerusalem, the Principality of Antioch, and the counties of Edessa and Tripoli. No more than seventy miles wide at its widest, the *Latin East*, as these feudal states came to be called collectively by the Crusaders, was an attempt to create units of politico-military rule that could stand against the Muslim hinterland and protect Christian pilgrims to the holy sites of Christianity.[78]

The conditions that prevailed in the Latin East and western Christianity's just war theory, which permitted the waging of war for the faith as a means to salvation,[79] gave rise to another form of feudal state: the ecclesiastical order-state. These states emerged from the military-religious brotherhoods that sprang up in the Latin East during the Crusades. The first of these was founded in 1120 by a Burgundian Crusader, Hugues de Payens (1070–1136), who persuaded seven fellow knights to help him protect pilgrims on the road from Jaffa to Jerusalem. The king of Jerusalem gave these knights the al-Aqsa mosque, which was believed to be the Temple of Solomon. Eventually, they transformed themselves into a religious order, took vows of poverty, and began calling themselves the Poor Knights of Christ and the Temple of Solomon, or Templars.[80]

The success of the Templars inspired several convents of monks of the Kingdom of Jerusalem to followed suit. In 1130, monks of the Hospital of St. John the Baptist, which had been founded to take care of poor and sick pilgrims, assumed military duties and came to be known as Hospitallers.[81] The monks of the Hospice of St. Mary of the Teutons, which had been established by merchants from Bremen and Lubeck during the siege of Acre in 1190, also began to assume military duties after they were joined by German-speaking Crusaders. This order became known as the Teutonic Knights. All three orders were the manifestation of the western medieval ideal of a warrior dedicated to Christ and to the protection of the weak.

The brotherhoods were organized for war and projected politico-military power in the same way that secular feudal rulers did. As the massed cavalry charge was the chief military formation of the age, the brethren, grouped into two ranks, knights and sergeants, wearing conical steel helmets and chain-mail surcoats and armed with long, two-edged broadswords, rode into battle on large war horses. Reflecting the feudal concept of the "stronghold," the orders built high, stone-walled fortifications at strategic locations, which provided safe haven for the brethren from which they sallied forth to strike the enemy quickly and to which they returned with captured booty, prisoners (for ransom), and livestock.[82]

The military brotherhoods copied the monastic life and organizational structure of the religious orders, such as the Cistercians, as well as those of the secular feudal kingdoms. The smallest unit, equivalent to the fief, was the commandery, a fortified stronghold occupied by a preceptor and his retinue, who was given the responsibility of controlling the surrounding territory. The commanderies were grouped into priories, and priories into provinces, ruled by a master. The entire order was ruled by a grand master.[83] Preceptors, priors, masters, and the grand master led the order in battle and administered its lands and castles. The preceptors, priors, masters, and grand master shared their military and administrative duties with an assemblage of senior brothers called a chapter. The brethren of the orders were recruited from among the younger sons of the European nobility who had no chance of inheriting the family fief. The orders also fell outside of the regular hierarchy of the Catholic Church and were directly accountable to the pope.[84]

In addition to fighting the infidel, the religious-military brotherhoods were engaged in charitable works, such as taking care of the sick and providing for the poor. The orders made the money they needed to support their military and charitable activities by selling the surpluses of livestock and crops they raised; levying fines within their territories; collecting rents on their properties; receiving papal indulgences; taking booty from defeated enemies; and collecting tribute from non-Christian rulers in adjacent territories. Through such activities, and through benefactions and donations, the military-religious orders amassed vast properties scattered around Christendom.[85] Although individual brothers had taken vows of poverty and owned nothing, the orders themselves eventually became extremely wealthy. Their commanderies became early banks where nobles could store their money, jewels, and documents safely.

The secular crusader states were unsustainable, however. By the fourth Crusade, Salah ad-Din (Saladin) (1138–1193), from the Baghdad Caliphate, had established himself and Mameluke politico-military rule in Egypt, whence he began a Muslim counteroffensive against the Christians. He conquered Jerusalem in 1187 and forced the Christians to coastal cities. In 1291, Acre, the last Crusader coastal stronghold in the Latin East, was besieged and fell after six weeks of fighting.

Despite being ejected from the Latin East, two of the ecclesiastical-military orders, the Hospitallers and the Teutonic Knights, were able to survive for several hundred years more by establishing order-states outside of the Latin East from which they continued to fight non-Christian peoples. The Templars, the richest and most powerful of these brotherhoods, was unable to establish an order-state because it had become the target of secular kings who could not tolerate within their domains an immensely powerful and wealthy independent entity of politico-military rule composed of aristocrats subject to monastic discipline who were armed and permitted by the Catholic Church to shed blood. The Templars were dissolved by the king of France, Philip IV (1268–1314), between 1307 and 1311. The grand master of the order, Jacques de Moly (1240–1314), was burned at the stake in 1314 for heresy, and the property of the Templars was either transferred to the Hospitallers or confiscated by the crown.[86]

Realizing that they could not successfully compete with the Templars and the Hospitallers in the Latin East, the Teutonic Knights decided to concentrate their religious and military activities in Europe, which was not yet fully Christianized. The Magyar-speaking King Andreas II (c. 1177–1235), who was being attacked by Turkish Kurmans, gave the brothers the Burzen district of southern Transylvania. Using fighting techniques learned in the Latin East, the Teutonic Knights defeated the Kurmans, pacified the district, and settled it with German-speaking peasants. King Andreas became frightened of the order's power and attacked it with a large host and evicted it from Armenia in 1225.

The order was forced to move on and eventually settled on lands east of the Elbe River, inhabited by polytheistic Slavonic-speaking tribes, among whom German-speaking tribes to the west had raided for slaves. When these German tribes were converted to Christianity by Charlemagne, the Slavonic-speaking area to the east became a *mark* (border) of western Christendom and slaving expeditions began to assume a religious character: the capture of "heathen" slaves was combined with their conversion to Christianity. By the end of the tenth century, present-day Bohemia, Silesia, and Poland had been converted. Gradually, a strong German presence was established beyond the Elbe and Oder to the Vistula. At the Vistula, the Germans encountered the Wends, Prussians, Courlanders, Lithuanians, Letts, who spoke Baltic dialects of Slavonic, and Estonians, who spoke a dialect of Fenno-Ugric. These tribes fiercely resisted the Germans and conversion to Christianity. In order to subdue and convert them, Pope Gregory IX (1145–1241) authorized a holy war against them.[87]

After having been expelled from Armenia, the Teutonic Knights joined the crusade against the "Northern Saracens," especially the Prussians,[88] a warlike people who practiced an extreme form of polytheism that included human sacrifice. In 1226 the Polish king offered the Teutonic Knights the province of Chelmo and any additional lands they could conquer. The Holy Roman Emperor granted them full sovereignty over these lands.[89] Two hundred brethren arrived in 1230 and immediately began their crusade against the Prussians. In 1231, they crossed the Vistula and stormed the fortress-temple of the Prussian chieftain and hanged him from his own sacred oak. Thus began a forty-year war against the Prussians, during which time extremely harsh methods were used to convert them to Christianity. Gradually, the Prussians were "reduced"—that is—conquered and Christianized. In 1223, Marienburg Castle, the future headquarters of the Teutonic Knights, was built.

After conquering the Prussians, the Teutonic Knights continued their crusade against the Rus in 1240, and campaigned against the Livonians and the Sams.[90] Revolts of the Prussians who wanted to return to their polytheistic religion were met with a policy of bloody extermination: chieftains were hunted down and burned alive, their followers were tortured and killed, crops uprooted, and villages razed. Whole clans disappeared. By 1283 only about 170,000 Prussians remained alive.[91]

Having finally pacified the Prussians, the order moved its headquarters to Marienburg in 1309, and the knights began to create "an ecclesiastical and military state of a unique type."[92] The order created its own bishoprics with the approval of the pope. The bishoprics were subject to the authority of the order's grand master, who, because his domain was outside of the Holy Roman Empire, was considered to be a sovereign prince. All bishops were priest-brethren of the order. The order built commanderies and convents for its brethren, established towns, granted municipal rights to burghers, and allied itself with the Hanseatic League. Gradually, the Teutonic Knights became a commercial and maritime power along the shore of the Baltic Sea.[93]

The order-state (*ordensstaat*) of the Teutonic Knights was, for its day, very bureaucratic, having been strongly influenced by Church administration, which had been influenced by Roman administration. Its administrators pioneered "scientific" bookkeeping, and kept meticulous archives; commanderies were built according to a standard design; taxes were collected systematically; roads were built and maintained on a regular basis; old and infirm knights were retired to the hospital at Marienburg. A system of uniform weights and measures was developed, put in place, and enforced, and the knights minted their own coins. Furs, salt, timber, falcons, horses, silver, wax, and amber were exported to other parts of Europe. Every commandery had a theologian and lawyer to handle religious and legal questions. A law school was established at Marienburg.[94]

The knights settled their order-state with German and Dutch peasants who were given land in exchange for rent in kind. German-speaking nobles were given vast estates in exchange for military service. Gradually, these nobles came to form a landed aristocracy, the *Junkers*, who were given official positions in the order-state and organized into a militia. Eventually, the indigenous Prussian population was reduced to serfdom and Germanized. Prussians were forbidden from living in German villages and Jews were prohibited from settling within the territory of the order-state.[95]

The grand master was a sovereign prince whose power within the order-state was limited by a council of bailiffs, which functioned like the great council in secular feudal kingdoms. Decisions taken by the grand master and the council constituted the law of the order-state. This uniformity of the law, administration, coordination of domestic policy, direct internal government, control of Church affairs, and support of external trade gave one historian to write that the order-state of the Teutonic Knights in Prussia was Europe's "first modern state."[96]

The desire of the Polish crown to have an outlet to the Baltic Sea, which was blocked by the order-state of the Teutonic Knights, which ran along the coast from the Holy Roman Empire in the west to the land of the Rus in the east, resulted in an attack by a large host of Polish knights who defeated the much smaller host of the knights at the Battle of Tannenberg in 1410. In 1411, the First Treaty of Thorn was signed between the brotherhood and the Polish crown, which gave the Polish monarchy Samaiten and Dobrzyn.[97] Despite having signed a peace treaty with the knights, the Polish crown attacked them again with a large pan-Slavic army in 1422. The knights were defeated, and the Second Treaty of Thorn (1466) divided the order state into two parts. The western portion (West Prussia), including the port city of Danzig, was absorbed by the Polish crown, and the eastern portion (East Prussia), continued under the control of the knights, but as a fief of the Polish king.

After the Second Treaty of Thorn, the Teutonic Knights tried to rebuild their order-state in East Prussia and gain independence from the Polish crown. In order to survive, the knights began to emulate the governing practices of the secular monarchies around them. In 1497, they elected a strong secular prince of the Holy Roman Empire, Friedrich of Saxony (1463–1525), as their grand master. This set the pattern for additional grand masters to be secular princes of the Holy Roman Empire. Margrave Albrecht von Branden-burg-Anspach (1490–1568), who was elected grand master in 1511, demanded the return of West Prussia from Poland and compensation for its fifty-year occupation.

At this point a new threat to the Teutonic order-state appeared, Protestantism, which had been spreading among the people of West Prussia. Martin Luther (1483–1556) called the Teutonic order a "hermaphrodite" institution (a reference to its religious *and* secular nature) and advised Prince Albrecht to "give up your vows as a monk; take a wife; abolish the order; and make yourself hereditary Duke of Prussia."[98] Albrecht eventually accepted Luther's advice, and, in 1524, he converted to Lutheranism and signed a treaty with the Polish crown that made West Prussia a secular duchy and Albrecht into a secular duke. He ruled over his dukedom as a secular ruler until his death in 1568, and his heirs until 1618, when the duchy was inherited by the

Hohenzollerns. During these years, many knights converted to Lutheranism, married, and founded Prussian noble families.[99]

The knights who refused to convert left West Prussia for East Prussia, where the order remained intact. Nonetheless, Lutheranism spread rapidly in East Prussia as well and, in 1526, the grand master was asked by the Diet of Worms to convert to Lutheranism and become a secular duke. The grand master refused and died a Catholic. In 1557, Czar Ivan IV, the Terrible (1530–1584), demonized the order and, using language reminiscent of the kind of language used today to describe aberrant forms of politico-military rule in the contemporary world, denounced it as a "criminal organization" and invaded East Prussia. The knights resisted but to no avail. By this time the order was bankrupt and almost without an army. Ivan's army easily overwhelmed the knights and occupied the southern portion of their order-state. In 1562, the northern portion was attacked and occupied by the Swedish crown while the Danish crown occupied its offshore islands. The grand master ceded all of the order-state's lands to the Polish crown. The grand master became the duke of Courland, which he held as an independent secular fief from the Polish crown. His descendants ruled Courland until the eighteenth century. As was the case in West Prussia, many knights converted to Lutheranism, married, and founded new noble families. The order-state of the Teutonic Knights ceased to exist by being transformed into two secular dukedoms.[100]

CONCLUSION

Europe was exceptional in that it contained diverse forms of territorial politico-military rule after the collapse of the Roman imperial state. The centralized formal-legal structures of the Roman imperial state were replaced by stateless Germanic tribes, which had no formal-legal structures and ruled themselves by personal loyalty. Essentially, politico-military power became privatized in that the kingdom was considered to be the patrimony of the king. Feudalism was the method devised to administer the successor Germanic kingdoms. In these kingdoms politico-military rule involved private, reciprocal personal obligations among individuals, not loyalty to formal-legal institutions. The most important social category in these kingdoms was the nobility, who exercised politico-military rule as a matter of right. The nobility consisted of mounted warriors who were expected to come to military aid of their king when called upon to do so, as well as render to him advice on important questions facing the realm. There were no formally organized armies, as had been the case with Rome. An army was a temporary coming together of various retinues of knights. The nobility built and ensconced themselves in high stone-walled castles from which they exercised politico-military rule over their fiefs. War was about the ownership of lands, towns, castles, and kingdoms. Feudal politico-military rule was fragmented, decentralized, personal, and chaotic. Eventually, feudal kings were able to establish internal hierarchies of direct control and administration over their kingdoms and free themselves from external control by the Catholic Church.

Portuguese kings were among the monarchs in Europe to accomplish internal hierarchy and external autonomy. The Portuguese feudal state began as a dependency of the Kingdom of León. Granted to Henri, the youngest son of the duke of Burgundy in 1093 as recompense for military service to Alfonso VI, king of León, it was able to free itself from León and become an independent kingdom with papal recognition. This involved several battles in which Portuguese nobility were led by Henri's son, Afonso Henriques, against the king of León and against his mother, Theresa, who had taken over the county of Portugal upon the death of her husband. After being recognized as king, Afonso Henriques made war on the Muslim peoples to the south. He captured Lisbon in 1147 and penetrated into the region south of the Tajo (Tagus) River, called the Alentejo. His successors were able to complete the *Reconquista* of the western portion of the Iberian Peninsula in 1249.

Although the early kings of Portugal had little direct politico-military power over the kingdom, later kings were able to consolidate kingly rule over the realm by investigating and challenging the Catholic Church over the rightful ownership of land, defeating the Castilians at Aljubarrota in 1385, and bringing the nobility to heel by making it a court nobility dependent on the king's largesse. The religious-military orders (Templars, Calatravans) and the monastic houses (Benedictines, Cistercians) were also suppressed and their lands and wealth absorbed into the royal patrimony. By the late 1400s and early 1500s, the Portuguese crown had established an internal hierarchy of direct rule over the kingdom and freed itself from external control by the Catholic Church, which laid the basis for the eventual development of the modern Portuguese state.

Unlike the Portuguese monarchy, the ecclesiastical order-state of the Teutonic Knights was a state-building blind alley. Secular centralized kingdoms, such as Portugal, gradually triumphed over them. The order-state was gradually suppressed by the growing power of secular kingly states, which increasingly sought to reproduce the secular kingly form of politico-military rule by disciplining the sovereignty of nonconforming (so-called aberrant, deviant, or rogue) states. Increasingly, European kingly states came to be a "management committee" seeking to maintain the system according to the prevalent conception of legitimate politico-military rule emerging in the European state system. The Teutonic Knights' order-state saved itself, as it were, by emulating the prevailing secular conception of legitimate sovereignty under pressure from the Polish and Swedish kingdoms, and imperial Russia, by becom-

ing two secular dukedoms, one of which grew into the future Prussian kingly
state, and, eventually, the German imperial state.

NOTES

1. Brendan Simms, *Europe: The Struggle for Supremacy from 1453 to the Present* (New York: Basic Books, 2013), pp. 2–3.
2. David Alvarez, *The Pope's Soldiers: A Military History of the Modern Vatican* (Lawrence: Kansas University Press, 2011).
3. Paul Kennedy, *The Rise and Fall of the Great Powers: Economic Change and Military Conflict from 1500 to 2000* (New York: Random House, 1987), p. 17.
4. Philip T. Hoffman, *Why Did Europe Conquer the World?* (Princeton and Oxford: Princeton University Press, 2015), pp. 120–21.
5. *Ibid.*, pp. 142–47.
6. *Ibid.*, pp. 132–33
7. *Ibid.*, pp. 52–53.
8. Hendrik Spruyt, *The Sovereign State and Its Competitors: An Analysis of Systems Change* (Princeton, NJ: Princeton University Press, 1994), p. 12.
9. *Ibid.*. p.16.
10. *Ibid.*, p. 23.
11. Norman Davies, *Europe: A History* (Oxford: Oxford University Press, 1996), p. 150.
12. J. M. Roberts, *A History of the World* (New York: Viking Penguin, 1983), p. 232.
13. William L. Langer (ed.), *Western Civilization: Paleolithic Man to the Emergence of the European Powers* (New York: Harper & Row, 1968), p. 222–23.
14. Azar Gat, *War in Human Civilization* (Oxford: Oxford University Press, 2006), p. 317.
15. Graham Webster, *The Roman Imperial Army*, third edition (Totowa, NJ: Barnes and Noble, 1985), pp. 1–27.
16. Jean Bethke Elshtain, *Women and War* (Chicago: University of Chicago Press, 1987), p. 121.
17. Kennedy, *op. cit.*
18. Keegan, *A History of Warfare* (New York: Vintage Books, 1994), p. 281.
19. *Ibid.*, p. 281.
20. Aurelio Bernardi, "The Economic Problems of the Roman Empire," and I. M. Finley, "Manpower Problems and the Fall of Rome," in Carlo M. Cipolla (ed.), *The Economic Decline of Empires* (London: Methuen, 1970), pp. 16–83 and pp. 84–91, respectively.
21. Langer, *op. cit.*, p. 294.
22. Herman Dörries, *Constantine the Great*, trans. by Roland H. Bainton (New York: Harper Torch Books, 1972), pp. 3–4.
23. *Ibid.*, p. 25.
24. Stewart C. Easton, *The Western Heritage: From the Earliest Times to the Present* (New York: Holt, Rinehart, & Winston, 1970), p. 170.
25. Elshtain, *op. cit.*, p 124.
26. William McNeill, *The Rise of the West: A History of the Human Condition* (Chicago: University of Chicago Press, 1963), pp. 338–39.
27. Dörries, *op. cit.*, p. 25.
28. Elshtain, *op. cit.*, p. 127.
29. *Ibid.*, p. 191 and p. 194.
30. Will Durant, *Caesar and Christ: A History of Roman Civilization and of Christianity from Their Beginnings to AD 325* (New York: Simon & Schuster, 1944), pp. 618–19.
31. Reinhard Bendix, *Kings or People: Power and the Mandate to Rule* (Berkeley: California University Press, 1978), pp. 21–35.
32. Langer, *op. cit.*, p. 349.
33. Herbert H. Rowen, *The King's State: Proprietary Dynasticism in Early Modern France* (New Brunswick, NJ: Rutgers University Press, 1980), pp. 29–30.

34. Joseph R. Strayer, *Feudalism* (New Brunswick, NJ: Krieger Publishing Co., 1965), pp. 29–30.

35. *Ibid.*

36. The breakup of Charlemagne's Carolingian is the most famous example. Charlemagne's son Louis the Pious, who had received the empire intact, having been made co-emperor before his father died, willed the empire to his eldest son, Lothar, and sub-kingdoms to his two younger sons, Charles the Bald, and Louis the German. When Louis the Pious died in 840, a war broke out among Lothar and his brothers for possession of the imperial throne. The dispute was settled in 843 with the Treaty of Verdun, which partitioned the empire into three new kingdoms: West Francia held by Charles the Bald, East Francia held by Louis the German, and the Middle Kingdom held by Lothar. The Middle Kingdom was itself divided into three entities: the Duchy of Burgundy, the Kingdom of Lower Burgundy, and the Kingdom of Upper Burgundy. See Norman Davies, *Vanished Kingdoms: The Rise and Fall of States and Nations* (New York: Viking, 2012), pp. 104–106 for more fragmentations.

37. Strayer, *op. cit.*, p. 34.

38. *Ibid.*, pp. 11–12.

39. Georges Duby, *The Three Orders: Feudal Society Imagined*, trans. by Arthur Goldhammer (Chicago: University of Chicago Press, 1978).

40. Elshtain, *op. cit.* p. 133.

41. Michael Howard, *War in European History*, updated edition (Oxford: Oxford University Press, 2009), pp. 2–3.

42. Keegan, *op. cit.*, p. 285.

43. Howard, *op. cit.*, p. 3.

44. Keegan, *op. cit.*, p. 286.

45. Davies, *op. cit.*, p. 311.

46. Keegan, *op. cit.*, p. 293.

47. Howard, *op. cit.*, p. 4.

48. *Ibid.*

49. Robert Bartlett, *The Making of Europe: Conquest, Colonization, and Culture Change, 950–1350* (Princeton, NJ: Princeton University Press, 1993), pp. 65–70.

50. See Geoffrey Hindley, *Medieval Sieges & Siegecraft* (New York: Skyhorse Publishing, 2014) for a detailed discussion of medieval siegecraft.

51. Maurice Keen, *Medieval Warfare: A History* (Oxford: Oxford University Press, 1999).

52. Howard, *op. cit.*, p. 5.

53. Desmond Seward, *The Monks of War: The Military-Religious Orders* (London: Archon Books, 1972), p. 12.

54. Andrea Hopkins, *Knights* (New York: Artabras, 1990), pp. 99–123.

55. Sidney Painter, *The Rise of the Feudal Monarchies* (Ithaca, NY: Cornell University Press, 1951), pp. 29–30.

56. Roberts, *op. cit.*, p. 32.

57. Jeffery Burton Russell, *Medieval Civilization* (New York: John Wiley, 1968), p. 204.

58. Davies, *op. cit.,* p. 313.

59. Painter, *op. cit.*, pp. 1–4.

60. A. H. de Oliveira Marques, *A History of Portugal, Vol 1: From Lusitania to Empire* (New York: Columbia University Press, 1972), pp. 34–38.

61. H. V. Livermore, *A New History of Portugal* (Cambridge: Cambridge University Press, 1969), pp. 9–10.

62. *Ibid.*, pp. 47–49.

63. According to Livermore, *op. cit.*, p. 52, there is considerable doubt as to the precise location of this legendary victory because the battle's location, Ourique, is too deep inside Muslim Iberia. Livermore suggests that the actual site is Chão de Ourique near the present city of Santarém

64. Marques, *op. cit.*, pp. 65–66.

65. Stanley G. Payne, *A History of Spain and Portugal*, Vol. 1 (Madison: University of Wisconsin Press, 1973), p. 113.

66. Marques, *op. cit.*, Vol. 2, pp. 83–84.

67. Livermore, *op. cit.*, p.73.

68. *Ibid.*

69. *Ibid.*, 83.

70. Payne, *op. cit.*, pp. 127–29.

71. Charles E. Nowell, *A History of Portugal* (New York: Van Nostrand, 1952), p. 48.

72. Livermore, *op. cit.*, p. 123.

73. Nowell, *op. cit.*, pp. 51–52.

74. Jonathan Riley-Smith, "The Crusading Movement in History," in Jonathan Riley-Smith (ed.) *The Oxford Illustrated History of the Crusades* (Oxford: Oxford University Press, 1997), p. 1.

75. Roberts, *op. cit.*, p. 148.

76. Friedrich Heer, *The Medieval World, 1100–1350*, trans. by Janet Sondheimer (New York: New American Library, 1961), p. 126.

77. Seward, *op. cit.*, p. 12.

78. *Ibid.*

79. *Ibid.*, p. 191.

80. Alan Forey, "The Military Orders, 1120–1312," in Riley-Smith, *op. cit.*, p. 191. See also John France, *Western Warfare in the Age of the Crusades, 1000–1300* (Ithaca, NY: Cornell University Press, 1999).

81. Anthony Luttrell, "The Military Orders, 1312–1798," in Riley-Smith, *op. cit.*, p. 342.

82. Seward, *op. cit.*, p. 26.

83. H. J. A. Sire, *The Knights of Malta* (New Haven, CT: Yale University Press, 1994), p. 191.

84. Forey, *op. cit.*, p. 191.

85. Sire, *op. cit.*, p. 29.

86. F. L. Carsten, *The Origins of Prussia* (Oxford, UK: Clarendon Press, 1954), pp. 1–4.

87. Sidney Bradshaw Fay, *The Rise of Brandenburg-Prussia* (New York: Henry Holt, 1937), p. 31.

88. Heinrich von Treitschke, *Origins of Prussianism* (London: George Allen and Unwin, 1942), p. 36.

89. Seward, *op. cit.*, p. 101.

90. *Ibid.*, p. 106.

91. J. A. R. Marriot and Charles Grant Robertson, *The Evolution of the Prussian State* (Oxford: Clarendon Press, 1946), p. 46.

92. *Ibid.*, p. 47.

93. Seward, *op. cit.*, p. 106.

94. *Ibid.*

95. *Ibid.*

96. *Ibid.*, p. 116.

97. *Ibid.*, pp. 127–31.

98. Quoted in Fay, *op. cit.*, p. 57.

99. Seward, *op. cit.*, pp. 127–31.

100. *Ibid.*

Chapter 3

Disciplined War and the Centralized Kingly State

As was shown in the previous chapter, after the collapse of the Roman Empire, politico-military rule in Europe fragmented into many competing territorial forms—monarchies, order-states, principalities, dukedoms, counties, city-states, etc.—despite the steady spread of Christian universalism. Attempts to reestablish coherent European-wide politico-military rule, such as Charlemagne's Holy Roman Empire, were quickly eroded by the steady disaggregating pull of feudal politico-military practices. As was also shown in the previous chapter, after the fall of the Western Roman Empire, the large, standing, infantry-based army of Rome was replaced by a multitude of small private armies consisting of the retinues of mounted aristocratic warriors. From about the eighth to the fourteenth centuries, an army was a temporary coalescence of many private retinues called into war service by the king. As was also discussed in the previous chapter, wars during the Feudal Age were mostly about *proprietary claims* because kings regarded their kingdoms as their private property. Therefore, the private quarrels of kings over who owned which throne by right of inheritance were legitimate reasons to go to war. This meant that disputes about the disposition of a kingdom upon the death of its king, especially when there was no heir apparent, were invariably resolved by war. [1]

For example, the Norman conquest of England in 1066 was the result of the proprietary claim of William, Duke of Normandy (1028–1087), to the English throne upon the death of Edward the Confessor (1003–1066); the Hundred Years' War (1337–1453) was fought over the ownership of land south of the Loire River (Aquitaine) that the English crown had acquired by marriage, which was also claimed by the French crown, as well as over the English king's hereditary claim to the French throne; the War of the Roses

(1455–1485) was a thirty-year struggle between the ducal houses of Lancaster and York over which family had the greater right by inheritance to the English throne.

Because war was a private matter that kings had to pay for from their own purses, they could not sustain an army in the field for long periods of time. Therefore, wars during the Feudal Age were a series of brief military skirmishes that took place episodically over a long period of time. In the words of one historian, "Armies were tiny, the theatres of operations vast. A defeated enemy would easily retire and recoup. Action was directed to local castles and strong points. Sieges were more common than set battles. The spoils of war were more desired than mere victory."[2]

Gradually, the introduction of new weaponry onto European battlefields had a revolutionary effect on the way that European war was fought and the way that the state was understood and organized.[3] The first innovation was the *longbow*, the traditional weapon of the Welsh. Archers using longbows could loose ten arrows per minute at mounted knights three hundred yards distant with great accuracy and penetrating power. The second was the sixteen-foot-long Swiss *pike*, which, when used by foot soldiers formed into squares (*phalanxes*), could break a cavalry charge by dislodging knights from their horses. To protect themselves from arrows loosed from longbows and from pikes, knights replaced their chain-mail surcoats with *plate armor*. Consequently, heavy cavalry became heavier, less maneuverable, and capable only of the forward charge. Because they were weighted down by their heavy plate armor, unhorsed knights could not regain their feet and were easily dispatched by lightly armed archers and pikemen who found chinks in their armor through which they could thrust a dagger. During the century and a half after 1300, battles at Courtrai (1302), Crécy (1346), Poitiers (1356), Aljubarrota (1385), and Agincourt (1415) showed that contingents of longbowmen and pikemen could defeat heavily armored aristocratic cavalry in this way. Gradually, feudal armies began to include contingents of archers and pikemen.[4]

The third, and by far the most revolutionary, developments were weapons that utilized gunpowder: *firearms* and *cannon*. Gunpowder, firearms, and cannon originated in China in the 1200s, spread to Europe, and began to be used in European warfare on a regular basis by the fourteenth century.[5] The first firearm was the *arquebus*, or harquebus. Although it was cumbersome to use and slow to fire, it could discharge lead balls at velocities capable of penetrating chain-mail armor. Knights responded by thickening their plate armor. Subsequently, large-caliber *muskets* capable of penetrating the thickest plate armor were invented and introduced onto the battlefield in about 1550.

The first cannons were made by bundling iron bars called *cana* together to form a long tube resting on a stand. Early cannons were inaccurate, cumbersome, and poorly made weapons that were dangerous to use because they frequently exploded when being fired and killed the men servicing them. Initially, primitive cannons could do no more damage to stone-walled castles than the mechanical siege engines that had been in use since Roman times. Gradually, metallurgical techniques learned from Europe's church-bell foundries were applied to the manufacture of cannons, which permitted the production of lighter, more powerful, and more accurate guns. Swiss gunfounder Jean Martz (1680–1743) saw that cannons could be made stronger by first casting them as a solid piece of brass or bronze then boring them out to make a tighter fit between cannonball and gun tube. His son, also named Jean (1711–1790), designed and built a machine that would revolve the whole cannon while keeping steady pressure against the cutting face. Jean's machines were installed in all the royal arsenals of France.[6] Brass and bronze cannons were followed by cannons of cast iron and, eventually, steel.

Boring out the tubes made cannons more accurate and powerful by reducing *"windage"* (lost propellant gas from the wide space between barrel and shot that was needed to avoid jamming caused by minor irregularities in the bore of cast guns), which increased the pressure of the expanding gas in the breech, resulted in higher muzzle velocities with a smaller powder charge, and gave greater accuracy and penetrating power to the projectile. Later, trunnions were added to the barrels to make it possible to raise and lower the angle of fire. Cannon were also made lighter by reducing the thickness and length of the barrels, and made mobile by attaching them to two-wheeled carriages drawn by teams of horses. Eventually, lead and iron replaced stone cannon balls. Improvements in the composition and manufacturing of gunpowder, called *"corning,"* increased muzzle velocities even more.[7]

The French general Jean Baptiste Vacquette de Gribeauval (1715–1789) introduced "a screw device for adjusting gun elevation precisely, and a new sight with an adjustable hairline made it possible to estimate accurately where a shot would hit before the gun was fired. . . . [And he] developed different kinds of shot—solid, shell, and canister—for different targets, thus assuring the guns' versatility."[8] Gribeauval made the transport of France's new field artillery the responsibility of the men who fired them, not civilian contractors who had been used previously; set up an artillery school for officers to teach gunnery; and integrated artillery side by side with infantry and cavalry. Gribeauval's artillery were an important element in France's victories from the cannonade at Valmy (1792) onward.[9]

Military engineers responded to gunpowder weapons by rebuilding and/or replacing high stone-wall castles, which had become hopelessly vulnerable to more powerful and accurate cannon fire, with a low-profile, artillery-resistant, earthen fortification, called the *trace italienne*. Stone-wall castles, which heretofore had held out for many months and even years against the battering of mechanical siege engines, were reduced to piles of rubble within days by the direct fire from accurate cannon firing large-caliber iron balls. The solution was to lower the castle's silhouette by replacing high stone walls and towers with low, massive, oblique earthen walls and bastioned traces. Fortifications with low-angled, star-shaped, projecting earthen bastions could absorb the shock of concentrated fire, even from the most powerful cannon, while exposing attacking troops to fire from defensive artillery emplacements, flank and rear. From the sixteenth century onward, kings built artillery-resistant fortifications at the most vulnerable places on the frontiers of their kingdoms. Such fortifications contributed to the defense of the realm and increasingly marked and fixed the borders of the kingdom.

DISCIPLINED WAR

The gunpowder weapons gradually transformed European armies, war-making, and the state. First, the feudal host of private contingents of heavily armored knights was gradually replaced by organized contingents of infantrymen armed with muskets and artillerymen to fire cannon. Knights despised these changes because they diminished the role of direct hand-to-hand combat and the muscular encounter of battle and put them at the mercy of those in society (commoners) whom they considered vile because they fought at a distance with cannon and firearms. According to one knight, gunpowder weapons allowed "valiant men to be killed by 'cowards' and 'shirkers' who would not dare to look in the face the men they bring down from a distance with their wretched bullets."[10] Although knights held fast to their old-fashioned ideas of battle and did not immediately abandon their romantic view of the fighting man and combat, they did, eventually, come to realize that there was no future in knightly war. Eventually, they shed their heavy armor for lighter breastplates and helmets, replaced their broadswords with *sabers*, and formed and integrated themselves into the new armies as *light cavalry*. By 1500, all European armies consisted of three basic fighting units: infantry, artillery, and cavalry.

Second, the men who made up these units were increasingly dressed in distinctive standardized clothes called *uniforms*, and issued standardized weapons produced in royal arsenals. The uniforms of the army's officers (usually former knights), non-commissioned officers, and enlisted soldiers were the same. Insignias, developed to determine a soldier's rank or position in the chain of command, were worn on the shoulder for officers and on the sleeve for enlisted men. Uniforms encouraged unit cohesion; reduced the social distance between officers and ordinary soldiers, despite differences in rank; identified friend from foe; and helped create the idea that the individual soldier was part of a large military institution brought together for a common purpose: to fight the king's wars. They also marked the wearers as servants of the crown, the "king's men," with diminished rights and liberties, licensed to kill for the crown when ordered to do so. The design and color of uniforms (e.g., red for the British crown, blue for the French, black for the Prussian, orange for the Dutch, etc.) and the armies who wore them became potent symbols of the kingly state. Increasingly, all European monarchs had armies that were set off from the civilian population of the realm. A kingly army was "a self-contained universe, a sub-culture with its own routine, its own ceremonies, its own music and dress and habits; that whole tedious but obsessive way of life known as 'soldiering' which has survived"[11] in armies to the present day.

Third, gunpowder weapons transformed the battle culture of knightly war. The warrior culture of knightly combat, which favored personal displays of fighting prowess and the headlong mounted charge, was replaced by a *battle culture of forbearance* because gunpowder weapons made war a test of wills. The victor in battle was the army that could absorb the heaviest casualties by gunfire and still maintain order, not the army that could inflict the greatest number of casualties. Therefore, battlefield heroics were discouraged and even punished because it undermined the fighting effectiveness of the king's army as a whole and jeopardized the lives of ordinary soldiers. The emphasis shifted to self-control, holding fire until ordered to fire, and taking casualties stoically. Soldiers were given orders to hold fire "until you see the whites of their eyes," because, in the age of slow-loading muskets, it was disadvantageous for an army to fire first because it was tantamount to being temporarily disarmed.

Fourth, and most important, discipline, which was essential to building a battle culture of forbearance, was introduced. Knights were notoriously undisciplined on the battlefield and troops were, in the main, the "dregs of society"—criminals, thugs, rogues, vagabonds, loiterers, misfits, beggars, derelicts, and drunks recruited in taverns, jails, and brothels. They were undisciplined, often arrived late for battle, fought in a desultory way, and deserted if they were not paid on time. They also regarded one another as equals, distinguished only by military function, not rank. The way to turn such undisciplined soldiers into disciplined ones and create forbearance under fire was to make them *drill* and *dig*.[12]

The first military commander in Europe to implement routines of drilling and digging into his army was Prince Maurice of Orange-Nassau (1567–1625), the captain-general of Holland and Zeeland from 1585 until 1625, who, when he studied classics at university, especially the two extant books of Publius Flavius Vegetius (?–?) who wrote about Roman military practices at the height of the Roman Empire, was impressed with his philosophy of self-sacrifice and self-discipline. Based on what he had learned of Roman military techniques from Vegetius, Maurice introduced three practices that had not been found in European armies since the collapse of Rome and the dissolution of its army. The first was the use of the spade to dig trenches and make ramparts behind which his army could protect itself from counterattack while continuing to press the attack. Digging became the soldiers' daily occupation, which eliminated idleness and reduced casualties from enemy fire.

The second novel practice was drilling. Maurice studied the movements required to load and fire matchlock muskets and compelled his troops to practice these motions in unison over and over again so that they could repeat them rapidly without thinking. This made firearms more effective than before by making volley fire easy and natural. Maurice also regularized marching together in step and turning together, left or right, on command. Drill made soldiers into obedient replaceable parts for his military machine.

Prince Maurice's third innovation was to divide the traditional infantry phalanx of pikemen into battalions of 550 men, which were subdivided into companies and these into platoons. This made for greater independence of maneuver on the battlefield and allowed a single voice, that of the commander, to coordinate the movements of all the units. He deployed his infantry into long linear ranks of musketeers, some ten deep, arranged side by side in close order to maximize the firepower of muskets. He perfected the countermarch, which allowed a well-drilled unit to deliver a series of volleys in quick succession: Musketeers countermarched in their files, reloading as they did, so that the front rank was always giving fire.[13] Disciplined, well-drilled musketeers, formed into linear ranks, ten deep, could deliver continuous fire more accurately than was heretofore possible when organized into phalanxes. Prince Maurice's reforms significantly altered war and soldiering:

> A well-drilled unit, by making every motion count, could increase the amount of lead projected against an enemy per minute of battle. The dexterity and resolution of individual infantrymen scarcely mattered any more. Prowess and personal courage all but disappeared beneath an armor-plated routine. Soldiering took on quite new dimensions and the everyday reality of army life altered profoundly. Yet troops drilled in the Maurician fashion automatically exhibited superior effectiveness in battle. As this came to be recognized, the old irregular and heroic patterns of military behavior withered and died, even among the most recalcitrant officers and gentlemen.[14]

Prince Maurice's reforms enabled the Dutch United Provinces, which had declared their independence from the Spanish Habsburgs in 1581 as a confederated republic, to transform their army into a disciplined fighting force that was able to win wars against the much larger Spanish army and keep their independence.

Maurice organized a military academy in 1619, the first in Europe, to train competent officers in his methods. A graduate of the prince's academy took up service in and brought drill to the army of the Swedish King Gustav

Adolf (1594–1632). On September 17, 1631, his army of 42,000, which had been reorganized and well drilled, delivered a crushing defeat on a battle-experienced Habsburg army at Breitenfeld near Leipzig. The victory of the Swedish army demonstrated that an army organized to allow volley-firing by its musketeers could "engage with and annihilate an enemy in a single battle or short campaign."[15] Prince Maurice's military reforms were quickly emulated by other European monarchs during the seventeenth and eighteenth centuries, first by the Protestant monarchs, then by the French, and last by the Spanish. Russian armies soon followed suit.[16]

Eventually, the cumbersome *matchlock musket*, which used a lighted "match" made of hemp to ignite the powder charge, was replaced by the simple and sturdy *flintlock musket*, which used a flint striking steel to make a spark to ignite the powder charge. Constant practice firing and reloading increased rates of fire to three rounds per minute. This allowed the reduction of the ranks from ten to three and the front rank to deliver volley fire continuously, and *salvos* (a simultaneous discharge of weapons) on rare occasions. This way of fighting demanded a high level of skill and discipline.

Gradually, the purpose of drill changed from imparting discipline, obedience, and restraint to engendering a state of mind. William McNeill has argued that physical movement in dance and drill enhances group cohesion through *"muscular bonding."* For McNeill, the result of drill was *esprit de corps* and group identity.[17] John Lynn has also argued that drill ensured effective battlefield performance by teaching soldiers to fear the consequences of disobedience. Being more afraid of one's officers than of the dangers of the battlefield gave greater steadiness under fire. In addition, the mechanical actions of drill distracted soldiers from the impulse to hide or flee the battlefield.[18]

The Gunpowder Revolution brought back a disciplined way of war that had not been seen in Europe since Roman times. By the end of the Thirty Years' War (1618–1648),

> European armies were no longer a mere collection of individually well-trained and bellicose persons, as early medieval armies had been, nor a mass of men acting in unison with plenty of brute ferocity but no effective control once battle had been joined, as had been true of the Swiss pikemen of the fifteenth century. Instead, a consciously cultivated and painstakingly perfected art of war allowed a commanding general, at least in principle, to control the actions of as many as 30,000 men in battle. Troops equipped in different ways and trained for different forms of combat were able to maneuver in the face of an enemy. By responding to the general's command they could take advantage of some unforeseen circumstance to turn a stubbornly contested field into lopsided victory. European armies, in other words, evolved very rapidly to the level of the higher animals by developing the equivalent of a central nervous system, capable of activating technologically differentiated claws and teeth.[19]

In sum, disciplined war resulted in the emergence of dramatically larger armies, new battlefield tactics, a new battlefield culture, a new type of fortification, the harnessing of science and engineering to warfare, and, eventually, the centralization, consolidation, and the monopolization of politico-military power by the kingly state.

Despite these changes, the common people living in European kingdoms were not directly involved in war as combatants. No king seriously entertained the idea of arming his subjects. Wars were, as never before, the "sport of kings" and his ministers. Since war had to be paid for by taxation, it was deemed wise to leave those who paid the taxes alone. The role of the people (i.e., the king's subjects) was to earn the money to pay the taxes that paid for the army and war. Most subjects of the crown viewed the onset of war as they would a coming of a natural disaster, a plague, or a famine; that is, having been sent by God as a harbinger of the Divine Apocalypse. Their exclusion from war also set a ceiling on the scale and intensity of war that would obtain until the French Revolution and the advent of the massive armies of "citizen-soldiers."

Instead, kings preferred to fill the ranks of their infantry armies with the "scum of the earth" from among their own subjects; that is, poverty-stricken peasants, vagabonds, outlaws, criminals, and debtors whom they could transform into soldiers through repeated drill. They also recruited their soldiers from the Europe-wide military manpower market composed of *freelancers*, or roving soldiers available for hire, and *mercenaries* (from the Latin *merces*, meaning wages or pay). Mercenary soldiering became a business in some of Europe's poor and overpopulated states. In particular, the German-speaking states, the Dutch state, and the Swiss cantons were Europe's premier suppliers of mercenary troops. Of these, the most sought-after mercenaries were the Swiss, who were grouped into regiments and placed at the disposal of any king or prince who had the money to pay the rates specified in a contract made with a particular canton. Mercenaries continued to serve any kingly master so long as they were paid regularly. Germans fought for the Spanish and French crowns, Italians fought for the English crown and the Dutch, the French fought for the Prussian king, and the Swiss fought for all crowns, even the pope! Kings also used mercantile companies, such as the East India, Royal Africa, and Hudson's Bay companies, to raise armies and navies, build fortifications, and make war in areas outside of Europe. And they used "privateers"; that is, ships "belonging to private owners, [that sailed] under a commission of war empowering the person to whom it is granted to carry on all forms of hostility permissible at sea and the usages of war."[20]

From roughly the sixteenth to the eighteenth centuries the recruitment of mercenaries was a major Europe-wide business. The main practitioners of this business were military *condottieri* (contractors) who signed *condotte* (contracts) with kings, princes, city-states, or bishops to provide groups of armed men of a specified number, length of time, and rate of pay to do military service. The most infamous of these was the Great Company, a band of 10,000 mercenaries drawn from across Europe founded by the Swabian Werner von Urslingen (1308–1354), which ran for fifteen years what today would be called a "protection racket." Another was the White Company of Englishman Sir John Hawkwood (1320–1394), which was composed of *routiers* (bands) of mercenaries unemployed by the ending of the Hundred Years' War. Another was the company of the Bohemian military leader, Albrecht von Wallenstein (1583–1634), who used his own financial resources and those of his backers to recruit, equip, and maintain an army of 100,000 men during the Thirty Years' War in the service of the Holy Roman Emperor, Ferdinand II (1578–1637).[21] Such armies were "off the shelf" and battle ready in that they came already trained, officered, and armed.

The use of mercenaries fostered

> a different kind of armed conflict: contract warfare. Contract warfare is literally a free market for force, where private armies and clients seek each other out, negotiate prices, and wage wars for personal gain. There were problems with this way of war . . . in the European Middle Ages, when bands of brigands sold their services to the highest bidder during wartime and became marauders in times of peace, raiding and ravaging the countryside.[22]

It also fostered many abuses: corrupt administration by the officers and the presence of *"rolling stones,"* men who passed from one army to another and enlisted in several different armies at the same time in order to collect enlistment bonuses.

At the end of the Thirty Years' War with the Peace of Westphalia (1648), European monarchs, believing that hired armies were incompatible with their status as sovereigns, began to put military contractors out of business and began to invest in their own state-raised, controlled, and administered standing armies. The transition from private armies to public armies and from private war to public war took several centuries. Kings began to monopolize military force initially by selling rights as officer-stakeholders in their armies. Regimental colonels and company captains were granted the "opportunity to buy and sell their units under proprietary contracts [which] gave them strong incentives to invest capital not just in purchasing the unit in the first place but in being prepared to enhance its capital value by further financial commitments."[23] Later, in the latter half of the 1700s, when the scale of warfare had become so great that the contracting-out approach to waging it was unsatisfactory, it was abandoned altogether and the making of war was completely taken over by the kingly state. The king's "recruiters enlisted soldiers for fixed terms of service with fixed pay and requisites. Purchase of commissions was phased out; and rules for promotion were made public and uniform. Regiments were made to conform to identical tables of organization."[24]

As war came to be a monopoly of the kingly state and the right to wage it was arrogated exclusively to states, private armies and private war were outlawed and suppressed. Mercenaries were forced underground and war became the exclusive monopoly of the state. The financial burdens of raising and supporting vast armies, building fleets of warships, and constructing artillery-resistant fortifications eventually forced kings to transform the weak, decentralized feudal state into the strong, centralized kingly state. How this happened in Europe is the subject of the next section.

THE CENTRALIZED KINGLY STATE

As was shown in the previous chapter, feudal kings were not all-powerful rulers. They faced the three estates of the realm—clergy, nobility, and bourgeoisie—who had their own privileges and rights as corporate groups. Kings were *primus inter pares* (first among equals) with respect to the nobility and had special responsibilities to the realm: providing justice, coining money, granting town charters, and defending the realm. As wars were private affairs during the Feudal Age, they had to be paid for from the king's private purse; that is, revenues collected by his bailiffs from his family's property and from tolls charged for the use of royal roads, bridges, fees for fairs and markets, fines levied in royal courts, customs placed on imports, and money given to him by his vassals called scutage, or shield money.[25]

As armies became larger and more expensive to recruit and arm, and fortifications became more expensive to build and maintain, kings increasingly found themselves in debt and in want of money. Feudal kings could not easily raise money because they did not have the unfettered right to tax or confiscate property, except that of Jews. Their powers in this regard were circumscribed by the ancient rights and privileges of the estates. In order to raise money to pay their war debts, kings resorted to borrowing, debasing the coin of the realm, and selling the family jewels.[26] They also met the expenses of war by using the services provided by mercenary military contractors and by selling regiments and companies to wealthy individuals. When these methods were no longer sufficient to cover the spiraling costs of war-making, kings began to ask for revenue from the estates. At first, the concessions granted to kings to levy taxes were valid only for the estate that had granted them (the third estate) and only for the purpose for which they had been granted (to fight a particular war). The idea of a general tax on all subjects to maintain the kingly state and support its army and wars came about slowly. Gradually, the financial institutions that kings used to collect taxes from their private lands became public institutions that collected taxes conceded by the estates.[27]

The burden of direct taxation fell most heavily on the third estate because it owned moveable property (that is, commodities bought and sold), which could be more easily taxed than fixed property (that is, land). The third estate "provided the monarchy with financial muscle. Monarchy repaid its debt by providing [the third estate] with military protection both within the country and later, outside its borders."[28] The third estate also benefited from the increasingly territory-wide legal and law-enforcement systems being developed by kings of the time. The third estate began to renounce its privileges and integrate itself into the emerging territory-wide system of kingly politico-military rule.[29]

For its part, the lower nobility of the second estate also favored the king's efforts to put his financial house in order because it created opportunities for enrichment not heretofore available to them. Kings recruited their tax collectors and judges from among the lesser nobles of the realm who were barely able to live as gentlemen because their lands were small and unproductive. They were paid good salaries and given greater titles and gifts of additional land. It was from the ranks of the lesser nobility and the bourgeoisie that medieval kings began to build up a corps of professional administrators loyal to them. This gave them the administrative capacity to bypass the estates and rule their kingdoms directly.[30]

Although certain practices of feudal politico-military rule remained within the kingly state, such as dispensing justice through personal rule, and dynastic politics based on family ties and feudal obligations, increasingly a new apparatus of politico-military rule—a new set of institutions, offices, and procedures for exercising power—emerged. These institutions were increasingly understood to be separate and distinct from the person of the king. The idea that there existed a *public weal* superior to private concerns began to reappear, having been lost with the collapse of the Roman Empire. Gradually, kingly politico-military rule began to be concerned with the efficient administration of the territory and population in order to ensure economic prosperity and military security. In effect, the kind of institutionalized, formal-legal territorial politico-military rule that had existed in the Roman Empire was being reconstructed within the kingly state. More and more, *"raison d'état"* (reason of state) became the justification for war, not the private concerns of the king. Increasingly, the kingly state monopolized the means of physical coercion.

As was mentioned in the previous chapter, all feudal lords, including kings, kept retinues of knights and stipendiary troops, and had household servants who helped them defend and administer their lands and castles. The most important members of the king's household were the chancellor, who was in charge of the chancel (the altar of the king's chapel), and the steward, who was in charge of the great hall of the castle or fortified manor house. The chancellor, in addition to saying Mass for the king and his family, kept the royal seal, wrote his business letters (in Latin) to other kings and the pope, and directed the work of the king's scribes, clerks, and messengers. The steward, who was in charge of the king's household and the management of his lands, acquired knowledge of accounting and document preparation. Stewards were assisted in their managerial tasks by several bailiffs, who were responsible for specific sections of the king's lands called bailiwicks.[31]

As the king's properties were scattered throughout his kingdom, revenues were collected from them by local noblemen, who were given a share for their effort. Therefore, kings did not receive all the revenue collected from their lands. As was shown in the previous chapter, shortfalls in revenue were made worse because kings were frequently defrauded of money by unscrupulous noblemen and the Catholic Church. The king's revenues were collected by estate managers called *reeves* in feudal England, *provosts* in feudal France, and *corregadores* in Portugal. Thus, revenue collection and providing justice were intertwined activities in the early kingly state.[32]

Gradually, kings began to see the administration of justice as more than a source of revenue. It came to be seen as a way of asserting kingly power. Therefore, kings began to increase the jurisdictions of their courts. Kings began to insist that serious crime, such as murder, be tried in royal courts, which allowed the king to intervene in locales where he did not have estates or rights of justice. In civil cases, special procedures were developed that allowed litigants to bypass the local court and present their cases directly to the royal court. This allowed the lesser nobility to protect themselves against their immediate lords. As the king was responsible for providing justice throughout the kingdom, appeals were allowed from local courts to royal courts as a way of assuring that injustice was remedied and the law made uniform throughout the realm.[33]

Gradually, from the fourteenth to the sixteenth centuries, throughout late feudal Europe the tasks of collecting revenue and providing justice were disentangled and two parallel sets of institutions and offices—legal and financial—developed. While the same individual might be both judge and tax collector, he followed different procedures and formalities when hearing cases and when collecting revenue. As the law became more complicated, individuals trained in the law, called lawyers, took charge of providing the king's justice. At the same time individuals trained in accounting began to take over the collection of the king's revenue.[34]

As legal and financial institutions evolved separately, the work that they did had to be coordinated. This was accomplished by the king's chancellor, who was always a high-ranking churchman, either a bishop or a cardinal. The king's scribes and clerks, under the direction of the chancellor, developed regular administrative procedures and routines. They drafted orders and instructions in the clearest language possible so that they would not be mis-understood. Gradually, the chancellery, or office of the chancellor, became the administrative center of the emerging kingly state.[35]

Slowly, a group of individuals appeared who spent their entire working lives as full-time administrators of the king's business. They were assisted by part-time agents who were willing to work for a portion of the year as the king's estate managers, tax collectors, and judges. Although their numbers were small at first, these individuals increased in number during the thir-teenth, fourteenth, and fifteenth centuries. This growing band of administra-tors was less and less recruited from the church and more and more recruited from the lesser nobility, who needed the extra income, and the bourgeoisie, who wanted the prestige and potential influence that came from being in the service of the king. Gradually, the king's officials were recruited from the lesser nobility and the bourgeoisie. Cardinal Thomas Wolsey (1473–1530) was one of the last churchmen to be chancellor of England when he was dismissed by Henry VIII (1491–1547) in 1525. His successor, Sir Thomas More (1478–1535), a lawyer who made his way into the king's service through Parliament, was the first layman to be appointed to that office. Louis XIV (1638–1715) of France stopped appointing churchmen to high positions in 1661.[36]

The development of financial and judicial institutions staffed by a small but growing number of professional judges, tax collectors, law-trained clerks, and scribes meant that kings were able to control and administer wide territories without the help of the aristocracy. Because the king's administra-tors were dependent upon the king for their livelihoods, they were increas-ingly loyal to him. Thus, the personalized vassalage system that loosely held the feudal state together was gradually replaced by a depersonalized, institu-tionalized system of offices and roles separate from the king's person that directly linked him to his realm.

The development of territory-wide law courts and direct systems of reve-nue collection, as well as the development of the general right to tax, aided the commercialization of economic life and the gradual decline of the nobil-ity as an effective military and political force. The aristocracy began to lose ground to the bourgeoisie and the king. It should be noted that this was an incremental development. Kings continued to support the nobility, although increasingly on the king's terms, usually as court nobility living on stipends paid by the king. The nobility was more and more subordinated to the king and his administrators. Those who were not transformed into court nobility were gradually integrated into the officer corps of the king's new infantry-based armies.

Thus, the need for money to raise and maintain large armies and navies, and to build large artillery-resistant fortifications, caused kings to create for themselves the instruments for effective, direct rule throughout their realms and transform feudal politico-military rule that had come into being after the collapse of the Roman Empire. They began to reverse "feudal entropy" and construct "new monarchies," within which they increasingly penetrated their realms by extended their politico-military rule across the territory and down to the local level without the help of the aristocracy. Gradually, these new monarchs gained a monopoly over the means of physical coercion by destroying the castles of the provincial lords, disbanding their private armies and integrating their fighting men into the king's army, and monopolizing the manufacture of weapons in royal arsenals. Larger and larger coherent, territorial kingdoms, marked out by large *trace italienne* fortifications, replaced fragmented feudal kingdoms as politico-military power was increasingly centralized and concentrated in the hands of the king and his administrators. Public officials gradually came into being and a distinction between the public and the private in the modern sense slowly appeared. Individuals who held power as a private possession were gradually replaced with public officials who held power on account of their position within the emerging formal-legal structure of the centralized kingly state.[37]

As the king's formal-legal institutions of territorial politico-military rule became more and more distinctive and visible, they gradually destroyed the feudal notion that humankind had been since the beginning of time divided into three functional but unequal categories of people, the three estates. This notion was increasingly replaced by the idea that the realm was peopled by a multitude of individuals of varying degrees of wealth and position who were equally the *subjects* of the king; that is, directly under the king's authority. Eventually, the three estates, which hitherto buffered individuals from the king, lost their distinctive rights and privileges. Individuals were increasingly direct subjects of the crown. In the words of one historian, "Everywhere monarchs raised themselves further above the level of the greatest nobles and buttressed their new pretensions with cannons and taxation."[38]

In sum, feudal kings who wished to stay competitive against other monarchs within the confines of Europe's militarily highly competitive geographical space had to gather to themselves the politico-military power that during the Feudal Age had been dispersed among their vassals. Kings stopped and then reversed "feudal entropy" by destroying the castles of the nobility, disbanding their private armies, and monopolizing the manufacture of weapons. Kings gained a monopoly over the means of physical coercion within their realms and created larger, centralized, and effective monarchies. The king's men replaced the nobility through which the king had previously ruled the kingdom indirectly. By the eighteenth century, kings stopped leading their armies in battle and appointed field commanders to lead them into war. By this time, "[s]uch tasks as recruiting the troops, enrolling them, paying them, clothing them, equipping them, and promoting them were centralized in the hands of the newly emerging war ministries."[39] It should be noted that these new ministries of war directed their military activities outwardly toward other kingdoms, not inwardly toward the kingdom's people. Gunpowder war had destroyed the social, economic, and political fragmentation of the Feudal Age and created the centralized kingly state that increasingly monopolized politico-military power.

By the end of the eighteenth century, European wars were being conducted by state-supported armies consisting of professional mercenary soldiers, not knights fighting private wars over property and feudal obligations, or military contractors doing a job for whichever crown would pay the going rate. Increasingly, soldiers were servants of the state that guaranteed regular pay and careers. Thus, by 1700,

> the essential outlines were there: a state machine responsible for, and capable of, maintaining a full-time force on foot in war and peace—paying, feeding, arming, and clothing it; and a coherent hierarchy of men with a distinct subculture of their own, set apart from the rest of the community not only by their function but by the habits, the dress, the outlook, the interpersonal relations, privileges, and responsibilities which that function demanded. [40]

Increasingly, war was more and more being conducted by a *hierarchically organized state-controlled institution* separate from civilian society. The basic structure of kingly armies was the regiment, consisting of two or more battalions, each of which was subdivided into two to four companies. The regiment was the focus of the lives and identity of the soldiers within the broader military institution. Regiments had an officially prescribed cadre of officers and enlisted men with clearly defined ranks and functions organized into a chain of command. Regiments were permanent organizations that lived beyond the particular officers and men in them at a particular time. The long life of these organizations brought forth regimental battle cultures typified by strong unit identity and intense devotion. Initially, regiments had large numbers of camp followers (wives, children, and concubines) who cooked for the troops, washed and repaired their uniforms, and nursed them when ill or wounded. By the late seventeenth century, camp followers were banished from armies and soldiers were completely isolated from civilian society. They began to cook their own food, do their own laundry, and sleep together in barracks. The regiment became an all-male community with its own masculine, misogynistic, and homophobic culture that isolated soldiers from civilian bonds and obligations and focused their loyalty on the unit. Drill and work details left soldiers with little time to spend with women, drinking, and getting into trouble. [41]

Thus, the emphasis on marching in step, close order drill, handling and using weapons in formation, unflinching obedience to commands, and synchronous firing and reloading shaped individual soldiers into exchangeable parts in a military machine, not unlike a clock, designed "to maintain complete control and order during battle."[42]

VARIETIES OF KINGLY STATES

As was discussed above, feudal kings ruled their realms jointly with the three estates: clergy, nobility, and bourgeoisie. Historians refer to this joint rule as being "constitutional" because the king's politico-military power was limited by the ancient rights and privileges of the three estates. The actions that feudal monarchs took to centralize and consolidate their rule (that is, to overcome feudal entropy), especially after the Gunpowder Revolution, which drove up the cost of war, upset the balance between the crown and the estates that had existed previously. The development of a centralized apparatus of judicial and financial institutions staffed by individuals beholden to the crown permitted kings to rule their realms directly without the help of the estates, which they saw as a serious threat to their ancient rights and privileges. The estates resisted the efforts by the crown to abrogate feudal "constitutionalism."[43]

The Gunpowder Revolution intensified the struggle between the crown and the estates in all European monarchies over whether the king was going to rule alone or jointly with the estates. The way that this struggle was resolved had a major impact on the way Europe's emerging new monarchies were governed. In realms where the king won the struggle against the estates, the king increasingly ruled the kingdom alone. In realms where the estates won the struggle, the assembly of estates became supreme and the power of the crown waned.[44]

Which of these two outcomes obtained in a particular realm depended on the relative politico-military power of the crown and the estates and the degree to which the realm was threatened by surrounding monarchies. If the environment was especially threatening the result was more often than not a strong monarchy that became increasingly stronger and stronger until all feudal constitutional constraints held by the estates were eliminated. Such monarchies were said to be absolute (from the Latin *absoluta*, meaning unbound). In effect, an absolute monarch was one who decisively won the struggle with the estates and freed himself from the limitations of feudal constitutionalism. As the king could rule the realm through an administrative staff of officials loyal to the crown, realms could be ruled without the help of the estates, so the assembly of estates was gradually "put to sleep" by the crown; that is, suppressed and no longer consulted by the monarch or needed to approve taxes for making war. Absolute monarchy was justified by reference to the need for the rational and orderly organization of government, and the position of the monarch as uncontested divine representative and sole seat of power."[45]

Victory of the estates over the crown, although a much less likely outcome, did occur in certain European monarchies, most notably in England but also in Poland, where the estates were in an especially strong position against the crown at the outset of the Gunpowder Revolution. In these monarchies the joint or "constitutional" rule by an assembly embodying the estates, the Parliament in England and the Sejm in Poland, defeated the crown and established itself as sovereign over the kingdom.[46]

France: From a Patchwork of Royal Fiefs to Absolute Monarchy

When Hugh Capet (940–996) was chosen to be the king of West Francia, that portion of Charlemagne's empire that had been ruled by his son Louis, he had no power over the kingdom beyond the prestige of his title. The entire kingdom, except for a small personal domain called the Île de France in what is today the city of Paris, was a feudal patchwork of so-called "royal fiefs," held by barons who recognized Hugh as suzerain but refused to do him homage or render military service. These barons were the count of Flanders, the duke of Normandy, the duke of France, the duke of Burgundy, the duke of Aquitaine, and the count of Toulouse. Although later Capetian kings, such as Philippe I (1052–1108) and Louis VI (1081–1137), increased the size of the royal holdings, West Francia remained for the next two centuries a loose aggregation of baronies protected by feudal constitutionalism; that is, the ancient rights held by the estates.[47]

Philippe II (1165–1223) was the first of four late Capetian kings who began to centralize and expand royal politico-military power. He reconquered Normandy from the English crown in 1204 and later annexed Brittany, Anjou, Maine, Touraine, and Poitou to his directly ruled domain. Philippe supervised local courts and made alliances with the bourgeoisie against the nobility. Many towns were given charters, and Philippe encouraged trade by granting privileges to merchants.[48]

Philippe's son, Louis VIII (1187–1226), gained portions of Aquitaine and Languedoc. His son, Louis IX (1214–1270), also known as St. Louis, did not add territory to the king's direct domain but centralized the crown's politico-military power. Although he respected the rights and privileges of the nobility, he did not tolerate infringements on royal authority. He suspended the baronial courts and replaced them with his own and gradually established a common law for the kingdom. The third strong king, Philippe IV (1268–1314), extended the boundaries of the kingdom to the Atlantic in the west, the Pyrenees in the south, the Alps in the east, and the Rhine in the north, thus establishing the territorial dimensions of the French kingly state.

Initially the administration of the kingdom was handled by members of the king's household. His steward supervised his lands, which were looked after by the king's provosts, who collected taxes, performed judicial functions, and kept the peace. His constable cared for his horses and led his host in battle. As the kingdom expanded, it was divided into bailiwicks, and bailiffs, who represented the king, controlled the provosts, sat as judges, and carried out policing functions. Provosts and bailiffs were recruited from the lower nobility and bourgeoisie. The French crown continued to centralize under Philippe IV's descendants, and by the beginning of the fifteenth century had an extensive administrative system in place supported by a regular tax called the *taille*.[49]

Like other feudal monarchs, Philippe IV convoked an expanded royal court called the *états généreaux* (Estates General), which consisted of representatives of the three estates of the realm, gave advice on major decisions affecting the realm as a whole, and approved requests for taxation. The Estates General was convoked only at the king's pleasure, usually during an emergency. Because each estate met separately in Paris and Toulouse, the Estates General was easily manipulated by the king's lawyers. The crown was thus able to bypass the Estates General and govern the realm directly using his own administrators.

Despite gaining the ability to rule the kingdom directly, French kings were slow to replace the feudal host with a standing army. It took the disastrous defeats of French knights in battles during the Hundred Years' War at Crécy (1346), Poitiers (1356), and famously at Agincourt (1415) where six thousand French knights were annihilated by a small English force armed with pikes and longbows led by Henry V (1387–1422), to move the French crown to modernize its military. In 1439, the Ordonnance sur la Gendarmerie created a regular military force consisting of cavalry, artillery, and infantry armed with longbows.[50] The army was not very effective, however, because it was small and officered by senior noblemen who refused to serve under each other's command and often conducted their personal quarrels on the battlefield.

By the time of the reign of Louis XIII (1601–1643) it was increasingly understood by French kings that a large, well-organized, and disciplined armed force was necessary if the crown were to have politico-military sway over the kingdom and to defend it against the armies of neighboring monarchs. In 1626, Louis XIII declared, "No place in France should be fortified except for the frontiers," and ordered his finance minister, Cardinal-Duke Armand Jean du Plessis Richelieu (1585–1642), to destroy the castles and fortified manor houses of the nobility. Richelieu also created a naval force of thirty ships of the line, fortified French harbors, and established royal arsenals. To pay for these forces, he reorganized the king's administrative system and imposed stringent taxes on the realm collected by *intendants*, appointed by and loyal to the crown. The *intendants* supervised local administration, finance, and law enforcement. These measures, and even more stringent ones taken by Richelieu's successor as finance minister, Cardinal-Duke Jules Raymond Mazarin (1602–1661), in order to fight a war against the Spanish Habsburgs, sparked a rebellion of the nobility, known as the Fronde (1648–1653). The *Frondeurs* were reacting to both the direction of the king's foreign policy and his centralizing tax policies to fight the war against the Spanish Habsburgs. According to one historian, the Fronde made the crown recognize that it "needed a foreign threat to maintain internal unity, as much as it needed internal unity to contain external dangers."[51]

The policies of Richelieu and Mazarin laid the groundwork for the establishment of royal absolutism by Louis XIV (1638–1715). Louis, who feared another Fronde and saw the kingdom encircled by the Habsburgs, believed that he needed a thorough reform of the kingdom's administration. Believing that he had been ordained by God to be the absolute master of France, which he justified by the "divine right of kings," Louis centralized all the functions of government at his palace at Versailles. He personally chaired meetings of the various councils that managed provincial affairs, taxation, and expenditures, and involved himself in every detail and decision, no matter how trivial. Louis XIV actively sought order and regularity within the French government "with reform achieved primarily through the instruments of law and *règlements*. Statistical and social surveys became an institutional practice of government, efforts were made to harmonize legislation across the territories, and the state bureaucracy was expanded and reformed to centralize power and weaken traditional allegiances other than to the king."[52]

In doing so, Louis became known as *le roi soleil* (the "Sun King") around whom everything in the realm revolved. In 1661, he instructed his finance minister, Jean Baptiste Colbert (1619–1683), to organize the French economy to serve the state. Colbert, a dedicated mercantilist, issued manufacturing standards, established new industries protected by high tariffs, and created state monopolies in certain economic sectors. He paid for scientific and technical education, kept wages low, abolished all internal tariffs, improved France's network of roads and canals, and added ships to the navy to protect France's commercial interests abroad.

In order to carry out Louis's policies, foreign and domestic, his minister of war, the Marquis de Louvois (1641–1691), the first non-churchman to serve the king in a high capacity, began to reform the army. He increased the size of the army to more than 100,000 men and armed them with the latest weapons. He replaced the old incompetent aristocratic officer corps with officers who had served as musketeers in the Royal Guard regiment commanded by Lieutenant Colonel Jean de Martinet (?–1672). Martinet implemented standards of drill and training in order to turn raw recruits into effective soldiers. Martinet "acquired fame by the bastinadores he inflicted

for every missing button and every ill-fitting garter."[53] His name has entered
the English and French languages to describe anyone who demands absolute
conformity to rules and regulations. Louis XIV also created a regular system
of inspection over the army and appointed Martinet inspector-general so that
he could spread his methods across the army as a whole.

In addition to their civilian duties, Louis's *intendants* supervised the recruitment of soldiers; the requisitioning of rations; and the procurement of
arms, equipment, and uniforms. The kingdom was divided into military districts whose economic potential was assessed and apportioned. Permanent
supply depots, magazines, and royal arsenals were established. By 1680 the
French army was 300,000 men strong and the most formidable fighting force
in Europe. Louis's marshal of France, Sebastian Le Prestre de Vauban
(1633–1707), arguably the greatest military engineer of his day, built a complete system of *trace italienne* fortifications that made the kingdom's borders
more defensible. For twenty-five years the French army was invincible on
the battlefield. The fear of Louis's army was so great that the monarchs of
Europe sought to build up their states as France had done. French military
and governing institutions were emulated with local variations by all kings of
Europe, as were French architecture, art, fashion, cuisine, and protocol. More
and more, the kings of Europe aped the French politico-military example in
order not to be overwhelmed by the French military juggernaut.[54]

The gradual monopolization of politico-military power by the French
crown beginning in the 1400s and culminating in the reign of Louis XIV
allowed French kings to increasingly ignore the Estates General. Between
1484 and 1560, the Estates General did not meet. In the words of one historian, "[a]fter having battled over three centuries to achieve . . . sovereignty
vis-a-vis foreign and domestic rivals, by the late 1400s the kings of France
were not prepared to share that sovereignty with the Estates General."[55] The
Estates General stopped being summoned after 1614. The French crown had
effectively freed itself from the limitations of feudal constitutionalism and
the king became the absolute sovereign of the French kingly state and ruled
alone.

England: From the Norman Conquest to Parliamentary Supremacy

In the English monarchy the intensified struggle between the crown and the
estates brought about by the Gunpowder Revolution had a different outcome.
In this case, the crown was unable to free itself from the limitations of feudal
constitutionalism. In 1066, William, Duke of Normandy, invaded the Anglo-
Saxon kingdom and defeated and killed Edward the Confessor's successor,
Harold II (1022–1066), at the Battle of Hastings (1066). Duke William, who
came to be called "William the Conqueror," became king and imported feudalism from France. He distributed among his Norman barons the choicest

lands in the kingdom as fiefs. The barons were required to supply the king a certain number of knights, whom they supported by dividing their lands into fiefs among their vassals.

Unlike the early Capetian kings of France, William was a strong monarch who did not hesitate to throw great barons into the dungeon and assert his right to appoint bishops and abbots of the Catholic Church. To finance his court, he did not hesitate to extract heavy taxes. When William died in 1087, his eldest son inherited Normandy as a separate dukedom, and a younger son, William II (1056–1100), a passionate, greedy ruffian, inherited the English throne. During Rufus's reign, justice was venal and expensive, his administration cruel and unpopular, and his taxation heavy. He was greatly disliked by the Church because he was satirical and suspected of being a homosexual. His harsh rule ended when he was murdered in 1100. He was succeeded by Henry I (1068–1135), who persuaded the barons to accept him as king by giving his word that he would stop the objectionable practices of his brother and return to the good rule of the Conqueror.

Henry restored Normandy to the English kingdom and expanded and differentiated the financial and judicial functions of the royal administration, and centralized both. The kingdom was divided into shires, and a reeve recruited from the ranks of the lower nobility was assigned to each one. His shire-reeves, or sheriffs, were made to appear before the barons of the exchequer to pay the taxes they had collected for the king. Henry's heavy-handed rule resulted in a series of revolts by the baronage, which he was able to put down.[56]

When Henry died he left no male heir and a dynastic war broke out among rival claimants to the throne. During the dynastic war that ensued, the barons were able to retain much local autonomy by promising support to the claimant who offered the most extensive privileges. By the time Henry I's daughter's son became king in 1154 as Henry II (1133–1189), the kingdom had been fragmented into numerous powerful baronies. Henry fought these barons and took away many of the privileges that they had gained during the fourteen years of dynastic war. He razed unlicensed castles, reconquered Northumberland from the Scots, reconstituted the exchequer and the Great Council, reduced Church encroachment on the royal courts, and reconquered Wales. Henry II's sons, Richard I, the Lion Heart (1157–1199) and John (1166–1216), continued to expand the power of the crown at the expense of the barons. Richard, who was a crusader, lived less than a year in England; nonetheless, he taxed his realm to the utmost to pay for his campaigns in the Holy Land. John was cruel, licentious, and weak of will. He levied heavy taxes to fight wars in Scotland, Wales, and Ireland; he violated many privileges of the estates; and he demanded high scutage (payments of money to the crown in lieu of providing military service) from the nobility. John's harsh rule resulted in a revolt by the barons to enforce their ancient feudal rights and privileges. They demanded a return to the rule of Henry I, which recognized these rights. On June 15, 1215, John accepted the demands of the barons and had drafted a document called the Magna Carta, sealed at Runnymede, in which he agreed not to levy taxes unless approved by the Great Council, or Parliament as it was called in the English realm. After the Magna Carta, the barons gradually gained the upper hand in their struggles with the crown. They were able to prevent the king's sheriffs from entering their lands; they took possession of his courts; and they usurped the powers of his administrators.[57] Rather than a victory for the common people, as is often claimed today, the Magna Carta was actually a feudal document that protected the rights and privileges of England's powerful baronage. Nonetheless, it laid the groundwork for the eventual supremacy of Parliament over the king and prevented the English monarchy from becoming absolute.

Henry III (1207–1272), who needed money to fight a war to recover Poitou and Aquitaine, expanded Parliament to include two knights from the shires, two leading merchants from the cities and towns, and the clergy. He consulted this "Model Parliament"—which was divided into an upper chamber called the House of Lords and a lower chamber called the House of Commons—when he needed money, especially for fighting wars. Parliament was able to exchange its approval of revenue requests for extensions of the rights and privileges of the estates. The power of Parliament was thus strengthened considerably during the Hundred Years' War by granting the king's requests for money to fight the French king over dynastic claims in the French kingdom in exchange for the right to meet regularly, to control royal ministers, and to examine the crown's accounts.[58]

The wars against the Irish, Welsh, and Scots extended the territorial dimensions of the English kingdom and had an important influence on the military defense of the realm. As in all feudal monarchies everywhere in Western Europe, heavy cavalry called into service by the king was the mainstay of the king's politico-military rule. However, wars against the Welsh and the Scots, who were able to defeat the king's heavily armored knights because of rough terrain and their guerrilla-style tactics, encouraged English kings to incorporate more foot soldiers into their armies. These foot soldiers were recruited by the barons, under whose control they remained as local militias. This meant that the crown was not able to build an infantry-based army from the top down and under its direct control. Moreover, the crown had come to depend on Parliament to agree to the taxes necessary to fight wars. The lack of an army under the direct control of the king did not, however, put the kingdom in danger of invasion and conquest by one of the increasingly centralized and powerful monarchies on the continent. England was an island kingdom separated from the other monarchies of Europe by the English Channel and regarded a strong army as an unnecessary expense.

Instead, it put its resources into a navy, upon which it came to rely to defend the realm.

During the reign of Henry VIII, the English crown sought to strengthen itself by forming an alliance with the landed gentry; that is, farmers who had become rich thanks to the gradual commercialization of English agriculture. Henry regularly sought the approval for his taxes and decisions from the Parliament, one of the most important taken during his reign being the reformation of the Catholic Church in England. Henry separated the Church from the Holy See, made himself the head of the English (Anglican) Church, and confiscated the lands and wealth of the great monasteries and convents. During this period the House of Commons became the site of the gentry's growing power.

Despite increasing involvement in wars on the continent, especially with the Spanish and French monarchies, the English king did not become an absolute ruler. Neither Henry nor his daughter, Elizabeth I (1533–1603), two of England's strongest monarchs up to that time, were able to put the Parliament to sleep and rule the realm alone, as Louis XIV had done in France. Parliament remained a force to be reckoned with. No large standing army was built and placed under the king's direct command. The English army consisted of mercenaries and freelancers, who were demobilized and sent home after a war. The navy, in large part, consisted of privateers—that is, ships belonging to private owners authorized by the crown to conduct hostilities in its name.[59]

The king's wars were paid for by selling crown lands, confiscating Church property, and borrowing money abroad. Additional money came from taxes granted by Parliament. Thus war-making, even during the reigns of strong Tudor monarchs, was conducted within the limits of England's feudal constitutionalism. Moreover, the reliance on a militia-based army and privateers for the navy lowered war-making costs because the crown did not have to support a large standing army and navy. Therefore, the English crown did not need to create a bureaucratic apparatus of direct rule as did the monarchies on the continent. This allowed Parliament to strengthen itself in relation to the crown by granting the king the money he requested in exchange for the recognition that certain forms of taxation were illegal.[60]

Eventually, Parliament strengthened itself so much as an independent institution that it was able go to war against the crown over taxation. The war, known as the English Civil War (1642–1648), was precipitated by a disagreement between Parliament and King Charles I (1600–1649) over a tax request by the king to put down rebellions in Scotland and Ireland, which Parliament was unwilling to grant. Charles, nevertheless, imposed the tax to pay for his campaigns against Scottish and Irish rebels without Parliament's consent. Parliament responded with the Petition of Right (1628), which restated its ancient right to be consulted. Charles responded to the Petition of

Right by dissolving Parliament and attempting to rule the kingdom alone. Consequently, Parliament organized itself for war against the king. As almost no effort had been made by earlier kings to monopolize military force, the king's army was small, poorly equipped, and irregularly paid. Moreover, Charles did not have control over the administrative institutions of the realm through which he could extract the money and manpower he needed to build up his army. Instead, he relied on donations from wealthy nobles and the proceeds from lands seized from the landed gentry who had aligned themselves with Parliament. Initially, the royalists had the upper hand in the English countryside. Parliament's forces held London and the administrative institutions of the government. Owing to its superior ability to raise money through taxation, Parliament, in due course, was able to organize a professional army, called the New Model Army, created and commanded by Oliver Cromwell (1599–1658), who gradually assumed a commanding position in military and political affairs. The New Model Army, which was organized along French lines, had a clear command structure, merit promotion, and regular pay, and was uniformed, highly trained, and disciplined. Parliament's modern army, better generals, and superior ability to raise revenues won the war against the crown. Cromwell decided to execute the king and Charles was sentenced to death and beheaded in 1649. England became what was called a Commonwealth.[61]

After the war, the unity of Parliament collapsed into factionalism and backstabbing. Cromwell, unable to stop the infighting, dissolved Parliament in 1653, and ruled as Lord Protector of England through colonels he appointed in eleven military districts. Cromwell's success as a military commander was founded on firm discipline, good administration, and organizational skills rather than tactical ability. Cromwell's rule is often described as a "military dictatorship" because his power base was the New Model Army, which he used to settle political disputes. Thus, Cromwell's "dictatorial" rule exacerbated the already strong distaste of England's landed gentry for strong standing armies.[62] Cromwell was never able to solve England's political disputes using the army and, when he died in 1658, there was no alternative but to restore both Parliament and the monarchy. Upon his death, the New Model Army was demobilized.

The monarchy was restored in 1660 and Charles II (1630–1685) of Scotland became king. Charles was succeeded by his brother James II (1633–1701). James, who was Catholic and had been greatly influenced by French absolutism, sought to centralize and modernize England's government.[63] He attempted to rule without Parliamentary consent by relying on loans, increased tariffs, and the taxation of religious dissidents. James was opposed by Parliament and driven into exile in 1688. A new royal house was founded when Parliament installed the Dutch Prince of Orange, William III (1650–1702), and his English wife, Mary (1662–1694), on the throne as joint sovereigns. William and Mary accepted the throne on terms set by Parliament in the Act of Settlement (1689). They ruled jointly until Mary's death in 1694, after which William ruled alone until his death in 1702. The ouster of James and the installation of William under Parliamentary tutelage, known as the Glorious Revolution, demonstrated the supreme power of Parliament and the utter futility of any king's challenging its authority. Parliament had become without question the absolute power in the English monarchy. Over the next two centuries, the power of the crown continued to decline and that of Parliament to increase, so that by the eighteenth century absolute politico-military rule had been acquired completely by Parliament.[64]

Prussia: From Dukedom to Militarized Kingdom

As was shown in the previous chapter, the Kingdom of Prussia developed from the order-state of the Teutonic Knights after Grand Master Albrecht converted to Lutheranism and transformed the order-state into a secular duchy owing fealty to the King of Poland. When Albrecht's line died out in 1618, the duchy was inherited by the Hohenzollerns who ruled as prince-electors of Brandenburg-Prussia. After the First, or Little Northern War (also known as the Second Northern War) (1655–1660), the duchy was granted sovereignty in its own right as the Duchy of Prussia and, in 1701, it became the Kingdom of Prussia.

In typical feudal fashion, the duchy was governed jointly by the Prussian estates, meeting in great council (Ständestaat), and the king. Surrounded by strong neighboring kingdoms—Sweden to the north, Russia to the east, and France to the southwest—and lacking protective geographical features, such as the English Channel, Prussian dukes and monarchs were well aware of the need to build a strong army in order to secure the realm. In many ways, the history of the development of the Prussian state is simultaneously the history of the development of the Prussian army.[65]

The first attempt to build an army was taken during the Thirty Years' War by Friedrich Wilhelm, known to history as the Great Elector (1620–1688), who saw that his realms (Brandenburg and Prussia), being noncontiguous, were exceptionally exposed to outside threats and required a strong army to defend them. Upon assuming the throne, he began to remedy Brandenburg-Prussia's military weakness. In 1653, faced with a growing Swedish threat, he cajoled the Ständestaat into granting him a small sum of money to raise an army of 8,000 men in exchange for the confirmation of existing privileges and rights. The nobility retained full feudal rights over the peasantry, judicial power within their lands, and a guarantee of control over appointments to ecclesiastical office, and the towns were confirmed in all their judicial immunities and guild restrictions.[66]

During the First (Little) Northern War, Friedrich Wilhelm demanded large sums from the estates. When the estates resisted, he imposed a land tax, which he collected by force. In 1662, he used his army to force the Junkers to submit to his authority. The Junkers agreed to allow the duke to place his officials throughout the realm to assess and levy taxes to support the army. Members of the nobility who were against these measures were arrested, imprisoned, and, in some cases, executed.[67] After the war, such draconian measures were abandoned and feudal constitutionalism reasserted itself.

The elevation of the duchy to a kingdom in 1701 did not unify the realm. When Friedrich Wilhelm I (1688–1740) assumed the Prussian throne in 1713, the kingdom still consisted of noncontiguous provinces stretching from Kurland in the east to Brabant in the west. He observed, "The worst thing [about the Kingdom of Prussia] was the irregular shape of the state. As a result of this fragmentation, the state had many neighbors but no inner strength and was exposed to far more enemies than if it had been rounded off more effectively."[68] Friedrich Wilhelm I was determined to remedy this situation. He was able to persuade the Ständestaat to agree to the formation of a permanent army. He proclaimed his right to raise taxes without the approval of the Ständestaat and to use the army to collect them. Following the reforms of Maurice of Orange, Friedrich Wilhelm I introduced drill and cadence marching to the Prussian army, for which he became known as the "Sergeant King." He completed the process of creating the central administrative structures that had been initiated by his grandfather, the Great Elector, in 1653—the Generalkreigkommissariat (General War Commission)—and increased the size of the army to 83,000 men, the fourth largest in Europe.[69] The crown also strengthened itself against the nobility by binding it to service to the crown through the "cantonal system," which tied peasants to a particular regiment and landed estate. Under this system, "a veritable military-agrarian complex developed, the nobility provided the civil servants and the officer corps, while the peasantry worked the land and provided the rank and file."[70] Gradually, the Ständestaat lost its say in how the emerging Prussian kingly state was to be governed.

The decline of the Ständestaat was paralleled by the rise of the king's bureaucracy and increased centralization of the state. The Generalkreigkommissariat was more an instrument of kingly control over the realm than were the emerging ministries of war in France and England. It came to oversee not only the recruitment, training, provisioning, and maintenance of the army, but also the collection of taxes, the administration of justice, and the control of local government. It consisted of a central office in Berlin, the capital of the kingdom, and an administrative structure that penetrated to the local level. Unity and identity within the kingly state were fostered through respect for military virtues: obedience, discipline, and heroism in battle.

According to one historian, the cantonal system and the Generalkreig-kommissariat militarized the whole of Prussia: "The whole of the country was a training school for soldiers. The rattle of muskets, the tramp of armed men was heard summer and winter from the Memel to the Rhine."[71] In effect, the Prussian state had been called into being to provide for the needs of the king's army.

The Sergeant King was followed on the Prussian throne by Friedrich II (1712–1786) in 1740. Friedrich built up the Prussian army and state well beyond anything his predecessor had imagined and came to be known as Friedrich the Great. Surrounding himself with many of the leading rationalists and philosophers of his day, Friedrich envisioned an army like a machine in which all the wheels and gears fit each other with precision, with the monarch as the mainspring that drives it in motion. Friedrich applied the laws of Newtonian science in a quest to discover the physical laws of warfare. He solved the problem of confusion on the battlefield by the application of strict discipline to his soldiers, from whom he demanded unconditional obedience and prompt execution of orders. Prussian soldiers were effectively mechanized by incessant close order drill and marching such that their movements became instinctive. The result was highly trained obedient troops who could deliver fire faster than the troops of other armies. Friedrich the Great engineered a formidable military machine of which there was no equal until the rise of French revolutionary and Napoleonic armies.[72] Prussia's survival against Austrian, French, and Russian armies is attributed to the efficiency of Prussian drill masters and the morale of the Prussian officer corps.

Poland: From Elective Monarchy to Partition

Unlike France and Prussia, Poland failed to build an effective response to the large modernized armies of the kingdoms around it by constructing an effective centralized kingly state. According to one historian, the history of "Poland demonstrates the tragic consequences of failing to build an effective response to modernized enemy armies. Polish [feudal] constitutionalism was the privilege of a large, lesser nobility whose number, paralyzing institutions, and diverse loyalties, prevented any measure of state centralization, until it was too late. The price was loss of sovereignty."[73]

In the Feudal Age, Poland, like other European monarchies, was governed jointly by the crown and the *szlachta* (nobility and landed gentry) but with a difference: the nobility was large, perhaps as much as 10 percent of the population, and it was organized into clans, not individual families. These clans were formidable entities with which the crown had to contend. In 1347, the crown negotiated a pact (the Pact of Koszyce) with the *szlachta* that exchanged the succession to the throne by the king's daughter for limitations on noble taxation, no other taxes without the approval of the Sejm (Great

Council), control of the mint and the judiciary, and the transformation of the hereditary monarchy into an elected monarchy. By the sixteenth century procedures had developed in the Polish Sejm that effectively paralyzed it on all bills of substance, which made it the most unwieldy in all of Europe. Each nobleman of the *szlachta* was entitled to vote, and a single negative vote (the infamous *liberum* veto) could scuttle not only the bill under discussion but all legislation enacted during a session. Over the following centuries, the Sejm was able to force concession from Polish kings in order to maintain *szlachta* rights and privileges against the crown. The principle of elective monarchy did not result in a strong monarchy because the *szlachta* invariably elected a weak nobleman from a minor clan. [74]

The subordination of the crown meant that the king was unable to circumvent the estates and centralize the kingdom as the French and Prussian crowns had done. Early on, feudal constitutionalism had been unbalanced in favor of the *szlachta*, and the Polish king was little more than an executive for managing its interests. Moreover, the Sejm was too large to be an effective decision-making body and its debates were interminable, directionless, and often inconclusive because of the *liberum* veto. Reform could be thwarted by a single member voting against the measure. [75]

Like those of other European feudal monarchies, Poland's military was based on knights called into military service by the crown. Polish knighthood fought well in the Middle Ages against the Teutonic Knights and the Hussites. However, it steadfastly opposed the monarch's attempts to raise a standing army consisting of modern infantry. The *szlachta* maintained the principle that the king had to pay for the army from his own purse. Thus, the military defense of the realm remained in the hands of the nobility, which consistently resisted reform, and Poland entered the seventeenth century without an infantry-based army, without a rational supply system, and without much artillery. Polish military successes on the battlefield in the sixteenth and seventeenth centuries were due to alliances with other kingly states, not the effectiveness of the Polish army. [76]

By the eighteenth century, Poland's protective alliances had lapsed and the kingdom was surrounded by increasingly strong hostile kingdoms—Russia, Prussia, and Austria. Following the Third Northern War, also known as the Great Northern War (1700–1721), Poland fell under Russian hegemony and lost territory. Poland's failure to build a strong, centralized monarchy because of resistance from the *szlachta* made it easy for Prussia, Russia, and Austria, in 1772 (First Partition), 1793 (Second Partition), and 1795 (Third Partition) to invade and partition the kingdom. By the end of the eighteenth century, Poland had ceased to exist and disappeared from maps of Europe. Efforts by Tadeusz Kosciuszko (1746–1817) between the First and Second Partitions to modernize the Polish army did not make up for the long neglect of military reform and inability of the crown to build a strong, centralized monarchy. Poland was reconstituted as a republic by the Allies after the First World War under terms set forth in the Treaty of Versailles (1919).[77]

CONCLUSION

This chapter has shown how the introduction of new weaponry onto the European battlefield revolutionized the conduct of war and transformed the organization of the kingly state. The introduction of three weapons—longbows, pikes, and cannon—transformed European armies, war-making, and the state. Armies increasingly became large, formally organized, well-disciplined, public institutions composed of artillery, infantry, and cavalry units officered by former aristocrats and under the command of the king. The costs of raising and supporting huge armies, building and maintaining fleets of warships, and constructing artillery-resistant fortifications encouraged kings to transform the weak, decentralized feudal state into the strong centralized kingly state. This was done by gradually breaking down the feudal system of personalized indirect rule and putting into place a set of institutions and offices separate from the person of the king, staffed by men of the king's choosing, which allowed him to rule the realm directly without the help of the nobility and the Catholic Church. Kings gained a monopoly over the means of physical coercion by destroying the castles of the barons, disbanding their private armies, integrating their troops into his own army, and monopolizing the manufacture of weapons in royal arsenals. By the end of the eighteenth century European armies were state-supported institutions whose ranks were filled by professional soldiers who fought for reasons of state, not private retinues of heavily armored knights who fought for property, revenge, honor, and glory.

The great costs of these new armies and fortifications resulted in challenges to the joint rule of the kingdom by the king and the estates ("feudal constitutionalism") in all European monarchies because the actions that monarchs took to overcome the limitations imposed by feudal constitutionalism meant that the ancient rights and privileges of the estates were seriously threatened. The struggle was essentially about whether the king was going to rule the realm directly and alone or jointly with the estates. The outcome of this struggle was determined for the most part by the threat environment of a particular kingdom. If the environment was especially threatening, the most likely outcome was absolute kingly rule because it was believed that *absolutism delivered the best politico-military rule domestically (internal hierarchy) and the best defense against threats from neighboring monarchies (external autonomy)*. Government by the great council was widely seen to be chaotic and corrupt. In other words, there was a general European belief that whatever curbed the power of the king inevitably weakened the crown's ability to defend the realm from foreign threats. Therefore, in most European monarchies centralization and coherence were achieved at the expense of the great councils.

The kings of France were able to transform a collection of royal fiefs into one of the most, if not the most, absolute monarchies in all of Europe. French kings gradually expanded royal power at the expense of the estates and built a large, well-disciplined standing army supported by an administrative apparatus of direct rule. The estates were increasingly ignored and eventually bypassed completely. In Prussia, which was exceptionally exposed to outside threats, the king was able to transform a weak duchy into one of Europe's most powerful states. Prussian kings cajoled the estates into supporting a standing army, gaining the right to raise taxes without their approval, created the central administrative structure necessary to collect them and recruit soldiers, and transformed the nobility into the officer corps of the army. In Prussia, as in France, the estates were increasingly ignored as the monarchy became increasingly absolute. Prussia became Europe's most militarized state.

There were exceptions to this rule, however. In England kings were unable to gain the upper hand over the estates and the kingdom was ruled jointly until Parliament won the English Civil War and established itself as the supreme institution of politico-military rule in the kingdom. On the continent, the kings of Poland were also never able to gain the upper hand against the estates. In fact, the estates were able to make the monarchy elective and force concessions that maintained the ancient rights and privileges of the estates. Polish kings were never able to circumvent the estates and rule the realm directly as French and Prussian monarchs had done. As the defense of the realm remained in the hands of the nobility, which resisted military reform, the Polish monarch was essentially defenseless against its powerful neighbors. The inability of Polish kings to build a strong, centralized kingly state resulted in the kingdom's disappearance from the map of Europe until it was reconstituted by the Allies after the First World War. The fate of Poland was not to be England's, primarily because the kingdom was separated from the continent by the English Channel, which mitigated its threat environment and reduced the need to build a strong army and centralized state to support it.

Despite the development of disciplined public war waged by large state-supported armies, warfare in all European kingly states remained the business of the king and the aristocracy, not the common people. In other words, the connection between the state, army, and people had not yet been made.

NOTES

1. Maurice Keen, *Medieval Warfare: A History* (Oxford: Oxford University Press, 1999) and Philippe Contamine, *War in the Middle Ages* (Oxford: Basil Blackwell, 1980).

2. Norman Davies, *Europe: A History* (Oxford: Oxford University Press, 1996), p. 440.

3. On the revolution in military affairs, see Lynn White Jr., *Medieval Technology and Social Change* (Oxford: Oxford University Press, 1962); Clifford J. Rodgers (ed.), *The Military Revolution Debate: Readings on the Military Transformation of Early Modern Europe* (Boulder, CO: Westview Press, 1995); and Geoffrey Parker, *The Military Revolution* (Cambridge: Cambridge University Press, 1989).

4. Contamaine, *op. cit.*, pp. 119–65.

5. Tonio Andrade, *The Gunpowder Age: China, Military Innovation, and the Rise of the West in World History* (Princeton and Oxford: Princeton University Press, 2016), p. 10.

6. William H. McNeill, *The Pursuit of Power: Technology, Armed Force, and Society since A.D. 1000* (Chicago: University of Chicago Press, 1982), p. 167.

7. Jack Kelly, *Gunpowder, Alchemy, Bombards, and Pyrotechnics: The History of Explosives that Changed the World* (New York: Basic Books, 2004).

8. McNeill, *op. cit.*, p. 170.

9. *Ibid.*, p. 171.

10. Max Boot, *War Made New: Technology, Warfare, and the Course of History* (New York: Gotham Books, 2006), p. 22.

11. Michael Howard, *War in European History* (Oxford: Oxford University Press, 1976/ 2009), p. 72.

12. *Ibid.*, pp. 55–56.

13. *Ibid.*, p. 56.

14. McNeill, *op. cit.*, p. 130.

15. David Parrott, "Had a Distinctive Template for a 'Western Way of War' Been Established Before 1800?" in Hew Strachan and Sibylle Scheipers (eds.), *The Changing Character of War* (Oxford: Oxford University Press, 2011), p. 48.

16. McNeill, *op. cit.*, pp. 134–35.

17. William H. McNeill, *Keeping Together in Time: Dance and Drill in Human History* (Cambridge, MA: Harvard University Press, 1995).

18. John A. Lynn, "Forging the Western Army in Seventeenth-Century France," in MacGregor Knox and Williamson Murray (eds.), *The Dynamics of Military Revolution, 1300–2050* (Cambridge: Cambridge University Press, 2001), p. 50.

19. McNeill, *op. cit.*, p. 123.

20. Janice E. Thomson, *Mercenaries, Pirates, and Sovereigns: State Building and Extraterritorial Violence in Early Modern Europe* (Princeton, NJ: Princeton University Press, 1994), p. 22.

21. Parrott, *op. cit.*, p. 57.

22. Sean McFate, *The Modern Mercenary: Private Armies and What They Mean for World Order* (Oxford: Oxford University Press, 2014), p. 28.

23. Parrot, *op. cit.*, p. 59.

24. McNeill, *op. cit.*, p. 164.

25. Howard, *op. cit.*, pp. 25–26.

26. Joseph A. Schumpeter, "The Crisis of the Tax State," in Richard Swedburg (ed.), *The Economics and Sociology of Capitalism* (Princeton, NJ: Princeton University Press, 1991), pp. 102–108; and Michael Mann, "State and Society, 1130–1815: An Analysis of English State Finances," in Maurice Zeitlin (ed.), *Political Power and Social Theory: A Research Annual*, vol. 1 (Greenwich, CT: JAI Press, 1980), pp. 165–208.

27. Schumpeter, *op. cit.*, p. 106.

28. *Ibid.*

29. Martin van Creveld, *The Rise and Decline of the State* (Cambridge: Cambridge University Press, 1999), p. 119.

30. Schumpeter, *op. cit.*, 106.

31. Joseph R. Strayer, *Feudalism* (Princeton: NJ: Van Nostrand, 1965), pp. 61–68.

32. Joseph and Francis Geis, *Life in a Medieval Castle* (New York: Harper and Row, 1979).

33. Joseph R. Strayer, *On the Medieval Origins of the Modern State* (Princeton, NJ: Princeton University Press, 1970), p. 28.

34. *Ibid.*

35. Ibid., p. 29.

36. *Ibid.*, pp. 33–34.

37. van Creveld, *op. cit.*, p. 70.

38. Gianfranco Poggi, *The Development of the Modern State: A Sociological Introduction* (Stanford, CA: Stanford University Press, 1978), pp. 77–79.

39. J. M. Roberts, *History of the World* (New York: Pelican, 1986), p. 545.

40. van Creveld, *op. cit.*, p. 160.

41. Howard, *op. cit.*, p. 54–55.

42. Antoine Bousquet, *The Scientific Way of Warfare: Order and Chaos on the Battlefields of Modernity* (New York: Columbia University Press, 2009), pp. 30–31.

43. Lynn, *op. cit.*, pp. 50–52.

44. Brian M. Downing, *The Military Revolution and Political Change: Origins of Democracy and Autocracy in Early Modern Europe* (Princeton, NJ: Princeton University Press, 1992), pp. 18–55.

45. Bousquet, *op. cit.*, p. 31.

46. Downing, *op. cit.*

47. David Judge, *The Parliamentary State* (London: Sage, 1993).

48. Sidney Painter, *The Rise of the Feudal Monarchies* (Ithaca, NY: Cornell University Press, 1951), chapter 2.

49. Hendrik Spruyt, *The Sovereign State and Its Competitors* (Princeton, NJ: Princeton University Press, 1994), chapter 5.

50. *Ibid.*

51. Downing, *op. cit.*, chapter 5.

52. Brendan Simms, *Europe: The Struggle for Supremacy from 1453 to the Present* (New York: Basic Books, 2013), p. 46.

53. Bousquet, *op. cit.*, pp. 51–52.

54. van Creveld, *op. cit.*, p. 160.

55. Bruce D. Porter, *War and the Rise of the State: The Military Foundations of Modern Politics* (New York: Free Press, 1994), pp. 73–78.

56. Thomas Ertman, *Birth of the Leviathan: Building States and Regimes in Medieval and Early Modern Europe* (Cambridge: Cambridge University Press, 1997), p. 93.

57. Otto Hintze, "The Emergence of the Democratic Nation-State" in Heinz Lubasz (ed.), *The Development of the Modern State* (New York: Macmillan, 1964), pp. 65–71.

58. Painter, *op. cit.*, chapter 2.

59. Ertman, *op. cit.*, p.167.

60. Thomson, *op. cit.*, chapter 2.

61. Downing, *op. cit.*, chapter 2.

62. Carl J. Friedrich and Charles Blitzer, *The Age of Power* (Ithaca, NY: Cornell University Press, 1957), p. 179.

63. André Corvisier (ed.), *A Dictionary of Military History*, trans. Chris Turner (Oxford: Basil Blackwell, 1994), p. 179.

64. Steven C. A. Pincus, *1688: The First Modern Revolution* (New Haven, CT: Yale University Press, 2009), p. 90.

65. Davies, *op. cit.*, p. 631.

66. Howard, *op. cit.*, p. 55.

67. *Ibid.*, p. 69.

68. Porter, *op. cit.*, pp. 114–15.

69. Simms, *op. cit.*, p. 96.

70. Corvisier (ed.), *op. cit.*, p. 287.

71. Simms, *op. cit.*, p. 90.

72. Downing, *op. cit.*, p. 95.

73. Bousquet, *op. cit.*, pp. 53–62.

74. *Ibid.*, p. 140.
75. *Ibid.*, pp. 141–42.
76. *Ibid.*, p. 145.
77. *Ibid.*

Chapter 4

People's War and the National State

As was shown in the previous chapter, eighteenth-century Europe contained a system of centralized kingly states with clearly delineated borders whose rulers were, with the exception of England, Poland, and the Dutch United Provinces, absolute monarchs. Their mutual relations had come to be conducted according to diplomatic conventions and their wars were fought within equally well-defined protocols by state-organized armies whose soldiers were professional fighting men recruited from the dregs of society, and mercenaries recruited from various places in Europe led by aristocratic officers who regarded themselves as being part of a trans-European politico-military elite based on noble birth.

All of this was to change with the French Revolution (1789), which transformed the kingly state from being the property of the king to being the instrument of the nation; that is, the people. According to Michael Howard, this "transformation was very largely the result of twenty-five years of almost uninterrupted warfare, from 1792 until 1815, between revolutionary France and her neighbors; warfare on a scale unprecedented since the barbarian invasions."[1] It was not a transformation of military technology as the Gunpowder Revolution had been, however. It was, rather, a transformation in thinking about the nature and purpose of the state, a new understanding of the purpose of war, and a complete alteration in the relationships of the people to the army and the state. Since well before the French Revolution, war had been accepted in Europe as an inevitable and ordinary aspect of human existence. Kings and the aristocracy saw war as their principal reason for being and they saw no difference between war and ordinary social life. Armies were small and major battles infrequent. Military commanders viewed their adversaries as honorable equals. Thus, there was no hard and fast distinction between the "military" and the "civilian" worlds. According to David Bell,

> This state of virtually permanent but restrained warfare seemed entirely natural
> and proper to the noblemen who led Europe's armies under the old regime, for
> it allowed the aristocratic values of honor and service to find full expression
> without serious threats to social stability and prosperity. Indeed, war operated
> as a sort of theater of the aristocracy, just as the royal courts of the period did.
> In war, aristocratic lives and values were put on display, amid splendor, polish,
> gallantry, and shows of utter self-assurance. European elites of the eighteenth
> century assumed that this world would last indefinitely. They did not realize
> that it was on the edge of total eclipse. [2]

The eclipse was brought about by the French Revolution, which overthrew the idea that legitimate politico-military rule flowed from God and was invested in an absolute hereditary monarch and replaced it with the notion that legitimate rule flowed from the people, and was vested in leaders chosen by and accountable to them. After the French Revolution, the state came to be seen as the embodiment of the nation dedicated to abstract concepts, such as *liberté, égalité,* and *fraternité,* as well as the fatherland, or motherland, for which no price was too high to pay and no sacrifice too great to make. According to one scholar, the "French Revolution . . . made war a 'concern of the people'"[3] for the first time in Europe since the collapse of the Roman imperial state.

The rise of nationalism also made war the test of a nation's moral worth, the ultimate test of whole peoples. As will be shown below, Romantic nationalism, in particular, saw war as a tonic for the rejuvenation of the state, a test of the moral fiber of the people, a redemptive experience, a corrective to the corruption and pettiness of commercial society. Such thinking about war was not possible before the French Revolution when kings saw war as a private concern and fought continuously over land, property, and thrones. Before the French Revolution, war was seen as natural and proper to Europe's monarchs; after the Revolution, war was increasingly viewed as a test of wills between whole peoples, whole nations. Nationalism made it possible to see enemy soldiers not as honorable adversaries but as enemies, and the populations of enemy states not as innocent bystanders, but as combatants. Thus, nationalism pushed war "*toward* a condition of total engagement and abandonment of restraints . . . that could end only in total victory or total defeat."[4] Therefore, nationalized states became increasingly militarized and bellicose and war became increasingly likely, and, when it came, increasingly violent and destructive.

Before the French Revolution, war was seen as part of the normal social order; after the Revolution it was seen as abnormal to the proper course of history. Before the French Revolution, there was no sharp line between the social identity of aristocrats and their role as fighters. After the French Revolution, the notion that the military was an *institution separate from the rest of society* with a distinctive culture (dress, norms, music, language, etc.) came into being. *Militarism* involves the imposition of military culture and values (discipline, self-sacrifice, unswerving patriotism) on the civilian world. Militarists believe in the moral superiority of the armed forces because they have been tested in combat. Militarists see civilians as weak, corrupt, unpatriotic, self-absorbed, narcissistic. Thus, after the French Revolution the idea of militarism, which requires a sharp line between civilian and military to make sense, and the words "military" and "civilian" gained their modern meaning. For the first time in history, war was split from normal life and it became possible to speak of "civil-military" relations.[5]

THE NATIONAL STATE

Originally, the word *nation* (from the Latin *natio*, meaning "place of birth" or "origin") had no political connotation whatsoever; it referred to groups of foreigners from the same place whose status was below that of Roman citizens. During the Middle Ages the word was used to designate groups of scholars and students from the same geographical locations attending Europe's medieval universities who had a common view and purpose. In the thirteenth century the word came to refer to scholars of the Catholic Church. In sixteenth-century England, the term was applied to the population of the kingdom and was a synonym for the lower social orders, the "rabble" or the "mob." Gradually, the word lost its negative connotations and came to have its contemporary meaning: "A socially mobilized body of individuals who believe themselves united by some set of characteristics that differentiate them (in their own minds) from outsiders and who strive to create or maintain their own state."[6]

This conception of the nation "locates the source of individual identity with a 'people' which is seen as the bearer of sovereignty, the central object of loyalty, and the basis of collective solidarity."[7] Nationalism recognizes the state as the ideal and only legitimate form of politico-military rule. Hence, nations seek to find political expression in sovereign states, the boundaries of which should ideally coincide with those of the nation, but rarely do. The nation, understood as a sovereign people, is always seen as being *fundamentally homogeneous and only superficially divided by status, class, and race.* Nationalism thus transformed the kingly state by connecting the king's subjects, who were increasingly understood to be a homogeneous national community, to the state.

The sacred universalism of the Catholic Church and feudal fragmentation made nationalism impossible before the rise of the kingly state. Recall that feudal kingdoms were ruled jointly by monarchs and the estates. Kings and the aristocracy often spoke languages and lived lives that were quite different than those of the common people they ruled. The king and the nobility of the feudal monarchy shared a common outlook and chivalric culture with the kings and nobility of other European kingdoms, despite the frequent dynastic wars they fought with one another. In the words of one scholar: "There was nothing illogical in any [noble] man's ruling over subjects who were alien to him. Germans lorded it in Italy, Frenchmen in Spain, Englishmen in France, with complete equanimity and limpid consciences; even such bizarre spectacles as English or Flemish knights installed in charge of Greek, Bulgarian, or Armenian communities in the Balkans were part of the natural order of things."[8]

As was made clear in the previous chapter, the king's subjects were excluded from ruling the realm and exempted from fighting in the king's wars. Ruling and making war were the linked responsibility of the king and the nobility. Common people did not identify themselves as belonging to a kingdom-wide community; rather, they "were conscious of belonging to their native village or town, and to a group possessing a local language whose members could communicate without recourse to Latin or Greek. They were aware of belonging to a body of men and women who acknowledged the same feudal lord; to a social estate, which shared the same privilege; above all, to the great corporation of Christendom."[9]

Therefore, in order for nations, as bodies of socially and politically unified individuals who believed that they were united by a set of shared characteristics that differentiated them from other peoples, to come into being, the sacred universalism of Christendom and the fragmentation and localism of feudalism had to be overcome. This became possible only after the coming to the fore of the centralized kingly state, which provided the intermediate politico-military framework *between* the universal Christian community of Christendom and the particular local communities of feudalism, within which nations could form.[10]

As was shown in the previous chapter, medieval kings in Europe were gradually able to emancipate themselves from the religious supervision of the Catholic Church, the political supervision of the Holy Roman Emperors, and the domestic restrictions of the "constitutional" rights and privileges of their estates.[11] Over time, absolute monarchy created a "unified and unlimited authority, owing no allegiance above and unhampered by any restriction below,"[12] especially after the Peace of Westphalia (1648).

The destruction of feudalism, which had exempted the common people from any military function and an active political existence, as well as the destruction of the universalism of medieval Christianity, allowed individuals to attach themselves to the centralized kingdom as a whole. As the power of kings increased and the estates were broken down into *equal* subjects under the king's direct authority, individuals began to regard the whole kingdom rather than their estate as their primary membership association. At first these attachments were personal and religious and were manifested as pride in the person of the king, as well as the literary, military, and artistic achievements of the kingdom. Gradually individuals came to identify with their kingdoms as a whole and came to believe that they had a common stake in its destiny. Eventually, loyalty to the king and identification with his kingdom was redirected to loyalty to the whole community of people living within its territorial limits, "a development that in time, led to the nation-state and the struggle for self-determination."[13]

Nationalism as a political movement appeared first in western Europe at the end of the seventeenth century. It spread from the west to central and eastern Europe in subsequent centuries. As it spread eastward, the way that it was understood and manifested changed because the form of politico-military rule in central and eastern Europe was different from that of the west. In the west the medieval ideal of local politico-military rule had been destroyed by the rise of the new consolidated and centralized kingly states. In central and eastern Europe, politico-military rule was imperial in nature. There existed three large, multi-ethnic imperial states: the Austro-Hungarian Empire, the Russian Empire, and the Ottoman Empire. The way that nationalism manifested itself in eastern Europe was strongly influenced by the presence of these empires. In the words of one scholar, the difference between the nationalism of western and eastern Europe was the

> inevitable result of the different process of historical evolution through which they had passed. The Breton or Provençal felt himself first and foremost a Frenchman no less than a Parisian; it was of a liberated France that he dreamed. It was far otherwise with the Slovenes [in the Austro-Hungarian Empire] who had never known a state of their own; with Bulgars and Roumanians [sic], whose states had undergone such vicissitudes that their ancient political boundaries had altogether ceased to correspond with their actual conditions; with the Slovaks, who were accustomed, indeed, to the historic state of Hungary, but had never known the day when they had been anything better than underlings within the [Austro-Hungarian imperial] state. . . . The state to most of them was something altogether alien. But what they did possess . . . was the personal bond of their *nationality*. The very policy of deliberate differentiation to which they had long been subjected had kept alive among them the consciousness of this tie. A Serb never felt that he was a citizen of the Ottoman Empire . . . [but] he had known that he was a Serb.[14]

As kingly power centralized in western Europe, a Europe-wide intellectual movement, known as the *Enlightenment*, emerged and began to challenge the theocratic worldview of the Catholic Church.[15] Enlightenment thinkers argued that human beings were capable of using reason to discover for themselves the laws of nature according to which they could construct the good society. These thinkers were opposed to monarchy as a form of politico-military rule because they saw it as unnatural and riven with privileges, sinecures, and nepotism. They saw kings, the nobility, and the Catholic Church as the enemies of humankind, especially the nobility, which they regarded as militaristic and the cause of Europe's many wars.

In stressing that all human beings were capable of deciding for them-selves, of using their reason to distinguish "good" from "bad," "right" from "wrong," Enlightenment thinkers created a new morality and a new way of considering the problem of "evil." They believed that human beings were naturally good and that by reason alone they could bring about the good society. In effect, these thinkers rejected Christianity's doctrine that all hu-man beings were possessed by the inclination to do bad because they were tainted by the original sin of Adam and Eve. Thus, ignorance, superstition, intolerance, exploitation, ancient customs, war, and vested interests associat-ed with the kingly state, the Catholic Church, and the nobility came to be seen as political and social evils that had to be eliminated. In the words of one historian, the Enlightenment's "new rationalism prepared the way for the modern state by its rationalization of all human relations; it cleared away all the underbrush of centuries which stood in the way of the growth of the united nation."[16]

Enlightenment ideals were manifested politically in a Europe-wide re-formist movement that appeared in the eighteenth century, which eventually came to be called "liberalism," with its supporters called "liberals," from the French *libéral,* meaning those who favored individual political freedom and the reform of the absolute kingly state. Liberalism is based on the idea of the autonomous individual:

> It believes that man has an unlimited capacity for self development and self improvement, provided he is free. Personal freedom is a precondition of all progress: with it man can create on this earth near perfect conditions. The purpose of liberalism is to remove all the shackles—political, legal, social, economic, and even aesthetic—that constrain man and prevent him from giv-ing full play to his personality.[17]

Enlightenment and liberal ideas were spread throughout western Europe by French aristocratic salons, and secret organizations, such as the Freemasons, whose members gathered to revel in their freedom from the old order and to discuss the creation of the "new order of the ages."[18]

In eastern and central Europe within the ethnically diverse dynastic em-pires, nationalism was manifested differently. Except for the exceptional case of the Russian Empire, there did not exist in eastern Europe a consolidated, coherent kingly state within which a singular national identity could crystal-ize. The dynastic empires were patchworks of different peoples distinguish-able from one another by language and culture to a degree unknown in

Europe's western kingdoms. In the dynastic empires, "the frontiers of an existing state and of a rising nationality rarely coincided; nationalism there grew into a protest against and in conflict with the existing state pattern—not primarily to transform it into a [liberal] state, but to redraw the political boundaries in conformity with ethnographic demands."[19]

Hence, the nationalisms of central and eastern Europe began from below as cultural movements that looked "into national history and philology; the collection of legends and folklore, the compilation of grammars and textbooks"[20] by intellectuals and priests of a particular ethnic group. Eventually, the cultural movements, influenced by the success of nationalism in western Europe, became political movements that sought escape from the dynastic imperial state and the formation of an independent state built on the liberated "captured" or "oppressed" nation. Thus, central and eastern European nationalism constructed itself in opposition to western nationalism, which arose to empower *individuals* within the political framework of the already centralized kingly state. In contrast, national movements in central and eastern Europe justified their political demands for a state by referencing the past and extolling the virtues and cultural peculiarities of an already existing *people* held together not by a social contract among individuals, but, rather, by natural ties of kinship and status. In ethnic nationalism, the legal concept of "citizen" was replaced by the concept of "folk."[21]

The philosophical foundations of ethnic nationalism were laid by an intellectual movement called Romanticism, which arose as a reaction to the Enlightenment. For romantic thinkers, the liberal state was a mechanical, juridical construction, the artificial product of politicians and political movements; therefore, it was a historical accident, not naturally occurring. In the minds of the romantics, the nation was sacred, eternal, organic, and primordial; a product of nature that lay beyond the influence of human beings[22]; an extension of the family, a natural unit bound together by ties of blood and soil. Although they believed that a nation had always existed, they believed that it had not always been conscious of its unity as a "*volk*." Nationalism appeared within such natural communities when the distinctive cultural unity they shared became self-conscious and sought a state of its own.

Romantics believed that each nation had its own unique culture that was manifested in dress, habits, and language. They also believed that all individuals possessing the cultural characteristics of a natural state had the right to belong to it, no matter where they happened to be born and live.[23] They rejected the liberal state's separation of the state from the nation. Essentially, they viewed the nation and the state as one and the same thing. They also rejected liberalism's preference for a limited state, preferring instead a strong state because they believed it was the only vehicle through which a nation could be expressed and survive. Romantics rejected the liberal state's emphases on individual equality and freedom. Instead, they saw freedom as the obligation of the individual to fulfill his or her naturally assigned purpose within the nation. Moreover, they argued that people were inherently unequal and that the preservation of a nation required the maintenance of social distinctions based on wealth and birth. Finally, romantics believed that the purpose of democracy was to provide a mechanism for the nation to realize its political ideals rather than individual freedom of choice. In the west, nationalism meant self-government and the actualization of individual freedom without regard to ethnicity. In central and eastern Europe, nationalism meant creating an independent state based on the "natural" ethnic characteristics of a particular people. The first duty of the state was to create a homogeneous national community, not to advance and protect the freedom of the individual.[24]

The theoretical marriage of the state to the nation conceived in this way was made by Georg Wilhelm Friedrich Hegel (1770–1831), who argued that the shaping of history was not due to humanity as a whole or the individuals of which it consisted, but the political communities or nations in which they lived. For Hegel, nations were strong, "world-historical" ideas incarnate. Imbued with sovereignty, national states were free to develop according to their own natures. History was, thus, a record of states rising, growing, clashing, reaching maturity, and dying in a search for the more perfect political order. Unlike liberals, who saw the state as a restriction on human freedom, Hegel argued that individual freedom was only possible within the state. Remove the state and individuals were reduced to insignificant biological creatures disconnected from the "world spirit." According to Hegel, the only way that states could play out their world historical destiny was to pit themselves against other states, especially in war, which became the principal means by which the world-historical spirit manifested itself. Therefore, war was seen as salubrious for the state because it called forth the qualities of heroism, self-sacrifice, and manliness. He believed that nations at peace would sink into "bovine contentment, its people gone soft, and inclined to surrender to their private interests." States, therefore, had to be as militarily strong as possible.[25]

Despite their differences with regard to war, both variants of European nationalism led to the militarization of the state. Preparing for war took precedence over all other responsibilities of the state. According to one historian, "Economic prosperity, commercial vitality, and social welfare were worthwhile goals; all of them contributed to the state's power and stability; but they counted for nothing if the existence of the state was not secure. Security meant creating and maintaining the kind of army necessary to win a modern war."[26] The type of army needed was the mass-reserve, standing army consisting of soldiers from all social classes of society, not just mercenaries or society's dregs and riffraff. Hence, national states, building on the administrative apparatus of the centralized kingly state, developed the bureaucratic infrastructure necessary to conscript, train, equip, maintain, and mobilize million-man armies. Increasingly, the national state's conscription and training apparatus penetrated society in order to transform citizens into soldiers in times of national emergency.

The army became the instrument not of the king but of the nation. The loyalty of men was being redirected from the monarch's person to the nation. Soldiers "no longer fought merely on behalf of a king, but for an ideal which encompassed the whole nation under the symbols of the Tricoulor and the *Marseillaise.*"[27] To connect themselves to the people through the army, European kings adopted military uniforms as their normal attire for public occasions; armies paraded on the main avenues of the state's major cities; national anthems, which projected militant nationalism, were adopted; every capital had its victory monuments and tombs of military heroes; and millions of young men had military training and hundreds of thousands had combat experience. In the words of one historian, the "mass reserve army made military service a part of the life experience of millions of European men and gave military institutions a central place in European society."[28]

The army was also a *nation*-building institution. In all European national states conscription brought men together from the cities, towns, and countryside for a single purpose, to defend the nation. Armies became schools for citizenship. Soldiers saluted the national colors, sang the national anthem, learned to read and write the national language, learned the value of soap and hot water, learned the feel of leather boots, learned toughness and discipline, learned to obey orders, and learned to pay the ultimate sacrifice in defense of the nation. In short, soldiers personified the military virtues on which the national state was increasingly based.[29] War was increasingly seen as the arbiter of national greatness and the army as the guardian of the nation. The rise of national consciousness "served to transform soldiering into an attainable and much admired profession."[30]

PEOPLE'S WAR

When a state is viewed by the population within it as the embodiment of the aspirations of "the people," however understood, it will be strengthened and its capacity to make war will be enhanced. In the words of one scholar of the state, war was a powerful catalyst in the creation and spread of the national state because it infused

> the collective consciousness of people with a sense of their national identity, while simultaneously linking that identity closely to the fate of the state itself. Nationalism in turn magnifies the unifying effects of wars, promotes a sense of shared destiny, and strengthens political bonds that might otherwise suffer centrifugal failure. The military origins of nationalism are reflected in the

military rituals and symbols that dominate national holidays, when military parades, fireworks, and many-gunned salutes herald a nation's glory.[31]

In effect, nationalism solved the problem that kingly states faced when they made war with mercenary armies. As was shown in the previous chapter, the ranks of early kingly armies consisted of men hired from across Europe and the dregs of the kingdom (criminals, drunks, social misfits, vagabonds, etc.) forced into the army as an alternative to prison. Such soldiers had to be watched over constantly and strongly disciplined so that they would not desert, mutiny, or turn their weapons on their officers. Also, the generals of armies made up of mercenaries tended to avoid directly confronting the enemy, preferring to outmaneuver rather than give battle in order to avoid casualties and the expense of recruiting replacements.[32]

An army conscripted from all social classes of the population of a national state proved to be cheaper and more reliable than one consisting of mercenaries and the "scum of the earth." Nationalism of both liberal and romantic variants provided an emotional attachment among the people living within the state to their fellow citizens and the political community as a whole that vastly increased their willingness to make sacrifices and bear hardships as soldiers in the service of the state when the state was seen as the instrument of the people. Intimidation, money, and physical coercion were no longer necessary to fill the ranks of the state's army and keep soldiers on the battlefield. The nation-at-arms was much more effective than professional mercenary armies at giving battle.

The transformation of the kingly state into the national state simultaneously transformed European warfare. As was mentioned in the previous chapter, before the rise of the kingly state war was mainly about *proprietary* and *dynastic claims* of the kings of Europe. With the coming to the fore of the kingly state, dynastic wars became increasingly anachronistic. More and more, wars were fought for *territorial gain*. Wars, such as the Seven Years' War (1755–1763) between Britain and France and the War of Jenkins' Ear (1739–1748) between Britain and Spain, as well as many others during the eighteenth century, were fought in order to wrest control of small pieces of territory from each other, principally outside of continental Europe.

With the development of nationalism, the purpose of war changed once again. Increasingly, wars were fought for *national objectives*. Wars, such as those that followed the French Revolution (1792–1799) and, later, the Napoleonic Wars (1800–1815), were fought to defend the revolution and to spread the ideology of popular sovereignty to surrounding kingly states; the wars of German and Italian unification (1850–1871), the Franco-Prussian War (1870–1871), the Balkan Wars (1912–1913), the First World War (1914–1918), and the Second World War (1939–1945) were fundamentally about the violent assertion of the principles of national identity, coherence, and self-determination of peoples in order to make the borders of nations and states in Europe coincide. More and more, wars were struggles not between kings but whole nations fighting for their survival as a self-governing people, or for an ethnically homogenized state of their own. With the rise of the national state, war had become the business of the common people for the first time in human history. In the words of one historian, "War was no longer considered a matter for a feudal ruling class or a small group of professionals, but one for the people as a whole."[33] Nationalism injected into European warfare a ferocity that far outstripped the religious wars of the sixteenth and seventeenth centuries. European national states were now pitted against one another in a succession of wars in which unprecedented amounts of human and economic resources were mobilized, extending over regions and over many months, with each new war. According to one scholar, two immense *global wars* resulted: the French War of 1792–1815 and the German War of 1914–1945.[34]

At the same time that nationalism was changing the kingly state into the nation-state, certain technological advances in weaponry encouraged changes in the way that armies were organized for war. The matchlock musket was replaced by the *flintlock musket*,[35] which could be reloaded and fired more quickly with fewer movements than the matchlock musket. In 1687, Sébastien Le Prestre Vauban (1633–1707), Louis XIV's chief military engineer, devised a bayonet that could be attached by a ring to the end of the musket's barrel, which allowed the weapon to be loaded and fired with the bayonet attached. Long, pointed bayonets replaced pikes and eliminated the phalanx from European armies for good.

These innovations required a new kind of soldier that nationalism provided. Recall that in kingly war soldiers engaged in combat were deployed in long ranks, up to six deep, which were rotated to make possible continuous fire with wheel-lock muskets. Long ranks required soldiers of great individual courage, proficiency, and iron discipline because it exposed them to the direct fire of the enemy. To be effective, soldiers had to be trained to march, load, and fire their weapons in unison. The replacement of matchlock muskets with flintlock muskets with fixed bayonets gave individual soldiers greater independent capacity for giving fire and defending themselves. This allowed their commanders to detach small groups of soldiers from the main body of the army as vanguard, rear, and flank guard units. Small units detached from the main body of the army required a degree of self-reliance, quick thinking, and reliability that troops trained to fight in ranks did not possess. Recruiters began to seek out hunters, who knew how to stalk game over broken ground, in forest, and in mountains, for the army's vanguard, rear, and flank guard units. Because such soldiers were dressed in distinctive green uniforms for camouflage and operated independently, out of touch from the main body of the army for long periods of time, they were considered by many aristocratic officers as little more than undisciplined brigands.[36] Granting "autonomy to individual units was easier and less risky in an army of conscripts dedicated to the revolutionary and national cause and whose loyalty could be relied upon far more than in the pre-revolutionary armies."[37]

After the Seven Years' War, it was realized by the French general and tactician Pierre de la Bourçet (1700–1780) that the entire army could be split into "autonomous 'divisions' of all arms, each moving along its own line of advance, mutually supporting but each capable of sustained action."[38] This kind of disaggregated fighting required a new kind of soldier: reliable, self-reliant, courageous, and loyal. Soldiers could now be trusted to fight alone away from the watchful eyes of their officers. Armies consisting of men who saw themselves as fighting for the nation brought to the European battlefield an enthusiasm for combat that had not been seen since Roman times. The potency of this new way of fighting and the enthusiasm of this new kind of soldier was demonstrated in 1792 at Valmy in the Argonne forest in north-eastern France, where a "rag tag French army under fire from the much better trained and better equipped Prussian infantry held its ground to the revolutionary battle cry of 'Vive la Nation,' [to which] Goethe, who was present, [declared] . . . that this 'date and place mark a new epoch in world history.'"[39]

In sum, after the French Revolution, wars no longer served

> the ambitions of an aristocratic class, wars were now the 'engines' of history, crucial junctures at which nations, peoples and classes revealed their true nature and purpose, fulfilling their historical destiny. Despite all the attempts by Metternich and the representatives of the Old Regime to turn the clock back in 1815 [at the Congress of Vienna], the forces unleashed by the [French Revolutionary and] Napoleonic wars had definitively set the world on a new trajectory.[40]

VARIETIES OF NATIONAL STATES

The French Revolution and the Napoleonic Wars created two varieties of national states throughout Europe: the liberal national state, exemplified by France, and the ethnic national state, exemplified by Prussia/Germany. Despite the philosophical differences in their underlying ideologies, liberalism and romanticism, respectively, both varieties of the national state became increasingly militarized and bellicose and declared enemies of the other.

Revolutionary and Napoleonic France: The First Nation-at-Arms

Although national identity emerged first in England, its appearance some-what later in France marked the beginning of what has been called the Age of Nationalism. During this age, the European states system was reconfigured from kingly to popular politico-military rule. France was, as was shown in the previous chapter, a large, powerful kingly state whose politico-military influence had been strongly manifested across Europe. The fact that French kings had constructed the most absolute monarchy in Europe affected greatly the way that nationalism appeared in France. In contrast to the gradual evolu-tion of national identity in England, French nationalism appeared as a revolu-tionary challenge to absolute monarchy. The result "was a see-saw history of alternating conservative and liberal regimes interposed with a series of vio-lent revolutionary outbreaks,"[41] the first of which was the French Revolution of 1789, arguably one of the most important, if not *the* most important, political events in the history of the world.

According to one historian, the French Revolution

> plunged Europe into the most profound and protracted crisis which it has ever known. It consumed an entire generation in its tumults, its wars, its disturbing innovations. From the epicenter in Paris, it sent shock waves to the furthest reaches of the Continent. From the shores of Portugal to the depths of Russia, from Scandinavia to Italy, the shocks were followed by soldiers in bright uniforms with a blue, white, and red cockade in their hats, and with 'Liberté, Égalité, Fraternité' on their lips. For its partisans, the Revolution promised liberation from the traditional oppressions enshrined in monarchy, nobility, and organized religion. For its opponents, it was synonymous with the dark forces of mob rule and terror. For France, it spelled the start of modern nation-al identity.[42]

The French Revolution began when Louis XVI (1754–1793) summoned the Estates General in 1789, the first time in 150 years that it had been called, in order to consider taxes to cover the extraordinary expenses associated with the Seven Years' War (1756–1763) and to support the War of American Independence (1775–1783). The third estate turned itself into the National Assembly and took decisions to transform and modernize the absolute kingly state, which it considered to be unnatural, backward, corrupt, and oppressive of human liberty, and the cause of French wars, into a peaceable republic. The National Assembly passed the Declaration of the Rights of Man and the Citizen (1793), and abolished the second estate (nobility) in order to establish a social order based on merit not birth. It abolished the first estate (clergy), disestablished the Catholic Church, and required the clergy to swear an oath of loyalty to the French republic; nationalized and confiscated Church lands and properties; forbade monastic vows and closed monasteries; and pres-sured France's linguistic minorities, Bretons, Flemings, Basques, Catalans, and Germans, as well as the various dialect groups especially in the south and west, to adopt the French language. The purpose of these actions was to forge all parts of France into a single nation.[43]

In addition, the National Assembly de-Christianized the calendar by giving the year's months descriptive names (e.g., August became Floréal); applied the metric system to all weights and measures; wiped the traditional provinces from the map and reorganized the French national territory into, more or less, equal-sized *départements* named after a geographical feature and administered by a single official of the state called a prefect; promulgated a written constitution; enfranchised men without property; abolished the mercantilistic practices of the kingly state and allowed free trade; created a new system of uniform taxation; abolished guilds; granted full citizenship to Jews and Protestants; introduced universal conscription; and revamped the judicial system by eliminating manorial and ecclesiastical courts.[44]

Despite its commitment to peace, the revolutionary government, called the Directory, was forced to defend the Revolution by making war on the European kingly states that were harboring French émigrés who were plotting with the deposed king to reestablish the monarchy. The Directory also believed that it had a historical mission to launch a war of peoples against kings. France's revolutionary armies made war on France's kingly neighbors who refused to accept liberty and equality. France's revolutionary armies conquered the Netherlands and annexed Belgium. Armies were also sent against Austria and Prussia. Another army, commanded by Napoleon Bonaparte, was sent against the Austrians and their Piedmontese allies in Italy. Although he was outnumbered, Napoleon defeated both and crossed the Alps and invaded Austria itself. The Austrians sued for peace, accepted the Rhine occupation, and gave the entire Italian peninsula to France. Lombardy was renamed the Cisalpine Republic, and the city-state of Genoa became the Ligurian Republic. Both of the new republics were modeled on republican France. For his victories in Italy, Napoleon was declared a national hero.

While the immediate cause of the wars of the French Revolution was their desire to defend the Revolution from the surrounding kingly states, the underlying cause was to determine the form of politico-military rule that was going to dominate the European continent—royal absolutism or people's republic. In the words of one historian, the French Revolution

> had ended feudalism, destroyed the pretensions of royal absolutism and founded new institutions on the principles of sovereignty of the people and personal liberty and equality. The old institutions, which had been overthrown in France, remained established in her continental neighbors. The influence of the Revolution was spreading, undermining the position of other rulers and implicitly challenging the survival of serfdom, feudalism, and absolutism everywhere.[45]

French military victories, and an attempt by Napoleon to sever the connection between Britain and India by establishing French hegemony over Egypt and Syria, sparked the major monarchies of Europe to form a new alliance against the French republic called the Second Coalition (1798–1801), composed of Russian, Prussian, British, Austrian, Portuguese, and Ottoman armies. Austria and Prussia pushed the French back from the Rhine and out of Italy. It appeared that the French monarchy was going to be restored by external military force. Napoleon, who had returned to France from Egypt in 1799, overthrew the weak Directory on November 9 (the 18 Brumaire according to the revolutionary calendar) and established a dictatorship.

Realizing that France needed strong leadership to quell the chaos in the streets, stabilize daily life, and prevent a return to absolute monarchy, Napoleon promulgated a new constitution that concentrated politico-military power into the hands of one official—the First Consul—who would be appointed for ten years. Napoleon had himself appointed the first First Consul. Firmly in the seat of power, Napoleon renewed the war against the Second Coalition. He crushed the Austrians in Italy and reestablished the Cisalpine and Ligurian republics. He signed a peace treaty with Britain. Having saved the Revolution from the Second Coalition, Napoleon turned his attention to the consolidation of the gains of the Revolution inside France.

He replaced the elected officials within the *départements* with individuals directly responsible to him in order to centralize and consolidate his control over the French state. In 1801 he signed an agreement (Concordat) with the Catholic Church that allowed him to put priests on the state payroll and to nominate all high Church officials in exchange for the Church's withdrawal of claims against the state for properties confiscated during the Revolution. In effect, the Concordat demoted the Catholic Church from being France's established church to being nothing more than the institution that represented the majority religion of the French people. In 1804, Napoleon unified the French legal system with the promulgation of the Code Napoleon, which was the culmination of a project launched during the Revolution to modernize the French legal system. He also introduced a system of state primary and secondary schools and universities. Through these schools, Napoleon intended to create a cadre of well-trained and loyal civil servants to replace the hereditary nobility of the *ancien régime*.

Finally, he put in place an efficient system of taxation, streamlined local government, and took the registration of births, marriages, and deaths out of the hands of the Church and gave it to local government, which gave the state data on the size and distribution of its population. These reforms made it possible for the French state to directly tax and conscript the largest population in Europe. Each *département* was given a quota of conscripts based on the size of its eligible male population. All Frenchmen were assigned a "class," which denoted the year they turned eighteen and were eligible for conscription. Resistance to conscription was countered by the strong-arm tactics of the Gendarmes, composed of veterans, which was dedicated to policing the French countryside. [46]

In 1802, Napoleon made himself consul for life and, in 1804, emperor of the French, having crowned himself in the cathedral of Notre Dame in Paris. Having stabilized the social and political situation within France, Napoleon launched a series of wars against neighboring kingly states, and in a few years of fighting, accomplished what France's absolute monarchy had endeavored to do for two hundred years: establish French hegemony over Europe. He transformed the Dutch Republic of Batavia into the Kingdom of Holland, he made the Cisalpine Republic into the Kingdom of Italy, and incorporated the Republic of Genoa into imperial France.

These actions brought forth the Third Coalition (1805–1814), consisting of Britain, Austria, Russia, and Sweden. Although his fleet was destroyed at Cape Trafalgar off the coast of Spain in October 1805, Napoleon's army defeated the armies of the coalition at Ulm and Austerlitz in the same year. After these two victories, he captured Vienna. Napoleon proceeded to strengthen the smaller German principalities and dukedoms by creating the kingdoms of Würtemberg and Bavaria and the Confederation of the Rhine, the latter consisting of all the small German-speaking states, except Austria and Prussia, under French protection. In 1806, Napoleon abolished the Holy Roman Empire.

After disposing of Austria and organizing the Confederation of the Rhine, Napoleon made war on Prussia. The Prussian king's mercenary soldiers, although well trained and equipped, were no match for Napoleon's army of patriotic conscripts, who were fighting for the ideals of the French Revolution and the French nation. Prussia's armies were overwhelmed at Jena and Auerstädt on October 14, 1806, after which Napoleon entered Berlin.

In an attempt to humble Czar Alexander (1801–1825) of Russia, who had sided with the Prussians against him, Napoleon marched his army from Berlin and defeated the Russian army at Friedland in 1807, after which he made peace with the czar at the expense of Prussia to make the new kingdom of Westphalia. Prussian holdings in Poland were reconstituted as the Grand Duchy of Warsaw. Now at the height of his power on the continent, Napoleon renewed his war with Britain. He devised an elaborate commercial blockade, called the Continental System, whereby he seized all British goods within French or allied territories and prevented all British ships from entering European ports in order to seal the continent against British trade.

The only kingly state on the continent to defy Napoleon was Portugal, which, being far from France and having been allied with Britain for centuries, refused to join the Continental System. Napoleon responded by invading the Iberian Peninsula in 1807, occupying Portugal, and driving out the royal family. His attempt to place his brother on the Spanish throne resulted in an insurrection against the French in Spain. The Spanish fought the French army with small bands, which attacked French military formations and then faded away into the countryside. These tactics came to be called *guerrilla* wars, which means "little war" in Spanish.

In an effort to unify Europe from the Atlantic to the Urals within the Continental System, Napoleon invaded the last kingly state on the continent that was independent of his authority, imperial Russia. In 1812, he assembled an army of 600,000 men—arguably the largest army under a single commander seen in Europe up to that time—and marched on Moscow. When he entered Moscow on September 15, he found that the Russians had abandoned the city and set fire to it in order to deny him his victory. After lingering in Moscow until October, Napoleon began his retreat to Paris. Before long his vast army was overtaken by winter weather, for which it was unprepared. Harassed by bands of Cossacks, lacking adequate provisions for his troops and horses, and suffering from disease, Napoleon's *Grande Armée* was reduced to fewer than 100,000 men by the time it straggled across the Niemen River into French-controlled territory.

Despite the Russian campaign, Napoleon raised, trained, and equipped a new army and made war on a new alliance of kingly states, the Fourth Coalition (Austria, Britain, Prussia, and Russia), which had formed against him. Napoleon's armies were driven out of German-speaking territories. At the same time, the British general, Sir Arthur Wellesley (1769–1852), later the Duke of Wellington, pushed the French army out of Portugal and Spain and pursued it across the Pyrenees into southern France. Coalition forces invaded France and captured Paris on March 13, 1814, and Napoleon capitulated. On April 11, the coalition granted Napoleon the island of Elba off the coast of Tuscany as a sovereign principality, where he was exiled with an 800-man guard of honor. The French monarchy was restored by placing the elder of Louis XVI's two surviving brothers on the throne as Louis XVIII (1755–1824).

After a few months in exile, Napoleon escaped from Elba with his guard of honor and formed a new army from his former troops, who rallied around him upon learning of his return to France. Louis XVIII fled France and Napoleon returned to power and resumed the war against the Fourth Coalition. The coalition organized a vast army commanded by the Duke of Wellington. Although Napoleon won some battles, Wellington defeated him decisively at Waterloo in Belgium on June 18, 1815. Narrowly avoiding capture, Napoleon fled to Paris, where he again abdicated. While planning an escape to the Americas, he surrendered himself to the British. The coalition made him a prisoner of war and banished him to St. Helena, a remote island in the mid-south Atlantic, where he lived under close supervision until his death on May 5, 1821. Louis XVIII reascended the throne and France was a kingly state once again.

Before he died, Napoleon said: "There are in Europe more than 30 million French, 15 million Spanish, 14 million Italians, and 30 million Germans. I would have wished to make each of these peoples a single united body."[47] The people living within the kingly states that Napoleon invaded, occupied, and reorganized along French lines saw things differently, however. What Napoleon failed to understand is that invasion by a foreign power, no matter the reason, usually ignites popular resistance and feelings of nationalism and patriotism against the invader. Thus, French armies inadvertently generated a patriotic response within the kingly states Napoleon invaded. In the words of one historian: "The whole of western Europe between the Pyrenees and the Baltic was infused with a strange mixture of general sympathy for the original ideals of the [French] Revolution and an immediate hostility to the practices of the French. It was a perfect mixture for nourishing the seeds of nationalism."[48]

Napoleon's successes on the battlefield were not due to new weapons. The muskets used by his troops had been in use since the end of the seventeenth century. Napoleon was successful first and foremost because his officers and soldiers were not mercenaries and the "scum of the earth" trained in the battle culture of forbearance as they had been during the *ancien régime*, but men from all social classes and regions of France officered by sergeants and corporals from the king's army who took the place of aristocratic officers who fled France after the Revolution. The soldiers of the Revolutionary army, a significant number of whom were the sons of peasants, saw themselves as free men fighting for a new social order in Europe.

Although revolutionary ardor played a role in Napoleon's victories, he was also successful because he perfected several strategic and tactical innovations known for decades but little used. Of these, four stand out. First, he divided his army into corps, each broken down into two or three divisions of 8,000 men each, which were further broken down into two brigades, which, in turn, were broken down into two regiments, each with two battalions. Breaking the army down into units gave it speed and flexibility because each division, brigade, and regiment could march along its own route simultaneously and be brought together at the last minute for the attack. The purpose was to maneuver the entire army into the best position to give battle. The success of this organizational strategy was demonstrated at Ulm, Austerlitz, and Jena, where, as was mentioned above, Napoleon dealt crushing defeats on Austrian and Prussian armies. Second, he employed free-moving, free-firing light infantry and light cavalry that operated independently in the front and on the flanks of the main army. These skirmishers went ahead of the main army to disorganize the enemy resistance. Third, he deployed his artillery on the battlefield to give concentrated fire from a great distance to breach the enemy's defensive line. Fourth, he attacked in columns of several thousand men rather than in long ranks to break through the breach created by the artillery.[49] The hallmarks of Napoleon's armies were speed of march, strategic concentration, aggressive tactics on the battlefield, and the effective coordination of artillery and infantry.

Napoleon's military success was due not only to these hallmarks and the enthusiasm and discipline of citizen soldiers who were fighting for France under the command of the greatest military genius since Alexander the Great, but also to the fact that Lazare Carnot (1753–1823), a member of the Directory who concerned himself with military matters and came to be known as "the Organizer of Victory," proclaimed in 1793 that "all Frenchmen are to be permanently requisitioned for the service of the armies."[50] Conscription (*levée en masse*) mobilized France's rural peasant population for the first time and gave French revolutionary armies and, later, Napoleon's armies more than a million men under arms, which gave them numerical superiority in every battle. Superiority in numbers was not the only advantage Napoleon's armies enjoyed. He was able to effectively control his vast army by advances in map making, the appointment of skilled officers from the ranks, the use of written orders, and the subdivision of his army into corps, divisions, and battalions each capable of operating as an independent fighting unit complete in itself.[51]

France's huge army required the extraction of vast quantities of men, money, and matériel to maintain it. In order to sustain an army of one million, Carnot

and his associates attempted to create planned war economy, based on the fear of the guillotine. All crops were requisitioned apart from those considered necessary for local consumption. A national bread was produced, *pain d'égalité,* and distributed against ration cards. A maximum price was fixed for all consumer goods. Stocks of luxuries were requisitioned for export against the importation of war materials, all foreign trade being regulated by a central commission. All transport and industrial output was nationalized and put to war needs. Evasions of the restrictions by hoarding or dealings on the black market were punished by death. The manufacture of arms, ammunition, uniforms, and equipment was organized on a national basis. Even scientists were conscripted to work on problems of metallurgy, explosives, ballistics, and other matters relevant to armaments manufacture. A research laboratory was set up at Meudon which devised the first military observation balloons. A semaphore telegraph system was established between Paris and the frontier. For the first time science was applied to warfare on a national scale.[52]

Under Napoleon, France was increasingly militarized and organized for war. Nearly all its institutions were organized for the purpose of recruiting, training, and maintaining its army. He sought to make the office corps the major component of France's post-revolutionary elite. The offices and rewards of state, such as the *Légion d'Honneur* (1802), were created and reserved primarily for army personnel of any rank. In order to lure the sons of France's notables into the army, Napoleon made it clear that the army offered careers open to talent in warfare and paid his officers very high salaries. [53]

The way Napoleon organized his *Grande Armée* was emulated by all European states for the next two centuries. Initiatives for reform usually came from young officers who realized that they were facing something new in European warfare against which they would have to react. They realized that war was becoming total, a conflict of whole peoples; therefore, armies consisting of reliable patriots who were fighting for their nation, the fatherland, or the motherland had to be raised to remain competitive on the European battlefield. As a consequence, all European states were organized and militarized along French lines, to a greater or lesser degree.

Bismarckian Germany: An Army with a National State

Napoleon's devastating defeat of the Prussian armies at Jena and Auerstädt in 1806 thoroughly discredited the "military-agrarian complex" that had served the Prussian crown so well up to that time. Prussia had to learn to win at war again, *or cease to exist*. A reform movement that sought to modernize the Prussian army and state was launched by barons Heinrich Friedrich Stein (1757–1831) and Carl August von Hardenberg (1750–1822) designed to systematically organize all aspects of Prussian society and state to prevent conquest by its powerful neighbors, France, Russia, and Austria. Although Friedrich Wilhelm III (1797–1840) was a staunch absolutist like his father, he bowed to necessity and

> improved decision-making by replacing the Byzantine system of unaccountable royal councillors with "responsible" ministers; opened the officer corps to bourgeois candidates according to the merit principle; abolished the guild system to liberalize the economy; emancipated the peasantry to create a free market in land and consequently abandoned the old cantonal system in favor of French-style universal military service; and lifted restrictions on Jews. Prussia's external vulnerability, formerly used to justify noble privileges and the separation of the army from society, was now advanced as an argument for a "real military state" in which they formed an indissoluble unity. [54]

This early connection of the Prussian people, understood in ethnic-linguistic terms, to the state and army and continued threats from France gave rise to efforts to unify all the German-speaking states of north-central Europe. Friedrich Wilhelm IV (1840–1861) sought to create a stronger national state not through liberal constitutionalism but, rather, through the revival of the estates and the glories of the divinely consecrated absolute monarchy. He dreamed of reestablishing the Holy Roman Empire within which Prussia would be the leading kingly state.

The 1848 revolution in Paris precipitated a widespread uprising of liberal nationalists in Prussia who demanded constitutional reform and the unification of the German-speaking states into a single empire. The liberals were motivated by the same fears as the king. The liberal David Hansemann (1790–1864) wrote that

> "the German [empire] must be mighty and strong" for we have dangerous neighbors. In the east was Russia, "the most consistently expansionist state since Roman times, which has already taken up a threatening position in the heart of Prussia [i.e., Poland]," and was threatening East Prussia. To the west lay France, "a state which is dangerous because of its internal cohesion, the warlike and excitable nature of its inhabitants and because of their tenacious and unhappy belief in the need to control the Rhine border sooner or later."[55]

Unlike the aristocratic reformers, however, the liberals believed that the only way to mobilize the nation against strong external enemies was to make internal reforms that would liberate the nation and harness the power of the bourgeoisie by giving it greater domestic political participation, which the king and the aristocracy were desperate to avoid.[56]

In 1846, Friedrich Wilhelm IV announced his willingness to collaborate with the liberals. He summoned a united *Landtag* (legislature) to write a constitution that would merge Prussia with other German states into a single united German state. The liberals wanted a unified constitutional Germany, not a federation. They were at odds over whether this united Germany should be a small Germany under Prussian leadership or a large Germany (*Grossdeutschland*) under Austrian leadership.[57] As the debate became increasingly radical, the king, encouraged by the restoration of absolutism in Austria, dissolved the *Landtag* and promulgated his own constitution, which maintained the absolute authority of the crown. Friedrich's constitution provided for a two-chambered legislature with an upper house consisting of the nobility and clergy and a lower house consisting of the bourgeoisie, based on tax-paying ability. Government ministers were responsible to the king, not parliament.

In 1861, Friedrich Wilhelm IV died and was followed on the throne by his brother, Wilhelm I (1861–1888) who, unlike his predecessor, was reform minded. He turned his attention first to universal military service, which for all intents and purposes had been abandoned by his brother. He was determined to make universal military service a reality in order to provide the state with a larger army. His minister of war, Albrecht von Roon (1803–1879), reintroduced compulsory military service consisting of three years of active duty followed by four years in the reserves, and fourteen years in the militia (*Landwehr*), which had been created during the wars against Napoleon.[58]

In 1862, Wilhelm appointed a Brandenburg Junker and staunch defender of royal power, Otto von Bismarck (1815–1898), as his chancellor. Bismarck was convinced that Prussia could survive only by destroying the German Federation created at the Congress of Vienna (1815) and by subduing the minor German states. Bismarck was able to achieve his objective by carrying out a series of military and diplomatic successes. The first was a quick victory in a war with Denmark in 1864 over the duchies of Schleswig and Holstein, which had been absorbed by the Danish monarchy. After crushing the Danes, Bismarck placed the duchies under joint Prussian and Austrian administration. The second was a victory in a war with Austria in 1866 after which Prussia annexed Schleswig-Holstein, Hanover, Hesse-Cassel, and Frankfurt. The third was the formation of a confederation of the German-speaking states to the north under Prussian leadership. The creation of a unified German state/people was still incomplete, however, because Bismarck allowed the four southern German-speaking monarchies (Bavaria, Württenberg, Baden, and Hesse) to form a federation of their own, albeit with a secret military agreement that tied them to Prussia. In the Prussian-led North German Confederation, the king of Prussia was the chief executive, and the legislative power was held by a Federal Council (*Bundesrat*), which represented the member states. The German people as a whole were represented in a parliament (*Reichstag*) elected by universal manhood suffrage.

Unification of the North German Confederation with the four southern German-speaking monarchies came about as a consequence of the Franco-Prussian War (1870–1871). The combined German armies quickly defeated the French and forced them to cede Alsace and part of Lorraine to Germany. The south German states entered the North German Confederation, which became the German Empire. The King of Prussia was named Emperor Wilhelm I on January 18, 1871 and Bismarck was elevated to the rank of prince and made chancellor of the empire.

In Germany, romantic nationalism had triumphed at the expense of liberal nationalism. The German state and nation were created simultaneously, not by liberals from below but by nationalizing aristocrats from above. The German nation finally found expression in a single state, the German Empire.

Prussia's quick victory in the Franco-Prussian War was due not only to the unification of the German people into a single state, but also to the reforms of the state and army made after 1806. Prussia created a system of primary and secondary education that began to produce citizen-soldiers who were able to master the complexities of industrial warfare. The army established schools for non-commissioned officers. In order to make merit, not birth, the most important factor in officer selection and promotion, many Junker officers were retired and replaced with graduates of the war academy (*Kriegsakademie*) who had been schooled in the new methods of war. An early director of the *Kriegsakademie* was Carl von Clausewitz (1780–1831), the author of the greatest book of military philosophy of all time, *Vom Kriege (On War)*, published posthumously in 1832 by his widow. In this work, Clausewitz stressed that the French Revolution had changed the nature of warfare from the wars of maneuver of the *ancien régime* to "absolute" wars carried out with the full force of national energies in pursuit of total victory.[59]

Prussian/German military success also resulted from the innovative application of industrial, technical, and managerial developments to war, such as the steam engine, railroads, the electric telegraph, and the creation of the General Staff (*Grosser Generalstab*) between 1803 and 1809, perhaps the greatest military innovation of the nineteenth century.[60] The invention of the steam engine and railroads eliminated long marches to the battlefield and increased the staying power of armies in the field. Armies no longer had to rely on stockpiles located in forward magazines. A continuous supply of war matériel extracted from the entire economy of the state provided for their needs. In addition, double-tracked railroads simultaneously brought troops to the battlefield well rested and immediately ready to engage the enemy, and evacuated the sick and wounded to hospitals. The electric telegraph brought news of the war to the home front, which allowed civilians to follow campaigns, giving them a sense of participation and intimacy in the war as never before.[61]

The General Staff (officers who provide the information necessary to plan military operations, assemble the required troops and matériel, and draft the orders necessary to carry out the intentions of the commander) was reorganized by Helmut von Moltke (1800–1891) in 1857, and became the model for all European armies. Much staff time was spent learning the lessons of past battles and devising plans for future ones. Moltke devised war games on maps or sand tables with metal symbols for opposing armies, red for the enemy and blue for friendly forces, a method still in use by all the armies of the world.[62] Moltke recognized that Prussia, being surrounded by powerful and hostile neighbors, needed time to mobilize its army. He saw railroads as a way of buying time to offset Prussia's geographical vulnerability. Moltke used railroads, the telegraph, and contingency planning to mobilize a very large army and go on the offensive on very short notice.[63]

Before Moltke, the work of supplying and deploying large armies was carried out by staff officers with little training, who were seen by line officers as nothing more than military bureaucrats out of touch with the real army and war. Moltke turned his staff officers into an elite force of military intellectuals by recruiting the most promising regimental officers to his staff and giving them the training they needed to become professional soldiers. He also rotated them between staff and command posts of increasing responsibility so that they would not lose touch with real soldiering. Moltke's bureaucratic method "made war a matter of scientific calculation, administrative planning, and professional expertise."[64] Prussian methods of conscription, strategic use of railroads, mobilization techniques, and the General Staff were copied by all the states of Europe in the years after the Franco-Prussian War, where they had been shown to be so effective. After the defeat of the Austrians at the battle of Königgrätz in 1866, it was common to say that Prussia "was not a state with an army, but an army with a state."[65] In other words, military service was the essence of citizenship itself. Germany had been militarized with a thoroughness that escaped Napoleon.

CONCLUSION

After the French Revolution, the environment in which European states existed became increasingly threatening as kingly states were transformed by war into national states. A strong national state was seen as the solution to the problem of external security because only a well-organized national state could mobilize the people for the defense of its existence in a Europe of predatory neighbors. The French Revolution enabled the state to wage war with the full power of the nation by transforming the relationship between the state, the army, and the people. Before the Revolution, kingly armies numbered in the hundreds of thousands and military service was seen as the calling of the few, those who were driven to it by poverty or born to it by social standing. After the Revolution it was increasingly understood and accepted that the state could require military service of all fit men, and all fit men understood and accepted that it was their duty to serve in the army in times of national emergency. The rank and file of armies no longer consisted of mercenaries and the dregs of society, but was increasingly representative of every social class and region. Armies numbered in the millions, and the vast majority of European men of military age experienced soldiering. The mass-reserve army became a central institution in all European national states. Eventually, all state resources were subordinated to building and sustaining the mass-reserve army in all European national states. European states were increasingly organized to transform citizens into soldiers who would fight not from fear, but from devotion to the nation, the fatherland, or the motherland.

Consequently, during the one hundred years after the French Revolution, European states became more and more *militarized* as military culture and values increasingly permeated civilian society. European states also became more and more bellicose with respect to one another. While these transformations were taking place in all European states, they were manifested most strongly in Prussia/Germany where the state/army/people were fused into a trinity not achieved in other European states and produced Europe's strongest, best organized, militarized, chauvinistic national state.

The political revolution that transformed the kingly state into the national state made the European states system more and more symmetrical and perilous as states emulated and replicated the technical and organizational innovations of their competitors. In the process, war fighting was transformed. The wars of position prior to the Revolution became wars of attrition after the Revolution. The armies of national states made war not for small territorial gains here and there, but to annihilate the enemy state's army and conquer its territory. The fusion of the state, army, and people unleashed tremendous military forces that made wars after the French Revolution unlike earlier wars in European history because millions of citizen-soldiers willing to sacrifice themselves for the nation could be mobilized with unprecedented speed, maintained on the battlefield for long periods of time, and replenished with new conscripts year after year. Nationalized war was made even more destructive by the application of science and technology to weaponry after the Industrial Revolution, which will be discussed in the next chapter.

NOTES

1. Michael Howard, *War in European History* (Oxford: Oxford University Press, 1976) p. 75.
2. David A. Bell, *The First Total War: Napoleon's Europe and the Birth of Warfare as We Know It* (New York and Boston: Houghton Mifflin, 2007), p. 5.
3. R. Harrison Wagner, *War and the State: The Theory of International Relations* (Ann Arbor: University of Michigan Press, 2007), p. 170.
4. Bell, *op. cit.*, p. 8.
5. *Ibid.*, p. 11.
6. Ernst B. Haas, *Nationalism, Liberalism, and Progress: The Rise and Decline of Nationalism*, vol. 1 (Ithaca, NY: Cornell University Press, 1997), p. 23.
7. Liah Greenfeld, *Nationalism: Five Roads to Modernity* (Cambridge, MA: Harvard University Press, 1997), p. 3.
8. C. A. Macartney, *National States and National Minorities* (New York: Russell & Russell, 1934), pp. 35–36.
9. Norman Davies, *Europe: A History* (Oxford: Oxford University Press, 1996), p. 382.
10. Hans Kohn, *The Idea of Nationalism: A Study in Its Origins and Background* (New York: Macmillian, 1944), p. 188.
11. *Ibid.*, p. 226.
12. Macartney, *op. cit.*, p. 39.
13. Philip Bobbitt, *The Shield of Achilles: War, Peace, and the Course of History* (New York: Anchor Books, 2003), p. 120.
14. Macartney, *op. cit.*, pp. 93–94; italics in the original.
15. J. M. Roberts, *A History of Europe* (New York: Allan Lane, 1996), pp. 235–38.
16. Kohn, *op. cit*, p. 217.
17. William L. Langer (ed.), *Western Civilization: The Struggle for Empire to Europe in the Modern World* (New York: Harper & Row, 1968), p. 293.
18. This phrase in Latin (*Novus Ordo Seclorum*) appears on the reverse of the Great Seal of the United States and has been printed on the one-dollar bill since 1935.
19. Kohn, *op. cit.*, p. 329.
20. Macartney, *op. cit.*, p. 94.
21. Kohn, *op. cit.*, pp. 330–31.
22. *Ibid.*, pp. 236–49.

23. Macartney, *op. cit.*, p. 97.

24. *Ibid.*, pp. 101–3.

25. Martin van Creveld, *The Rise and Decline of the State* (Cambridge: Cambridge University Press, 1999), pp. 195–96.

26. James J. Sheehan, *Where Have All the Soldiers Gone? The Transformation of Modern Europe* (Boston/New York: Houghton Mifflin, 2008), xix.

27. George L. Mosse, *Fallen Soldiers: Reshaping the Memory of the World Wars* (New York: Oxford University Press, 1990), p. 18.

28. Sheehan, *op. cit.*, p. 13.

29. *Ibid.*, p. 17.

30. Mosse, *op. cit.*, p. 19.

31. Bruce D. Porter, *War and the Rise of the State: The Military Foundations of Modern Politics* (New York: Free Press, 1994), p. 19.

32. John D. Weltman, *World Politics and the Evolution of War* (Baltimore, MD: Johns Hopkins University Press, 1994), pp. 36–45.

33. Howard, *op. cit.*, p. 110.

34. Williamson Murray and MacGregor Knox, "Thinking about Revolutions in Warfare," in MacGregor Knox and Williamson Murray (eds.), *The Dynamics of Military Revolution, 1300–2050* (Cambridge: Cambridge University Press, 2001), p. 8.

35. The matchlock was a mechanism invented to facilitate the firing of a musket. It removed the need to lower the hand-lit match into the flash pan, which freed the hands to aim and fire the weapon. The flintlock replaced the match with a flint fixed to the hammer that produced a spark and ignited the charge.

36. Howard, *op. cit.*, p. 76.

37. Antoine Bousquet, *The Scientific Way of Warfare: Order and Chaos on the Battlefields of Modernity* (New York: Columbia University Press, 2009), p. 77.

38. *Ibid.*

39. Rogers Brubaker, *Nationalism Reframed: Nationhood and the National Question in the New Europe* (Cambridge: Cambridge University Press, 1996), p. 1.

40. Bousquet, *op. cit.*, p. 77.

41. Davies, *op. cit.*, p. 803.

42. *Ibid.*, p. 677.

43. Simms, *op. cit.*, p. 143.

44. Robert E. Holtman, *The Napoleonic Revolution* (Philadelphia: J. B. Lippincott, 1967), chapter 1.

45. *Ibid.*, p. 181.

46. Michael Broers, "Changes in War: The French Revolutionary and Napoleonic Wars," in Hew Strachan and Sibylle Scheipers (eds.), *The Changing Character of War* (Oxford: Oxford University Press, 2011), pp. 73–74.

47. David Thomson, *Europe since Napoleon*, 2nd Edition (New York: Knopf, 1962), p. 15.

48. *Ibid.*, p. 31.

49. Howard, *op. cit.*, pp. 76–78, and p. 84.

50. Simms, *op. cit.*, p. 151.

51. William H. McNeill, *The Pursuit of Power: Technology, Armed Force, and Society since A.D. 1000* (Chicago: University of Chicago Press, 1982), p. 163.

52. Howard, *op. cit.*, p. 81.

53. MacGregor Knox, "Mass Politics and Nationalism as Military Revolution: The French Revolution and After," in Knox and Murray, *op. cit.*, pp. 67–68.

54. Simms, *op. cit.*, 167.

55. Quoted in Simms, *op. cit.*, p. 204.

56. *Ibid.*, p. 210.

57. *Ibid.*, p. 216.

58. Howard, *op. cit.*, p. 100.

59. Max Boot, *War Made New: Technology, Warfare, and the Course of History, 1500 to Today* (New York: Gotham Books, 2006), p. 121.

60.   Jeremy Black, in *The Battle of Waterloo* (New York: Random House, 2010), p. 155, attributes Napoleon's defeat at Waterloo, *inter alia*, to poor staff work and personal command in contrast to the superior Prussian general staff system that gave more coherent control, direction, and unity of command.

61.   Howard, *op. cit.*, p. 97–99.

62.   Boot, *op. cit.*, p. 122.

63.   André Corvisier (ed.), *A Dictionary of Military History*, trans. Chris Turner (Oxford: Basil Blackwell, 1994), p. 528.

64.   Howard, *op. cit.*, p. 101.

65.   Boot, *op. cit.*, p. 141.

Chapter 5

Industrial War and the Managerial Welfare State

The Industrial Revolution, which began when non-animate forms of energy (water, steam, chemical, nuclear) were harnessed to drive machines, brought the industrialization and mechanization of war. At the end of the nineteenth and beginning of the twentieth centuries, the design and manufacture of diverse kinds of machines of war, especially warships, became a major aspect of the economies of European states. Naval and ground forces became increasingly machine dependent. Soldiers and sailors increasingly became less and less fighting men and more and more operators of complex machines of war that engaged similar enemy machines of war on land, at sea, and in the air. Industrialization and mechanization made war vastly more costly and destructive than it had been in previous eras because it combined "industrial firepower and logistics with the fighting power and staying power that nationalism could generate."[1]

The confluence of the transformations in war-making wrought by the French Revolution with those of the Industrial Revolution gave European states unprecedented military capabilities, which culminated in the two most expensive, wide-ranging, deadly, and destructive wars ever fought by human beings, the First and Second World Wars. Both wars, which can be seen as a single war with a temporary truce among the belligerents from 1919 to 1939, brought about what William McNeill called a *"managerial metamorphosis"* that changed the nature of the European state in a profound way: the state's "innumerable bureaucratic structures that had previously acted more or less independently of one another in a context of market relationships coalesced into what amounted to a *single national firm for waging war."*[2] Private business corporations, labor unions, and government ministries came to jointly manage the affairs of the state through an alliance among top-level government, labor union, and business bureaucrats during the war years.

The industrialization of war increasingly *militarized* European states and put them on a war footing. From the end of the nineteenth century they built armies, navies, and air forces of unprecedented size and equipped them with more and more complex, destructive, and expensive machines of war. They developed the bureaucratic and financial structures necessary to mobilize all of their human, economic, scientific, and political resources, such that "every aspect of social life—production, administration, and culture—[was] directed toward war and all social change translated into battle potential."[3]

National war combined with industrial war made European war *total*. Increasingly, whole societies and economies were militarized and organized for war. Immense loans were raised, women took the place of men in factories and on farms, and civilians gave up luxuries, submitted to rationing of necessities, and did without consumer goods. Military imperatives overrode all others. States nationalized firms, took control of industrial production and regulated labor, postponed elections, and censored the media.[4] In order to organize their societies and economies for total industrial war, states increasingly centralized their bureaucracies and increased the number of administrative personnel. Taxes were increased and money borrowed to pay for the increasingly expensive machines of war.

Total war also established the principle that states are not only responsible for organizing their societies for war but also for managing the welfare of their peoples. The state's concern about the well-being of its soldiers, sailors, and airmen spread to encompass the health and well-being of the entire population. Essentially, the state made a bargain between itself and its people: *social discipline and sacrifice in time of war in exchange for social welfare programs after the war.*

Total war required European states "to guide and manage the entire society, because without the total effort of all sectors of society modern [industrialized] warfare could not be successfully waged. Not only the power of the state but its responsibility as well were extended into virtually all areas of civil life."[5] Thus, industrialized war brought forth a new form of the state in Europe, the managerial welfare state.

INDUSTRIAL WAR

The Industrial Revolution required three things: (1) the harnessing of non-animate forms of energy by human beings; (2) the invention and construction of machines to do the jobs of skilled workers; and (3) the grouping together of such machines and their operators in a single "factory." These conditions took hold first in the United States where there was no well-organized class of skilled handworkers who resisted mechanization because it was a threat to their traditional way of life. American pioneers in mechanization, such as Eli Whitney (1765–1825), best known for inventing the cotton gin, said that mechanization was necessary in order "to substitute correct and effective operations of machinery for that skill of the artist which is acquired only by long practice and experience; a species of skill which is not possessed in [the United States] to any considerable extent."[6]

The grouping of manufacturing machines and their operators into factories began in the government arsenal at Springfield, Massachusetts, between 1820 and 1850, where milling machines (lathes, drills, and files), initially powered by water wheels, which could do the same task in exactly the same way repeatedly, were developed for the mass-production of small arms. Springfield's machines cut gun parts to exact specifications, which made them interchangeable and allowed muskets to be mass-produced on assembly lines without the filing and adjustment of each piece by skilled gunsmiths. By the middle of the nineteenth century, Springfield's assembly-line method of small arms manufacture, known as the "American System," was copied in Britain in a new plant at Enfield. Soon after, American milling machines were imported by the Russians, Spanish, Turks, and Swedes. Artisanal methods of gun manufacture disappeared. Mass production of small arms meant that "[a]n entire army could be reequipped [with a new gun design] about as quickly as soldiers could be trained with the new weapon. The door was thus opened wide for further improvements in the design of small arms."[7] Mass production of small arms made it possible to arm the vast conscripted armies that followed the French Revolution and made soldiers "much more expendable, as individuals, than they had ever been . . . [and a] new emphasis was placed upon the material ability to kill as many men as possible."[8]

After flowing water, the next form of non-animate energy harnessed by human beings was steam, which was first used to drive pumps to remove water from coal mines in Wales and later to power the spinning and weaving machines of the burgeoning cotton industry in England. It was, however, the *steam-powered locomotive* and the road of rails on which it traveled that had a transformative impact on European war-making because it permitted the moving of vast numbers of men, weapons, and supplies to the battlefield on an unprecedented scale. Instead of having to march to the battlefield, whole armies could be loaded onto carriages pulled by steam engines to staging areas behind the front lines and then sent into battle in good physical shape and fully rested. Front-line troops could be continuously resupplied with war matériel and, when wounded, they could be taken by train to hospitals well removed from the fighting. Moreover, trains made it possible for individual soldiers to go home on leave for rest and relaxation, during which time they mixed with the civilian population and told of their experiences at the front. Their presence in uniform on the streets and in the beer gardens and cafés of their towns and villages and the experiences they related of life at the front brought the war home to civilians as never before. Railroads came to be seen as essential for the defense of the state. As early as "1842, Prussia planned the construction of a strategic railway network in preparation for the eventuality of a simultaneous war against France and Russia."[9]

The third form of non-animate energy to be harnessed by human beings was *electro-magnetism*. As a consequence, slow and inefficient optical beacons and semaphores, such as Claude Chappe's (1763–1805) semaphore signaling system, that were used to send messages over long distances were replaced by the *telegraph* in the 1830s. The introduction of a coded signaling system and the telegraph key by Samuel Morse (1791–1872) in 1844 made it possible to speedily send accurate messages over great distances no matter the weather or time of day. The telegraph, adapted for military use, made it possible for generals in the field to communicate instantaneously with civilian leaders in the capital to tell them of enemy troop movements and to manage the logistical demands of industrial war. This allowed the civilian leadership to involve itself in the conduct of the war as never before. The telegraph also made it possible for war correspondents to file their stories within hours of a battle. Newspapers were able to print stories of the success or failure of battles and campaigns within days. Civilians were thus able to follow the progress of the war, battle by battle, campaign by campaign, with critical interest. Newspaper stories about the war gave civilians a sense of involvement in war as never before.

Innovations and improvements in the design and manufacture of gunpowder weapons in the nineteenth century made firearms and cannon more reliable, more powerful, and more accurate than previously. *Percussion caps*, which made guns fire more consistently, replaced flints in the first quarter of the nineteenth century. *Rifling* (spiral grooves inside the barrel), which improved accuracy by a factor of five, began to be applied to guns used by ordinary soldiers, not just snipers. In the 1820s, a German gunmaker, Johann Nikolaus von Dreyse (1787–1867), attached the percussion cap onto the base of the bullet and designed a gun that ignited the powder charge by driving a needle through the paper casing of the cartridge. Von Dreyse's gun, known as the "needle gun," represented a new design because the round was inserted into the breech, not the muzzle, and locked into place with a bolt and fired with a pin. About the same time, elongated bullets, hollow at the base and rounded to a point at the nose, that could be dropped down the bore were patented in 1849 by Claude-Étienne Minié (1804–1879), a French army captain.[10]

Needle guns and rifles that used *Minié* bullets had rates of fire six times that of muzzle-loaded flintlock muskets. The development of metal cartridges that held a percussion cap, powder charge, and bullet in a metal case, and the invention of the *magazine* that could hold several cartridges, improved the speed of loading and firing even more. These mechanical improvements to firearms made it possible for infantrymen to carry more ammunition and to reload and fire more rapidly even from the kneeling and prone positions. This meant that for the first time in the history of gunpowder warfare, soldiers did not have to stand erect to fire their weapons and could take cover and kill the enemy at a distance of several hundred yards without exposing themselves to enemy fire.[11]

In the 1850s, standard smooth-bore, muzzle-loaded, bronze cannon, which were ineffective beyond 1,500 yards, were replaced by *rifled, breech-loaded, steel cannon*, which were effective up to 5,000 yards. The development of *high explosives* by the French chemist Paul Marie Vieille (1854–1934), made of nitroglycerin, acetone, and mineral jelly, brought the replacement of solid cast-iron cannon balls with hollow *shells* filled with high explosives and fitted with *point-detonating fuses*. High explosives also replaced gunpowder as propellants in cannon because they combusted totally and made no smoke to reveal the location of the cannon firing the round, left little residue in the barrel to slow down the rate of fire, and increased the range and accuracy of the pieces to an extent not seen before. *Smokeless high-explosive powder* (known as *Poudre B*) eliminated the thick smoke that had clouded battlefields since the introduction of gunpowder weapons.

The invention of the *hydraulic recoil cylinder*, which allowed artillery pieces to return automatically to their firing positions after each discharge, made it unnecessary to re-aim them after each firing, and increased rates and accuracy of fire substantially. In the nineteenth century, the best artillery pieces were developed and built by the German arms manufacturer Alfred Krupp (1812–1887). Known as the "cannon king," Krupp manufactured artillery pieces with rifled steel barrels that could fire high-explosive shells up to 3,000 yards. Krupp's artillery pieces contributed significantly to Prussia's victory over the French in the Franco-Prussian War (1870–1871).[12]

The invention of the *field telephone* and the increased range of artillery made it possible to locate guns in concealed positions well behind the front lines and fire indirectly on unseen targets. Heavy artillery was able to fire shells 20 miles or more, and in the case of some exceptionally large-caliber pieces, up to 60 miles.[13] Despite these advances, artillery did not at first enjoy wide esteem in European armies because it was seen as an improper way to wage war and many senior officers did not believe that artillery could be used effectively against an enemy that gun crews could not see and fire upon directly. A few even believed that concealing artillery showed cowardice. Nonetheless, by the beginning of the First World War, the effectiveness of indirect artillery fire in decimating advancing enemy troops at great distances had been demonstrated and artillery become known as the "queen of the battlefield." It remained dominant until the middle of the twentieth century when aircraft were designed and built that were capable of bombing behind enemy lines.

In 1861, Richard Jordan Gatling (1818–1903), a dentist from North Carolina who had an unshakable belief in the benefits of technological and industrial progress, invented a gun capable of continuous fire, the hand-cranked, multi-barrel eponymous *Gatling gun*. In a letter written in 1877 explaining why he invented his gun, he wrote that it "occurred to me that if I could invent a machine—a gun—that would by its rapidity of fire enable one man to do as much battle duty as a hundred, that it would to a great extent, supersede the necessity of large armies, and consequently exposure to battle and disease would be greatly diminished."[14]

In the 1880s, another American, Hiram Maxim (1840–1916), invented the first gun capable of true automatic continuous fire, the *machine gun*. Maxim's gun used the mechanical force of recoil from the first round fired to operate its ejection, loading, and firing mechanisms repeatedly until a belt of ammunition was expended. The barrel was encased in a metal tube-like jacket filled with water to keep it from overheating. Maxim's water-cooled machine gun was heavy and cumbersome and required a crew of three to fire. Other American inventors followed with their own machine-gun designs. William Browning (1855–1926) invented a gun that used escaping muzzle gases to operate the mechanism, which surpassed Maxim's mechanical recoil design. A United States Army colonel, Isaac Newton Lewis (1858–1931), designed a gas-operated machine gun, which was much lighter than either the Browning or the Maxim guns. After retiring from the army, Lewis manufactured his eponymous Lewis gun in a factory he established in Liège, Belgium, the Armes Automatique Lewis.

The Gatling gun made its appearance on the battlefields of the American Civil War, the world's first industrial war. Machine guns were, like artillery, slow to be adopted by European armies, however, because they were dominated by conservative aristocratic officers who were suspicious of mechanical killing machines that left little room for individual feats of courage and valor. Into the early twentieth century, the officer corps of European armies were romantics in the industrial age and "still believed in the glorious cavalry charge and, above all, the supremacy of man as opposed to mere machine."[15] Europeans were, however, willing to use machine guns in colonial expeditions in Africa from the 1880s until the 1920s against tribal warriors who did not hold European ideas of chivalrous combat and resisted the "benefits" of European civilization.[16] Machine guns were not used by European armies against each other until the First World War, when trench warfare made them a military necessity.[17]

The third form of non-animate energy that was harnessed by human beings during the Industrial Revolution was *chemical*. The invention that used this form of energy to great effect, eventually in war, was the *internal-*

combustion engine, the first commercially successful model of which was built in 1859 by Jean-Joseph Lenoir (1822–1900), a Belgian engineer and inventor working in Paris. By the 1880s, Lenoir's engine had been installed on four-wheeled carriages. Various mechanics added carburetors, radiators, steering wheels, crank-starters, pedal brakes, and rubber tires. Within a few months of the start of the First World War, it was realized that the internal-combustion engine could be used to power fighting machines as well as vehicles for transportation. The first motorized fighting machine, the *tank*, was put in operation by the British in 1916 and was used with varying degrees of success as mobile firepower to break through the enemy's defenses. Increasingly, armies consisted of "tens, later hundreds, of thousands of machines [powered by internal-combustion engines] ranging from light reconnaissance vehicles (jeeps) all the way to personnel carriers, motorized or self-propelled artillery, and tanks."[18]

The first steam-driven warship was a paddle wheeler, the *Demologos*, built by the American steamboat pioneer Robert Fulton (1765–1815), for use against the British in the War of 1812. In the years immediately following the war, paddle wheelers were used by navies only to patrol and defend their coastal waterways because their steam engines did not produce sufficient power to propel them in the open ocean where high waves made the ship plunge in and out of the water, which damaged the paddle wheels and strained the machinery. The steam engines they used were operated at low pressure because sea water corroded their boilers, which would explode if pressure in the boiler exceeded about twenty-five pounds per square inch.[19]

Although it was known by engineers that increasing the operating pressure in a steam engine would increase its power, the technology to do so safely in marine steam engines was not invented until the 1830s. In 1834, Samuel Hall (c.1782–1863) developed the *surface condenser*, which recycled steam back to the boilers in the form of salt-free distilled water that reduced boiler corrosion and allowed higher pressures to be generated within the engine. Hall's invention and the invention of the marine *compound steam engine* by John Elder (1824–1869), which had several pistons in tandem through which high-pressure steam from the first, then subsequent, pistons was fed resulting in less loss of power, allowed the construction of very large steam-powered ocean-going ships capable of sailing from Europe to the Far East without coaling.[20]

In the 1830s a new method of propulsion, the *screw propeller*, was introduced. The screw propeller, located on the underside of the hull, made ships more maneuverable and seaworthy and opened up deck space for turrets housing very large-caliber guns that could rotate 180 degrees and fire shells up to 20,000 yards. By the 1880s, sails and paddle wheels had been replaced by screw propellers, and wood hulls by *iron* and *steel* hulls, which made ships larger, lighter, stronger, and faster. Iron and steel hulls also made ships safer from sinking from a break in the hull because they could be constructed with watertight bulkheads that would limit flooding to a single compartment.

At the end of the nineteenth century, *battleships* became the symbol of national pride, the embodiment of national industrial power. Britain, which had always relied on its navy for national defense, and imperial Germany, which wanted to demonstrate its industrial achievements and aspirations to become a great power, competed to build fleets consisting of the biggest battleships (called dreadnaughts after the super-battleship, the HMS *Dread-naught*, propelled by oil-burning turbine engines and armed with ten twelve-inch guns, launched in 1906) and the largest number of battle cruisers, destroyers, mine layers, and mine sweepers. The invention of the wireless telegraph, or *radio*, at the turn of the twentieth century, created a means for ships at sea to communicate with one another and with their home ports, which made possible coordinated naval warfare.[21]

Also by the end of the nineteenth century, armed, steel-hulled, shallow-draft, screw propeller–driven boats carrying pivot-mounted cannon capable of sailing upstream in navigable rivers were designed and built. In the late nineteenth and early twentieth centuries such boats, which were called *gun-boats*, carried Europeans deep into Africa and Asia by sailing up rivers such as the Ganges, Irrawaddy, Indus, Niger, Tigris, Euphrates, and Yangtze, attacking inland towns and villages along the way. Gunboats and machine guns were the main means by which Europeans conquered Asian empires and subjugated African peoples.[22]

Another oceangoing machine of war that used the internal-combustion engine when surfaced and battery-powered electric motors when submerged was the *submarine*. Originally designed for coastal protection, it was transformed into an offensive weapon during the First World War and used extensively to attack enemy shipping. Submarines were vulnerable when they surfaced; therefore, their captains tended to sink ships on sight and asked questions later. In order to defend against submarines, navies developed fast ships called "destroyers," equipped with locating devices (sound navigation and ranging [SONAR]) and powerful *depth charges* (water bombs) that could be dropped on submarines with devastating results.[23]

Industrial war in the air began when French and German reconnaissance aircraft began to fire at one other with handguns while carrying out their primary task of observing for commanders of artillery batteries during the First World War. First World War *biplanes* built of cloth-covered wood framing were replaced in the 1930s with true flying machines of war: powerful, fast-climbing *monoplanes* built of aluminum, capable of carrying heavy machine guns and several bombs. By the Second World War it became clear that the air superiority over the battlefield could become a substitute for artillery. This resulted in the design and construction of tens of thousands of several types of fast fighters and large bombers by the warring states of

Europe in order to achieve air superiority over the battlefield. *Tactical fight-er-bombers* provided close air support for troops on the ground; medium and heavy *strategic bombers* flew over the front lines and relentlessly bombed the enemy state's cities, towns, and factories in order to break the will of the people to fight; and *long-range escort fighters* accompanied bombers on their missions in order to protect them from the enemy's *interceptors*, which flew out to meet them. Although Germany tried to bomb Warsaw, Rotterdam, and London (the *blitz*) into submission during the Second World War, its air force, having been built with a different war in mind, did not have sufficient heavy, long-range bombers necessary for the task. The United States and Britain designed and built the requisite type of aircraft in great numbers. The United States built thousands of heavy bombers, the B-17 (Flying Fortress), the B-24 (Liberator), and the B-29 (Superfortress), which were used by the American Army Air Corps and the British Royal Air Force to bomb German and Japanese cities and factories on a massive scale. The British and the Americans believed that "mighty fleets of aircraft, each propelled by four engines and each carrying perhaps three to five tons of explosives could win the war against the Axis almost unaided."[24]

By the time of the Second World War, supplying armies, air forces, and navies was extremely complicated, not so much because of their large size but because of their complexity:

> The armies of 1914 consisted basically of great numbers of infantry with a limited range of standard weapons, whose logistical needs could be met very largely by railways and a simple shuttle service between the railheads and what was in most cases a fairly stable front line. In the Second World War fighting units were highly diversified. The inventory of a simple infantry battalion contained not only rifles and grenades but two types of mortar, two kinds of machine gun, light tracked vehicles, anti-tank guns, hand-held anti-tank weapons, and several types of mine. The demands of armoured units were many times more complex; those of amphibious and airborne units more complex still. So a far greater portion of the manpower in . . . Western armies was absorbed in servicing and supplying fighting units than in manning them: in repairing and maintaining vehicles, weapons, and communications systems, in driving supply vehicles, manning depots and hospitals, and ensuring that the whole drab mass was administered, fed, and paid.[25]

In the years between the First and Second World Wars, European states began to mobilize and conscript scientists and engineers for the purpose of designing and building the machines of war instead of leaving it to private entrepreneurs, as had been the case before 1914. During the Second World War tens of thousands of scientists and engineers were set to work designing and building more powerful machine weapons and weapon systems. For example, German scientists and engineers designed and built short-range, liquid-fueled ballistic missiles (the *Vengeance Weapon 2*, or *V-2*), which were used against London, Antwerp, and Liège, and developed the first operational jet-powered fighter aircraft (the *Messerschmitt Me 262*); British scientists and engineers perfected radar (radio detection and range [RADAR]); an American engineer, Carl Norden (1880–1965), designed and built the first gyroscopically stabilized bombsight; American electrical engineers designed and built the first electronic computer (*electronic numerical integrator and computer* [ENIAC]) to calculate ballistics trajectories; and an American team of scientists, engineers, and mathematicians working at Los Alamos, New Mexico, designed and built the first thermonuclear bomb, which was employed in war against Japan at Hiroshima on August 6, 1945, and then at Nagasaki three days later, killing more than 100,000 civilians.[26]

THE MANAGERIAL WELFARE STATE

As the militarily more competitive European national states replaced the kingly states after the French Revolution, and as wars became struggles between whole peoples, the idea that the state existed not only to protect the nation from foreign aggression but also to better the life of its people as a whole spread across Europe. While nationalism eliminated the need to use intimidation and coercion to get people to serve the state in wartime, especially through service in the armed forces, by substituting an emotional attachment to the nation (i.e., feelings of patriotism), continued loyalty and willingness to serve the state also came to depend upon the degree to which the state concerned itself with the economic prosperity and social welfare of its people. This was especially the case toward the end of the nineteenth century when wars became national struggles for survival. According to one historian, the first place that the state showed concern for the well-being of the people was on the battlefield: "The first systematic use of battle dress to *hide rather than advertise* a soldier's presence dates from this period. In contrast, the [kingly state's] exaltation of sacrifice to the State had caused uniforms to reach their ornamental peak. The British adopted khaki for colonial campaigns in 1880 and for home service in 1902. The Germans went to field gray in 1910."[27]

Thus, the marriage of the nation with the state and the industrialization and mechanization of war fundamentally changed the relationship between the rulers of the state and the people whom they ruled. In the words of one historian, "European rulers and politicians could no longer claim to rule according to their own interests, or even, as in the late eighteenth century, in the interest of the state itself. Instead, they increasingly acknowledged their role as servants of the general welfare, ultimately responsible for the well-being of the whole society and guarantors of the peoples' basic rights."[28]

After nationalism transformed the people from impassive and inert subjects into active participants in war as citizen-soldiers, the state came to rely more and more not only upon the extent to which it was viewed as representing its people but also upon the extent to which it was seen as providing for their well-being; that is, their physical fitness, economic prosperity, and welfare. With the rise of the national state, "rulers mattered less, and people mattered more,"[29] and the legitimacy of the European state rested more and more on the approval of its people.

Although kings were concerned with the economic productivity of their realms and invested in vital infrastructure, such as roads and bridges, the advent of the national state increased concern for the general economic and social well-being of the people because the rulers of national states began to see themselves as servants of the general welfare, but also because the growing importance of large conscript armies made the size and health of a state's population a national defense issue. In addition, industrial war with rival states was beginning to reduce populations and upset the natural ratio between males and females in European populations.

Serious concern for the size and health of the state's population began toward the end of the nineteenth century and the beginning of the twentieth century when industrialization made war increasingly destructive. Such concern was especially high after the First World War because millions of soldiers were killed or wounded. Thus, the idea that the "nation needed racially sound progeny, that the state should therefore intervene in private life to show people how to live . . . ran right across the political spectrum of interwar Europe, reflecting the tensions and stresses of an insecure [continent] in which nation-states existed in rivalry with one another, their populations decimated by war and threatened by the prospect of another."[30]

It was during the years between the First and Second World Wars that the birthrate, physical fitness, and mental health of the state's people became a major concern of the rulers of European national states, many of whom were influenced by theories of *scientific racism*; that is, the use of scientific theory and methods to support racist theories of national superiority. This concern led to the establishment of ministries of health and the training of cadres of social workers, school psychologists, public health nurses, and family-planning experts. Thus, "welfare and warfare were intimately connected, and social policies to improve population numbers and health reflected the anxieties of nation-states keen to defend or reassert themselves in a world of enemies."[31]

The purpose of economic institutions is to produce and distribute the material goods (food and shelter) to sustain human life. In the feudal state, economic production was based on manors owned by the noble families. Serfs worked the lord's land in exchange for protection. Which crops were to be planted, where they were to be planted, when they were to be harvested, and how much of the harvest was to go to the lord, were regulated by ancient norms and customs that had been built up over the centuries. In the towns, guilds regulated various trades (cobblers, pullers, weavers, coopers, bakers, butchers, thatchers, tanners, wheelers, and smiths of various kinds), their levels of production, and the training and licensing of those who worked in them. Each guild established detailed regulations concerning the method of manufacture, price, quantity, and quality of goods.[32]

As kings became increasingly in need of money and material resources to support large infantry armies and artillery, to build *trace italienne* fortifications, and to fight wars, they became more concerned with the economic productivity of their realms. In the sixteenth and seventeenth centuries, kings began to intervene actively in the economies of their kingdoms to improve them. Such kingly intervention came to be called "mercantilism" by eighteenth-century economists.[33]

Mercantilism assumed that a kingdom's wealth was based on the amount of gold and silver it could accumulate, and that the quantity of these precious metals that one king could accumulate was an equivalent loss by another. Kings, therefore, wanted to accumulate as much gold and silver as possible. They did this by maximizing exports of manufactured goods in exchange for gold and silver, and by minimizing imports in order to keep accumulated gold and silver in the kingdom's treasury. To make sure that exports exceeded imports, kings levied high tariffs (i.e., taxes) on imports in order to keep foreign-made goods out of their kingdoms. They also subsidized domestic industries by granting them monopolies, and by founding, owning, and managing industries themselves. All kingly states in Europe restricted imports by raising high tariff walls against imports and chartered industries that enjoyed a monopoly in a particular economic sector, especially those relating to war-making: arms and munitions manufacturing, shipbuilding, sail-making, etc. Therefore, all European national states have some tradition of purposeful state intervention into and management of their economies.

War and preparing for war has been a major driver of state intervention in economic and social life. During the First World War, the belligerent states raised taxes, borrowed massive amounts of money, nationalized certain industries (shipping, armaments, coal, steel, chemical), controlled raw materials and commodities, imposed price controls, instituted rationing, regulated consumption, and controlled gold and currencies. The industrialization of war required European states to penetrate their societies and economies more deeply than they had in the past. According to Porter,

> the belligerent states of Europe literally [had] to reinvent and redefine themselves in order to compete more effectively with each other. During World War I, they achieved a more radical degree of penetration of their societies and economies than anything contemplated or indeed possible in the mercantilist

age. The intensity of total warfare made this imperative, while technical advances in communications, transportation, financial controls, and administration made it feasible.[34]

Despite the ending of some wartime controls at the end of the First World War, European states continued to intervene and manage their economies to greater or lesser degrees during the inter-war years. The Great Depression (1929–1939) ensured continued state intervention into the economy, and the Second World War brought even more intervention into the economy and more stringent wartime controls than in the First World War. After the Second World War, wartime controls were relaxed but European states continued to manage "the economic growth of the society in order to provide a continuous improvement in the material conditions of life for all [social] classes."[35]

In the feudal state, the starving and destitute had been assisted by the charitable institutions of the Catholic Church. The Church also provided education in cathedral schools primarily to educate young men for the priesthood. As the centralized kingly state emerged, the responsibility of providing education and assistance to the destitute shifted from the Church to the state. Three epochs in this development can be identified.

The first is the period before the Industrial Revolution when the primary concern of the kingly state was relieving poverty among the peasantry and urban poor. Such relief was usually provided by the Catholic Church's hospitals and charitable foundations. The state's role was marginal, going no further than occasionally providing bread to beggars and vagabonds and distributing a small portion of the king's revenues to the rural poor to supplement their meager earnings.

The second epoch began with the Industrial Revolution and lasted until the beginning of the twentieth century. In this epoch, the state began to address the social and economic problems created by industrialization and concomitant urbanization. During this period the idea that the state's responsibility to provide poor relief was a temporary concession to the indigent, was gradually replaced with the idea of helping the working class by providing it with a panoply of social services. This new way of thinking about the role of the state was a consequence of the social dislocation and poverty created by early industrialization *and* by the demands of industrial warfare. It was increasingly recognized by all European states that the working class had to be well nourished in order to have a healthy and happy industrial work force as well as a healthy pool of patriotic men from which the state could conscript soldiers, sailors, and airmen for its armed forces.[36] Therefore, states began to establish standards of sanitation in the new industrial towns, regulate the conditions of employment in the new factories, guarantee a minimum standard of living, and ensure against illness and unemployment, as well as provide social security for the aged.

The third epoch began during the last decades of the nineteenth century, during which time the state came to be responsible for the education, health, safety, and general well-being of its entire population.[37] Thus, "from about 1885 [to] 1950, with major spurts of activity occurring during the periods following both world wars . . . in almost all European [states], the major forms of social insurance were adapted and extended to the entire population."[38] One hundred and fifty years of purposeful management of the economy and society in European states produced "a dense tissue of social benefits and economic strategies in which it was the state that served its subjects, rather than the other way around."[39]

After the Second World War, it was widely believed in Europe that the state would always do a better job dispensing social justice, distributing goods and services, applying strategies for social cohesion, and creating cultural vitality than if such matters were left to the individual citizen and the workings of the unregulated market mechanism of the capitalist economy. By the 1960s, all European states were managing their economic prosperity and social well-being with varying degrees of success.[40]

Thus, industrial war, not the Industrial Revolution per se, transformed states into "fulcrums for waging *total war*, for marshaling the whole of a nation's capacity—all social strata, all fiscal resources, and all industrial production—for military ends."[41] While industrial war made all European states managerial and welfarist, the degree to which states managed their economies and provided for the welfare of their peoples varied. Some states intervened more than others. In all European states preparing for war usually brought some state intervention to resolve long-festering social, political, and economic problems in order to achieve the domestic social harmony and economic and political equality necessary for mobilizing the population for total industrial war. During wartime, all European states took extraordinary measures to ensure total control of industry, raw materials, prices, wages, consumption, and currency flows. After wars such controls were usually relaxed, but the cumulative effect of state intervention to make war with machines over time resulted in the permanence of the managerial welfare state.

VARIETIES OF MANAGERIAL WELFARE STATES

The following brief case histories illustrate the various ways that preparing for industrial war and fighting war with machines brought into being the managerial welfare state across Europe.

Liberal Britain

In Great Britain, as in other national states, "wars, depression, and other crises . . . have been a source of social program expansion. [During the Second World War] a bargain was made, almost explicitly, between government and the public that if they endured the hardship of the war, they would be rewarded with a better Britain."[42] Like other European national states, war and preparing for war brought forth the managerial welfare state in Britain; nonetheless, the British case is different from others in Europe because the British managerial welfare state did not develop until relatively late in the state's history, and when it did it was never as pervasive as on the continent.

As was discussed in previous chapters, the English monarchy came to be dominated by Parliament and never created a highly centralized state apparatus under the direct control of the king. The kingly state was primarily engaged in enforcing the law, maintaining internal order, and defending the realm. There was little kingly involvement in the economy and ample opportunity for private initiatives.[43] After the defeat of Napoleon at Waterloo in 1815, the British scaled back their army from 600,000 to 100,000 men and allowed the market mechanism to "manage" the economy. In 1846, influenced by the liberal doctrine of laissez-faire, Parliament repealed the Corn Laws, which had put high tariffs on imported grain in order to protect domestic producers. The repeal of the Corn Laws was followed by the repeal of high duties on manufactured goods. By the 1860s there were few dutiable goods left in Britain, the most important of which were wine, tea, and tobacco. Essentially, Britain turned away from mercantilism, and committed itself to a free-trade economy.[44]

However, by the late nineteenth century, owing to the increasing need to build up the state's economic and military power to counteract similar developments on the continent, Britain began to intervene in the economy and society to alter their general condition. Many in Britain thought that more, not less, government was needed to deal with new threats. Income taxes were imposed, the colonies were more tightly integrated into the metropolitan economy, and electoral reform bills were passed in 1867 and 1884 to increase political participation in order to mobilize the nation to defend its vital interests. In 1901 the Army Reform Bill increased the size of the army to make it more equal in size to the conscripted armies on the continent, and, in the same year, established the Home Fleet to respond to the growing German naval challenge. The poor physical condition of British soldiers, which revealed itself by their poor performance during the Boer War (1899–1902), gave rise to the "national efficiency" movement, which was designed to make Britain more productive and rational, and thus a more powerful national state. In 1902 the National Service League agitated for the introduction of conscription in order to distribute the burdens of national defense more equally.[45]

Throughout the nineteenth and early twentieth century, the British state used classical liberal methods to strengthen the British economy and society. As an alternative to conscription and to stiffen the "moral and physical sinews" of Britain's youth, the Territorial and Reserve Forces Act was passed in 1907 that introduced military training in schools and universities. The working class was increasingly reconciled with the state by the passage of social and welfare reform, especially with the introduction of health insurance and pension schemes. In 1909 questions of how national security was to be funded and how British society should be reformed and reshaped to meet the military challenge of a rising Germany were raised in Parliament. At the same time women began to demand the right to vote. Gradually it was realized that women represented a vast human resource that could be tapped. It was also realized that the provision of healthy young males was linked to women's health.[46]

During the First World War, the British state took extraordinary measures to strengthen its military capacity. Conscription was introduced to replace the all-volunteer army that Britain used at the beginning of the war; a Ministry of Munitions was organized to oversee the production of artillery shells and small arms ammunition; soldiers were mobilized from its colonial armies; working-class women were encouraged to work in munitions factories; aristocratic women were encouraged to do volunteer service; and welfare programs were accelerated.

In the years after the First World War, the British state began an ambitious effort to achieve economic growth and full employment. The approach used to manage economic growth was inspired by the economist John Maynard Keynes (1883–1946), who had become well known for his economic theories pertaining to the ending of the Great Depression and preventing future depressions. Contrary to the economic orthodoxy of the day, which held that states should *decrease* spending and live within their means during depressions, Keynes argued that governments should *increase* spending during hard times in order to boost aggregate demand to stimulate investment and economic growth. "Keynesian economics" (i.e., countering the downward movement of the business cycle with government spending and monetary policies) became the new orthodoxy in Britain after the Second World War.[47] At the same time, the British state also sought to manage the economy by *nationalizing* (that is, taking into state ownership) coal mines, gas and electricity production, public transportation (railroads, canals, and some trucking companies), and the steel industry.[48]

Before the rise of the national state, the European kingly state with the most developed system for providing poor relief was England. During the Tudor period (1536–1603) Parliament passed several poor-relief acts. These acts required each shire of the realm to raise money in order to pay the indigent an allowance to supplement their meager wages. By the end of the eighteenth century, this system of poor relief came under strong criticism because it depressed rural wages and inhibited the mobility of the rural poor, who could not seek better employment elsewhere without losing their allowances. Therefore, in 1834, Parliament passed the Poor Law Amendment Act which removed poor relief from the shires and placed it under the management of the central government. In 1929, Parliament abolished the poor-relief system and replaced it with a national system of public assistance funded by the state but administered by the county councils.

The idea that the state had a responsibility to help the working class came first in Britain because Britain was the first European state to industrialize and urbanize. In the nineteenth century, Parliament passed a series of acts to regulate the industrial sector. The first was the Factory Act of 1833, which created a system of factory safety inspection. The Mine Regulation Act of 1842 protected miners; the Factory Act of 1847, the so-called Ten Hour Act, limited the workday to ten hours; the Merchant Shipping Act of 1876 protected merchant seamen; and the Regulation of the Railways Act of 1889 protected railway workers. The British state's concern with the health of its working class was manifested in 1848 with the passage of the Public Health Act, which set standards for sanitation in factories and dwellings.[49]

The creation of a system of social insurance began when Parliament passed the Workman's Compensation Act in 1897 that required employers to insure employees against the dangers of their employment. In 1908, the Old Age Pensions Act introduced a pension system paid for by the state for workers over the age of seventy who were unable to support themselves in retirement. The next year, Parliament passed the Trade Boards Act, which established a minimum wage for workers in jobs that did not have union representation. In 1911, the National Insurance Act introduced a health insurance scheme to which workers, employers, and the state made equal contributions. This act also provided unemployment insurance in certain industries such as iron founding and ship building.[50]

In Britain the idea that the state had a responsibility to manage the health, safety, and welfare of the entire population began after the First World War when the Widows, Orphans, and Old Age Contributory Pensions Act of 1925 extended unemployment insurance to cover most wage earners in the population. A series of housing acts gave the state the responsibility of constructing housing for people who could not afford to build their own. In order to offset the losses of the Second World War and to live up to promises made to the British people in exchange for their perseverance and loyalty during the war, Parliament passed the Family Allowance Act in 1946, which paid benefits to families with two or more children. In the same year, Parliament passed the National Insurance Act, which provided substantial payments for sickness and unemployment, as well as maternity benefits, widows' allowances, and pensions for the entire population. The National Assistance Act of 1948 required local governments to make housing available for the old, the infirm, and the poor. Finally, also in 1948, Parliament created the National Health Service, which brought together private, local, and national health services and providers (doctors, hospitals, and clinics) into a single system under the authority of the state and available to the entire population. By the beginning of the 1950s the institutions by which the British state provided for the physical and social well-being of the entire British population were well entrenched.

Dirigiste France

The tradition of purposeful state intervention in and management of the economy was stronger in France than in Britain. As was discussed in previous chapters, efforts by French kings to gain control of the kingdom resulted in the most absolute kingly state on the continent, which became a model emulated by other continental monarchs. Louis XIV's finance minister, Jean Baptiste Colbert (1619–1683), intervened mightily into the French economy in order to develop it and build up state power. He built canals and roads, issued detailed standards for manufacturing, encouraged exports, discouraged imports, recruited skilled craftspeople from across Europe, abolished internal tariffs, and provided scientific and technical education.[51]

Despite the liberal ideas of the revolutionaries, the French Revolution was followed by much state intervention in order to eliminate the vestiges of feudalism and to rationalize economic structures. The Directory and, later, Napoleon, decreed a metric system of weights and measures; reformed the currency; reformed the legal system (the Code Napoleon of 1804); reorganized the tax system; abolished internal tariffs, inaugurated a national system of education; founded engineering and technical schools; constructed an extensive system of national roads; and encouraged the development of industries, especially those related to the production of weapons.[52]

Owing to France's militarily more-threatening environment, the government continued many mercantilistic policies and never allowed the market to be the sole manager of the economy. Throughout the nineteenth century, the French state continued to subsidize technical and scientific education, build roads, and operate certain industries. During the Third Republic (1871–1945) a series of laws was passed that reinstated conscription and lengthened military enlistments to five years, and huge sums were spent on the military. The problems of sustaining a large army during the First World War caused the French state to become increasingly *dirigiste* (directed) with respect to its economy and society. It set up a consortium to run the economy more efficiently, took over the supply of raw materials, set prices, and regulated the movement of capital. Integrated national planning was introduced after the war to raise French productivity and protect the French people from the ravages of the free market. Ambitious plans were also introduced for the French colonies to compensate for France's economic weakness in Europe. In the 1930s, France returned to the gold standard, sought to accumulate a substantial reserve, and built a string of fortifications (the Maginot Line) along its eastern border to prevent a German invasion. The French state also embarked on an ambitious program of social transformation: the school-leaving age was raised; the Bank of France was placed under state control; the price for wheat was fixed; and, in 1936, the arms industry was national-ized.[53] After the Second World War, more French industries were national-ized—railroads, electricity generation, petroleum refining, coal mining, insu-rance companies, large-deposit banks, aircraft manufacturing, aviation (Air France), and the Renault automobile works because its owners had collabo-rated with the pro-German Vichy government. The state also embarked on a program of national planning.[54]

Until the French Revolution, the French monarchy had relied on the Cath-olic Church to provide poor relief through its hospitals and charitable foun-dations. The king occasionally provided bread (*pain du roi*) to the beggars and vagabonds of Paris, and his *intendants* were permitted to give a small share of the king's revenues to the rural poor in their *généralités*. The French Revolution abolished the charitable foundations of the church and the distri-bution of royal revenues. Poor relief was transferred to the new local author-ities, the *départements* and *communes*, created by the revolutionary govern-ment to rationalize local administration. The *préfects* of the *départements* were required to alleviate rural destitution and, after Napoleon's rise to pow-er, to undertake local public-works projects, such as road building, in order to build up the infrastructure of the state and to provide work for the rural poor. In 1871, the National Assembly passed a law that required each *département* to provide public assistance to all who were unable to work because of old age, mental incapacity, and illness.[55]

Social insurance came later in France than other European states. The first such program was not initiated until 1905, when the aged poor and incurably ill were provided with small state pensions. In 1910, the National Assembly passed the Old Age Pension Act, which provided pensions for wage earners from a fund contributed to by employers, employees, and the state. A second act was passed in 1913 to aid families with more than three children in order to encourage the growth of the French population and to lower the then-high infant mortality rate. In order to offset the losses of men during the First World War, the French state encouraged Italian and Spanish immigration, established workplace nurseries, and established social housing in order to boost the birth rate.[56]

After the Second World War, the French state strengthened its social insurance programs and extended coverage to the entire population. The French system was paid for by contributions from employers and employees, and covered illness, disability, widowhood, and retirement. In order to rebuild the French population, which had been reduced by the war, the state's insurance program included very generous family benefits that increased as families got larger. Large families also received income tax rebates, reduced fares on public transportation, and larger pensions for their breadwinners. After the war, France also built an extensive system of state-run hospitals, orphanages, retirement homes, and mental institutions. Although the French state did not create a national health service, as the British state had done, it did enhance its extant fee-reimbursement plan, which reimburses patients— who are free to choose their own physicians—for 80 percent of the cost of medical care.[57]

From *Volksgemeinschaft* to Social Market Germany

Germany's unification from above by Bismarck rather than from below by liberal nationalists meant that liberal economic doctrines there were even less significant than in France. Mercantilism was well entrenched in Prussia and other German-speaking principalities and duchies. The Prussian state built roads, canals, bridges, and railroads. It promoted industrialization by founding technical schools and sending people abroad to learn manufacturing techniques, and used taxes and government subsidies to expand the economy. From the end of the Franco-Prussian War (1870–1871) businesses owned by the Junkers were taken over by the state governments that comprised the German Empire: breweries in Bavaria, porcelain factories in Prussia, and tobacco factories in Alsace.

During the First World War, the Hindenburg Program mobilized the entire society for war: all men between the ages of eighteen and sixty not already serving as workers or agricultural laborers were recruited for the war effort. The resources of the Austro-Hungarian Empire, a German ally, were also mobilized. This "'war communism' ensured that the [Second] Reich was able to go on fighting even though it was outnumbered, surrounded and cut off from global sources of raw materials and foodstuffs."[58]

After the war the Weimar Republic (1919–1930) turned to liberal economic policies to manage the German economy. This was halted with the naming of the Nazi Party's leader, Adolf Hitler (1889–1945), as reich chancellor in 1933. Under Hitler's leadership, the Nazi government instituted a massive program of state intervention and control in economic life as well as a massive program of rearmament in order to pull Germany's economy out of depression and rebuild German military power. According to one scholar, during the Nazi period deficit financing was used for the extensive construction of public works projects, including the famed autobahns, and business activity was tightly regulated. In 1936, a four-year plan was initiated for the proclaimed purpose of guiding basic production, controlling imports and exports, allocating basic resources, overseeing orders and credit, and strengthening foreign-exchange controls in order to achieve "autarchy"; that is, self-sufficiency in food and raw materials.[59]

During the war, the entire economy was organized for war by Reich Minister for Armaments and War Production Albert Speer (1905–1981). Speer was able to increase the production of armaments and increase industrial production by innovation and organizational changes, as well as the ruthless use of slave labor, despite massive bombing of German factories and cities by the Allies.

Hitler also intervened in German society, because he believed that Germany could survive a war only if its people were unified and racially pure. He sought to create a German nation that would exclude Jews, Gypsies, and other "undesirables." He established a compulsory Labor Service for ideological indoctrination and military mobilization. He introduced conscription in 1935. Class distinctions were to be suppressed by national solidarity. Germany was to be reconstructed as a pure racial community (*Volksgemeinschaft*) instead of aristocrats, bourgeoisie, and proletariat. Women were encouraged to marry and stay at home, have babies, and raise the next generation of "people's comrades" (*Volksgenossen*). In order to encourage procreation, Hitler introduced a celibacy tax on unmarried men and women. As is well known, he moved against Jews by passing racial purity laws that excluded them from employment in public services, schools, universities, and hospitals. Eventually, their property and businesses were confiscated. Later, he forced them into ghettoes and, finally, began a program of systematic extermination (the Final Solution). Hitler hoped to reward the German people after the war with a massive welfare state consisting of autobahns, guaranteed employment, housing, and packaged holidays.[60]

After the defeat of Germany by the Allies in 1945, massive state intervention into the economy was rolled back by Konrad Adenauer (1876–1967), West Germany's first post-war chancellor. Adenauer, a Christian Democrat, moved West Germany toward a mixed system of economic management that came to be called the "social market"; that is, an economy in which the market allocates goods and services while the state limits its intervention to ensuring that all Germans have a minimum level of economic security. Most of the controls on the economy put in place by the Nazis were lifted, and certain state-owned concerns, such as the Volkswagen automobile company, were privatized. Nonetheless, the German state "continued to own very considerable parts of the economy, including 40 percent of the coal and iron sector, 62 percent of electrical-power generation, 72 percent of the aluminum industry, and 62 percent of the banking industry exclusive of the central bank."[61]

Germany is credited with having the first system of social insurance against illness, unemployment, and old age. It was started in the 1880s when Bismarck, motivated partly by a desire to woo workers away from the revolutionary Social Democratic Party, which was gaining followers at a rapid rate, and by his view that such programs would make the workers support the state, put several bills through the Reichstag that created a system of social insurance for the working class. The first bill, passed in 1883, required employees and employers to contribute to a fund that insured against illness. Premiums were collected by insurance societies approved and regulated by the state. The second bill, passed in 1884, created a fund, also approved and regulated by the state, that paid claims for workplace injuries. The last of Bismarck's bills, passed in 1889, insured workers against invalidism and old age. Workers and employers as well as the state contributed to this fund.[62]

After the Second World War, the West German state broadened its social insurance to include all German working people. Legislation passed in 1954 made it possible for old-age pensioners to have the same standard of living that they had enjoyed during their working years by indexing pensions to reflect earnings and by giving cost-of-living adjustments to counteract inflation. The Federal Employment Office made payments to unemployed workers to cover expenses incurred while looking for work, and paid for vocational retraining for new jobs. German workers were given subsidies from the employment office, called "bad weather money," to cover days not worked on account of rain, snow, or sub-zero temperatures. In 1996, bad weather money was replaced with a system that guaranteed workers 75 percent of their gross pay per hour for inclement days. The German state continues to provide health insurance through the system established by Bismarck in the 1880s, although it was overhauled in order to bring it up to current expectations and standards. The system is still supported by joint contributions from workers, employers, and the state, and is still administered by welfare funds that reimburse hospitals and physicians of the patient's choosing.[63]

Socialist Russia

The most managerial European welfare state was Russia during the period of the Soviet Union when the state owned, planned, and managed *all* aspects of economic, social, and political life. State management of the economy began well before the Bolsheviks took over the Russian state in 1917, however. Seeking to overcome Russia's backwardness, Peter the Great (1672–1725) traveled incognito to western Europe in 1697 in order to learn how he could transform Russia's traditional, medieval state into a western-oriented, scientific, rational state that could compete more effectively on the battlefield with

European states. Peter modernized Russian society and copied western European mercantilistic practices to modernize the economy. He founded schools of mathematics, engineering, science, and medicine. He created Russia's first standing army in 1699 and also built a navy. During his reign, mining and manufacturing industries of all types were founded and railroads were built. In mercantilistic fashion, the state used tariffs and subsidies to protect Russia's nascent industries.

Peter's reforms transformed Russia into a major European power, which created anxiety among the states of western Europe, especially Prussia. Catherine the Great (1729–1796) declared Russia to be a European power, and claimed that it had become one by "introducing the manners and customs of Europe," and that the intention of her absolute rule was territorial expansion and military success.[64]

Russia defeated the Ottoman Empire in 1770; participated in the first partition of Poland in 1772; began to meddle in the internal affairs of the Austro-Hungarian Empire; annexed the Crimea in 1783; participated in the second partition of Poland in 1793; joined the second and third coalitions (1798–1802 and 1803–1806, respectively) of European monarchs against Napoleon; turned Napoleon back when he invaded Russia in 1812; and helped defeat Napoleon at Waterloo in 1815. After 1815, czarist Russia continued to involve itself in European affairs and was increasingly seen by liberals as a despotic, expansionist colossus. Russia went to war against the Ottomans in 1854, which resulted in a humiliating defeat of Russian forces in the Crimea by Britain and France in 1855.

The defeat in the Crimea brought a series of domestic reforms in the Russian Empire. Serfdom, which prevented the czar from mobilizing Russia's vast rural population for war, was abolished in 1856 by Czar Alexander II (1818–1881). In order to restore its standing in Europe, Russia began to develop its economy by becoming increasingly mercantilistic and building up the army and navy in order to be militarily competitive with Germany. At the same time, the Russians made an alliance with the French. Another humiliating defeat in the Russo-Japanese War (1904–1905) again made the monarchy a target of criticism by those who believed that Russia's military weakness was due to the absolutist nature of the state. Under pressure from liberal critics, the czar agreed to a consultative assembly, the Duma, to be elected by a very restrictive franchise. At the same time, the "state sought to create a more reliable and effective conscript army. The purpose behind this programme of limited political modernization was to harness the potential of Russian society to the great project which lay ahead; rebuilding Russia's international standing and vindicating her strategic interests."[65]

After 1900, the critics of the monarchy continued to argue that Russia would never realize its full military potential without social and political reform. The problem was that the "political nation demanded a more active foreign policy, but refused to give the executive [the czar] the means to pay for it; the government wanted to raise taxation to fund armaments but would not countenance the political reforms which would have persuaded the Duma to agree to it."[66]

The assassination of the Austrian archduke, Franz Ferdinand (1863–1914), in June 1914 in Sarajevo led the Russians to back the Serbians and mobilize their army. On August 1, Germany mobilized its army and declared war on Russia. This action brought a French mobilization and a subsequent attack on France by Germany by way of Belgium. The violation of Belgian neutrality brought a declaration of war on Germany by Britain. In Russia, the Duma rallied to the cause and voted for the necessary taxes to support the war. Constitutionalists used the war to make claims for greater political participation. The czar refused and took over the management of the war himself. Defeats of Russian armies in 1916, and the sinister influence of the monk Rasputin on the czar and his wife, made the monarchy even more vulnerable. By 1917 the monarchy had lost all credibility and legitimacy. Strikes and mutinies in February 1917 brought the collapse of the monarchy and the establishment of a weak government that continued the war. Russian losses in July 1917 sparked debate among the various parties in the Duma about the future of Russian foreign policy. One of the factions, the Bolsheviks, gradually gained the upper hand and, in November 1917, seized control of the Russian imperial state.

After seizing power and extricating Russia from the war by giving up large swaths of Russian territory in the west in exchange for peace at Brest-Litovsk (1918), the Bolsheviks commenced to abolish capitalism and establish a socialist *command economy*; that is, an economy in which all decisions affecting the economy were made by the state. In 1920, the State Commission for Electrification was created, and, in 1921, GOSPLAN (the State Planning Commission), which was concerned with managing the economy and establishing production goals. In 1928, the first Five-Year Plan was promulgated and the collectivization of agriculture began. From this point onward, the entire economy was managed by the state. The Soviet command economy remained unchanged until the 1960s, after which, in response to the growing complexities of its advanced industrial economy and demands for more consumer goods, Soviet economists began to use the market mechanism in a limited way.[67]

Until the Bolshevik Revolution, the state's role in providing for the well-being of the Russian people was minimal. The earliest social legislation was passed in 1893 and was designed to give miners and railroad workers some protection against financial losses incurred by job-related illness and injury. In 1912, the Duma passed a comprehensive health and accident law that made benefits available for work-related accidents, illness, and death and guaranteed maternity-leave payments to female workers. At that time, Russian social legislation covered less than one-fourth of the workforce and paid benefits so small that the working class was essentially left to face the hardships of industrial employment on their own, without state assistance.[68]

Owing to the Bolsheviks' Marxist ideology, which blamed the poverty of the workers on the capitalist economy itself, their coming to power in 1917 radically changed the Russian state's approach to social welfare. The Bolsheviks aimed to provide full social assistance to every Soviet citizen as a matter of right. Although their attempts to do so were delayed by the civil war (1917–1922), by the late 1920s the Bolsheviks were able to guarantee unemployment insurance, free medical care in state-run hospitals, and old age and disability pensions, as well as compensation for illness. Unemployment was dropped in 1930 because unemployment had been, at least theoretically, eliminated in the Soviet Union's socialist state-managed economy.[69]

The Soviet Union's social insurance program was supported by contributions based on a percentage of payroll from the employing establishment according to state norms. Benefits were disbursed centrally by the state. Special benefit programs existed for persons with permanent disabilities. The Soviet state also operated homes for orphaned, neglected, and emotionally disturbed children.[70]

Before the Bolshevik Revolution, medical care in Russia was rudimentary. After the Revolution a massive program of preventive and curative medicine was launched. In relatively short order a system of free clinics and hospitals was established for the general public. Large factories and the military established their own medical facilities. While the system was a vast improvement over the health-care situation as it had existed before the Revolution, the Soviet system was far from satisfactory. The vastness of the Soviet Union meant that medical resources were spread too thinly across the national territory, and health-care professionals, the vast majority of whom were women, who were, as most state employees, poorly paid.[71]

In sum, the Bolshevik Revolution brought forth a directly managed economy and society that wrenched the inefficient, absolutist monarchical state into the modern era. Rapid industrialization during the 1930s made the Soviet economy strong enough to successfully defend itself against German invasion. When Germany attacked in June 1941 (Operation Barbarossa) with the aim of conquering the Soviet Union, the offensive, at first wildly successful, stalled on the outskirts of Moscow. Thanks to the rapid industrialization of the 1930s and the reorientation of the Soviet economy toward military production, the Soviets had numerical superiority in tanks, artillery, and aircraft. Gradually, the Germans' initial advantage of surprise, better weaponry, generalship, and troops was overcome by the sheer weight of Soviet arms production and manpower. This was the result of the Soviet Union's greater military assets, the total mobilization of the people for a war to defend "Mother Russia," the dismantling of and reassembling of critical industries east of the Urals, the drafting of millions of men, and improvements in Soviet military leadership by the release of thousands of officers from the Gulag (the forced labor camp system that operated in the Soviet Union from the 1930s to the 1950s). After four years of hard fighting, the Soviet army was able to push the German army back to Berlin, which fell to Soviet troops in May 1945. Although it was able to survive the Second World War, the Soviet state was unable to survive the Cold War, and collapsed in 1991.

CONCLUSION

In this chapter it has been shown that the combining of people's war with industrial war transformed the national state into the militarized managerial welfare state. As machine war raised the cost of war in terms of men, money, and matériel to stratospheric heights, states were increasingly forced to concern themselves with the size and health of their populations, the wealth of their economies, and the social well-being of their people. The combination of national and industrial war required states to become increasingly bureaucratic, managerial, and interventionist, no matter their legitimating ideology—liberalism, socialism, or fascism. Even the most liberal capitalist European state, Britain, found it impossible to wage national-industrial war successfully without considerable intervention into its economy and society. The industrialization of war demanded that states transform themselves in order to mobilize their full military, economic, social, technological, and industrial energies to wage it successfully.

The military competition for supremacy among Europe's national states culminated in the twentieth century, during which time Europe was convulsed by a nearly century-long inter-state war (the First and Second World Wars). The use of the atomic bomb against Japan during the Second World War marked a turning point in war itself, which transformed the militarized managerial welfare state into two different, but related forms of the state—the national security state and the civilianized neoliberal state—which will be discussed in the next two chapters, respectively.

NOTES

1. Williamson Murray and MacGregor Knox, "Thinking about Revolutions in Warfare," in MacGregor Knox and Williamson Murray (eds.), *The Dynamics of Military Revolution: 1300–2050* (Cambridge: Cambridge University Press, 2001), p. 10.

2. William H. McNeill, *The Pursuit of Power: Technology, Armed Force, and Society since A.D. 1000* (Chicago: University of Chicago Press, 1984), p. 317.

3. James J. Sheehan, *Where Have All the Soldiers Gone? The Transformation of Modern Europe* (Boston and New York: Houghton Mifflin, 2008), p. 172.

4. Martin Shaw, *The New Western Way of War: Risk-Transfer War and Its Crisis in Iraq* (Cambridge: Polity Press, 2005), p. 73.

5. Philip Bobbitt, *The Shield of Achilles: War, Peace, and the Course of History* (New York: Anchor Books, 2002), p. 204.

6. Quoted in John Ellis, *The Social History of the Machine Gun* (Baltimore, MD: The Johns Hopkins University Press, 1975), p. 22.

7. Bobbitt, *op. cit.*, p. 235.

8. Ellis, *op. cit.*, p. 25.

9. Antoine Bousquet, *The Scientific Way of Warfare: Order and Chaos on the Battlefields of Modernity* (New York: Columbia University Press, 2009), p. 80.

10. Max Boot, *War Made New: Technology, Warfare, and the Course of History, 1500 to Today* (New York: Gotham Books, 2006), pp. 127–28.

11. Martin van Creveld, *The Rise and Decline of the State* (Cambridge: Cambridge University Press, 1999), p. 250.

12. *Ibid.*, pp. 250–51.

13. Michael Howard, *War in European History*, updated edition (Oxford: Oxford University Press, 2009), pp. 103–4.

14. Ellis, *op. cit.*, p. 27.

15. *Ibid.*, p. 49.

16. Daniel R. Headrick, *The Tools of Empire: Technology and European Imperialism in the Nineteenth Century* (New York/Oxford: Oxford University Press, 1981), chapter 6.

17. Boot, *op. cit.*, pp. 150–52.

18. van Creveld, *op. cit.*, p. 255.

19. Headrick, *op. cit.*, p. 147.

20. *Ibid.*, pp. 147–48.

21. Howard, *op. cit.*, pp. 123–24 and Boot, *op. cit.*, p. 173.

22. Headrick, *op. cit.*, chapters 1 and 2.

23. Howard, *op. cit.*, pp. 125–26.

24. van Creveld, *op. cit.*, p. 256.

25. Howard, *op. cit.*, p. 133.

26. John Keegan, *A History of Warfare* (New York: Vintage Books, 1994), p. 379.

27. Bobbitt, *op. cit.*, p. 204.

28. David Kaiser, *Politics and War: European Conflict from Philip II to Hitler* (Cambridge, MA: Harvard University Press, 1990), p. 273.

29. Ernst B. Haas, *Nationalism, Liberalism, and Progress, Vol. 1, The Rise and Decline of Nationalism* (Ithaca, NY: Cornell University Press, 1997), p. 18.

30. Mark Mazower, *Dark Continent: Europe's Twentieth Century* (New York: Knopf, 1999), p. 77.

31. *Ibid.*, p. 103.

32. Sidney Painter, *The Rise of the Feudal Monarchies* (Ithaca, NY: Cornell University Press, 1951), pp. 79–84.

33. On mercantilism, see Benjamin J. Cohen, *The Question of Imperialism* (New York: Basic Books, 1973).

34. Bruce D. Porter, *War and the Rise of the State: The Military Foundations of Modern Politics* (New York: Free Press, 1994), p. 161.

35. Bobbitt, *op. cit.*, p. 208.

36. On the influence of war on the development of social services, see Richard M. Titmuss, *Essays on the Welfare State*, 2nd Edition (Boston: Beacon Press, 1963), chapter 4.

37. Ernest Barker, *The Development of Public Services in Western Europe, 1600–1930* (Hamden, CT: Archon Books, 1966), pp. 68–70.

38. B. Guy Peters, *European Politics Reconsidered* (New York: Holmes & Meier, 1991), p. 228.

39. Tony Judt, *Postwar: A History of Europe since 1945* (New York: Penguin, 2005), p. 360.

40. Bobbitt, *op. cit.*, p. 208.

41. Porter, *op. cit.*, p. 150, italics in the original.

42. Peters, *op. cit.*, p. 227.

43. Stanley Rothman, *European Society and Politics* (Indianapolis, IN: Bobbs-Merrill, 1970), p. 734.

44. Ferdinand Schevill, *A History of Europe from the Reformation to the Present Day* (New York: Harcourt, Brace, 1930), pp. 573–74.

45. Brendan Simms, *Europe: The Struggle for Supremacy from 1453 to the Present* (New York: Basic Books, 2013), *passim*.

46. *Ibid.*, pp. 280–82.

47. Mark Kesselman, *et al.*, *European Politics in Transition*, 5th Edition (Boston: Houghton Mifflin, 2006), p. 25.

48. Rothman, *op. cit.*, p. 748.

49. Barker, *op. cit.*, pp. 73–74.

50. *Ibid.*

51. Norman Davies, *Europe: A History* (Oxford: Oxford University Press, 1996), p. 631.

52. Rothman, *op. cit.*, p. 740.

53. Simms, *op. cit.*, pp. 351–52.

54. Rothman, *op. cit.*, pp. 740–41.

55. Barker, *op. cit.*, pp. 70–73.

56. Simms, *op. cit.*, p. 324.

57. Rothman, *op. cit.*, pp. 767–68.

58. Simms, *op. cit.*, p. 302.

59. Rothman, *op. cit.*, p. 742.

60. Simms, *op. cit.*, p. 343 and p. 373.

61. Martin van Creveld, *op. cit.*, p. 357.

62. Barker, *op. cit.*, pp. 75–78.

63. Rothman, *op. cit.*, p. 772.

64. Simms, *op. cit.*, p. 119.

65. *Ibid.*, pp. 275–76.

66. *Ibid.*, p. 288.

67. Rothman, *op. cit.*, p. 744.

68. *Ibid.*, p. 747.

69. *Ibid.*

70. *Ibid.*, pp. 780–81.

71. *Ibid.*, p. 782.

Chapter 6

Air-Atomic War and the National Security State

The advent of atomic weapons at the end of the Second World War transformed warfare, which in turn transformed the managerial welfare state. The transformative effect was not felt in the first years after the war, however, because there were few atomic weapons at that time and they were possessed by only one state, the United States. It was assumed by American military planners that conventional, industrial war would not change very much despite the development of atomic weapons. Atomic weapons fit existing ideas and procedures for employing strategic air power that had evolved during the Second World War.[1] Military planners believed that states would continue to fight each other with large conscripted armies using large numbers of conventional machine weapons, and that atomic weapons would be used only occasionally and in a limited way to eliminate specific armed forces.[2] Thus, in the first decades after the Second World War, "labor-intensive militarism" was still strong and there was little realization among military planners that atomic weapons were apocalyptic *"out-of-ratio"* weapons "that enable a tiny number of people (one, fifty-three, or two hundred twelve) to annihilate millions of people."[3] One man, President Harry Truman (1884–1972), decided to drop the first atomic bomb on Hiroshima, which flattened ten square miles of the city and killed more than 100,000 Japanese men, women, and children.

When it was realized that atomic weapons could replace conventional "labor-intensive" armed forces, the United States began to design and build large numbers of atomic weapons of increasingly destructive power, as well as the means to deliver them by air. In response, the Soviet Union did the same. However, because of the extreme destructiveness of atomic weapons, their actual use was prevented by the difficulty, if not the impossibility, of mounting an effective defense against them. An attack by one state armed with atomic weapons on another state similarly armed would result in a retaliatory strike and the certain annihilation of the attacking state. According to Martin Shaw, the advent of atomic weapons modified

> the way in which war and war-preparation affected societies. In particular, it undermined classical militarism and its role in society. [The] advanced industrial world (especially in Europe) has [undergone] a profound transformation in the relationship of warfare to society. . . . Most members of these societies have not experienced them as militarized. There has therefore been a huge disjuncture between the knowledge people have had of the ultimate dangers of nuclear war, and the general irrelevance of this to their daily lives. As [nuclear] war-preparation . . . [became] separated from the areas of social life which involve the majority of society, so it . . . [became] more politically insulated from mass involvement.[4]

Thus, atomic weapons transformed war from classical industrial inter-state war with conventional weapons and mass-reserve armies to *deterrent air-atomic war* with nuclear weapons deliverable by aircraft and missiles. The nuclear arms race between the United States and the Soviet Union also permitted the transformation of both states from militarized managerial welfare states in which the civilian populations are closely tied to their states through military service and welfare programs into *national security states* in which the people are no longer required to be active participants in the defense of their states, beyond giving their passive consent and generalized support to its preparations for atomic war. Essentially, political elites gradually realized that they did not need the people to fight atomic war. Consequently, they constructed a super-secret, almost invisible, national security apparatus, separate from the people, to conduct such war.[5] Atomic weapons and the prospect of atomic war, therefore, began to undermine the managerial welfare state by uncoupling the people from the state and the armed forces. The development of atomic weapons opened "up a large gap between the military branches of the state and the underlying society."[6]

DETERRENT AIR-ATOMIC WAR

Two extremely powerful states emerged from the Second World War, the United States and the Soviet Union. The United States dominated western Europe and the Soviet Union dominated eastern Europe. Politico-military rivalry between the two with regard to which state, the United States' liberal capitalist state or the Soviet Union's socialist state, would prevail was manifested in a military standoff called the Cold War (1945–1991), during which time both states built up huge arsenals of atomic weapons and maintained substantial conventional forces against one another but did not directly engage on the battlefield, although they did "fight" one another indirectly in other states, as will be discussed in chapter 8.

The United States had a nuclear monopoly from 1945 until 1949, when the Soviet Union tested a nuclear device. In 1952, the United States developed and tested a "super," or thermonuclear weapon 3,000 times more powerful than the bombs that were dropped on Hiroshima and Nagasaki. In 1953, the Soviet Union exploded its own thermonuclear bomb. Early atomic bombs were heavy and cumbersome and had to be carried to their targets by the B-50 (a modified B-29 Superfortress) or the recently introduced B-36 Peacemaker, the first manned bomber with un-refueled intercontinental range. Aircraft technology underwent rapid improvement in the late 1940s and early 1950s. Jet engines replaced piston engines and swept-back wings and vertical stabilizers (i.e., tails) replaced straight wings and straight vertical stabilizers, which enabled bombers to fly faster and higher than hitherto. In 1951, the B-36 was replaced by the jet-engined B-47 Stratojet and, in 1955, by the B-52 Stratofortress, capable of carrying 70,000 pounds of conventional and atomic bombs to the Soviet Union. At the height of the Cold War, the United States had about 650 B-52s organized into forty-two squadrons stationed at bases in the United States and abroad. During the nearly half-century of the Cold War, twenty-four hours each day, seven days each week, the United States had twelve B-52s carrying several atomic bombs each on *airborne alert*; that is, flying toward their targets inside the Soviet Union ready for immediate action should they receive the "go code" before reaching their "*fail-safe*" points.[7]

In 1960, in order to penetrate Soviet air defenses using speed and altitude, the United States put into service the B-58 Hustler, a delta-winged supersonic bomber capable of flying at Mach 2 (i.e., twice the speed of sound) at 60,000 feet. During the 1960s, the United States even built a prototype of a supersonic bomber, the B-70 Valkyrie, that could fly at Mach 3, had a ceiling of 70,000 feet, and could carry one or two atomic bombs. The Soviets also built jet-powered aircraft capable of dropping atomic bombs on the United States, beginning in 1954 with the M-4 Bison A and the twin-engined TU-16 Badger, and later, in 1955, the M-6 Bison B and, in 1956, the turboprop TU-95 Bear. None of these could fly as fast, as far, or as high as United States' bombers, however.

In very short order, American and Soviet weapons designers, using captured German V-2 rockets and the knowledge of captured German scientists and engineers who designed and built them, were able to develop a reliable intercontinental ballistic missile (ICBM) capable of carrying an atomic warhead from the United States to the Soviet Union. Ballistic missiles, which flew much faster and higher (about 15,000 mph above the atmosphere) than conventional aircraft, were less vulnerable to Soviet air defenses and did not require crews. In the 1960s and 1970s, the multiple independent reentry vehicle (MIRV) was developed, which made it possible to mount as many as ten independently targeted atomic warheads on a single ICBM. By the end of the 1970s, miniaturization and improvements in weapons design that reduced the weight of atomic warheads made it possible to pack three times as much explosive power as the Hiroshima and Nagasaki bombs inside a warhead weighing only five hundred pounds.[8] The doctrine of "instant readiness" led to the replacement, in 1962, of cumbersome and dangerous liquid-fueled surface-launched missiles, such as the Atlas and Titan, with a solid-propellant missile that could be launched at a moment's notice, the Minuteman. In the United States, hundreds of Minutemen were stored vertically in atomic-bombproof underground silos scattered around the western United States so that they would survive a surprise attack and provide a retaliatory second strike against the Soviet Union. Initially, ICBMs complemented the higher flying and faster jet-powered bombers of the 1960s. By the 1970s, however, ICBMs began to replace manned bombers and assume a major role in air-atomic warfare.

Nuclear-powered submarines, which could stay submerged for months at a time, were developed by both the United States and the Soviet Union. They carried submarine-launched ballistic missiles (SLBMs) that could be fired from a submerged submarine. The Polaris, Poseidon, and Trident SLBMs formed the third leg of the United States' *strategic nuclear triad* consisting of jet-powered bombers, ICBMs, and SLBMs, from the 1960s until the end of the Cold War. The purpose of the nuclear triad was to reduce the possibility that the Soviet Union could destroy all of the United States' nuclear forces in a *first-strike* attack and to ensure that the United States could deliver a powerful retaliatory atomic attack on the Soviet Union, thereby increasing nuclear deterrence.

By the 1980s, the United States had about 30,000 atomic weapons and the Soviet Union had as many as 20,000 deliverable by bomber, missile, and submarine. In both states these nuclear weapons systems were linked together by vast radar detection systems, such as the American Distant Early Warning Line (DEW Line) located in the high-arctic regions of Alaska, Canada, and Greenland, and command-and-control networks consisting of atomic-bombproof underground command centers, such as the North American Aerospace Defense Command (NORAD) facility beneath Cheyenne Mountain near Colorado Springs, Colorado, to warn of nuclear attack in time to launch a retaliatory strike.[9]

The accumulation of vast nuclear arsenals and three systems of delivery came about because it was realized early on in the Cold War that the conventional armed forces of the United States and its allies were too small to prevail over the extremely large conventional armed forces of the Soviet Union and its allies, and would be forced to respond to a conventional attack with a massive response with atomic weapons. It was also realized that such weapons could accomplish their defensive objective not by their *actual* use but by the *threat* of their use in massive numbers. These understandings, and the United States' desire to reduce the size and cost of conventional forces, impelled President Dwight Eisenhower (1890–1969) and his air-atomic war planners to build up a massive strategic nuclear arsenal and develop the three means of delivery discussed above so that the United States could inflict "unacceptable damage" on the Soviet Union. Known as *mutually assured destruction* (MAD), this doctrine sought "to deter a deliberate [nuclear] attack . . . by maintaining at all times a clear and unmistakable ability to inflict an unacceptable degree of damage upon any aggressor—even after absorbing a surprise first strike."[10] The Soviet Union developed a similar doctrine and built the same types of atomic weapons systems.

The MAD doctrine was partially abandoned by President John Kennedy (1917–1963) in 1961, however, because the air-atomic doctrine of MAD was too confining. Kennedy's thinking on this matter was strongly influenced by a book titled *The Uncertain Trumpet*[11] written by a retired general, Maxwell Taylor (1901–1987), who argued in it that, *inter alia*, MAD was endangering national security of the United States because it limited the American military response in crisis situations, such as the Berlin Crisis (June 4–November 9, 1961) and the Cuban Missile Crisis (October 14–28, 1962), to a massive strike on the Soviet Union, whose retaliatory strike would annihilate the United States itself. President Kennedy recalled General Taylor to active duty as military adviser to the president and, in 1962, appointed him to the chairmanship of the Joint Chiefs of Staff (JCS). During his time as chairman, General Taylor articulated a new approach to atomic war called *"flexible response,"* which required the development of tactical atomic weapons that could be delivered by fighter-bombers, and artillery and tank shells.

Flexible response gave the United States two atomic war-fighting options: the first was unrestricted air-atomic war using *strategic* weapons in a massive first strike, which would destroy the entire Soviet Union (and, perhaps, the United States as well from the Soviet retaliatory strike). The second option was atomic war using less destructive *tactical* atomic weapons in a limited area of military operations without launching a direct attack on the Soviet Union. Those who advocated the second option were convinced that war could be fought using both conventional and atomic weapons on the same battlefield, despite the dangers posed by radiation from exploded tactical atomic shells.

Finally, the development of the extremely fast and accurate Pershing II missiles in the late 1970s and early 1980s gave rise to another atomic war-fighting doctrine called *decapitation.* Pershing IIs were to be stationed in Europe to counter Soviet mobile SS-20s where they could be used to eliminate the Soviet Union's political and military leadership in a single swift attack, thereby disabling its command-and-control capabilities and prevent an effective response.[12]

During the Cold War, the closest that the United States and the Soviet Union came to an actual air-atomic war was the Cuban Missile Crisis of October 1962. This crisis was brought about by a United States–sponsored failed invasion of Cuba by exiled counter revolutionaries, known as Brigade 2506, at the Bay of Pigs in April 1961, and the installation by the United States of Jupiter intermediate-range ballistic missiles in Turkey aimed at targets in the Soviet Union. The Soviets responded to these provocations by installing intermediate-range nuclear missiles in Cuba to prevent an invasion from the United States and to offset the military advantage of American missiles in Turkey. The crisis was defused at the last minute by the United States agreeing to remove its Jupiter missiles from Turkey as well as from Italy and the Soviet Union agreeing to remove its missiles from Cuba. The United States also agreed not to invade Cuba.

The Cuban Missile Crisis was a turning point in the relations between the two superpowers during the Cold War. Having brought the world to the brink of nuclear Armageddon, they became more cautious in their dealings with one another. So-called hotlines between the White House and the Kremlin were installed so that their leaders could confer directly in case of a crisis. It also resulted a general easing of geopolitical tensions (known as *détente*) between them in 1969, as well as the signing of several bilateral treaties to regulate their respective atomic arsenals. In 1972 and in 1977, the Strategic Arms Limitation Treaties (known as SALT I and SALT II, respectively) established the number of ICBMs each side was permitted to have at then-existing levels; in 1975, the Helsinki Agreement curtailed the manufacture of new atomic weapons; and, in 1987, the Intermediate Range Nuclear Forces Treaty forbade nuclear weapons within Europe.[13]

By the time the Cold War ended in 1991, it was clear that atomic weapons could not be used for war fighting because a war between nuclear-armed states would escalate and lead to the virtual annihilation of both. Thus, the only function of atomic weapons was to deter war from breaking out. According to the military historian Walter Millis, military leaders who oversaw the design, production, and employment of "giant weapons of mass destruction cannot learn much from Napoleon, or Jackson, or Lee, or Grant—who were all managers of men in combat, not of 'weapons systems' about which the most salient feature is that they must never . . . be allowed to come into collision."[14]

In 1969, the Nuclear Non-Proliferation Treaty was agreed upon to prevent the spread of atomic weapons technology to "undesirable" states. However, the spread of nuclear technology has proven to be difficult to stop. At the end of the Cold War in 1991 there were eight states with deliverable atomic weapons: the United States, the Russian Federation (the successor state of the collapsed Soviet Union), Britain, France, China, India, and Pakistan. Israel is also believed to have deliverable atomic weapons, but neither denies nor concedes that it has; South Africa claims to have had atomic weapons, but dismantled them; North Korea is known to have tested an atomic device; and Iran is arguably seeking to build one. Argentina, Brazil, Canada, Taiwan, Japan, Australia, and New Zealand are capable of building atomic weapons but have refrained from doing so, but could if they decided they were needed.[15] To date, the only atomic weapons used in war were the ones dropped by the United States on Hiroshima and Nagasaki.

The subsequent decline in major inter-state war after the introduction and development of atomic weapons at the end of the Second World War led many people, politicians and scholars alike, to conclude they had ended inter-state war. For example, Winston Churchill (1874–1965), in his last speech to Parliament, said that "it may well be that we shall by a process of sublime irony have reached a stage in this story where safety will be the sturdy child of terror, and survival the twin brother of annihilation."[16] The military historian and theorist Martin van Creveld concurs: "By far the most important factor behind the waning of major inter-state war has been the introduction of nuclear weapons."[17] For van Creveld, atomic weapons have had an inhibiting influence on nuclear-armed states. The fear of escalation has prevented them from making war on one another. Because of this, he argues, major inter-state war is "slowly abolishing itself."[18]

This view is disputed by many scholars, however. Evan Luard says that there is little evidence that highly destructive atomic weapons alone are capable of deterring war;[19] Steven Pinker points out that the theory of nuclear peace cannot explain why many non-nuclear states have also forsaken war.[20] John Mueller believes that the reason for the waning of major inter-state war is not atomic weapons per se but changing attitudes about the value and efficiency of war over the last century. He says that attitudes toward war have changed much like those toward slavery, torture, and dueling, which most people today find repugnant.[21] Jeremy Black says that Western states have become noticeably less bellicose;[22] and Martin Shaw says that formerly militarized western states have become increasingly civilianized but not necessarily more pacific.[23] Kalevi Holsti and others have argued that the properties of the post–Second World War international system have made major inter-state war obsolete, not atomic weapons.[24] The decline in inter-state war and the changes in the global system of states that have brought it about will be discussed in greater detail in chapter 8.

THE NATIONAL SECURITY STATE

While the casual relationship between atomic weapons and the waning of major inter-state war is debatable, the casual relationship between such weapons and the development of the national security state is not. As was shown in the previous chapter, the nationalization and industrialization of warfare during the last years of the nineteenth century and the first decades of the twentieth century brought forth the militarized managerial welfare state and transformed the inert subjects of the kingly state into the militarily active citizens of the national state. Making war and mobilizing for conventional war were major activities of industrialized national states and the top priority of their leaders. For some leaders, war was a tonic for the rejuvenation of the nation and victory in war an indicator of national greatness. For others, war was not glorious but inevitable and had to be prepared for in order to defend the state's people against powerful predatory neighbors. In industrial total war, there was no aspect of the state, society, and economy that was unaffected by preparing for and making war. States become increasingly managerial and their societies and economies became increasingly militarized. As armies became larger and their weapons and equipment became more technologically sophisticated, industrialized national states became more and more managerial, interventionist, and welfarist.

Atomic weapons transformed the industrialized managerial welfare state by fundamentally altering the trinitarian relationship between the state, the army, and the people. Nuclear-armed states do not need large armies and vast arsenals of conventional weapons for their security. Instead, they need large numbers of powerful atomic weapons and the reliable means to deliver them by air swiftly and accurately to the cities, towns, industries, and military facilities of the enemy state. As reliable atomic technology is more important than mass-conscripted armies, nuclear-armed states need scientists and engineers, research laboratories, high-technology manufacturing facilities, and skilled technicians. And they need a new kind of soldier: the *military technician* who knows how to operate increasingly complex, advanced weapons systems, not rude conscripts. In nuclear-armed states there is a shift from old-fashioned soldiering to complex weapons-systems operations.

Nuclear-armed states also need a new kind of citizenry. They need *passive citizens* who are happy to forego military service, accept their exclusion from an active role in the security of the state, and willingly *leave national security in the hands of a small elite of high-level defense intellectuals and high-ranking military officers* educated in the arcane technicalities (such as throw-weights, payload fraction, and para-nuclear capability, for example) of air-atomic war. As Shaw, quoting Michael Mann, has written: "Where the first half of the twentieth century saw the direct involvement of the masses in war, [which broke] down the separation of limited war and society in the previous two and half centuries, the nuclear age sees a re-privatization of war by the elites. War-preparation becomes not just a private but secret activity of political and military leaders, in which populations acquiesce but do not actively participate."[25]

These developments have been summed up by Michael Howard as follows:

> [States] have to keep their preparations for thermonuclear war and the clandestine activities connected with ideological confrontation as secret from their own people as from their putative enemies. There can be no sense of mass participation by citizen-soldiers in nuclear and clandestine warfare as there was in the great military acts of the two world wars. . . . The state *apparat* becomes isolated from the body politic, a severed head continuing to function automatically, conducting its intercourse with other severed heads according to its own laws, sometimes it even directs its activities against its own people.[26]

Thus, atomic weapons removed the military necessity that brought forth the militarized managerial welfare state. They reduced the role of the people to that of *passive subjects*, not participants in the war-making function of the state. Essentially, nuclear weapons *uncoupled* the state from the people. There has been little change in this state of affairs despite the ending of the Cold War. In the United States the habits, routines, procedures, and bureaucratic structures that evolved during the Cold War have persisted to the present. American presidents still act within the national security paradigm built up by deterrent air-atomic war.[27]

THE UNITED STATES AS A NATIONAL SECURITY STATE

As the examples of national security states are limited to those states possessing atomic weapons (the United States, the United Kingdom, France, the Russian Federation, China, Israel, India, and Pakistan) and as the national security apparatus of these states is very similar, this section presents only one case, that of the United States, without doubt the premier example of the national security state among the examples that could be used. What follows is the history of the way that war in general, and deterrent air-atomic war in particular, transformed the United States from a militarily weak decentralized state into a militarized managerial welfare state and then added to it a permanent national security apparatus.

The United States: From Jeffersonian Democracy to Thermonuclear Monarchy

Throughout most of its history, the United States has had a weak national government, a consequence of one central fact: its geographical isolation from enemy states. The Atlantic and Pacific oceans acted as protective barriers against attack until the development of jet-powered strategic bombers and ICBMs after the Second World War. In addition, no state in the Western Hemisphere has ever been militarily powerful enough to be a serious existential threat to the United States. Thus, for most of its history, the United States has existed in a militarily non-threatening environment. Therefore, it has not needed to build up a large army nor has it had to build up a strong central government to extract the men, money, and matériel to support it. Historically, only during wartime did the United States temporarily build up its armed forces and centralize its state apparatus. During the Civil War, the Federal state in the north transformed its small, weak army into a powerful military machine, built up its administrative and managerial capacity, and intervened in the economy in order to defeat the Confederacy and save the Union. After the war and the salvation of the Union, the huge army assembled by the Federal government was demobilized and many, but not all, of the governmental structures built up during the war were dismantled.

However, the First and Second World Wars, and the Cold War, shattered the United States' deep-rooted sense of insular security and brought into being for the first time a powerful managerial state. The marriage of atomic warheads with ICBMs, which could reach the continental United States from the Soviet Union within fifteen minutes, removed the protection provided by the United States' geographical location. Such weapons have changed the American state in profound ways. According to Elaine Scarry, the technology of deterrent air-atomic war, especially ICBMs, has transformed the United States from a constitutional republic into a *"thermonuclear monarchy,"* not unlike that of Louis XIV, because the president can make

> foreign policy decisions without enlisting the consent of the home population. It makes him independent of the will of the people. Since no human beings are needed to carry the weapons onto the battlefield, there is no need to persuade that population of the wrongdoing of the foreign country, no need to persuade them that all avenues of diplomacy are useless, no need to persuade them that stopping this foreign wrong is even more important than saving their own lives. . . . Thus the ordinary features of civic life—speech, contestation, debate, persuasion—disappear and are replaced with secret meetings in the leader's private chambers.[28]

At the end of the Cold War in 1991 the United States did not dismantle the national security apparatus, however. The attacks on the twin towers of the

World Trade Center in New York City on September 11, 2001 (known as 9/11) did much to increase its extent and pervasiveness in certain areas of American life. Essentially, the apparatus of the American national security state built up during the air-atomic age and all that it entails has been institutionalized and made permanent.

Most Americans are ignorant of the fact that many of the most important political reforms that expanded democracy and made life better are consequences of American wars. Every constitutional amendment that expanded the franchise was enacted either during or in the aftermath of a war. The Fifteenth (1870) gave the vote to freed slaves after the Civil War; the Nineteenth (1919) gave women the vote after the First World War; and the Twenty-Sixth (1971) gave the vote to eighteen-year-olds at the end of the Vietnam War. Americans are also ignorant of the way that war has reshaped American political institutions, stimulated their managerial capacity, encouraged their intervention into the economy, and shifted the actual power, if not the constitutional right, to declare war and make war from Congress to the executive. As with European states, war also drove the American state to concern itself with the welfare of the people.

The United States was brought into being by war. The American War of Independence (1775–1783) started as a revolt against taxes levied by the British to maintain a permanent military force in the western territories of the colonies to protect them from French encroachments. The Sugar Act of 1764, the Stamp Act of 1765, and the Townshend Revenue Act of 1767 were passed by the British Parliament to raise money to pay for British frontier garrisons whose presence was deemed necessary to maintain the security of western areas of the colonies after the French and Indian Wars (1754–1763). The Quartering Act of 1765 shifted the cost of maintaining British troops to the colonists.[29]

George Washington (1732–1799) wanted a regular professional army to fight the British. Many other leaders of the revolution had a deeply ingrained aversion to standing armies, which they associated with European absolute kingly rule. They wanted to fight the British with militias, guerrilla-style, because they were strongly influenced by the classical idea of armed civic virtue and glorified yeoman farmer militias, the so-called Minutemen. Washington won the debate, however, and, in 1775, the Continental Congress voted to form a Continental Army. By 1777 a regular system of recruitment was in place. Washington was helped by a coterie of European (mostly French) military advisers in the organizing, training, and deployment of this new army.[30]

The first institutions of the future state came into existence during the War of Independence. With the exception of the Post Office Department, they were exclusively about state security and raising the revenue necessary to maintain the Continental Army and fight the British: the Department of

State, the Department of War, the Department of the Treasury, and the Department of Military Supply. Congress also founded an arsenal in Springfield, Massachusetts, known today as the Springfield Armory, as well as the Bank of North America. During the war, more than half of the thirteen soon-to-be independent colonies lowered tax-paying and property-owning restrictions on the franchise to allow more men to vote. The war also had a leveling effect on American society because it brought together big plantation owners, tradesmen from the cities, and yeoman farmers from the countryside. It also broke down racial barriers in the North where freed slaves joined the ranks of the Continental Army. The departure of the Tories (colonists who remained loyal to Britain) after the war helped level the class structure of post-revolutionary society even more.[31]

After the War for Independence was won, the Continental Army was mostly demobilized. In 1784 it numbered only seven hundred men. The Continental Congress, still distrustful of standing armies, soon disbanded the army altogether, leaving two minuscule garrisons of twenty-five and fifty-five men each. Much of the administration set up by the Confederation government to fight the war was also dismantled. The newly independent states began to go their separate ways as if the Articles of Confederation did not exist. Certain leaders of the day began to argue for a stronger central government largely for military reasons: they argued that the individual states could not wield sufficient military force to defend themselves and maintain internal order. Increasing unrest in certain states (such as Shays' Rebellion in 1786–1787 in Massachusetts) exposed the weakness of state militias. Shipping interests worried about how trade could be conducted without the protection of a strong navy, which no one state could afford to build and maintain alone. "Hostile" native peoples in the western parts of the states had to be suppressed. Revolutionary War veterans, who were the most nationalist minded, pushed for a stronger central government because they were worried about their pensions being paid by the states. They, and those who had loaned money to the Continental Congress to help pay for the war, pushed for a central government that would assume the full debt of the war and continue to pay pensions.[32]

The mounting concerns over national security, civil unrest, and war debt culminated in a gathering of delegates from the states (except for Rhode Island) in Philadelphia in the summer of 1787 in order to consider changes to the Articles of Confederation that would strengthen the Confederation government, which had no power to tax and was, therefore, reliant on contributions from the states to conduct its affairs. Strong nationalists, like James Madison (1756–1836) and Alexander Hamilton (1755–1804), wanted to create a new stronger government rather than fix the old one. Those who favored a new government won the day, and the Articles of Confederation were abandoned and a new constitution written.

Military and security concerns were foremost in the minds of the delegates who wrote the new constitution; consequently, much of the Constitution is dedicated to building up the military power of the national government. The Constitution's Preamble states that two of the purposes of the document are to "insure domestic tranquility" and "provide for the common defense." Specifically, the Constitution stripped the states of the right to maintain standing armies, conduct foreign policy, and engage in wars, unless invaded. Article I, Section 8, grants Congress the power to provide for the common defense, declare war, raise and support armies, provide and maintain a navy, make rules for the government and regulation of the land and naval forces, provide for the calling up of the militia to suppress insurrection and to repel invasion, provide for the organization and discipline of the militia, and appoint officers of the armed forces. The Constitution also made the president commander-in-chief of the armed forces and gave him authority over the state militias when called into national service.

The Constitution's strengthening of the war-making capacity of the national state was simultaneously tempered by the conditions that had to be met before the state could make war. The Constitution ensured that the American state could fight no war unless it was *declared* by the national legislature (both houses of Congress in joint session) and without the *active involvement of the adult male population of military age* organized into "well regulated" state militias, as is the clear intent of the Second Amendment to the Constitution.[33]

Although the international situation in the first decades after the Revolution was volatile (quarrels with Britain and Spain) and the internal situation tumultuous (the Whiskey Rebellion [1791] instigated by the first tax imposed on domestic production levied by the newly formed Federal government, and skirmishes with Native American tribes), the Federalists, who wanted a strong national government, lost to the Jeffersonians, the faction of the Founding Fathers led by Thomas Jefferson (1743–1826), which favored a limited state. After being elected the third president of the United States, Jefferson signed a bill in 1802 to found a military academy at West Point, New York, to educate and train officers for the regular army. Nonetheless, he kept the army small. The United States was the least militarized, least centralized, and least managerial of all the major states of the day.

Until the Civil War, the United States remained wedded to the Jeffersonian ideal of a limited state with a small military establishment. There were two wars between 1800 and 1860, the Anglo-American War (1812–1815), known to Americans as the War of 1812, and the Mexican-American War (1846–1847). The United States managed to win the War of 1812 not because its army was bigger and more powerful than its opponent's, but because the British were tied down in Europe fighting Napoleon. The Anglo-American War resulted in the abandonment of tax-paying and property-owning restrictions on white males in almost all of the states. The United States defeated Mexico in part because of superior military performance but also because the Mexican army was using inferior weapons (Napoleonic War–vintage muskets) and experiencing serious internal political divisions.

Even after the election of General Andrew Jackson (1767–1845) in 1828, a certified hero of the War of 1812, the army continued to be neglected. During his administration Congress even attempted to close the United States Military Academy at West Point. State militias degenerated into social clubs of marginal military utility. The national government remained small with no more than 1,000 personnel scattered across the national territory, most of whom were patronage appointees in the Post Office Department (1792–1971). It can be said that at that time, the essential purpose of the United States government was delivering the mail![34]

The Civil War (1861–1865) was the watershed in the transformation of the weak American state into the military colossus that it is today. At the beginning of the Civil War, in 1860, the army numbered only 16,000 men, had a budget of $63 million, and employed 2,191 civilians in the Department of War in Washington, DC. At the end of the Civil War the army had more than one million men and a budget of $1.2 billion, and had become the largest, best-equipped army put on the battlefield to that date by any state in the world. The Civil War fostered the building of the American state by:

1. settling the question of whether or not the national state was dissoluble by confirming the supremacy of the national government over the states;
2. stimulating the growth of key industries, such as iron, textiles, and meat-packing, by massive Federal procurement of war matériel;
3. creating Federal clothing factories, pharmaceutical laboratories, and arsenals;
4. stimulating the creation of new taxes (stamp taxes, excise taxes, inheritance tax, value-added taxes, luxury taxes) and creating the Internal Revenue Service (IRS) to collect them;
5. creating a national paper currency (the Greenback) still in use today;
6. raising money to pay for the war by selling war bonds;
7. stimulating the creation of new government administrative departments (the IRS, Department of Agriculture, National Academy of Sciences, Bureau of Immigration, and the federally chartered Union Pacific and Central Pacific Railroad Companies);
8. gaining the power to extract by coercive methods the men, money, and matériel to make war by suspending the writ of *habeas corpus* and arresting people for disloyalty without judicial process, introducing conscription, and seizing railroads and operating them as U.S. Military Railroads; and

9. diminishing regional and local loyalties and creating a sense of national identity by service in the army.[35]

The Civil War had other transforming effects. It revived the labor movement, and gave impetus to the budding women's suffrage movement because hundreds of thousands of women had replaced men in factories and went to work for the national government. It also stimulated the development of the welfare state by creating the Bureau of Refugees, Freedmen, and Abandoned Lands (1865), referred to simply as the Freedmen's Bureau, which gave social assistance to freed slaves during Reconstruction, and by giving wounded veterans disability pensions, which eventually became an old-age/ disability-pension program for all veterans over the age of sixty-two. And it stimulated the creation of national cemeteries in 1862, which was the first time that any state accepted the responsibility of burying its war dead. Before this, the corpses of ordinary soldiers who were killed in battle were ignored. If they were buried at all, they were buried anonymously where they had fallen in combat, or in mass graves. National cemeteries where "[t]hose who gave their lives in the defense of the Republic during the Civil War must rest in perpetuity within the 'securely enclosed' confines of a national cemetery" became shrines of national worship and did much to create a sense of American nationhood.[36]

Thus, in the process of preserving the Union and eliminating slavery, the Civil War transformed the American state: before "1861 'United States' was a plural noun: The United States *have* a republican form of government. Since 1865 'United States' is a singular noun: The United States *is* a world power. The North went to war to preserve the *Union*; it ended by creating a *nation*."[37]

After the Civil War, owing to the fact that the United States did not have any enemy states nearby, the army was demobilized and reduced to 24,000 men, and many, but not all, of the special agencies created to conduct the war were eliminated, and the power that had accrued to the president during the war returned to Congress. Although the American state had been transformed from near non-existence to an organization to be reckoned with domestically, especially during Reconstruction in the states of the defeated Confederacy, it was still relatively weak from the perspective of European states. The Post Office Department, with 30,000 postmen, still dwarfed the federal workforce of 15,341.

After the Civil War, the army of the United States was not used to defend the national territory per se but was used internally to protect settlers in the western territories, to suppress wars between Native American tribes, and to round up bands of Native Americans who had left their reservations. The army was reduced to 57,000 men in 1867, then to 26,000 in 1876, where it remained until the Spanish-American War in 1898. During the Spanish-

American War the army was increased to 65,000 regulars and 135,000 temporary service volunteers. As the Spanish-American War lasted only ten days, it did little to transform the American state.

This was not the case with the First World War, during which the United States drafted four million men, shipped two million of them to Europe, and lost 100,000 in the trenches.[38] Federal spending increased by 1,000 percent, and the federal bureaucracy doubled in size. During the war the American state regulated industry, imposed price controls, and intervened in labor disputes. It encouraged the construction of ships, submarines, machine guns, artillery pieces, airplanes, tanks, and an assortment of small arms. It created a complex of Federal agencies to mobilize the economic resources necessary to support its vast army, navy, and budding army air corps: the War Industries Board, the Fuel Administration, the Shipping Board, the War Finance Corporation, the Railroad Administration, the War Trade Board, and the Bureau of Aircraft Production. The American state mobilized the manpower and industrial might of the United States in order to support what was at that time the largest overseas military expedition undertaken by any state.[39]

This generated a big fiscal and bureaucratic expansion of the Federal government. Federal spending increased from $713 million in 1914 to $1.9 billion in 1917, $12.7 billion in 1918, and $18.5 billion in 1919. The Wartime Revenue Act increased taxation, and the Wartime Revenue Act of 1918 went farther and was more progressive. These acts established the principle of progressive taxation that survived until the end of the twentieth century. Liberty Bonds were sold to raise even more revenue.[40] The National Defense Act (1916) gave the Federal government the authority to intervene in the economy. It compelled factories to sell to the government on a priority basis at a price determined by the government. The Army Appropriations Act authorized seizures of transportation. The Lever Act (1917) imposed Federal authority over fuel (coal, oil, natural gas) and food. It created the Food Administration and the Fuel Administration to regulate these sectors. The Department Reorganization Act of 1918, also known as the Overman Act, gave the president the authority to restructure the executive branch. President Woodrow Wilson (1856–1924) used the act to create the War Industries Board, which centralized government control over raw materials, regulated prices, froze wages, and prohibited strikes; the National War Labor Board, which arbitrated disputes between workers and owners for the sake of the war effort and national unity, and threatened any unemployed male with being drafted; and the Committee on Public Information, which made sure that all publications and works of art contained no anti-war sentiments.[41]

As during the Civil War, the state's power to quash internal dissent was increased. Socialists and anti-war protesters were arbitrarily arrested and jailed under the Espionage Act (1917), which is still the law of the land, and the Sedition Act (1918), which extended the Espionage Act to cover a broader range of offenses, notably speech and writings that cast the government or the war effort in a negative light, and forbade disloyal language directed at the United States, its flag, or its armed forces. Quasi-governmental organizations came into being, such as the National Security League that supported a greatly expanded military based on universal military service; the Home Defense League; and the Anti-German League, which espoused a virulent brand of anti-German nationalism, forcing German-Americans to profess their patriotism publicly and renaming sauerkraut "victory cabbage."[42]

Like the Civil War, the First World War helped build a more uniform national community. Military service broke down class distinctions, trade unions grew, and women joined the workforce in large numbers. Women were given the right to vote in 1919 (Nineteenth Amendment) not because of the suffrage movement, but because of their contribution to the war effort in hospitals and factories. The ratification of the Eighteenth Amendment in 1919, which prohibited the manufacture and sale of alcoholic beverages, came about because of war-buttressed moral conservatism and efficiency concerns.[43] About 100,000 Native Americans were granted citizenship as a reward for fighting in the war. Demobilized African-American soldiers began to demand their civil rights.

The First World War also paved the way for the statist approach to economic recovery during the Great Depression (1930–1941). Progressive reformers wanted a strong state to intervene in the economy. President Franklin Roosevelt (1882–1945), who had been secretary of the navy under President Wilson, saw the Depression as a crisis comparable to war. Much of what he did to end it was inspired by Wilson's wartime administration, and he patterned his New Deal agencies after their First World War predecessors. One of the most popular and successful was the quasi-military Civilian Conservation Corps (CCC), which recruited unemployed, unmarried men between the ages of eighteen and twenty-five to do unskilled manual labor on jobs related to the development of natural resources in rural areas on land owned by federal, state, and local governments. Recruits were provided shelter, food, clothing, and a small wage, most of which they were required to send home to their families. More than three million men served in the CCC during its existence from 1933 until 1942. Another program was the Works Progress Administration (WPA), which also employed millions of young, unskilled men to construct public works projects, such as public buildings, roads, schools, bridges, dams, and parks. It also employed writers, artists, and musicians.

The final step in transforming the United States into a national security state was taken during the Second World War. When war broke out in Europe in 1939, the United States began to re-arm. The threat of war caused the office of the president to grow by leaps and bounds. Before the United States entered the war, President Roosevelt created the National Defense Advisory

Commission, the Office of Emergency Management, the Office of Price Administration, the Office of Economic Stabilization, and the Supply Priorities and Allocations Board to mobilize the economy and society in case of hostilities. In 1941, he created a super-agency called the Office of War Mobilization to coordinate the efforts of these agencies and boards. Controls were put on prices, wages, and rents. Food and fuel were rationed. The Second War Powers Act (1942) gave the president enormous power over the American economy, including the right to seize any and all resources deemed necessary for the war effort. Conscription (the draft), the first in peacetime, was introduced in the same year, which increased the size of the armed forces to 1.8 million men by June 1941. At the same time, federal employment exploded and surpassed 3.8 million by war's end. The largest office building in the world, the Pentagon, was built to house the burgeoning war and navy departments, which had doubled in size from 1939 to 1941. By 1943, the American state was consuming one-half of the national economic output. Washington, DC, was transformed from a sleepy town on the Potomac to a bustling metropolis and power center almost overnight.[44]

The Second World War, like the Civil War and the First World War, had a unifying effect on the nation. It broke down class, race, and gender barriers as millions of women and minorities were hired to take the place of men in factories. The "We Can Do It!" poster showing Rosie the Riveter flexing her muscular right arm by J. Howard Miller (1918–2004) in 1942 and the *Saturday Evening Post's* Memorial Day cover by Norman Rockwell (1894–1978) in 1943, depicting a tough-looking Rosie the Riveter in coveralls cradling her rivet gun, have become feminist icons of the period. Native Americans left the reservations for the first time in great numbers and some 25,000 served in the armed forces, especially in the United States Marine Corps, as "code talkers." Some 900,000 African Americans also served in the armed forces, mostly in segregated units, the most famous being the 332nd Fighter Group and the 477th Bombardment Group of the United States Army Air Corps, better known as the "Tuskegee Airmen." After the war, military service by African Americans legitimated their patriotism and their claims to full citizenship rights and stimulated the development of the civil rights movement of the 1950s and 1960s. In sum, the Second World War made the American state more centralized, bureaucratic, interventionist, and inclusive than it had ever been in its history.[45]

At war's end, the United States had 12.5 million men and women (8.6 percent of the American population) in its armed forces. By 1946 the number had shrunk to three million, and by 1948 to 1.5 million. It rose to 3.6 million at the height of the Korean War (1950–1953) in 1952 then declined again at war's end. This downward trend stopped and reversed itself when the Cold War started, the number of service personnel reaching about three million.[46] It stayed, more or less, at this number until the collapse of the Soviet Union in 1991, after which it began to decline. While the state's involvement in the economy was reduced significantly after the Second World War, the power that had accrued to the presidency did not flow back to Congress. In fact, the president's war-making powers increased substantially during the Cold War.

During the Second World War it became evident that having a Department of War, which contained the army, and a Department of the Navy, which contained the navy and the marines, as separate entities was chaotic and inefficient. President Truman, convinced that the armed forces needed to be unified, sent to Congress in December 1945 a proposal that would bring all branches together into one department under a single chief of staff. After eighteen months of study, a subcommittee of the Senate Armed Services Committee recommended a coordinating advisory council, to be called the National Security Council (NSC), be created, which would be headed by an executive-director appointed by the president and confirmed by the Senate. Truman's advisers believed that the Senate's proposal would undermine the president's role in the defense policy-making process; therefore, they re-drafted it such that the NSC became an entity within the Executive Office of the President solely under the authority of the president with an executive-director who did not report to Congress and whose staff was to be chosen entirely at the discretion of the president. This redrafted proposal passed Congress as the National Security Act of 1947.[47]

The National Security Act created four coordinating bodies: the National Military Establishment (NME), the Central Intelligence Agency (CIA), the National Security Council (NSC), and the National Security Resources Board (NSRB). Each of these bodies was designed to correct problems that arose during the Second World War and deal with the perceived needs of the Cold War. None of these worked as intended, however. Amendments made to the National Security Act in 1949 eliminated the MNE and created the Department of Defense (DoD), a secretary of defense, and the Joint Chiefs of Staff (JCS). The NSRB disappeared in 1953. The DoD contained the Army, Navy, and Marine Corps as well as the newly created Air Force. The chiefs of these four branches of the armed forces composed the JCS, and a high-ranking military officer from one of them was appointed chairman by the president with the "advice and consent" of the Senate.

During the Eisenhower administration, changes were made to the DoD that gave the chairman of the JCS more authority and subordinated the military departments to the secretary of defense. Eisenhower also enhanced the role of the NSC and created the position of national security assistant. Stoked by the perception that the Soviet Union was an expansionist power, the victory of the communists in the Chinese civil war, and the outbreak of the Korean War, these institutions grew and flourished during the 1950s. In 1952, the most secretive agency of the American national security state, the National Security Agency (NSA), was created to bring together all of the signals-intelligence-gathering capabilities (SIGINT) scattered among the agencies of the federal government and the military services.[48]

When John Kennedy assumed the presidency he made certain changes that strengthened the national security apparatus of the American state. First, he upgraded the national security "assistant" to the national security "adviser." Second, he directed his national security adviser, McGeorge Bundy (1919–1996), to assemble a policy staff to assist him and the president. Third, he created the White House Situation Room, which still exists today and houses a twenty-five-person, round-the-clock staff that monitors information flows from American diplomatic and military missions abroad. Kennedy ignored the Department of State, which he regarded as stodgy and slow moving, and increasingly relied on his national security adviser and the NSC staff for foreign and military policy recommendations. After the Kennedy administration, the Department of State was never able to regain its supremacy in the making of American foreign policy. Kennedy also relied heavily on his secretary of defense, Robert McNamara (1916–2009), who surrounded himself with a group of experts in operations research and management from the RAND Corporation known as the "Whiz-Kids." Under McNamara the role of the DoD in American national security policy was greatly enhanced.[49]

Although President Lyndon Johnson (1908–1973) made no major changes to the apparatus of the American national security state, the Vietnam War (1955–1975) expanded the influence of the CIA and the DoD over American national security policy and solidified the role of president as commander-in-chief. During the presidency of Richard Nixon (1913–1994) and his national security adviser Henry Kissinger (1923–), the White House absorbed more State Department security policy functions and completed the ascent of the national security adviser to the top rung of the national security apparatus. No president since Nixon has lowered the national security adviser on the national security ladder, despite intentions to do so. For example, President Jimmy Carter (1924–) attempted to move away from the obsession with the Soviet Union and emphasize human rights and arms control, but his national security adviser, Zbigniew Brzezinski (1928–), who came of age during the height of the Cold War and thought in terms of anti-Soviet geopolitics, resisted. For him, the Soviet Union still had to be contained. President Ronald Reagan (1911–2004) set the general direction of national security policy and delegated the details to the six national security advisers who served him during his eight years in office.[50] Presidents George H. W. Bush (1924–), Bill Clinton (1946–), and George W. Bush (1946–), did little or nothing to change Cold War habits, nor has President Barack Obama (1961–), despite the ending of the Cold War.

In sum, the vulnerability of the United States to nuclear attack by the Soviet Union justified the extraordinary security measures put in place during the Cold War: super-secret facilities, special levels of clearance, and concealment of certain defense budgetary information from Congress and the American people. According to Gary Wills, the whole

> history of America since World War II caused an inertial rolling of power toward the executive branch. The monopoly on the use of nuclear weaponry, the cult of the Commander-in-Chief, the worldwide web of military bases to maintain nuclear alert and supremacy, the secret intelligence agencies, the whole National Security State, the classification and clearance systems, the expansion of state secrets, the withholding of evidence and information, the permanent emergency that welded World War II with the Cold War and the Cold War with the war on terror—all these make a vast intricate structure that may not yield to efforts to dismantle it. Sixty-eight years of war emergency powers (1941–2009) have made the abnormal normal.[51]

The 9/11 terrorist attacks have caused power to continue to roll to the executive branch and reinforced the American national security state. In the aftermath of the attacks, existing agencies were expanded. The Defense Intelligence Agency, the Federal Bureau of Investigation (FBI) Joint Terrorism Task Forces, and the White House Military Office experienced significant increases in personnel. This was followed by large increases in the Federal budget for national security. The size and complexity of existing security agencies were expanded. For example, the FBI established a new unit called the Directorate of Weapons of Mass Destruction that combined law enforcement, intelligence analysis, and technical expertise. A new super-sized cabinet-level department was created, called the Department of Homeland Security (DHS), with more than 180,000 employees drawn from part or all of twenty-two preexisting agencies, including the Coast Guard, Secret Service, Department of Justice, Internal Revenue Service (IRS), and the Customs and Naturalization Service, and was given the responsibility of encouraging state and local governments to fight terrorism. The DHS was divided into four directorates: Border and Transportation Security, Emergency Preparedness and Response, Science and Technology, and Information Analysis. In addition, there has been a massive increase in government surveillance of citizens, especially by the NSA, which has the technical capability to monitor all telecommunications, domestic and foreign.[52] Essentially, the so-called "global war on terror" has justified the continuation and strengthening of the American national security state.

War also stimulated the development of the American welfare state. Theda Skocpol has argued that the first national welfare program in American history was the Army Disabilities Pension Act of 1862, which provided pensions for invalid veterans of the Civil War and their survivors. The Arrears Act of 1879 and the Dependent Pensions Act of 1890 expanded the 1862 act into a de facto old-age and disability pension for all veterans over the age of sixty-two, Union and Confederate.[53] Her findings sustain the argument that war has been a major factor in the formation of the American welfare state.

Neither the pensions and disability programs for Civil War veterans nor the Depression-era Social Security Act (1935), which extended similar benefits to all Americans sixty-five or over, brought the full-blown European-style welfare state to America, however. That had to wait until the "permanent emergency" created by deterrent air-atomic warfare, the ideological and military rivalry with the Soviet Union, as well as the revelations in the late 1950s and early 1960s about the large number of Americans living in poverty. The transformation of the United States into a managerial welfare state began in the early 1960s with the anti-poverty programs initiated during the presidency of John Kennedy, and greatly accelerated when Lyndon Johnson, a child of the Depression, assumed the presidency after Kennedy's assassination in November 1963. Called the "Great Society," these programs were the largest expansion of welfare programs in American history. They included Medicare and Medicaid; food stamps; the Work Incentives Program (WIN), which provided adults with vocational training; and Supplemental Security Income (SSI) for the elderly, blind, and disabled, as well as a large number of programs aimed at specific groups, such as single mothers and minorities. It is possible to see these programs as "payment" to the American people for their loyal service to the state and patriotism during the Second World War and the Cold War. It can also be argued that they were created to prove that America's capitalist economy was superior to the Soviet Union's socialist one at eradicating poverty and unemployment. It is not coincidental that they were brought into being at the height of the Cold War (1955–1970) when ideological rivalry between the United States and the Soviet Union over which system—socialist or capitalist—produced the highest standard of living, the greatest technical achievements, and the most social equality for its people was the most intense.

There is little doubt that the ending of segregation can be understood in this way as well. Racial segregation was a liability in the post-war world. It embarrassed America's allies and gave the Soviet Union a stick with which it could beat the United States. The intense ideological and atomic rivalry with the Soviet Union demanded that racial segregation and other forms of discrimination be ended. The Kennedy administration eventually allied itself with African-American civil rights groups against southern states to end segregation and outlaw racial discrimination. In 1964, President Johnson pushed a Civil Rights Act through Congress that made segregation illegal and abolished discriminatory voter registration practices designed to disenfranchise African Americans.[54]

The collapse of the Soviet Union in 1991 altered the threat environment of the United States by removing its most implacable foe. If war in general and the threat of air-atomic war in particular have driven the formation of the

American managerial welfare/national security state, what would the disappearance of the existential Soviet threat mean for the future of the American state? In this regard, Bruce Porter has written:

> The post-Cold War era is likely to be not an era of good feeling, peace dividends, and economic boom (à la the post 1945 era), but an era of political turmoil and divisiveness. . . . We can expect growing public disdain for the political process, rising unrest in the inner cities, proposals for radical constitutional change, third-party movements, one-term presidents, and a serious national identity crisis over what it means to be an American. We may see a variety of attempts to solve all these problems through foreign diversions: finding and inventing enemies . . . against which united efforts can be directed. But unless an actual military foe arises, or the United States becomes embroiled in a serious war, the problem of keeping America unified in the face of profound centrifugal tensions is likely to be *the* political problem of the 1990s and beyond.[55]

Much of what Porter predicted would happen has come to pass. In addition, Benjamin Ginsberg has argued that, not having a major state to fight, the United States has turned its military power inward and uses its "now superfluous coercive capacity against its own citizens."[56] Increasingly, it seeks internal enemies to substitute for external foes.

CONCLUSION

The national security state was brought into being by the development of atomic weapons. Not all states in the global states system are national security states, but the eight that have such weapons have the characteristics of the national security state: arsenals of nuclear weapons ready for instant use; intelligence agencies operating in secret; self-perpetuating groups of national security intellectuals consisting of military officers, academics, and bureaucrats; a specialized national security apparatus; a shift of war-making power away from legislatures to executives; and a disconnect between the state's war-making function and the people. The national security state will survive as long as such states have clearly identifiable enemy states similarly armed. At the same time, the transformation of the trinitarian relationship between war, the state, and the people brought by atomic weapons has undermined the managerial welfare state and brought forth a new form of the state, the neoliberal state, which is quickly becoming the dominant form of the state on planet Earth. The coming to the fore of this form of the state will be the subject of the next chapter.

NOTES

1. Edward Kaplan, *To Kill Nations: American Strategy in the Air-Atomic Age and the Rise of Mutually Assured Destruction* (Ithaca: Cornell University Press, 2015).
2. Martin van Creveld, *The Rise and Decline of the State* (Cambridge: Cambridge University Press, 1999), p. 338.
3. Elaine Scarry, *Thermonuclear Monarchy: Choosing between Democracy and Doom* (New York/London: W. W. Norton, 2014), p. 5.
4. Martin Shaw, *Post-Military Society: Militarism, Demilitarization and War at the End of the Twentieth Century* (Philadelphia: Temple University Press, 1991), p. 23.
5. Martin Shaw, *Dialectics of War: An Essay in the Social Theory of Total War and Peace* (London: Pluto Press, 1988), p. 40.
6. *Ibid.*, p. 106.
7. This strategy was brilliantly depicted and mocked in Stanley Kubrick's film *Dr. Strangelove or: How I Learned to Stop Worrying and Love the Bomb* (1964).
8. Martin van Creveld, *The Changing Face of War: Lessons of Combat from the Marne to Iraq* (New York: Ballantine Books, 2006), p. 176.
9. *Ibid.*, pp. 175–76.
10. John Keegan, *A History of Warfare* (New York: Vintage Books, 1994), p. 382. See also Kaplan, *op. cit.*
11. General Maxwell Taylor, *The Uncertain Trumpet* (New York: Harper, 1960).
12. van Creveld, *The Rise and Decline of the State*, p. 341.
13. *Ibid.*, p. 342.
14. Quoted in van Creveld, *The Changing Face of War*, p. 174.
15. Martin van Creveld, *The Rise and Decline of the State*, p. 343.
16. Quoted in Steven Pinker, *The Better Angels of Our Nature: Why Violence Has Declined* (New York: Viking, 2011), p. 268.
17. Martin van Creveld, "The Waning of Major War," in Raimo Väyrynen (ed.), *The Waning of Major War: Theories and Debates* (London and New York: Routledge, 2006), p. 97.
18. van Creveld, *The Rise and Decline of the State*, p. 344.
19. Evan Luard, *The Blunted Sword: The Erosion of Military Power in Modern World Politics* (New York: New Amsterdam, 1988), pp. 24–31.
20. Steven Pinker, *The Better Angels of Our Nature*, p. 269.
21. John Mueller, "Accounting for the Waning of Major War," in Väyrynen, *The Waning of Major War*, pp. 64–79. See also James L. Payne, *A History of Force* (Sandpoint, ID: Lyntton Publishing, 2004) and Pinker, *op. cit.*, pp. 268–78.
22. Jeremy Black, *Why Wars Happen* (New York: New York University Press, 1998), pp. 225–26 and 231–33.
23. Shaw, *Post-Military Society, passim.*
24. Kalevi J. Holsti, "The Decline of Interstate War: Pondering Systemic Explanations," in Väyrynen (ed.), *The Waning of Major War*, pp. 135–59. See also, Hendrik Spruyt, "Normative Transformations in International Relations and the Waning of Major War," in Väyrynen (ed.), *The Waning of Major War*, pp.185–206.
25. Shaw, *Post-Military Society*, p. 76.
26. Michael Howard, *The Causes of Wars and Other Essays*, 2nd Edition, Enlarged (Cambridge, MA: Harvard University Press, 1984), pp. 30–31.
27. Andrew J. Bacevich (ed.), *The Long War: A New History of U.S. National Security Policy since World War II* (New York: Columbia University Press, 2007), p. ix.
28. Scarry, *op. cit.*, p. 149.
29. Bruce D. Porter, *War and the Rise of the State: The Military Foundations of Modern Politics* (New York: Free Press, 1994), p. 249.
30. *Ibid.*, p. 250.
31. *Ibid.*, p. 251.
32. *Ibid.*, pp. 252–54.
33. Scarry, *op. cit.*, p. 31.
34. *Ibid.*, pp. 256–57.

35. *Ibid.*, pp. 259–62.

36. George L. Mosse, *Fallen Soldiers: Reshaping the Memory of the World Wars* (Oxford: Oxford University Press, 1990), pp. 45–46. See also Drew Gilpin Faust, *This Republic of Suffering: Death and the American Civil War* (Waterville, ME: Thorndike Press, 2008).

37. James McPherson, *The War That Forged a Nation: Why the Civil War Still Matters* (New York: Oxford University Press, 2015), p. 6.

38. Brendan Simms, *Europe: The Struggle for Supremacy from 1453 to the Present* (New York: Basic Books, 2013), p. 316.

39. Porter, *op. cit.*, pp. 269–72.

40. Simms, *op. cit.*, p. 316.

41. Porter, *op. cit.*, pp. 269–72.

42. James Burke, "The Changing Moral Contract for Military Service," in Bacevich, *op. cit.*, p. 420.

43. Robert H. Zieger, *America's Great War: World War I and the American Experience* (Lanham, MD: Rowman & Littlefield, 2000), pp. 2–3.

44. Porter, *op. cit.*, pp. 279–81.

45. *Ibid.*, pp. 284–85.

46. *Ibid.*, p. 286.

47. Anna Kasten Nelson, "The Evolution of the National Security State," in Bacevich, *op. cit.*, pp. 268–69.

48. *Ibid.*, pp. 272–73.

49. *Ibid.*, pp. 280–82.

50. *Ibid.*, pp. 285–91.

51. Gary Wills, *Bomb Power: The Modern Presidency and the National Security State* (New York: Penguin, 2010), p. 238.

52. Sidney Tarrow, *War, States, and Contention* (Ithaca, NY: Cornell University Press, 2015), pp. 171–76.

53. Theda Skocpol, *Protecting Soldiers and Mothers: The Political Origins of Social Policy in the United States* (Cambridge, MA: Harvard University Press, 1992).

54. Simms, *op. cit.*, p. 440.

55. Porter, *op. cit.*, p. 295.

56. Benjamin Ginsberg, *The Worth of War* (Amherst, NY: Prometheus Books, 2014), p. 216.

Chapter 7

Unmanned War and the Neoliberal State

The period from 1945 to 1991 was a time of transition between the industrialized, labor-intensive mode of war of the twentieth century and the capital-intensive, unmanned way of war of the twenty-first century. The first half of the twentieth century saw an unprecedented buildup of conventional military power that peaked in Europe's second Thirty Years' War (1914–1945).[1] During that time, European states took control of their economies and societies and forged an extremely tight connection between the state, the army, and the people. The states of Europe, the United States, Japan, and other states were more or less *militarized*. Military culture and values infused the civilian world of these states and the people in huge numbers participated directly in war. Martin Shaw sums up the age of total war militarism thusly:

> The years before 1914 were dominated by the build-up to war, their popular nationalism and militarism utterly innocent of the slaughter to come. The First World War involved the most dramatic transformation of world society in history: an unprecedented international upheaval in social structure, state organization, economy, class struggle. The "inter-war" years were but a period of war preparation, in which the political fissures opened by the first war fed into the unresolved conflicts of states and led toward a new general conflict. The Second World War was an even more global struggle, more politicized, more destructive, even more complete in its mobilization and murderous effects on civilian populations.[2]

As was shown in the previous chapter, the advent of atomic weapons began to undermine the nationalized and militarized welfare state and the labor-intensive, industrial way of war by substituting air-delivered atomic weapons for mass military participation.[3] War was increasingly unmanned as atomic

179

weapons and skilled military technicians began to replace mass-conscripted armies and large infantry formations. These trends were accelerated with the waning of inter-state war in general and the ending of the Cold War in particular. As Charles Moskos has written: "Without the threat of invasion, Western states no longer need to buttress armed forces so distinctive from the social values of the larger society."[4] Clausewitz's remarkable trinity forged during the era of nationalized/industrialized war has been broken and a new relationship between the state, armed force, and the people has come into being. Unmanned war has also brought forth a new form of the state: the neoliberal state.

Although the neoliberal state represents a new version of an old form of the state, it retains certain aspects of the national security state that preceded it. In the neoliberal state the secret and invisible war-making apparatus of the national security state built up during the Cold War remains unchanged. War-making is still in the hands of national security professionals, and the people of the neoliberal state are still not expected to participate actively in the defense of the state through military service and economic sacrifice. Rather, they are expected to tacitly support the decisions regarding war taken by national security elites in their name.

Unmanned war has tightened the relationship between the neoliberal state and basic scientific research. In the neoliberal state the line between military and civilian technologies has been blurred and large numbers of civilian researchers and research firms are tied together into a public-private system of unmanned weapons design and procurement. One scholar has estimated that fully one-third of American scientists and engineers work in jobs direct-ly or indirectly related to the military, specifically the design and construc-tion of advanced unmanned weaponry.[5]

The neoliberal state still makes war, but it utilizes sophisticated aerial and terrestrial unmanned weapons and so-called "smart munitions," made pos-sible by the Revolution in Computing, and small all-volunteer armed forces instead of large conscripted armies and conventional machine weapons. It also does not make inter-state war and has no interest in conquest, the acqui-sition of territory by force of arms being forbidden in the current global order and no longer being necessary to enhance state power and wealth. Rather, it fights "[i]ndividual targets—fixed, mobile, and . . . even individual hu-mans—[who] are identified, and validated and located and tracked from the ground and the sky"[6] using unmanned weapons that rely on civilian technol-ogy and the Internet to do their work. Essentially, the armed forces of the neoliberal state do not fight wars; they seek out and kill "high-value targets, foreign regime elements, [and] violent extremists."[7]

UNMANNED WAR

As with the transformations of the state discussed in earlier chapters, the transformation of the militarized welfare state into the national security state and the transformation of the national security state into the neoliberal state were driven by new military technologies, organization, and culture.[8] Unmanned war and the neoliberal state were brought into being by the technological imperatives made possible by the Revolution in Computing that began at the end of the Second World War. It can be argued that this revolution was as important for the post-war transformation of the militarized welfare state into the neoliberal state as the Gunpowder Revolution was for the transformation of the feudal state into the centralized kingly state during the late Middle Ages in Europe because it made it possible to fight war (actualize violence) from unprecedented distances (thousands of miles) while reducing the risks to one's own armed forces to nearly zero for the first time in human history.

The Revolution in Computing began in the 1930s with the invention of mechanical data-processing machines that used punched cards (called "IBM cards" after the manufacturer of the machines, the International Business Machines Corporation [IBM]), and the invention of the electro-mechanical cypher machine (Enigma) by the Germans at the end of the First World War and electro-mechanical machines for breaking the coded messages sent by these machines by the British and the Americans (the Ultra and Magic machines, respectively) during the Second World War. These machines were very sophisticated mechanical calculators that used cogs and gears, not electronic computers.[9]

The device that revolutionized information technology was the *electronic computer*, the first prototypes of which were built at the University of Pennsylvania's Moore School of Electrical Engineering in the 1930s. Between 1943 and 1945, under contract from the United States Army's Ballistics Research Laboratory, the school's engineers built the first general-purpose, programmable computer, the Electronic Numerical Integrator and Computer (ENIAC). The machine's primary purpose was to perform the complex calculations needed to make ballistics-firing tables for gravity bombs and artillery shells faster than was possible at that time by the laboratory's small army of mathematicians using hand-operated electro-mechanical calculators. The British and the Germans also built working computers, but both were destroyed during the war—in Germany by Allied bombing, and in Britain by their operators for security reasons. The ENIAC's successor, the Electronic, Discrete, Variable Automatic Computer (EDVAC), was designed with the assistance of the Hungarian-American polymath John von Neumann (1903–1957), who understood that a computer's essential function was to perform operations that could be broken down into sequences of discrete logical steps that could be programmed into the computer and stored in its "memory." The EDVAC became the prototype of all future computers.[10] It should be noted that computers themselves do not perform physical work but can be used to control servo-mechanisms in other machines that do the actual work by transmitting instructions to them.

The computer, created for military purposes, continued to evolve as a military technology for the first twenty years of its existence. Its development was driven by the needs of the United States armed forces during the Cold War as "embedded means of fire control for artillery and anti-aircraft guns; solvers of long, complex technical and engineering problems; elements of advanced command and control; basic tools for strategic analysis and war gaming; or embedded and programmed controllers for self-guided weapons."[11]

Until the 1970s, computers were large and difficult to program. They weighed thousands of pounds and filled entire rooms. They contained thousands and thousands of vacuum tubes that consumed large quantities of electricity and generated much unwanted heat, which required heavy-duty air-conditioning to dissipate. By today's standards, they were very slow, only capable of making a few thousand calculations per second. Compared to the electro-mechanical calculators then in use, however, they were amazingly fast. The invention of three ingenious devices—the transistor, the semiconductor, and the microprocessor—made it possible to build smaller and faster computers. The first, the transfer resistor, or *transistor*, could perform the same switching functions as vacuum tubes but without the need for the glass dome filled with filaments like a lightbulb. The second, the *semiconductor*, allowed an entire electronic circuit to be reduced to microscopic size and etched onto a wafer of silicon, called a "chip." The third, the *microprocessor*, was essentially a programmable microchip.[12]

Miniaturization was supported by money from the Department of Defense (DoD), which needed lightweight digital computers for the inertial guidance systems of ICBMs, and for the space program. The incredible destructive power of atomic weapons and the speed of their delivery by missiles made it necessary to ensure tight control over their use. This led the Pentagon to support the development of computerized command-and-control systems. In the late 1950s the United States Air Force created the first computer-based command-and-control system designed to provide a centralized air defense network, the Semi-Automated Ground Environment (SAGE) system. SAGE was followed by numerous computerized systems, the most notable being the World Wide Military Command and Control System (WWMCCS), which was initially developed for the Strategic Air Command (SAC) and gradually extended to the rest of the military via a broad spectrum of communications systems and military satellites, which had been put in earth orbit by 1965. The first satellite navigation system, the Naval Navigation Satellite System

(NAVSAT), was designed to give nuclear submarines the ability to locate themselves on the globe with the precision necessary to launch SLBMs. In order to gain greater precision in the aiming of ICBMs and SLBMs the Pentagon perfected the Navigation Signal Timing and Ranging Global Positioning System (NAVSTAR), which came to be the Global Positioning System (GPS).[13]

By the end of the twentieth century, high-speed electronic computers were linked to optical and acoustic sensors fitted on military satellites encircling the Earth in a mesh of geocentric orbits that picked up the spectral "signatures" that could identify a piece of equipment, activity, individual, or event.[14] Providing all types of intelligence—audio, visual, and spectral, which could be transmitted instantaneously from any location on Earth to the Pentagon—these satellite systems enclosed the planet within a surveillance network and gave American generals the ability to "see" a "battlefield" as large as Korea, Iraq, or Afghanistan with fidelity, comprehension, and timeliness, day and night, in all sorts of weather.[15] These systems gather electronic and biometric data (gait, body markings, heartbeat, odor, etc.) and enter it into vast databases that can be accessed later to identify individual "bad guys" and target them for elimination.[16]

The Revolution in Computing has reshaped weapons, armed forces, and warfare, as well as changed the trinitarian relationship between the citizen, the army, and the state. Increasingly, weapons have been unmanned in order to permit armies to wage war without suffering casualties. In neoliberal states in general, and in the American neoliberal state in particular, the focus has been on the development and procurement of sophisticated, unmanned weapons and weapons systems utilizing all-weather "smart" bombs, known as Joint Direct Attack Munitions (JDAMs), to substitute for "boots on the ground." That is, to transfer as many of the risks of war to the enemy as possible by *actualizing violence from a distance* in such a way as to *reduce to a minimum* casualties to the armed forces of the American state.[17]

The most well-known unmanned weapon that actualizes violence at a distance is the *unmanned aerial vehicle* (UAV) or "drone." Originally designed for aerial surveillance and intelligence gathering, UAVs have been modified for killing the "enemy." Drones are remotely controlled by crews (a "pilot" and a sensor operator) sitting in padded chairs at consoles equipped with computer screens, keyboards, and joysticks in ground-control rooms thousands of miles away from the "battlefield." The environment is militarily risk-free for the "crew."

The most widely used UAVs are the medium altitude, long-endurance vehicles manufactured by General Atomics Aeronautical Systems: the MQ-1 Predator and the MQ-9B Reaper. The Predator, developed in the 1990s, provides intelligence, surveillance, and reconnaissance. It can fly at 45,000 feet and carry a 750-pound payload, usually two laser-guided Hellfire missiles. The MQ-9B Reaper is twice as large as the Predator and carries four times the payload, usually four laser-guided Hellfire anti-tank missiles and two JDAMs, the 510-pound GBU-12 or the 500-pound GBU-38. Northrop Grumman manufactures the Global Hawk UAV, which can fly at 65,000 feet, twice as high as the Predator and the Reaper, and can loiter for twenty-four hours over and make images of a geographic area the size of the state of Illinois (40,000 square nautical miles). The Global Hawk is completely autonomous. It can be programmed to take off, fly a programmed computer-controlled flight path, and land by itself. In addition, the United States armed forces have used many different handheld short-range UAVs (Pioneer, Shadow, Pointer, Flashlight, Pathfinder, Puma, Buster, Silver Fox, Swiper, and Raven) that are used by troops to look "over the hill" and "put eyes on the battlefield." There are about 11,000 drones in the United States UAV force, the majority of which are Ravens because they are simple to use. Ravens are used by the militaries of eighty-eight states, fifty-four of which manufacture their own.[18]

UAVs are not very fast, not very nimble, and lightly armed. Despite these shortcomings, they are powerful weapons because they

> can take off, land, and fly by themselves. The operators can program a destination or a desired patrol area and then concentrate on the details of the mission while the aircraft takes care of itself. Packed with sensors and sophisticated video technology, UAVs can see through clouds or in the dark. They can loiter for hours or even days over a target. . . . Of course, the most significant fact about drones is precisely that they do not have [on board] pilots.[19]

The Defense Advanced Research Projects Agency (DARPA) is working on nuclear-powered UAVs that can fly at 70,000 feet and stay in the air for months on end. DARPA is also working on UAVs with the agility and appearance of small birds. For example, the Nano Hummingbird contains a video camera and audio sensors, can fly forward, backward, and side to side, hover, and perch on power lines to capture audio and video undetected. Development has also begun on *fully autonomous* UAVs that rely on spectral signatures and biometric data to hunt, select, and destroy stationary or mobile targets *without human intervention.*[20]

Although UAVs have received the most attention in the press because of the legal and moral issues their use raises,[21] there are actually more *unmanned ground vehicles* (UGVs) being used by the armed forces of the American state than aerial vehicles. Mounted on treads or wheels, UGVs, such as the PackBot tactical robot built by iRobot and the TALON and SWORDS robots built by Foster-Miller, can detect and disarm IEDs; search and clear buildings, bunkers, caves, and tunnels; sniff chemical agents; localize gunfire and give azimuth, elevation, and range for return fire; and kill enemy combatants. UGVs are controlled remotely by military technicians using video-game-style consoles. QinetiQ North America has developed a larger, heavier version of the TALON/SWORDS UGV that is armed with an M240B 50-caliber machine gun and M203 grenade launcher, and carries 450 rounds of 50-caliber ammunition and four grenades. The camera and 50-caliber machine gun on this UGV can be perfectly synchronized so that its accuracy is 100 percent.[22]

Finally, DARPA is trying to develop a self-powered robotic suit, called an exoskeleton, that could enable soldiers to carry heavier loads, move much faster, and even jump over low buildings. The United States Navy is experimenting with an unmanned jet ski designed to intercept attackers trying to sneak up on American ships underwater, and an unmanned sailboat packed with high-tech surveillance equipment that can sail around the world. Unmanned remotely controlled submersibles (ARIES) are also being developed that could park themselves on the bottom of enemy harbors, observing the movement of ships in and out.

Electromagnetic weapons have been developed that can neutralize unexploded ordnance (Zeus), and laser weapons are being developed that are capable of shooting down cruise missiles, mortar rounds, and artillery shells while in flight. JDAMs already exist and have been used in combat, most recently and extensively in the First Persian Gulf War (August 1990–February 1991) and the combat phase of the Second Persian Gulf War (March–April 2003) and in Afghanistan (2001–2014). Other electromagnetic weapons can fry the electrical circuits of enemy aircraft and missiles. An Active Denial System, which emits electromagnetic waves that can cause an intense burning sensation, is being developed for crowd control as well as "electrical weapons that shock and stun; laser weapons that cause dizziness or temporary blindness; acoustic weapons that deafen and nauseate; chemical weapons that irritate, incapacitate, or sedate; projectile weapons that knock down, bruise, and disable; and an assortment of nets, foams, and sprays that obstruct or immobilize."[23]

So-called "cyber war" is also waged by the neoliberal state. Cyber war must be distinguished from *cyber espionage*, which is the "science of covertly capturing e-mail traffic, text messages, and other electronic communications, and corporate data for the purpose of gathering national-security or commercial intelligence." *Cyber war*, on the other hand, "involves the penetration of foreign networks for the purpose of disrupting or dismantling those networks, and making them inoperable."[24] In cyber war there is no instrumental act of violence (soldiers on battlefields firing rounds and rockets into enemy positions). Rather, "well-fed technicians [essentially, hackers in military uniforms] in air-conditioned rooms, operating in the safety of their home state . . . attack a facility in another state that is of a scale and effect as to constitute an armed attack."[25] Although non-violent, a cyber attack could lead to massive disruption and loss of life by activating so-called logic bombs that were pre-installed in . . . electricity grid[s]. Financial information on a massive scale could be lost. Derailments could crash trains. Air traffic systems and their backups could collapse, leaving hundreds of planes aloft without communications. Industrial control systems of highly sensitive plants, such as nuclear power stations, could be damaged, potentially leading to loss of cooling, meltdown, and contamination.[26]

Such an attack would be an act of war, and the state attacked would have the right to respond in self-defense, and not necessarily just by computer.

In 2010, the Pentagon created the United States Cyber Command (CYBERCOM) to protect American military computer networks from attack and to develop the ability to destroy enemy computer networks by burrowing into such systems anywhere in the world, where they would hide for years completely undetected, during which time a low and slow "data gathering paradigm" would operate. There is a professor of computer science and software engineering at the author's former university who has a classified grant from the Department of the Air Force to "adapt new protocols to fight known and future Internet intruders that could threaten everything from combat missions to mundane communications tasks."[27] The objective of such protocols is to "stealthily exfiltrate information."[28] CYBERCOM is training a cadre of "cyber warriors" for the cyber wars of the future. China, Russia, India, North Korea, and other states are also training cyber warriors for the same purpose.

Thus far, known cyber attacks can be counted on the fingers of one hand. The most violent of these, if it actually happened, took place in 1982. It is supposed that a malicious code was inserted, probably by the Central Intelligence Agency (CIA), into the programmable logic controllers of Russia's Urengoy-Surgut-Chelyabinsk oil pipeline. After a certain period of normal operation, the code reset the pumps, turbines, and valves to produce pressures far beyond those acceptable to pipeline joints and welds. This resulted in an explosion and fire large enough to have been observed from space. Data gathered by American air force satellites indicated that the explosion was the equivalent of the detonation of a three-kiloton atomic bomb.[29]

In 2007, the banking and government websites of one of the world's most connected states, Estonia, were attacked, presumably by Russian cyber warriors in response to the removal of a Soviet Second World War memorial of the Unknown Soldier from the center of the capital, Tallinn, to the outskirts of the city by the Estonian government.[30]

In August of 2008, Russia attacked the websites of the Georgian government and financial institutions at the start of the brief war between Russia and Georgia over South Ossetia. Georgia's prominent websites were defaced; two- to three-hour denial-of-service attacks were made against government, commercial, and news media websites; and malicious software was distributed via Russian-language forums in order to deepen and widen the number of attackers. As not much of Georgia's vital infrastructure is tied to the Internet, the attacks did little more than make some websites temporarily inaccessible, however.[31]

In 2010, it was revealed that the Israelis, probably with American help, attacked Iran's nuclear enrichment program at the Bushehr Nuclear Power Plant and the Natanz Nuclear Facility. This attack, known as "Stuxnet," is considered to be the most sophisticated known cyber attack to date. The cyber warriors were able to infect the logic controllers of the uranium enrichment centrifuges at these facilities, probably using a removable flash drive containing a "worm" that stealthily varied the rotation speeds of the electric motors that turned the centrifuges. Unnoticed by the operators, the slight variations in rotational speeds over several months slowly damaged many of the centrifuges and retarded Iran's enrichment program.[32]

Cyber espionage is much more common than cyber war, however. In 2003, it was revealed that Chinese hackers had gained access to fire-walled, but unclassified, networks at the United States Departments of Defense, State, and Homeland Security, as well as those of certain defense contractors. In 2008, spyware believed to have originated in Russia was unknowingly inserted through a flash drive at a base in the Middle East that penetrated at least one American classified military computer network. In March 2009, computer scientists at the University of Toronto discovered "GhosNet," an international spying operation, probably of Chinese origin, that was able to take control of the computers in embassies, ministries of foreign affairs, and international organizations in 103 states. In January 2011, the information technology system in the British Foreign Office was penetrated by a foreign intelligence agency.[33] In 2014, the Sony Pictures Entertainment computer network was attacked, presumably by North Korean hackers, in an attempt to stop the release of the film *The Interview*, a ribald, raunchy, political comedy that depicts the attempted assassination of the North Korean leader, Kim Jong-un (1983–), by an American television personality and his producer.

Cyber attacks do not always come from a state. Attempts by the American state to silence WikiLeaks after it released 250,000 classified State Department cables in 2010 brought forth a popular uprising among hundreds of thousands of tech-savvy leaderless Internet "hacktivists," known as "Anonymous." Hacktivists conceal their identities and unite in favor of free speech and against censorship. Anonymous has targeted the Church of Scientology and the HBGary technology security company.[34] In 2008, it launched "Operation Avenge Assange," referring to WikiLeaks founder Julian Assange (1971–), and temporarily brought down the websites of credit card giants MasterCard and Visa, as well as PayPal and Amazon, in retribution for their withdrawal of services to WikiLeaks, owing to intense pressure from the American state.[35] After the terrorist attacks in Paris on November 15 in which 129 people were killed, Anonymous declared online war on the Islamic State of Syria and the Levant (ISIL), which claimed responsibility. Cyber attacks by Anonymous have brought down ISIL-related websites and exposed Twitter accounts used by ISIL supporters.

Finally, the "relentless march of technoscience" is bringing to the fore "human-machine weapons systems," or "cyborg soldiers."[36] For example, using nanotechnology, the Massachusetts Institute of Technology (MIT) is developing a combat uniform with tiny wires embedded in it to keep the wearer "connected" 24/7 to his or her unit. The helmet would receive and send video, audio, and text messages. The wearer would have night-vision capability, a GPS system, and a laser finder. The suit's sensors could adjust its camouflage to make the wearer "invisible" as his or her surroundings change. The suit could be made as strong as Kevlar.[37]

The composition of the armed forces, military culture, and the relationship between the armed forces and the people are being profoundly changed by unmanned weapons and weapons systems and the technology needed to support them. The shift from industrial-era conventional warfare to information-age unmanned warfare has *civilianized the military and joined war to civilian life in a manner reminiscent of the pre-industrial age.* The line between the military and civilian worlds is blurring. Increasingly, the military is becoming more and more an "occupational" military, which is less and less distinguishable from civilian institutions and more and more being "brought under the same standards as consumerist civil society."[38] In the neoliberal state, service in the military is seen as another way to get ahead rather than as doing one's patriotic or civic duty.

Unmanned weapons make the training of military personnel more and more a matter of developing technical expertise and managerial skills and less and less about learning combat skills and battlefield survival; that is, training has moved "from soldiering to weapons system maintenance."[39] Military uniforms have become less military and more civilian in appearance. Unmanned weapons "flatten" the hierarchical nature of the military command structure by collapsing the professional distance between officers, who give orders, and enlisted personnel who carry them out. They have changed the tradition of "heroic leadership" by single individuals to a new form of team leadership. Instead of officers making decisions, telling soldiers what to do, and leading them in the doing of it, "teams" of soldiers are given problems to solve and not told how to solve them. The team is expected to come up with the solution itself.[40] Unmanned weapons make it possible to increase the number of women in the military who are increasingly able to move from support to "combat" military occupational specialties (MOSs). Unmanned weapons change the ratio of technicians to those doing the actual fighting significantly because they require the support of vast numbers of military and civilian information technologists to do the "planning, scheduling, monitoring, scanning, collating, translating, geolocating, data-pulling, processing, formatting, chatting, and briefing"[41] necessary to make digital, unmanned war.

As a consequence of the increasingly occupational nature of the armed forces, many American women are fighting hard to take their place in the military on equal terms with men. Their success is indicated by the increasing numbers of women in the armed forces and the increasing number of women into MOSs from which they were hitherto barred. The presence of large numbers of women in the armed forces has challenged and demanded changes in the misogynistic, hyper-masculine subculture of the military built up over the two and a quarter centuries since the advent of the institutionalized armed forces separate from civilian society.

As more and more women have volunteered for military service and entered combat MOSs, the numbers of sexual assaults by male soldiers has increased substantially over previous years when women were few in number and relegated to serving in non-combat MOSs, such as nursing and administration. It is well known that sexual assault is about power, not sex; therefore, sexual assault in the military can be understood as a form of resistance by men against the feminization of what has been historically an all-male preserve separate from civilian society, which many men in the military believe is necessary for an effective defense. This way of thinking is especially prevalent in the United States Army and Marine Corps.

Recently, certain members of Congress have attempted to pass legislation that would bring the American military's unique legal system (the Uniform Code of Military Justice [UCMJ]), in alignment with civilian law, which does not permit bosses (i.e., commanding officers) to decide if a female employee (i.e., a female soldier) was sexually assaulted or not. In 2014, Senator Kirsten Gillibrand (D-New York) introduced a bill in Congress that, if it had become law, would have shifted the responsibility for prosecuting sexual assault cases from commanding officers to a prosecutor outside of the chain of command. The bill failed to pass, not because those who voted against it do not want to see women in the military or harbor sexist ideas about sexual assault, but, rather, because it would have forced much broader changes in the Second World War–era UCMJ and disrupted the command structure of the armed forces.

Since the end of the Cold War, the United States and other neoliberal states have moved from the classical form of labor-intensive military organization to a post-modern, civilianized form. In the current era, all states are seeking to transform their armed forces

> of conscripted lower ranks or militia and a professional officer corps, war-oriented in mission, masculine in makeup and ethos, and sharply differentiated in structure and culture from civilian society [into a] postmodern military, by contrast, [which] undergoes a loosening of the ties with the nation-state. The

basic format shifts toward a volunteer force, more multipurpose in mission, increasingly androgynous in make up and ethos, and with greater permeability with civilian society. [42]

Therefore, since the end of the Cold War, the armed forces of the neoliberal state increasingly have the following characteristics: first, an increasing interpenetration of civilian and military sectors of society, structurally and culturally; second, a diminution of differences within the armed forces based on branch of service, rank, and combat versus support MOSs; third, a change in the basic purpose of the military from fighting inter-state wars to what the Pentagon calls "Military Operations Other Than War" (MOOTW), such as interdicting drug traffickers, killing terrorists, arresting war criminals, or providing humanitarian assistance; fourth, an increasing deployment of military forces in international peacekeeping missions authorized and/or legitimated by entities beyond the state, in particular the United Nations; and fifth, the internationalization of the military forces of certain states, such as the European Eurocorps and the binational divisions of the North Atlantic Treaty Organization (NATO) states. [43]

The advent of unmanned weapons has brought a metamorphosis of war from modern war to postmodern war. The armed forces of the neoliberal state still seek to defeat the "enemy," but they define the enemy differently than was the case during the era of the managerial welfare state, and they fight the enemy in a different way. Owing to the fact that the Cold War has ended and major inter-state war is waning, the armed forces of the neoliberal state no longer prepare to fight other states, except in a few places such as on the Korean peninsula. Instead, its armed force is directed at terrorist networks and armed movements within states, and the like.

The neoliberal state seeks to kill only individual armed combatants, usually called "terrorists" or "bad guys," using high-tech, unmanned weaponry. It seeks to kill as many terrorists and bad guys as possible without collateral damage (unintended civilian casualties), while avoiding as much as possible the deaths of its own soldiers. Martin Shaw calls postmodern war *risk-transfer war*, which he says operates according to the following rules:

1. Wars must respond to plausible perceptions of risk to Western interest, norms, and values;
2. Wars must be limited in the risks they create for Western polities, economies, and societies;
3. Wars are exercises in political risk-taking, therefore they must minimize electoral risks for governments and (if possible) maximize their gains;
4. Wars must anticipate the problems of global surveillance;
5. Wars must be strictly time-limited;

6. Wars must be limited spatially to distant zones of war;
7. Wars must, above all, minimize casualties to Western troops;
8. Western forces should rely heavily on airpower and look to others—as far as possible—to take risks on the ground;
9. The enemy must be killed: efficiently, quickly, discreetly;
10. Risks of "accidental" civilian casualties (collateral damage) must be minimized, but small massacres must be regarded as inevitable;
11. Wars must be fought with "precision" weaponry to sustain their legitimacy;
12. Suffering and death must be unseen: indirect, less visible, and less quantifiable life-risks are more acceptable;
13. Longer-term post-war risks must be spread as widely as possible through an international division of labor;
14. "Humanitarianism" and "humanitarian" organizations must be annexed to compensate for violence against civilians; and
15. Media management is essential: it maintains the narratives that explain the images of war.[44]

The advent of unmanned, risk-transfer war has changed the people's connection to its military and to war in fundamental ways. Increasingly, the people in the neoliberal state are spectators *of* war not participants *in* war. Unmanned risk-transfer wars are media events, not qualitatively different from the Super Bowl or the Olympic Games, and the people are now "the equivalent of sports fans watching war, rather than citizens sharing in its importance."[45]

James Der Derian contends that unmanned risk-transfer war has elevated war morally in neoliberal states by making it not only virtual but virtuous. He writes, "War is ascending to an even 'higher' plane, from the virtual to the *virtuous*. . . . At the heart of virtuous war is the technical capability and ethical imperative to threaten and, if necessary, actualize violence from a distance—*with no or minimum casualties.*"[46] Christopher Coker says that cybernetics has profoundly changed the way that war is thought about and fought in neoliberal states. Cybernetics has reversed the deep skepticism toward all organized violence that developed in the wake of the Second World War and has "re-enchanted" war in the neoliberal state because it permits deadly combat with no risk and optimal destruction.[47]

Moreover, war is being rejoined with normal life in the way that it recruits military personnel and trains them. Roger Stahl has argued that war-themed video games and personal computer simulations, for example, are being produced by the Pentagon and commercial game makers to recruit and train military personnel. Games such as *Full Spectrum Warrior*, *Close Combat: First to Fight*, *Doom*, *Conflict: Desert Storm*, *Splinter Cell*, *Rainbow Six*, *Ghost Recon*, *Raven Shield*, and *Command and Conquer: Generals* code war as an object of consumer play. In the process, such games transform the players of these games, the vast majority of whom are teenage boys and young men, into *"virtual citizen-soldiers."* They also merge the "home front" with the virtual "battle front." When recruited by the armed forces, these virtual citizen-soldiers will have undergone, not unlike medieval knights, the required apprenticeship during boyhood to become "warriors" of unmanned, risk-transfer cyber war.[48]

THE NEOLIBERAL STATE

Unmanned war changed the relationship of the people to the army and state by opening up a "political space which has been successfully occupied by 'anti-statist' forces of the right."[49] As was shown in previous chapters, conventional mechanized war drove European states to become more managerial with respect to their economies and societies. Gradually, during the first half of the twentieth century, states increasingly became managerial welfare states that provided a "dense tissue of social benefits and economic strategies in which it was the state that served its subjects, rather than the other way round."[50]

After the Second World War it came to be widely believed in Europe and other regions of the world that the state could always do a better job providing social justice, distributing goods and services, applying strategies for social cohesion, and creating cultural vitality than would be the case if such matters were left to the enlightened self-interest of the individual citizen and the workings of the market mechanism. The state had become

> a good thing; and there was lots of it. Between 1950 and 1973, government spending rose from 27.6 percent to 38.8 percent of the gross domestic product in France, from 30.4 to 42 percent in West Germany, from 34.2 percent to 41.5 percent in the Netherlands. . . . The overwhelming bulk of the increase in spending went on insurance, pensions, health, education and housing. In Scandinavia the share of national income devoted to social security alone rose 250 percent in Denmark and Sweden between 1950 and 1973. In Norway, it tripled. Only in Switzerland was the share of post-war GNP [gross national product] spent by the state kept comparatively low (it did not reach 30 percent until 1980), but even there it stood in dramatic contrast to the 1938 figure of just 6.8 percent.[51]

European managerial welfare states were

> responsible, directly or indirectly, for the employment and remuneration of millions of men and women who thus had a vested interest in it, whether as professionals or bureaucrats. Graduates from the . . . [states' most prestigious universities] typically sought employment not in [the private sector] . . . much

> less industry and commerce, but in education, medicine, the social services, public law, state monopolies, or government service. . . . The European state had forged a unique market for the goods and services it could provide. It formed a virtuous circle of employment and influence that attracted near-universal appreciation. . . . Faith in the state—as planner, coordinator, facilitator, arbiter, provider, caretaker, and guardian—was widespread and *crossed all political divides.*[52]

Although the political right has always resisted the welfare portion of the managerial welfare state, it acquiesced to it because it understood that welfare programs were necessary to reward the people for their contribution to and sacrifice for the defense of the state. After the Second World War, power in Europe "shifted from warrior elites to merchants and manufacturers" and Europeans constructed "civilian states [that] were organized for peace, not war; in them social change was translated into economic production, not battle potential."[53] By disconnecting the people from war, the state became less managerial and the welfare programs of the state put in place after the Second World War as payment for the great sacrifices made by the people in defense of the state came under challenge by conservatives and libertarians.

By the 1980s, these attacks began to become "most evident at the core of the Anglosphere—in Britain under Margaret Thatcher . . . and in the United States under Ronald Reagan."[54] Margaret Thatcher (1925–2013), a grocer's daughter, began to blame Britain's economic malaise and decline as a world power on British welfare programs. During her years as prime minister (1979–1990), Thatcher successfully reduced the power of Britain's labor unions, privatized public housing, sold off nationalized (i.e., state-owned) industries, eliminated social programs, and replaced the Keynesian approach to the management of the economy and began to rely on the market mechanism to distribute goods and services. By the end of her time in office, Britain had been transformed into a neoliberal state.

In 1980, President Ronald Reagan (1911–2004), an actor and former pitchman for the General Electric Corporation, was elected on a similar anti-welfare state agenda. During the eight years of his presidency, he was able to put the anti-big government/anti-welfare agenda so firmly in place that all subsequent presidents, Democrat and Republican, have followed suit. The only exception has been President Barack Obama (1961–), who was able to make medical insurance available for millions of Americans by getting the Affordable Care Act passed by Congress, despite a vicious anti-Obama campaign waged by the Republican party, especially its Tea Party faction. The efforts to overturn "Obamacare" have not stopped, and it is probably a matter of time before they are successful, given the absence of inter-state war and the need for social programs to ensure the loyalty of the people and payment for their service in war.

The success of the neoliberal right was also made possible by the withdrawal of the Soviet Union from Eastern Europe in 1989 and, in 1991, its collapse as a unified state, which ended the Cold War. America's primary military threat had disappeared, and its successor, the Russian Federation, became increasingly a neoliberal state itself, although with strong authoritarian impulses. Subsequently, the anti-welfare agenda articulated by Thatcher and Reagan began to spread from and be spread by the United States and European states to the states of Eastern Europe, and beyond, to states in Asia, Latin America, and even Africa as rightist parties, which promised lower taxes, less state intervention, and greater prosperity, won elections with American help and came to power. Since then, neoliberal theory and practice, which has come to be known as the "Washington Consensus," has become the dominant ideology in the current global order and the neoliberal state the only acceptable form of the state within that order.[55] States that do not conform to this form of the state (North Korea, Iran, Myanmar, and Cuba, for example) are under heavy pressure to do so.

In the neoliberal state the relationship of the people to the armed forces and the state has been reconfigured because unmanned weapons have reduced to a minimum the *demands the state needs to make on its people in order to make war* against the entities the national security elites define as enemies of the state. War-making continues to be the exclusive concern of national security elites rather than of the people as a whole. The national security apparatus of the neoliberal state is like "a severed head continuing to function automatically, conducting its intercourse with other severed heads according to its own laws."[56]

In the neoliberal state, conscripted mass-reserve armies employing mass-produced industrialized weapons are replaced by small all-volunteer armed forces employing very lethal unmanned weapons. In the neoliberal state, national defense is no longer every citizen's duty. In the neoliberal state, war-making is a matter for national security elites, soldiers, civilian contractors, and technicians (male and female) who are paid to assume the relatively low risks to life and limb and bear the burdens, such as they are, that come with their jobs, not unlike police officers and firefighters. In the neoliberal state, the sharp and clear line that used to exist between the military and civilian worlds becomes increasingly indistinct. In the neoliberal state, the military becomes less and less masculine and more and more androgynous in makeup and ethos. In the neoliberal state, there is an increasing penetration of civilian values and habits into the armed forces. In the neoliberal state, military personnel are rarely seen in uniform and the uniforms they wear have become increasingly less military and more civilian in appearance, not unlike those of the police, firefighters, bus drivers, letter carriers, and train conductors. In the neoliberal state, monuments are built to the victims of war, human and animal, not to its military heroes.[57] In the neoliberal state, citizens are spectators of, not participants in, war.

Unlike the managerial welfare state that undertakes the task of maintaining and improving the health and material well-being of the people, the neoliberal state "promises instead to maximize the opportunity of the people and thus tends to privatize many state activities and to make voting and representative government less influential and more responsive to the market."[58] The neoliberal state

> depends on the international capital markets and, to a lesser degree, on the modern multinational business network to create stability in the world economy, in preference to management by national or transnational political bodies. Its political institutions are less representative (though in some ways more democratic) than those of the nation-state. . . . Like the nation-state, the [civilianized neoliberal] state assesses its economic success or failure by its society's ability to secure more and better goods and services, but in contrast to the nation-state it does not see the State as more than a minimal provider or distributor. Whereas the nation-state justified itself as an instrument to serve the welfare of the people (the nation), the [neoliberal] state exists to maximize the opportunities enjoyed by all members of society. For the nation-state, a national currency is a medium of exchange; for the [civilianized neoliberal] state it is only one more commodity. Much the same may be said of jobs: for the nation-state, full employment is an important and often paramount goal, whereas for the [civilianized neoliberal] state, the actual numbers of persons employed is but one more variable in the production of economic opportunity and has no overriding significance.[59]

In addition, the neoliberal state pursues its objectives by incentives and sometimes draconian penalties, rather than impartial rules and regulations. The neoliberal state is indifferent to matters of justice. It does not champion particular ethnicities or cultural values. The neoliberal state replaces state managerialism with the market mechanism to allocate private goods and services and, increasingly, "public" goods. In the neoliberal state the people are transformed from citizens into consumers. The neoliberal state deemphasizes the programmatic and legal aspects of governance and emphasizes electoral competition (e.g., who's winning, who's losing, who's up, who's down, etc.), not policies. Above all, the neoliberal state is presented as a mechanism for "enhancing opportunity," for "creating possibilities." This does not mean making sure that no one becomes poor. It means opening opportunities to maximize the growth of personal wealth generally. Redistribution of wealth is not a concern of the neoliberal state. The neoliberal state is an enabler and umpire, not a provider.[60] Welfare programs, to the extent that they exist in the neoliberal state, are seen as temporary "safety nets" for those who fail to prosper.

In the neoliberal state, government is weakened because it has devolved its authority to other institutions, such as churches and corporations, and because it has contracted out and privatized many traditional state responsibilities, such as running prisons, educating children, and fighting wars. In the neoliberal state, the military becomes a tangled mass of soldiers, civilian information technologists, and private contractors.

As the neoliberal state does not need its citizens for its military defense, could not rely on its citizens' sense of patriotic duty if it needed them, or demand military service by conscripting them to fill the ranks of its armed forces, it has brought back the age-old practice of recruiting the dregs of society (ex-cons, the physically and mentally unfit), children,[61] and the "troubled, truant, tattooed ranks of the population"[62] to fill the ranks of its armed forces.

As the armed forces of the neoliberal state have become all-volunteer and narrowly recruited, they have increasingly become less representative of the people of the state in terms of religious affiliation, race, class, and education. For example, while the American military is officially neutral with respect to religion, its personnel have increasingly become more and more religiously fundamentalist than the general population because of changes made during the waning years of the Reagan administration to regulations pertaining to recruitment of chaplains for the armed forces. Before these changes, chaplains were recruited from the mainline Protestant denominations (Presbyterians, Methodists, Lutherans, Episcopalians, etc.) and priests from the Catholic Church in rough proportion to the numbers of each denomination in the armed forces, and they were required to minister to troops of all faiths. The new regulations stopped making distinctions among Protestant denominations and lumped them together as "Protestant." At the same time, the

> Pentagon began crediting hundreds of evangelical and Pentecostal "endorsing agencies," allowing graduates of fundamentalist Bible colleges—which often train clergy to view those from other faiths as enemies of Christ—to fill up nearly the entire allotment for Protestant chaplains. Today, more than two-thirds of the military's 2,900 active-duty chaplains are affiliated with evangelical or Pentecostal denominations.[63]

Many of these chaplains are, essentially, undercover missionaries for Christian fundamentalists who seek to transform the secular American armed forces into a Christian missionary organization to the world. Groups like the Officers' Christian Fellowship and the Campus Crusade for Christ's Military Ministry have an excessive influence on many military bases. Ending mandatory military ceremonies with Christian prayers, holding official military retreats at off-base churches, appearing in uniform at religious events, displaying crucifixes in military chapels, and dipping the American flag at the altar in the Naval Academy chapel are indications of improper religious influence that has begun to permeate the American armed forces. [64]

The same problem has appeared in the Israeli Defense Forces (IDF). In the early years of the Israeli state, religious young people were a small percentage of the IDF, which was dominated by secular Ashkenazi (Jews of European extraction), and its elite battalions were dominated by soldiers raised on *kibbutzim* (collective agricultural communities). As the Israeli economy has become more developed and high-tech, many young people from Ashkenazi backgrounds no longer want to serve in elite units or become officers. Their places are being taken by new groups of immigrants and religious soldiers who have gravitated to infantry battalions in which they not only serve but also lead. Some 30 percent of the officer corps are openly orthodox, and about 50 percent of the enlisted ranks of the IDF are religious. As a result, religious soldiers now see themselves as leading the Israeli army. Increasingly, the IDF is becoming a bastion of the Israeli religious right. [65]

In addition to its narrowly recruited all-volunteer armed forces, the neoliberal state outsources much of its war-making function to companies from the global private military industry: (1) combat arms companies, (2) combat security companies, and (3) combat general contractors. *Combat arms companies*, commonly known as private military companies (PMCs), such as Executive Outcomes (now dissolved), Sandline International, Sterling Corporate Services, Blackwater/Academi, DynCorp International, and Triple Canopy, receive government contracts to deploy military units to engage and defeat the enemy and achieve wartime objectives, such as force projection, offensive and defensive operations, reconnaissance, and special operations. *Combat security companies*, such as the Titan Corporation, the Lincoln Group, Total Intelligence Solutions, and SAIC, receive government contracts to establish and manage command-and-control and communications operations in combat environments, collect intelligence, develop threat analyses, plan and disseminate propaganda, and engage in cyber-warfare. *Combat general contractors*, such as DynCorp International, Swift Global Logistics, SOS International, and ITT Corporation, equip and supply soldiers and civilians in the field with food, water, ammunition, and various types of equipment; maintain equipment; transport personnel, equipment, and supplies; and construct military bases. [66]

Although the individuals who manage and staff these companies are drawn from all over the world, they tend to come from among retired and former American, British, French, South African, and Australian military personnel, who need the work, wish to supplement their retirement pay, or seek the excitement of combat. Once called "mercenaries" or "soldiers of fortune," such individuals are now called "military contractors" because the use of mercenary troops is prohibited by the United Nations Mercenary Convention (2001). For the same reason, the firms that recruit and employ them are called private security companies (PSCs), private military companies (PMCs), and private security providers (PSPs).[67] The largest private military companies are publicly traded on world stock exchanges.

In addition to private military contractors, neoliberal states use private contractors to recruit and hire thousands of third-country nationals (TCNs) from the world's poorest states to work on bases in war zones as cooks, cleaners, fast-food clerks, electricians, and beauticians. The recruitment, transportation, and working conditions of some TCNs by some contractors has been likened to human trafficking because of widespread abuses, including the illegal confiscation of workers' passports, deceptive hiring practices, excessive recruiting fees, and substandard working conditions.[68]

The American state employed an estimated 180 private military contractors in Iraq to secure American bases and supply routes, protect American officials, and train Iraqi security forces. They were not subject to government oversight, military authority, or Iraqi law. They maintained thousands of armed men under secret command. Like military recruiters, private military contractors entice new hires with promises of adventure and the chance to "democratize" the world.[69]

Thus, the neoliberal state, in which there is a greatly diminished direct involvement of the people in war and increased use of private military contractors, can be seen as a return to the practices of the centuries before the French Revolution when war was fought without the direct participation of the people. Some scholars characterize the rise of the private military industry as "neomedievalism," by which they do not mean a literal return to the medieval period but a *restoration* in the contemporary global order of the kind of private war that was characteristic of the Middle Ages in Europe before the kingly state monopolized military force and made war a public matter.[70] What this means for the state, armed force, and the people in today's world will be discussed in chapter 9.

A CIVILIANIZED NEOLIBERAL STATE

There are many examples of neoliberal states in the current states system. This section presents only one case, that of Japan, because its transformation from a militarized warfare state into a neoliberal state has been more thoroughgoing than any other example that could be chosen, except, perhaps, that of Prussia/Germany. What follows is a history of the way that war first transformed the Japanese feudal state into a militarized Western-style state and then into a neoliberal state and mainstay of the current neoliberal global economic order.

Japan: From a Feudal State to a Civilianized Pacifist Neoliberal State

The Japanese archipelago consists of four main islands: Honshu, the largest; Kyushu and Shikoku to the south; and Hokkaido to the north, as well as thousands of smaller islands. The history of Japanese state-making on these islands can be divided into three broad periods.[71] The first is the period of indigenous war-driven state-making from roughly 300 to 1867 CE, during which time feudal entropy was gradually overcome and a strong centralized state created. The second is the period of reflexive state-making from 1867 to 1945, during which time Japan transformed itself from a weak feudal state into a powerful Western-style state. The third is the period of demilitarization and civilianization of the Japanese state by the Allies after Japan's defeat in the Second World War and its transformation into a major civilianized neo-liberal state.

Historians usually date the beginning of the Japanese centralized feudal state from the "old tomb" or Kofun period (300–710 CE) when horse-riding aristocratic warriors established themselves on the Japanese archipelago. These warriors wore armor, carried swords, and used the military tactics of Northeast Asia. Kofun society was clan-based. Each clan was headed by a patriarch who was to see to the long-term welfare of the clan. War among them was incessant. Gradually, one clan (the Yamato) was able to suppress the others and established a court in Asuka (near present-day Nara) and established a centralized administration based on the Chinese model as well as Chinese-based fiscal policies. The Yamato clan ruled over other clans by bestowing titles on rival clan patriarchs and acquiring agricultural lands.

War among three important clans—the Soga, the Nakatomi, and the Mononobe—raged for a century until the Soga clan emerged ascendant. The Soga intermarried with the imperial family. Soga Umako (551–626 CE), the clan's patriarch, was powerful enough to install his nephew as emperor and later assassinate him and replace him with Empress Suiko (554–628 CE). Suiko, the first of eight empresses, was a figurehead for Prince Regent Sho-toku Taishi (474–622 CE), who was a devout Buddhist and had been strongly influenced by Chinese Confucianism. During his regency Confucian ideas of rank and etiquette were introduced into Japan. He also introduced the Chi-nese calendar, developed a system of roads, built many Buddhist temples, and established relations with China. Official missions were sent to China in the seventh century. Shotoku came to see himself as the equal of the Chinese emperor, which was resented by the Chinese.

After his death in 622, and the death of Empress Suiko in 628, palace intrigues and the threat of invasion by China led Prince Naka to seize control of the court from the Soga family. Prince Naka issued the Taika Reform (meaning Great Change), the purpose of which was to centralize the state and end the system of landholding by the great clans and their control over the people living on them. Hereditary right to land was revoked; taxes were levied on silk and cotton cloth; a corvée (forced labor system) was set up for military conscription and building public works; three ministries were established to advise the throne, the minister of the left, minister of the right, and minister of the center, or chancellor; the realm was divided into provinces and the provinces into districts and villages. Prince Naka assumed the post of minister of the center. During the Naka period, Japan began referring to itself as Nippon or Nihon (Japan). In 662 Naka took the throne himself as Emperor Tenji and assumed the title "Heavenly Sovereign" to emphasize the divine origins of the imperial family and to raise it above the power struggles of the court. Naka's reforms were consolidated in 701 with several additional codes that established a Confucian-model penal system that used light not harsh punishments; a Chinese-style civil service examination system; and additional government ministries (administration, state, imperial household, justice, military affairs, treasury, and people's affairs).

In 710 CE a permanent imperial capital was established at Heijokyo, or Nara, after which economic and administrative development quickened. Roads were built from Nara to provincial capitals, taxes were collected on a routine basis, and coins were minted. Despite reforms, factional fighting continued within the imperial court. By the late 800s, the financial burdens of the court increased beyond the revenues of the treasury, and district governors were allowed to establish private militias and authority was decentralized. In an effort to return control to the center, Emperor Kammu (737–806) moved the capital to Nagaoka and then to Heiankyo (Kyoto) in 794, where it remained for the next thousand years. Having the capital in one place for so long a period of time consolidated the authority of the emperor.

Nonetheless, after Kammu's death succession struggles ensued and the Fujiwara family rose to prominence. During the reign of Emperor Daigo (897–930), however, imperial authority was temporarily reestablished. Soon after Daigo's death the Fujiwara clan regained control of the imperial court, governed Japan, and decided such matters as succession to the imperial throne. Private family matters and public functions were thoroughly intertwined. Essentially, clan solidarity was stronger than the centripetal pull of the imperial throne. This was because clans held *shoen* (estates) from which they derived the wealth necessary to build military force.

Gradually, military service became central to the aristocratic way of life and aristocrats were transformed into military elite based on a code of conduct called *bushido*, which emphasized good deeds, bravery in battle, and unswerving loyalty to one's lord. The most powerful of the aristocratic *samurai* families was given the title *shogun* by the emperor. *Shoguns* were both stewards and constables of the empire. Wars for the shogunate among the major aristocratic families, such as the Fujiwara, Taira, and Minamoto clans,

were many and bloody. During these centuries, the imperial power was limited to ceremonial functions, while administrative, judicial, and military affairs
were controlled by *samurai* aristocrats, the most powerful of whom became
the de facto ruler of Japan. Japan was essentially a feudal society, not unlike
that of Europe during the Middle Ages. Both had land-based economies, the
vestiges of a previously centralized state, and the concentration of military
force in the hands of a specialized fighting class.

In 1274, Japan was attacked by a powerful Mongol army, which was
defeated not by superior Japanese military force but by the forces of nature.
Two fortuitous typhoons destroyed the Mongol invading fleet. The invasion
and defeat of the Mongols had a lasting impression on the Japanese. It reinforced long-standing fears of invasion from China and imparted to the *samurai* a sense of martial superiority that remained with them until Japan's defeat
in the Second World War.

The Mongol invasion was a drain on the economy, and taxes had to be
raised to pay for it and to make defensive preparations against future invasions. This led to disaffection among those who expected recompense for
their help in defeating the Mongols, but there were no lands to be given.
Chaos ensued. An arrangement was worked out whereby two contending
imperial lines—known as the Southern Court and the Northern Court—alter-
nated on the throne. This worked well for a time until one emperor decided to
name his own son heir rather than turn the throne over to the other line. A
war that lasted from 1336 until 1339 broke out between the Southern and
Northern Courts for control of the imperial throne. The Northern Court won
the war and patriarchs of the Ashikaga clan were made *shogun*. Although the
third *shogun* of this clan, Yoshimitsu (1358–1408), was able to reunify the
Southern and Northern Courts, regional rulers, known as *daimyo*, become too
strong, which gradually undermined the central authority of the shogunate.

During the Yoshimitsu shogunate, central authority ceased to exist. A ten-
year-long war broke out among the *daimyo*, called the Onin War
(1467–1477), for control of Japan. This "warring states" phase of Japan's
history stimulated the growth and development of infrastructure as roads
were built and mines opened for military purposes. It also stimulated the
construction of walled castles and fortified towns. Emphasis was put on
success in war, estate management, and finance. Aristocratic society became
increasingly military in character.

Between 1560 and 1600 three powerful *daimyo*—Oda Nobunaga
(1534–1582), Toyotomi Hideyoshi (1536–1598), and Tokugawa Ieyasu
(1542–1616)—arose in succession and took strong military actions that finally united Japan. Nobunaga defeated another overlord's attempt to capture
Kyoto and, in 1568, marched on the capital himself and gained control of the
central government. By 1573 he defeated local *daimyo* and the last Ashikaga
shoguns. He built a new stone-walled castle capable of withstanding cannon

fire at Azuchi (the arrival of the Portuguese in 1543, the Spanish in 1587, and the Dutch in 1609 had introduced western muskets and cannon into Japan), which became the symbol of a unified Japan. He gained control through large-scale warfare, systematic administrative practices, and regularized tax collection. He also stimulated economic development by breaking down barriers to trade and establishing standardized weights and measures.

In 1577, Nobunaga sent his chief general, Toyotomi Hideyoshi, to subdue western Honshu. During the war Nobunaga led an army to assist Hideyoshi in the campaign but died in the attack on Kyoto in 1582. Hideyoshi defeated the forces of Akechi Mitsuhide, the warlord responsible for Nobunaga's death, and became the undisputed successor to his late overlord. He made an alliance with the major *daimyo* and continued the war of reunification in Shikoku and northern Kyushu. In 1590, with an army of 200,000, he defeated his last main rival. The remaining *daimyo* capitulated and all of Japan came under the control of Hideyoshi directly or indirectly through his vassals. In 1577 he seized the port city of Nagasaki, which was Japan's major point of contact with the outside world. Hideyoshi invaded the Korean peninsula in 1592 in an attempt to conquer China. He was defeated by a combined Korean and Chinese army, however.

Upon Hideyoshi's death in 1598, Tokugawa Ieyasu, already a rich and powerful *daimyo*, seized control of the Toyotomi family's holdings and made war on and unsubdued lesser vassals. In 1600, he achieved a significant military victory at Sekigahara over them and was able to establish himself as the shogun of the Japanese islands. The Tokugawa family ruled the Japanese archipelago as military governors from its castle at Edo (modern-day Tokyo) from 1603 until 1867. During the Tokugawa period Japan was stable and relatively peaceful. The government had been centralized and was administered through a large bureaucracy. The Tokugawa shoguns controlled the emperor.

The period of reflexive state-making began during the Tokugawa shogunate after Europeans arrived in the sixteenth century. Initially, contact between Japanese and Europeans, principally the Portuguese, who arrived in Japan in 1543, was forbidden, except for carefully regulated trade through the port of Nagasaki. The Tokugawa shogunate's policy of isolation was based, first, on the fear that Christianity, which had been introduced to Japan by Portuguese Jesuit missionaries, would spread and subvert traditional Japanese religions, Buddhism and Shintoism; and, second, on the fear that certain of the shogun's vassals could become powerful enough to challenge the Tokugawa family's dominance if they had access to European military technology. The isolationist strategy succeeded until the middle of the nineteenth century, because contact between Japan and Western states was intermittent.

After the arrival of the American Commodore Matthew Perry (1794–1856) in 1852, however, contact became more regular, which changed

Japan's external threat environment significantly. Increasingly, Japan found itself under great pressure by Western states, such as Britain, France, and Russia, as well as the United States, that desired to enter the archipelago, by force if necessary. Faced with the superior military technology of the Europeans, the thirteenth Tokugawa shogun, Iesada (1824–1858), capitulated and signed unequal treaties with Russia, Britain, France, and the Netherlands, which regulated trade and diplomatic relations through the port of Nagasaki. For this capitulation the Tokugawa shogunate was castigated by young *samurai* from feudal domains historically hostile to its rule, certain nobles at court, and wealthy merchants, who were concerned about foreign encroachment. The Emperor Komei (1831–1867) sided with the challengers and began to assert himself and regain the power and authority lost to the Tokagawa clan.

Upon Komei's death in 1867, his son, crown prince Mutsuhito, assumed the imperial throne as Meiji (Enlightened Ruler). Emperor Meiji (1852–1912), like his father, recognized the need for Japan to transform itself into a Western-style state by emulating European politico-military practices so as to be able to resist the Western challenge to Japan's independence. He adopted Western attire, ate Western-style food, and took the "Charter Oath of Five Principles," which put Japan on course to become a European-style state.

The young *samurai* who led the Meiji Restoration also realized that Japan's survival as an independent state against the European threat depended upon eliminating Japan's feudal military system and replacing it with a Western-style army. Therefore, Japanese elites worked to build a well-trained army and navy equipped with European weapons supported by an industrial economy and an educated, loyal, and patriotic population. Soon after the Meiji Restoration, Japan's new elite began to invite Western experts to Japan to teach the people European military and industrial techniques. At the same time, Japanese students were sent to Europe and the United States on "learning missions" to acquire Western scientific and engineering knowledge. Railroads were built and a telegraph system was created. Factories were set up and strategic industries were subsidized by the state. Schools and universities were built and compulsory education decreed. A modern banking system was created. In 1871, feudal castes were abolished and, inspired by France's centralized system of administration, the feudal domains were replaced by a prefecture system of territorial administration. In the same year a national army was organized and, in 1873, universal conscription was instituted. A standard coinage was adopted and internal feudal barriers to trade were eliminated. Finally, a system of courts and a legal code were copied from those of European states.[72]

The revenue needed to build a European-style state was raised by borrowing and taxing the people, especially rice farmers. Farmers began to resist the many taxes that were being levied, which they saw as benefiting the urban industrial sector, and resorted to armed uprisings. The restoration elite responded by using the new national army to suppress these uprisings, arrest and jail their leaders, and censor newspapers. Eventually, the elite made a bargain with the rebellious farmers. In exchange for their cooperation, a parliament would be created and a constitution promulgated. The government sent a commission to Europe to study various constitutions and returned most impressed with that of imperial Germany. With the assistance of Prussian legal scholars, a constitution was drafted in 1889. It created a bicameral legislature, called the Imperial Diet, consisting of a House of Peers and a House of Representatives, the members of which were elected by a very small electorate defined by high tax-paying requirements. The Imperial Diet met for the first time in 1890.

If Japan were to successfully defend itself against European encroachment, a sense of nationhood also had to be developed. To do so, certain traditional Japanese institutions and practices, especially those focusing on the emperor, had to be created and imposed on the people. In 1890 a law was passed that called on all subjects to practice filial piety, to be loyal to the emperor, to obey the law, and to offer oneself to the state.[73]

Japan's military had a strong influence on Japanese political and economic life after the Meiji Restoration because almost all of Japan's new elite were former *samurai* who shared the warrior values and outlook of *bushido*. Moreover, the implementation of conscription enabled the military to indoctrinate thousands of young men from across various backgrounds and social classes with militaristic-patriotic values and unquestioning loyalty to the emperor. Military values and practices were further enhanced when the Prussians defeated the French in the Franco-Prussian War (1871), which persuaded the Japanese that the Prussian army model was superior to that of the French. Thereafter, the Japanese requested and received military and technical help from the Prussians who replaced French military advisers. A Prussian major, Jakob Meckel (1842–1905), worked closely with high-ranking Japanese officers to reorganize the army by subdividing it into divisions and regiments, strengthening support and logistics structures, and connecting major military bases by railroad. He introduced the Japanese to Clausewitz's theories of military organization and strategy.

The Japanese military was also free from direct civilian control. The Japanese Army General Staff and the Japanese Navy General Staff were independent of the Ministries of War and of the Navy, and reported directly to the emperor. In addition, the minister of the army and navy were, by law, active-duty officers nominated by their respective services. The lack of civilian oversight of the military emboldened the army to take unauthorized action when it believed that Japan's vital interests were being threatened.

By the end of the nineteenth century, the Meiji elite had built a formidable Western-style state with Japanese characteristics. It also believed itself to be increasingly threatened by the imperial states around it, especially by China and Russia, as well as by the United States, Britain, and France. In 1894–1895 Japan fought a war with China (the First Sino-Japanese War) over which state was to dominate Korea, and, in 1904–1905, a war with Imperial Russia (the Russo-Japanese War). In the Russo-Japanese War Japan defeated the czar's army and navy in a series of battles on land and sea, which humiliated the Russians and contributed to the eventual collapse of Romanov rule in 1917. The Russo-Japanese War was the first time that a non-European state had defeated a European one. The victory greatly enhanced the prestige of the Japanese military, which increasingly became the most important institution in the Japanese state.

The Great Depression, which devastated the Japanese economy; the imposition of trade embargoes, especially the oil embargo by the United States; increasing radicalism in Japanese domestic politics; growing economic woes; an attempted assassination of the emperor; and several attempted coups d'état by ultra-nationalist secret societies, gave rise to the idea that the military was the only Japanese institution that could solve Japan's internal problems.

The control, albeit indirect, of the Japanese state by the military began in earnest after the civilian government signed the London Naval Treaty in 1930, which regulated submarine warfare and limited Japan to twelve heavy cruisers. The treaty was strongly opposed by the Japanese admiralty, which portrayed the treaty as having been foisted on Japan by a hostile United States. In 1932, the prime minister, Inukai Tsuyoshi (1855–1932), was assassinated by a group of junior naval officers. Although the assassins were tried and jailed for fifteen years, the military was increasingly emboldened. In 1932, the army waged a three-month undeclared war in Shanghai. They also blew up a few yards of railroad track in Manchuria, blamed it on Chinese saboteurs, and invaded Manchuria, which they wanted to use as a staging ground for war with the Soviet Union. In 1936, the army's elite First Infantry Division attempted a coup. Although the coup's leaders were arrested and executed, the civilian leadership capitulated to the army's demands for increases in military spending and navy ship construction, in part to satisfy the military, and, in part, to counter the effects of the worldwide economic depression.

As Japan militarized, the government became more and more concerned with the conservation of human resources for military purposes. In 1937, it organized a Ministry of Public Health and Welfare to promote the health and welfare of the nation. The new ministry had bureaus devoted to health (improving physical strength, public hygiene, sanitation, housing inspection, and food supply), social affairs (military relief, protection of mothers and children, and employment), labor, and social insurance. A national health-insurance law was passed in 1938 that provided for the establishment of health-insurance associations in towns and villages to render medical care to their members.[74]

During the 1930s, Japan fought several wars with the Soviet Union over the border between Japanese-occupied Manchuria and the Soviet Union. In 1937, a skirmish between Chinese and Japanese troops at the Marco Polo Bridge near Beijing escalated into a full-scale war, the Second Sino-Japanese War (1937–1945). In the late 1930s Japan began its wars of imperial expansion in the Pacific. The territories conquered during these wars were organized into the Greater East-Asian Co-Prosperity Sphere, which was to bring Asia together economically and politically under Japanese leadership as a bulwark against Western domination. Japan's attack on Pearl Harbor on December 7, 1941, brought the United States to declare war on Japan. From 1941 until the dropping of the atomic bombs in 1945, the United States, using amphibious operations developed by the United States Marine Corps, pushed the Japanese imperial army inexorably back to Japan by amphibious assault against one Japanese-occupied Pacific island after another. Although planned, the invasion of the Japanese archipelago was not required because the Japanese capitulated after the atomic bombs were dropped on Hiroshima and Nagasaki on August 6 and 9, 1945, respectively.

The occupation of Japan (1945–1952) by the Allies after its defeat marks the beginning of the transformation of the Japanese state into a civilianized neoliberal state.[75] The Supreme Commander for the Allied Powers (SCAP), General Douglas MacArthur (1880–1964), was the de facto ruler of Japan from the end of the war until 1952. Initially, American policy vis-à-vis Japan after the war was punitive. However, America's fear of the victory of communism in China caused officials to rethink this policy and shifted away from punishment to reconstruction. Japan was to become the workshop of democracy in Asia and an American ally against China. To prevent a recurrence of war and to expedite reforms, the occupying authorities began a purge of officials who had supported the war. They abolished the ministries of the army and navy and reassigned their military functions to the national police agency. Twenty-eight military and civilian leaders were tried for war crimes. Seven were sentenced to death and eighteen sent to prison. In addition to removing those likely to oppose change, the Allies made six major reforms in the following areas: landholding, labor organization, the *zaibatsu*, education, constitution, and local government.

The purpose of land reform was to create a yeoman farming class that would be the backbone of democracy in the rural areas. Their counterparts in the cities were to be the members of Japan's new labor unions. Japanese labor law, which had prohibited strikes and collective bargaining before the war, was rewritten to allow workers to organize and join unions and go on strike. Organized labor was to offset the power of the *zaibatsu*, the large combines of capital in steel, shipbuilding, chemicals, and aircraft manufacturing that had supposedly collaborated with the military and landlords and profited from the war. The *zaibatsu* were broken up and their stocks and bonds confiscated and sold to private investors. The education system was reorganized according to American liberal norms and practices. The most important act of the Allies was to abolish the Meiji constitution and write and impose on Japan a new constitution.

The constitution was designed to eliminate the political autonomy of the military and to reduce the political authority of the emperor. The constitution made clear that sovereignty rested with the Japanese people and created a ministerial form of elective government. It preserved the emperor as the ceremonial and ritual head of state. The prime minister and the cabinet formed the executive branch of the government, half of whom were elected members of the Diet (Parliament). The government was aided in its work by the national civil service. Suffrage was given to all men and women at the age of twenty. They were empowered to elect representatives to both of the Diet's two chambers, the House of Representatives and the House of Councillors. The constitution also established a supreme court with the power to determine the constitutionality of laws. The principles of popular democracy were applied to local government. At the city, town, and village level, mayors and local assemblies became elective offices.

The constitution addressed the excessive role of the military in the prewar Japanese state. Article 9 of the constitution demilitarized the state by prohibiting Japan from making war to solve international disputes and from having an armed force with war-making potential. Nonetheless, in the early 1950s the United States signed a security pact with Japan that permitted the stationing of American military forces on Japanese soil and obliged the Japanese to defray some of the costs. The security pact obliged the United States to defend Japan against external attack. Japan was permitted to create a small military force composed of ground, sea, and air elements, called the Japan Self-Defense Force (JSDF) that operated under the American nuclear umbrella. In order to remain within Japan's pacifistic constitution, the JSDF was not technically an armed force. All JSDF personnel are legally civilians who work for the cabinet-level Defense Agency within the Office of the Prime Minister headed by a director-general directly responsible to the prime minister. JSDF personnel are volunteers because conscription would be politically impossible to impose owing to strong anti-militarist sentiments in post-war Japan. JSDF personnel are not called "soldiers" but "self-defense group members." Most come from rural areas of the archipelago where employment opportunities are limited. Since 1992, women have been permitted to take up MOSs other than nursing. Because all JSDF personnel are civilians, they can resign at any time. Therefore, recruitment and retention are major problems for the JSDF because a military career has little prestige in contemporary Japan. The vast majority of university graduates prefer to make careers in the civilian sector of the economy, especially in one of Japan's transnational corporations (TNCs). Because they are special civil servants, any crimes that JSDF members may commit, on or off base, in uniform or out, are tried in civilian courts, there being no special military courts and no military law equivalent to the United States' UCMJ. Civilian control of the JSDF is guaranteed by the constitution.

The JSDF is defensive in orientation. It, therefore, lacks offensive weapons systems, such as aircraft carriers, long-range surface-to-surface missiles, ballistic missiles, or strategic bombers. It also has no marine corps or amphibious capability. It has no atomic weapons and prohibits them on Japanese soil or on ships in its harbors. Japan has strict limits on arms exports. The JSDF has about 250,000 self-defense group members and consumes only 3 percent of the state's annual budget. Despite these modest numbers, the JSDF is the fifth largest armed force in the world. During the Cold War, its defensive orientation was directed at the Soviet Union. Since the collapse of the Soviet Union in 1991, it has been redirected toward China and North Korea.

Initially, SCAP was opposed to the rebuilding of Japan's industries and wanted to keep it isolated from international markets. However, the outbreak of the Korean War (1950–1953) and the decision by the United States to rely on Japanese suppliers for wartime needs stimulated demand and brought a resurgence in Japan's industrial sector. Military demand increased profits, increased profits encouraged investment in new factories, new factories created more jobs, more jobs meant steadier incomes, and steadier incomes meant more consumption and increased family savings, which went into productive investment. The Japanese government decided to focus its resources on four strategic industries: coal mining, steel making, shipbuilding, and chemical production. Certain manufacturers, such as Toyota and Nissan, won contracts to build trucks, and Toshiba and Hitachi benefited from Korean War demands. By 1955 Japan's industrial output was at pre-war levels; agricultural output had also recovered its pre-war highs; and urban consumption levels returned to those of 1935.

The Japan that emerged from the war was markedly different from that of the pre-war years. Wealth, status, and power had been radically reconfigured. The aristocracy, which had been implicated in the war effort, was eliminated; the super-rich *zaibatsu* families had been stripped of their assets; large landowners lost their lands and were replaced by a new class of yeoman farmers; and the pre-war military establishment had been eliminated. Japan entered a period of high-speed growth during which time it was fully transformed into an economically powerful neoliberal state.

Political stability was provided by the Liberal Democratic Party (LDP) that dominated Japanese politics from the 1950s until the 1990s. Supported by big business, small- and medium-sized enterprises, retail trades, interest groups, farmers, and some industrial workers, the party made economic growth the nation's first priority and pursued policies to realize it. Pre-war high-ranking bureaucrats provided most of the party's leadership. These individuals were well connected, politically adroit, and experienced technocrats. The LDP pursued economic development through the Income-Doubling Plan that set broad targets for growth in various sectors. The government provided tax breaks and direct assistance to achieve the targets set forth.

The most important government ministry in this endeavor was the Ministry of International Trade and Industry (MITI), which controlled foreign exchange and imported technology. MITI steered economic resources toward the large firms that it believed would use them most effectively to achieve national economic goals. The result was rapid economic growth between the 1950s and 1970s. Japan's spectacular economic growth during these years was helped by the fact that economic resources did not have to be diverted to supporting a large military establishment. Japan did not develop a generous welfare system, either. No industries were nationalized. Manufacturing remained in private hands. The government never became a large consumer of goods and services. These facts meant that the government had the financial means to invest in new factories.

Under American tutelage, Japan successfully transformed itself into a neoliberal state and successfully integrated its economy into the developing post-war global economy by becoming a low-cost producer of high-quality manufactured goods (ships, precision equipment, automobiles, business equipment, and audio and video appliances) that it exported to the world. It was aided in this endeavor by the Bretton Woods settlement of 1944 that created stable currency-exchange rates, the International Monetary Fund (IMF), and the General Agreement on Tariffs and Trade (GATT). Although China recently replaced Japan as the second-largest economy after that of the United States, it remains one of the most powerful neoliberal states in the current global order.

CONCLUSION

The transformation of the managerial welfare state into the neoliberal state was, like other transformations of the state, brought about by a transformation in war. As was shown above, the advent of atomic weapons, followed by the development of unmanned weapons, changed the relationship between the people, army, and state. Huge conscripted armies no longer being needed to make war, states no longer need to exchange welfare programs for military service. Therefore, political forces opposed to the welfare portion of the managerial welfare state have been able to undo much of what was built up over the last century to improve the health and well-being of the people. The waning of inter-state war, the ending of the Cold War, and the spread of the neoliberal state across the globe have changed the international threat environment significantly. Small, all-volunteer armed forces using unmanned weapons are sufficient to maintain the security of the state in today's world. This means that the state does not need to concern itself with the general well-being of the people. Thus, the fulminations of rightists against "big government social programs" have been increasingly successful, even in the states of Europe where the welfare state reached it apogee, but especially in the American state, which has a long history of opposition to "big government" programs. These developments have undermined the welfare state, reprivatized war, and blurred the line between the military and the civilian worlds.

Japan is the epitome of the neoliberal state. It has a civilianized armed force and a market economy thoroughly integrated into the global capitalist economy. Although the JSDF is not permitted to engage in military operations outside of Japan, a law passed in 1992 allows deployments under United Nations auspices as peacekeepers, and for medical and refugee relief, hospital support, reconstruction, election monitoring, and anti-piracy operations. More recently, efforts to remove Article 9 from the constitution have been made by conservatives in Japan as a consequence of China's increasing military strength in the region and disputes in the East China Sea and China's claims to the ownership of the uninhabited Senkaku islets (known as the Diaoyu in Chinese). In 2004, Prime Minister Junichiro Koizumi (1942–), who was associated with the nationalist and revisionist group Nippon Kaigi, which denies Japanese war crimes, promotes patriotic education, and advocates for a return to militarism, was able to pass legislation that permitted the JSDF to deploy to "noncombat areas" of Iraq to support reconstruction after the American-led invasion. Shinzo Abe (1954–), who is also associated with Nippon Kaigi, is the most nationalist Japanese prime minister since the Second World War. Pointing to Japan's changing threat environment, Abe has advocated lifting the constitutional ban on collective defense and has said that he would "reinterpret" Article 9, which has been interpreted by legal experts to mean that the JSDF can open fire only if fired upon. In 2015, Abe's cabinet approved the biggest-ever defense budget, which includes money to buy twenty P-1 maritime surveillance aircraft, six F-35 fighters, five vertical-takeoff Ospreys, several Global Hawk drones, two Aegis radar-equipped destroyers, and thirty amphibious assault vehicles. Abe is expected to introduce legislation this year that would allow Japanese troops to fight alongside allies on foreign soil, forbidden since the end of the Second World War.

The Japanese people, for obvious reasons, are intensely anti-military and suspicious of efforts to give the JSDF an offensive capability. Many Japanese believe Article 9 is the reason that Japan has been at peace for sixty-eight years, and a majority of the population remains in favor of retaining it. Many civil society groups, such as the Article 9 Association founded by Nobel Prize–winning author Kenzaburo Oe (1935–), have been organized to preserve Article 9. Another, the Organizing Committee for the Nobel Peace Prize for Article 9 of the constitution, led by a housewife, Naomi Takusu (1974–), garnered 26,000 signatures on a petition that nominated Article 9 for the Nobel Peace Prize. The petition eventually gathered about 80,0000 signatures from around the world and was accepted by the Nobel Committee.[76] It remains to be seen if Abe will be successful in overcoming the resistance of the Japanese people to his efforts to give the JSDF a greater role in policing the neoliberal global order.

NOTES

1. Ian Kershaw, "Europe's Second Thirty Years' War," *History Today*, September 2010, pp. 10–17.

2. Martin Shaw, *Post-Military Society: Militarism, Demilitarization and War at the End of the Twentieth Century* (Philadelphia: Temple University Press, 1991), p. 22.

3. *Ibid.*, p. 110.

4. Charles C. Moskos, John Alan Williams, and David R. Segal, "Armed Forces after the Cold War," in Charles C. Moskos, John Alan Williams, and David R. Segal (eds.) *The Post-Modern Military: Armed Forces after the Cold War* (New York/Oxford: Oxford University Press, 2000), p. 2.

5. Keith Krause, *Arms and the State: Patterns of Military Production and Trade* (Cambridge: Cambridge University Press, 1992), p. 82.

6. William M. Arkin, *Unmanned: Drones, Data, and the Illusion of Perfect War* (New York/Boston/London: Little, Brown, 2015), p. 112.

7. *Ibid.*, p. 281.

8. Shaw, *op. cit.*, p. 65.

9. These machines are briefly depicted in two recent films about the code-breaking efforts at Bletchley Park, the home of Britain's Code and Cypher School: Michael Apted's *Enigma* (2001) and Morton Tyklum's *The Imitation Game* (2014).

10. Antoine Bousquet, *The Scientific Way of Warfare: Order and Chaos on the Battlefields of Modernity* (New York: Columbia University Press, 2009), p. 99.

11. *Ibid.*, pp. 122–23.

12. Max Boot, *War Made New: Technology, Warfare, and the Course of History, 1500 to Today* (New York: Gotham Books, 2006), pp. 308–11.

13. Bousquet, *op. cit.*, pp. 128–34.

14. Arkin, *op. cit.*, 191.

15. Bousquet, *op. cit.*, 128–34.

16. Arkin, *op. cit.*, p. 202.

17. James Der Derian, *Virtuous War: Mapping the Military-Industrial Media-Entertainment Network* (Boulder, CO: Westview Press, 2001), p. xv. See also Michael Ignatieff, *Virtual War: Kosovo and Beyond* (New York: Viking, 2000).

18. Arkin, *op. cit.*, pp. 1–10 and illustration legends on unnumbered pages.

19. Christian Caryl, "Predators and Robots at War," *New York Review of Books*, September 29, 2011, p. 55.

20. Peter J. Singer, *Wired for War: The Robotics Revolution and Conflict in the Twenty-First Century* (New York: Penguin, 2011).

21. See, for example, Kenneth Roth, "What Rules Should Govern US Drone Attacks?" *New York Review of Books*, April 4, 2013, and Mark Bowden, "Drone Warrior: Has It Become Too Easy for the President to Kill?" *Atlantic Magazine*, September 2013.

22. *The New York Times*, November 28, 2010.

23. Ando Arike, "The Soft-Kill Solution," *Harper's Magazine*, March 2010, p. 39.

24. Seymour M. Hersh, "The Online Threat," *The New Yorker*, November 1, 2010, p. 48.

25. Alastair Gee, "The Dark Art of Cyberwar," *Foreign Policy*, November 12, 2008. Accessed from http://foreignpolicy.com/2008/11/12/the-dark-art-of-cyberwar.

26. Thomas Rid, "Cyber War Will Not Take Place," *Journal of Strategic Studies*, 35 (No.1), 2012, pp. 5–32.

27. "Cyber Security," www.oswego.edu /news/index.php/campusupdate /story/Cyber_security.

28. Mark Thompson, "U.S. Cyberwar Strategy: The Pentagon Plans to Attack," *Time*, February 2, 2010, http://content.time.com/time/nation/article/0,8599,1957679,00.html.

29. Rid, *op. cit.*

30. *Ibid.*

31. *Ibid.*

32. *Ibid.*

33. *Ibid.*

34. *Ibid.*

35. Siobhan Gorman and Julian E. Barnes, "Cyber Combat: Act of War?" *The Wall Street Journal*, May 31, 2011.

36. Chris H. Gray, "Posthuman Soldiers and Postmodern War," *Body and Society*, 9 (No. 4), 2003, pp. 215–26.

37. Max Boot, *op. cit.*, p. 410.

38. Jean Bethke Elshtain, *Women and War* (Chicago: Chicago University Press, 1987), p. 242.

39. Shaw, *op. cit.*, p. 84.

40. General Stanley McChrystal, *Team of Teams: New Rules of Engagement for a Complex World* (New York: Penguin Random House, 2015).

41. Arkin, *op. cit.*, p. 264.

42. Moskos, *op. cit.*, p. 1.

43. *Ibid.*, p. 2.

44. Martin Shaw, *The New Western Way of War: Risk-Transfer War and Its Crisis in Iraq* (Cambridge: Polity Press, 2005), chapter 4.

45. Peter W. Singer, "Robots at War: The New Battlefield," in Hew Strachan and Sibylle Scheipers (eds.), *The Changing Character of War* (Oxford: Oxford University Press, 2011), p. 348.

46. Der Derian, *op. cit.*, p. xv. Italics in the original.

47. See Christopher Coker, *Waging War without Warriors? The Changing Culture of Military Conflict* (Boulder and London: Lynne Rienner, 2002); *The Future of War: The Re-enchantment of War in the Twenty-First Century* (Oxford: Blackwell, 2004); *The Warrior Ethos: Military Culture and the War on Terror* (London and New York: Routledge, 2007); and *Warrior Geeks: How 21st Century Technology Is Changing the Way We Fight and Think about War* (London: Hurst, 2013).

48. Roger Stahl, "Have You Played the War on Terror?" *Critical Studies in Media and Communication, Vol.* 23, No. 2, June 2006, pp. 112–30.

49. Martin Shaw, *Dialectics of War: An Essay in the Social Theory of Total War and Peace* (London: Pluto, 1988), p. 116.

50. Tony Judt, *Postwar: A History of Europe since 1945* (New York: Penguin, 2005), p. 360.

51. *Ibid.*, p. 361.

52. *Ibid.*, p. 362.

53. James J. Sheehan, *Where Have All the Soldiers Gone? The Transformation of Modern Europe* (Boston and New York: Houghton Mifflin, 2008), p. 172.

54. Stephen J. Rosow and Jim George, *Globalization and Democracy* (Lanham, MD: Rowman & Littlefield, 2015), p. 37.

55. *Ibid.*

56. Michael Howard, *The Causes of Wars and Other Essays*, Second Edition, Enlarged (Cambridge, MA: Harvard University Press, 1984), p. 31.

57. Sheehan, *op. cit.*, pp. 179–80. For example, the Animals in War Memorial unveiled in 2004 in Hyde Park, London, dedicated to the "animals that have served and died under British command throughout history."

58. Philip Bobbitt, *The Shield of Achilles: War, Peace, and the Course of History* (New York: Anchor Books, 2002), p. 211.

59. *Ibid.*, p. 229.

60. *Ibid.*, pp. 229–35.

61. Matt Kennard, "Wanted in Any State," *The Guardian Weekly*, September 21, 2012, p. 25.

62. Michael Massing, "The Volunteer Army: Who Fights and Why?" *New York Review of Books*, April 3, 2008, p. 35.

63. Jeff Sharlet, "Jesus Killed Mohammed," *Harper's Magazine*, May 2009, p. 38.

64. Eric Lichtblau, "Questions Raised Anew about Religion in the Military," *New York Times*, March 1, 2009.

65. Eyal Press, "Israel's Holy Warriors," *New York Review of Books*, April 29, 2010.

66. Christopher Coker, "Outsourcing War," *Cambridge Review of International Affairs*, 13 (No. 1), 1999, pp. 95–113, and Sean McFate, *The Modern Mercenary: Private Armies and What They Mean for World Order* (Oxford: Oxford University Press, 2014), pp. 16–17.

67. Charles Glass, "The Warrior Class," *Harper's Magazine*, April 2012, p. 28.

68. Sarah Stillman, "The Invisible Army," *The New Yorker*, June 6, 2011, pp. 56–65.

69. Daphne Eviatar, "Contract with America," *Harper's Magazine*, October 2007, pp. 74–75.

70. McFate, *op. cit.*, chapter 8.

71. The historical details of this section are taken from *Japan: A Country Study* (Washington, DC: U.S. Government Printing Office, 1992), *passim,* except where otherwise noted.

72. Eleanor D. Westney, *Imitation and Innovation: The Transfer of Western Organizational Patterns in Meiji Japan* (Cambridge, MA: Harvard University Press, 1987), and Marius B. Jansen, *The Making of Modern Japan* (Cambridge, MA: Harvard University Press, 2000).

73. Sheldon Garon, *Making Japanese Minds: The State in Everyday Life* (Princeton, NJ: Princeton University Press, 1997).

74. Hugh Borton, *Japan since 1931* (Westport, CT: Greenwood Press, 1973), pp. 103–4.

75. This discussion of the transformation of Japan into a civilianized market state relies on Gary D. Allinson, *Japan's Postwar History* (Ithaca, NY: Cornell University Press, 1997), *passim.*

76. Ankit Panda, "Article 9 of Japan's Constitution: Nobel Peace Prize Laureate Material?" *The Diplomat*, April 25, 2014, http://thediplomat.com/2014/04/article-9-of-japans-constitution-nobel-peace-prize-laureate-material. The Peace Prize was awarded jointly to Kailash Satyarthi of India and Malala Yousafzai of Pakistan.

Chapter 8

Internal War and the Weak State

While the frequency of inter-state war has been trending decidedly down-ward since 1945, many states situated "in an arc that extends from Central and East Africa through the Middle East, across Southwest Asia and northern India, and down into Southeast Asia"[1] are wracked by various kinds of low-intensity wars inside them: wars between the government and lightly armed insurrectionist or secessionists; wars among lightly armed militias, guerrilla bands, and paramilitaries, often aligned with ethnic groups or religious sects; and wars on unarmed civilians. Until the end of the Cold War, such conflicts were held in check by local tyrants, strongmen, and dictators supported by the two superpowers, the United States and the Soviet Union.

Wars inside states are not caused by poverty, or by "ancient hatreds" between ethnic groups as is commonly believed. Rather, the problem is that most, but not all, states in the "arc of conflict" described above are weak. In a few cases they are so weak that they are no more than "geographical expressions." Their central governments have not pacified their populations; they do not have a monopoly on the means of physical coercion within their territories; they have almost no sense of nationhood; and they have not built up their capacities to regulate society and provide for the well-being of their people. According to Harrison Wagner, this has created a puzzle for students of international politics today who

> look at the Balkans or Afghanistan and are puzzled, and this puzzlement has produced the growing literature on "state failure." But Europe in the sixteenth and seventeenth centuries was much like the Balkans or Afghanistan today, and the important puzzle is how it came to be so different. The process by which states with the properties of Hobbes's commonwealth were created in Europe was a long and violent one. The question it poses for us today is whether people now living in the "state of nature" must follow the same

215

violent path out of it that the Europeans did and whether the outcome will ultimately be as welfare enhancing as Hobbes claimed it would be.[2]

The purpose of this chapter is to challenge the standard explanations given for state failure and weakness: that is, states fail and/or are weak because (1) they suffer from the legacies of Western conquest and colonization, (2) they contain within them groups adhering to religious and cultural values that are incompatible with the state, or (3) they are cursed with a valuable resource, such as oil, which frees their governing elites from the hard work of state building. The chapter presents an alternative explanation: to wit, states fail and are weak because they exist in a world that *forbids* them from engaging in the kind of war that built strong European states. The inconvenient truth that the chapter seeks to impart is that if weak states were left alone to make wars of conquest and annexation against one another, they might, in the fullness of time, create new states within which domestic coercive power would be monopolized, external involvement neutralized, and nations brought into being that correspond to the state's boundaries. Those that could not compete successfully in this local inter-state war system would be conquered and eliminated.

WAR AND STATE FORMATION OUTSIDE OF EUROPE

The new military history shows that Europeans were not the only peoples on the planet to build strong states, organize effective armies, conquer territory, and subjugate peoples. In Africa, ancient Egyptians built an empire stretching from the Nile Delta on the Mediterranean Sea to the Kingdom of Kush located at the confluences of the Blue and White Nile rivers in today's Sudan. In the eighth century BCE the Kushites conquered the Egyptians and ruled them as their pharaohs. In the fifteenth century, Sunni Ali (?–1492) conquered Timbuktu and became the first king of the Songhai Empire that stretched across the Sahel from present-day Senegal to Sudan. The Ashanti people built a confederacy between the Gulf of Guinea and Lake Volta in West Africa in the seventeenth century and the Zulu people rose to prominence in Southern Africa under the leadership of Shaka (1787–1828).

In ancient Mesopotamia several large empires arose, beginning with the Sumerians, followed by the Akkadians, then the Babylonians under Hammurabi (?–1750 BCE), and finally the Assyrians. Muhammad (?–632), the founder of Islam, conquered the Arabian peninsula and his successors built several large caliphates that stretched from Arabia across north Africa to the Iberian peninsula. Turkic peoples created the Ottoman Empire that lasted from 1300 until 1922.

Chandragupta Mauryu (340–298 BCE) unified the Indian subcontinent and, later, Zahiruddin Babur (1483–1530), a Chaghatai Turk, conquered the

Hindustan and established the Mughal Empire. In China, Qin Shi Hung (259–210 BCE) unified the Chinese warring states into the first Chinese Empire. Gwanggaeto (374 –413 BCE), the king of Gongutyeo, the northern-most of the three kingdoms on the Korean Peninsula, expanded his kingdom to include most of the peninsula, Manchuria, and parts of Inner Mongolia. Bayinnaung (1516–1581) conquered the many small kingdoms in Myanmar to build the largest empire ever to appear in Southeast Asia.

The warring states of the Japanese archipelago were unified by Tokugawa Ieyasu (1543–1616), and the Mongol warrior Genghis Khan (1162–1227) conquered most of Eurasia. Mayas, Incas, and Aztecs built great empires in South and Central America. In Oceania, Maoris dominated present-day New Zealand and Kamehameha (1758–1819) conquered the Hawaiian Islands and established the Kingdom of Hawaii in 1810.[3]

In addition to large empires, non-European peoples have built strong armies supported by the state and introduced new weapons onto the field of battle. The world's first large standing army was organized by the ancient Akkadians. They introduced horse-drawn chariots, which they used as mobile platforms from which an archer could loose arrows into the ranks of the enemy. The Akkadians were equipped with composite bows, metal armor, helmets, shields, and metal-tipped spears. The armies of the Sumerian Empire (5300–2000 BCE) advanced in close-order formation similar to the phalanx used by the Greeks many centuries later (see below) and they were the first to use cavalry in support of infantry. Their armies could be expanded in size with conscription. The buried terra-cotta army discovered in 1974 near Xi'an in China gives archaeological evidence that ancient Chinese armies were large; organized into infantry, cavalry, and archery units; and well-equipped with chariots, metal-tipped spears, crossbows, bronze armor, and swords as early as the Qin dynasty (220–210 BCE). During the Han dynasty (206 BCE–220 CE), all Chinese males received military training for one month a year and were required to serve in the militia thereafter. The Mycenaeans developed large and intricately organized Bronze Age armies that relied on massed chariots and infantry. Ancient Greek soldiers (*hoplites*), wearing full body armor, carried spears (*sarrisae*) up to twenty feet long, as well as swords, and fought in solid ranks with overlapping shields to engage the enemy head-on. This type of fighting required regular drill, discipline, and great courage.[4]

The military historian Victor Davis Hanson has argued that the Greek way of war, with its disciplined fighting in ranks and preference for shock battle, not military technology, brought into being a singularly lethal "Western Way of War" that, eventually, brought about the West's dominion over the Rest.[5] While there may be some truth to this assertion, the eventual superiority in the quantity and quality of Western weapons cannot be dismissed as irrelevant.

On this question, the learned view has been that China invented gunpowder but Europeans developed gunpowder weapons. Recent scholarship has shown that gunpowder *and* gunpowder weapons were both born in China in the 1200s and spread to Europe by the 1300s, not the other way around.[6] Moreover, the military capabilities of Europeans and non-European peoples were for many centuries after the invention of gunpowder and gunpowder weapons more or less the same. Many non-Europeans were proficient at manufacturing gunpowder weapons. Those they could not manufacture themselves were procured from European stocks of obsolete weapons sold throughout the world by private entrepreneurs. Many non-European peoples also learned how to use gunpowder weapons effectively and how to raise, train, and support well-drilled and disciplined armies through systems of regular recruitment and taxation. Therefore, early clashes between European and non-European armies were often closely fought, with Europeans barely winning, and occasionally losing. This was especially true in Asia, where the indigenous Indian states emulated British military practices, which made the conquest of the subcontinent very costly to the British in military terms, and Chinese, Japanese, and Koreans built large armies and developed gunpowder weapons that evenly matched those of Europeans. In other places, however, such as sub-Saharan Africa where there were few indigenous states of consequence, the military balance was grossly unequal in favor of Europeans, and war between Europeans and indigenous peoples "resembled hunting more than war."[7]

Nonetheless, "by the late seventeenth century, if not before, Chinese, Japanese, and Ottoman military technology and tactics all lagged behind what one found in western Europe. They could adopt the latest military innovations and at times improve the gunpowder technology on their own too. But they could not keep up with the relentless pace of military innovation set by the Europeans."[8] Europeans advanced gunpowder technology without interruption from the fourteenth century onward because Europe entered a period of intense, existential inter-state war. Thereafter, a "Great Military Divide" opened up between the West and the Rest. Gunpowder technology and military expertise advanced in Europe and flowed outward from Europe, not the other way around and, by the late nineteenth century, the global balance of military technology had shifted decisively in favor of Europeans. The result was Europe's conquest of the world.

The development of two weapons facilitated this conquest: the *machine gun* and the shallow-draft, iron hull, steam-powered *gunboat* that could speedily sail up navigable rivers. The machine gun was used extensively in the conquest of Africa south of the Sahara and the gunboat in the conquest of Asia and Southeast Asia by carrying overwhelming European firepower up rivers such as the Ganges, Irrawaddy, Tigris-Euphrates, Indus, and Yangtze. The machine gun and the gunboat "dramatically widened the power-gap between Europeans and non-Western peoples and led directly to the outburst of imperialism at the end of the [nineteenth] century."[9] The result was the gradual establishment of European hegemony over vast numbers of non-European peoples and the conquest of large swaths of the terrestrial surface of the Earth. A few non-European peoples were spared direct European conquest and occupation—the Japanese, Chinese, Persians, Siamese, Afghans, Saudis, and Koreans, for example—because their indigenous forms of politico-military rule and their armies were strong enough to resist the European onslaught and/or because European states were diverted from making full-on war against them as they were devoting most of their military resources to fighting one another in Europe.

Without doubt, then, the European success at subjugating the non-European peoples of the planet was primarily the result of the formidable lead the former eventually gained in military technology over the latter, a lead that was produced by Europe's own long history of incessant war and constant military innovation. Europeans, especially the British, developed fleets of warships supported by extensive industrial and logistical resources that dwarfed the navies of non-European peoples. Europeans were able to dispatch gunboats and armies armed with machine guns worldwide and sustain them for long periods of time because they were supported by strong, well-organized, centralized states with impressive bureaucracies capable of mobilizing a wide range of human and non-human resources necessary to support such an endeavor. In addition to having the most advanced weapons and military technologies of the day, they had large, conscripted, well-trained, and disciplined armies, and their peoples had a well-developed sense of nationhood that increased their willingness to accept deprivation and even death for its ends, whether it be the defense of the state from the predation of other European states or the conquest and colonization of non-European peoples.

For the most part, the above was not the case in the non-European world, except in a few places, such as Ming China and Mughal India. Despite their many wars, military rivalries among non-European peoples were as not as great as they were among European states. Most non-European states did not face military competition of sufficient intensity to advance weapons innovation and to change their politico-military institutions and cultures. For example, China, which had maintained military parity with the West, began to lag behind when it no longer faced serious military threats from Mongols, Turks, and Russians after 1760 and became free of warfare. The Chinese army atrophied and China's military technology fell behind that of the West. The result was the defeat of China by the British in the Opium Wars (1839–1842; 1856–1860).[10] Apropos of this fact, Jeremy Black has observed that neither "China nor Japan had any immediate rivals facing them or appeared to have any need to match European developments in military technology."[11]

However, in some cases, non-European peoples under threat from the West did attempt to modernize (i.e., Westernize) their armed forces, but with limited success. Attempts to build up armies organized along Western lines were often met with resistance by established warrior elites, such as China's mounted archers and the janissaries of the Ottoman Empire. Even after their armies were defeated by European military forces, most continued to rely on elite warrior troops who, not unlike the warrior nobility in medieval Europe, valued individual bravery and courage, and did not build large, well-drilled, disciplined armies recruited from the general population, as Europeans had done. While they did adopt European gunpowder weapons, non-Europeans, in general, did not improve upon them or use them as effectively as did Europeans. As Jeremy Black has written:

> Qualitative European military changes, such as the bayonet, the flintlock musket and accurate and mobile grape-and canister-firing field artillery, opened up a major gap in capability among militaries supplied with firearms from the late seventeenth century. The introduction of close order formations firing by volley was also very important: an individual on his own with a musket, and even a crowd of individuals, were of limited effectiveness. [12]

In general, it can be said that most non-European peoples were not capable of producing a "scale and regularity of resources sufficient to sustain military competitiveness in the context of mounting European pressure"[13] to the level necessary to make war effectively enough to defend themselves against European states and prevent conquest and subordination.

However, a few non-European states, when faced with the military threat from the West, were able to successfully adopt and effectively use European military systems. Beginning in 1868, as was discussed in chapter 7, Emperor Meiji (1852–1912) Europeanized Japan's society and Westernized its military so successfully that it was able to defeat imperial Russia in the Russo-Japanese War (1904–1905), and, in 1941, make war on the United States. After seizing power in a coup in 1913, the Young Turks were able to reform the Ottoman state and army sufficiently to make it a formidable foe for Europeans during the First World War. Nonetheless, the vast majority of non-European peoples were not able to resist so successfully and were conquered, subjugated, and enclosed within European colonial empires.

The empires created by Europeans did not last forever. The first to break apart was the British Empire in North America where, in the late eighteenth century, thirteen of its colonies successfully fought a war of independence (the American Revolutionary War [1775–1783]) and emerged, after fourteen years of confederation, as the federal United States of America. Beginning in the early nineteenth century, *criollo* (locally born individuals of Spanish descent) elites in Spain's colonies in South and Central America, encouraged by the success of the independence movement in British North America, began demanding and fighting for their independence. By 1825 all of Latin America (except Puerto Rico and Cuba) had achieved independence from Spain or Portugal. Many of Latin America's independence leaders, such as Simón Bolívar (1783–1830) and José de San Martín (1778–1850), favored the organization of the independent Spanish-speaking Latin American states into a federated republic much like that of the United States. Unlike the United States, however, none of the attempts to form such a federation were successful because the elongated shape of Spain's Latin American empire and variations in topography and climate within it had imparted to the *criollo* elite of each colony a strong sense that their colony was distinct from the others. Therefore, Latin America was balkanized into competing independent states. This resulted in about a century of inter-state wars, interventions, territorial predations, and arms racing similar to that of Europe. In short, Latin America in the years immediately after independence was a region of warring states.

The Latin American threat environment began to change after the Congress of Lima (1848) at which Latin American states agreed to accept each other's borders. At first, however, this agreement did not alter the Latin American threat environment because the borders of Latin American states were hard to demarcate, owing to the formidable physical geography of the continent. Hence, border tensions remained high and caused several limited wars in the late nineteenth century. By 1945, however, military solutions to border disputes were no longer acceptable and Latin America became a region of inter-state peace. Excluding the war between Argentina and Britain over the Malvinas/Falkland Islands in 1982, there has not been a war in Latin America since 1941 and only two since 1903. In terms of inter-state war, Latin America has been the most peaceful area of the world outside of North America. It has become a no-inter-state-war zone where mutual peaceful relations and non-violent modes of conflict resolution among states are the norm.

Therefore, according to Miguel Angel Centeno, the states of Latin America did not receive the structural boosts produced by a very long period of incessant inter-state war. The warring states phase was relatively brief and the wars that Latin American states fought against one another were few in number and limited in scope. Latin American inter-state wars, such as the Chaco War (1832–1835) and the War of the Triple Alliance (1864–1870) were simply too limited to "produce powerful states or help consolidate national identity."[14] Limited wars produced weak states. In addition, Cameron Thies has found that Latin American states borrowed money on the world market to fight their wars. Hence, war among Latin American states did not produce the internal state structures necessary to extract the financial resources to make war. It is safe to conclude that war in Latin America did not produce states with the same extractive and regulative capacities as those of European states.[15]

Like Latin American states, African states, except Ethiopia (formerly Abyssinia) and Liberia, came into being as European colonies. Unlike Latin American states, however, they gained their independence, for the most part, without having to fight for it.[16] Also unlike Latin America, the leaders of the former colonial African states, for the most part, did not contest the boundaries of their states as laid down by Europeans at the Berlin Conference of 1884–1885. Instead, they embraced them. Also unlike the states of Latin America, the boundaries of African states were declared immutable and recognized by the international community, the United Nations (UN), and the Organization of African Unity (OAU) (now the African Union [AU]) at the moment of independence. This meant that the newly independent African states were born without armed struggle into an international environment in which their governing elites did not have to worry about predation from neighboring states. Therefore, unlike Europe, where weak states disappeared, weak states survive in Africa today because their sovereignty and territorial integrity are guaranteed by global norms.[17]

As there is no link between war and state formation in Africa, Africa's political elites have not had to build up state capacities to extract the resources necessary to defend their states nor to weld the many ethnic groups within their states into a single people willing to give of itself and make big sacrifices to defend the nation against predatory neighbors. Wars in Africa since independence have been wars among various groups (ethnic, political, religious) *within* states not wars *between* states. Essentially, Africa has not had a "warring states" period since independence. Even the Second Congo War (1998–2003), also known as Africa's World War One, was basically several internal wars, not a single inter-state war, and did nothing to strengthen the capacities of the states within which it took place, Congo, Rwanda, and Uganda.[18] Hence, African states have not built up the same extractive and regulative capacity as Latin American states, much less European ones.

While war has not had the same state-forming effects in states in postcolonial Latin America and Africa, it has made a difference in a few non-European states in other regions of the world. For example, Brian Taylor and Roxana Botea found that the French Indochina War (1946–1954) and the American war in Vietnam (1955–1975) had the effect of transforming a non-European people (the Vietnamese) into a modern national state with considerable capacity to extract the resources to make war.[19] Although Taylor and Botea conclude that "relative homogeneity" is the key variable in Vietnam's state-building success, it could be argued that the key variable is the fact that Vietnam had a history of war-driven state-building *before* being colonized by the French. The French colonizers, who returned to Indochina after the Second World War, were seen as aggressors by Vietnam's nationalist elites, who had been "liberated" from French colonialism by the Japanese during the war, and wanted a modern, independent Vietnamese state. The injection of Cold War rivalries among the Soviet Union, China, and the United States drove a wedge between Vietnam's nationalist elites who aligned themselves with these states. The war in Vietnam was thus essentially an internal war between competing nationalists seeking to take control of the Vietnamese state, which had been built much earlier by indigenous Vietnamese state-makers before being colonized by the French. The victory of the North over the South unified the already existing Vietnamese people within one state.

Since the departure of American forces in 1975 and the unification of the North and South within a single state, tensions between China, Vietnam, and Thailand that were submerged during the Cold War have reappeared. From 1978 to 1991 Vietnam fought several brief border wars (collectively known as the Third Indochina War) with China, Cambodia, and Thailand.

In the Middle East, some states were formed by indigenous war-making—Iran and Afghanistan, and arguably Saudi Arabia, for example. Most Middle Eastern states, however, were produced by the defeat and dismemberment of the Ottoman Empire by the British and the French, who expanded into the region after the First World War and carved it into several states. Owing to the manner of their formation, these states are not states with the characteristics of fully developed states given in chapter 1. Rather, they are "social fields" within which competing elites have struggled to establish hierarchical power among diverse competing groups.[20] Ian Lustick argues that Arab states in the Middle East have not been able to become more than social fields because they have been denied inter-state wars on a scale grand enough to weld their populations and territories into strong states. He writes that indigenous Middle Eastern state-builders, from the Ottoman army commander Muhammad Ali Pasha al-Mas'ud Ibn Agha (1789–1849) in the nineteenth century to Colonel Gamal Nasser (1918–1970) of Egypt and President Saddam Hussein (1937–2006) of Iraq in the twentieth, who attempted to build strong states using aggrandizing wars have been frustrated and thwarted in their state-building projects by the powerful states of the West for their own political and geo-strategic reasons.[21] Lingyu Lu and Cameron Thies also found that the many intra-state wars in the Middle East have jeopardized the ability of the governments of these states to penetrate society for the purpose of resource extraction.[22] However, Syrd Zaidi *et al.* found that Pakistan's wars with India have stimulated state-building[23] and Michael Barnett found that wars between Egypt and Israel stimulated the growth of state power in both states.[24]

Despite isolated cases like Iran, Afghanistan, Vietnam, Pakistan, Egypt, and Georgia,[25] states beyond Europe, in general, have either not desired (as in Africa) or have been denied (as in the Middle East) the state-building benefits of war with other states. Inter-state war for acquiring new territory is forbidden by international anti-belligerency norms, and states that wish to enter the club of "great powers" using state-building wars are not permitted to do so by the global community of states. In other words, the *link between war-making and state-making has been broken in the contemporary world*. The vast majority of non-European states exist in a global order dominated and regulated by the well-established, strong, mostly Western states, which function as a management committee for the global order. Non-European states have been prevented by this committee from making the kind of war (inter-state) that would, perforce, make them into organizations that monopolize the means of physical coercion within their territories and give them the administrative capacity to break down the strong tribal societies within them and transform them into coherent nations.[26]

In conclusion, the major reason for the weakness of many non-European states, in general, is the fact that *they have not had to fight existential inter-state war, not the fact that they are the direct successors of colonial states, and not because the religious and cultural values of groups within them are incompatible with the modern state*. In Latin America, as the threat environment became less threatening during the nineteenth century, the initial incentive for the governing elites to build strong states to prevent predation from neighbors gradually disappeared. African states were born into a non-threatening environment; consequently, there has been no need for their governing elites to build strong states against potential predators on that continent. In the Middle East, serious existential threats have been limited to Israel from Arab states (especially Egypt, Syria, and Jordan) and to Iran from Iraq. Since the signing of the Egypt-Israel Peace Treaty (1979), the Israel-Jordan Treaty of Peace (1994), and the cease-fire between Iran and Iraq brokered by the United Nations that ended the Iraq-Iran War (1980–1988) these threats have been eliminated.

In general, then, non-European states have been, for the most part, free from external threats because their existence is guaranteed and enforced by the states system itself. Therefore, wars in these states are essentially struggles among domestic groups, often ethnically and religiously defined, seeking to monopolize their power within the state and prevent other groups from challenging that monopoly. Groups within weak states seek to defend themselves by taking control of the state, or seceding from it using violent means, if necessary. The weakness of and wars within most non-Western states are a consequence of the current global *threat trough*, which denies *all* states within the current global order the state-building benefits of inter-state war. Therefore, the biggest threats "to individual security in many countries come not from foreign armies, neighbors, or members of other ethnic, religious, or language communities, but from the state itself. Since 1945 more people have been killed by their own governments than by foreign armies."[27]

THE GLOBAL THREAT TROUGH

It has been shown in previous chapters that the threatening environment of Europe produced centralized, coherent, viable, well-functioning national states on that continent. The development of *norms* within the states system in recent times with regard to when states may go to war have changed the global threat environment for all states. Evan Luard has written that in earlier eras European

> [c]ompetition took place, for example, for succession, the right to a throne elsewhere—probably the most frequent cause of war from the Middle Ages to the eighteenth century. Or, particularly in the sixteenth century, states disputed about religion: usually, which religion could be practised in a particular territory. In other cases they fought essentially for territorial objectives: again, assets which both could not simultaneously control. Finally, in the nineteenth century many wars were fought about the right of people to secure national independence (if they are ruled by another state), national unity (if they are scattered among several states), or national preeminence.[28]

Luard goes on to say that these reasons for going to war gradually disappeared and were replaced with *political* reasons, such as going to war against states with different ideologies, governing systems, and modes of economic organization. The overall purpose of these wars was to make the world safe for one type of state by eliminating its political rivals; that is, to make the threat environment less threatening. An example of this thinking is exemplified by the reason President Woodrow Wilson gave to Congress in 1916 that the "world must be made safe for democracy" to justify the participation of the United States in the First World War.

Nowadays, states are forbidden by the norms of the contemporary global order from making war on one another. Full stop. States that violate the no-war norm are universally condemned. There are several reasons for this state of affairs. First, the pre-First World War unrestricted right to wage war as an inherent right of sovereignty to conquer foes and acquire territory has been delegitimized, repudiated, and replaced with the norm that war may be engaged in by a state only for individual or collective self-defense or to uphold international peace by fulfilling obligations under Chapter VII of the United Nations Charter after the Security Council has determined that there has been a threat to international peace, a breach of the peace, or an act of aggression.[29] No statesman today would even think of saying, as Abraham Konig (1846–1925), Chile's minister plenipotentiary in La Paz, said in 1900 of Chile's victory over Bolivia in the War of the Pacific, also known as the Saltpeter War (1879–1883): "Chile occupies this coastal territory, and took possession of it in the same way that Germany annexed Alsace-Lorraine. Our rights are rooted in victory, the supreme law of nations."[30]

Second, the pre-Second World War idea of war as a heroic and virtuous endeavor or as a regenerative tonic for states has been replaced by a strong global anti-war ethic.[31] In the current global order *all* forms of war (inter-state and intra-state) are strongly condemned by the states within the states system. According to Martin Shaw, the "idea that war is justified only as a response to a manifest threat is now deeply ingrained."[32]

Third, the territorial state as a form of politico-military rule "was eventually extended to encompass the globe."[33] No other form of rule is considered legitimate, and the state takes precedence above all other forms of politico-military rule on planet Earth. Every square mile of Earth's terrestrial surface (except Antarctica) is seen as being under the theoretical politico-military jurisdiction of one state or another, even if its government and territory are being contested by internal warring groups. In the period before the Second World War, other forms of politico-military rule, such as empire, existed and were regarded as legitimate forms of governance.[34] Beginning in the early twentieth century, empire, as a legitimate form of politico-military rule, began to be challenged and replaced by the sovereign national state.[35] Essentially, the current global order is a "closed system" in which the state is an "independent, isolated unit possessing a freedom of will to do as it pleased."[36]

After the First World War, a war that pitted the national states of Western Europe (France, Britain, etc.) and their colonial appendages against the empires of central and eastern Europe (German, Austrian, and Ottoman), the victorious Allies applied the principle of "self-determination of peoples" to break up the multiethnic empires in Eastern Europe and replace them with ethnically defined independent nation-states (e.g., Poland, Hungary, Romania, Czechoslovakia, etc.). After the Second World War the principle of self-determination further delegitimized colonialism, which eventually resulted in the breakup of the overseas empires that some European states (e.g., Britain, France, and Portugal, for example) had acquired over the previous centuries. By 1975, nearly all of these empires had been dismantled and replaced by juridically sovereign states. The last empire to disappear was that of the Russians, in the guise of the Soviet Union, which collapsed in 1991 into fifteen sovereign states. According to Kalevi Holsti, "We are witnessing the creation of a genuinely global international system whose essential and primary units are states constructed upon distinct social communities."[37] Thus, the global system now contains a standard form of politico-military rule, the territorial state. Hence, wars over the type of politico-military units the system is to have are no longer necessary. *The world has been made safe for the territorial state. No other form of politico-military rule is permitted on planet Earth.*

Fourth, Robert Latham has shown that the current global order is unique in that after the Second World War, under the "overlordship" of the United

States, the Western powers were able to make the neoliberal variety of the territorial state the only type of state "through which just political outcomes can be pursued."[38] All other varieties are seen as illegitimate in the current states system for most but not all states, China being an obvious exception to this rule. Thus, the current global order has increasingly become a system in which the dominant organizational logic is that of the *neoliberal, secular territorial state.* As will be shown below, one form of war in the contemporary world is about "liberal order making"[39] by which the strong correcting states of the system, the United States and certain states of the European Union acting in concert, regulate and discipline the sovereignty of non-conforming states, not unlike Napoleonic France in regard to the European state system in the early nineteenth century (see chapter 4).

The compartmentalization of the globe into more than two hundred juridically recognized sovereign territorial states is reinforced in several ways: (1) sovereignty is reciprocally shared and recognized by the states of the current global system; (2) international organizations, such as the United Nations, uphold and respect the sovereignty of member states; and (3) violations of sovereignty are universally condemned by the states of the system.[40] Thus, the current global order of sovereign states and the strong commitment present within it by states in support of the territorial integrity norm[41] have created what Michael Desch has called a "*threat trough*—a period of significantly reduced international security competition [which] may reduce the scope and cohesion of many states."[42] Thus, each of the states extant in the present global system holds an "insurance policy against mortal danger."[43]

States in the current global order no longer have territorial ambitions, except in a few places where borders and territories are in contention, such as the above-mentioned border wars in Indochina, the long-running dispute between India and Pakistan over Kashmir, the 1982 dispute over the ownership of the Malvinas/Falklands by Britain and Argentina, the current dispute over the Senkaku/Diaoyu islands by Japan and China, and the conflict between Ukraine and Russia over Crimea and the Donbass. It can be argued that the global states system resembles that of Latin America after the Congress of Lima, which limited inter-state war to conflicts among states over *unsettled borders and disputed territories.*

Finally, the current threat trough has been produced by changes in the structure of global power: the development of global governance since 1945, and the "growing economic costs of war in conditions of global interdependence."[44] The consequence of these changes in the global threat environment is that the amount of predation by states in the current global order has been reduced to such a degree that many scholars believe that Clausewitzian war between major states has become "obsolete." As John Mueller has written:

War lacks the romantic appeal it once enjoyed, and . . . has been substantially discredited as a method. Moreover, there has been a major shift in values: prosperity has become something of an overriding goal, and war—even inexpensive war—is almost universally seen as an especially counterproductive method for advancing this goal. Finally, prosperity and economic growth have been enshrined as major status, and even power symbols in the international arena, occupying much of the turf previously claimed by military powers and by success in war.[45]

Even General Charles Krulak (1942–), 31st commandant of the United States Marine Corps (USMC), has claimed that "the days of armed conflict between nation-states are ending."[46] Thus, war as a confrontation between states no longer describes war in the current global order. War, more often than not, takes place *within* and *across* the borders of states not *between* them.

INTERNAL WAR

In the twenty-first century war has been transformed from "pitched battles between organized forces into more fragmented, uncontrolled, and indeterminate series of military events";[47] that is, wars that take place within and across the borders of weak states among various lightly armed fighting units and groups (remnants of the state's armed forces, self-defense groups, foreign mercenaries, paramilitary groups, and regular foreign troops, usually under international auspices) seeking to (1) gain and/or retain control of the state (Syria), (2) secede from the state (Tamil Tigers), (3) break the state apart into two or more states (Sudan–South Sudan), or (4) form a non-Westphalian variety of state (the Islamic State of Syria and the Levant [ISIL]).

The most common fighting units are "autonomous groups of armed men generally centered around an individual leader."[48] Often paramilitary groups are connected to extremist parties. In large part, they are composed of redundant soldiers or entire breakaway units of the state's armed forces. They rarely wear uniforms, although they often sport certain articles of clothing or patches that indicate their political allegiances. In Africa, it is not uncommon for such fighting units to include contingents of child soldiers.[49]

In major part, light weapons (assault rifles, hand grenades, machine guns, land mines, anti-tank rockets, and various kinds of improvised explosive devices) are used by these groups. Of these, the weapon of choice is the *AK-47*, the automatic assault rifle invented during the Second World War by Mikhail Kalashnikov (1919–2013), a sergeant in the Soviet army tank corps, while he was in the hospital convalescing from a gunshot wound he sustained in combat. Since the AK-47 (Avtomat Kalashnikova-1947) was adopted by the Soviet armed forces in 1947, an estimated 80 to 100 million have been manufactured, making it the most widely used weapon in the world. It has been adopted by many armies and is the undisputed firearm of choice of non-state guerrilla bands, drug cartels, insurgents, rebels, and militias, because it is cheap, reliable, and readily available. Ironically, its ubiquity across the planet is a consequence of the nuclear stalemate between the United States and the Soviet Union, which resulted in proxy wars in non-European states. During the Cold War, the AK-47 became a symbol of socialist resistance to capitalist domination. It appears on the flags of many non-Western states, especially in Africa. The AK-47 is the most lethal weapon on the planet. It is used to kill about 250,000 people each year. Moreover, "in destabilized areas, owning an AK-47 is a sign of manhood, a rite of passage. Child soldiers in Congo, Myanmar, Sri Lanka, and dozens of other countries proudly display their AKs for all to see."[50]

Another weapon favored by non-state fighting units is the *improvised explosive device* (IED). An IED is any explosive device made in an improvised manner to destroy vehicles and kill or maim personnel. A vehicle-borne IED refers to a car or truck bomb, but can refer to a bomb transported by bicycle, donkey, or motorcycle. Such devices were used in the Second World War by guerrilla groups against German troops in states occupied by the German army. They were used extensively by the Viet Cong against American troops during the American war in Vietnam, and the Irish Republican Army (IRA) used roadside IEDs extensively against British security forces during the Troubles in Northern Ireland from the late 1960s until 1998. The Afghan multinational Mujahideen used IEDs made from unexploded ordnance against Soviet forces during the Soviet Union's invasion and occupation of Afghanistan (1979–1989). IEDs have been the most common method of attack against NATO forces by the Taliban in Afghanistan, and Hezbollah made extensive use of them against Israeli forces during its invasion of Lebanon in 1985. Finally, they have been used against Coalition troops in Iraq since the invasion and occupation of that state in 2003. IEDs have been used by non-state groups in India, Nepal, Libya, and Syria. They have been delivered by boat, car, animal, suicide bomber, and rocket. An IED can be set off by wire, radio, cell phone, or by the person carrying it. Conventional forces counter IEDs with bomb-disposal robots.[51]

Another weapon commonly used by non-state fighting units against each other and opposing conventional forces is the *rocket-propelled grenade* (RPG). The RPG is a shoulder-held, anti-tank weapon that fires a rocket equipped with an explosive warhead. RPGs date from the Second World War, during which time Americans used the bazooka, Germans the Panzerfaust, and Russians the "*ruchnoy protivotankovy granatomyot* (RPG)," meaning handheld anti-tank grenade. The Soviet-developed RPG-7 is the most widely used RPG in the world. Like the AK-47 it is cheap, easy to use, and readily available. They have been used by non-state fighting units in Afghanistan, Angola, Chechnya, Iraq, Northern Ireland, and El Salvador.[52]

It is claimed by one scholar of war that low-intensity internal war is more brutal and involves far higher civilian casualties than conventional inter-state war because in such wars little attempt is made "to distinguish between qualitative and quantitative warfare, for political objectives may lead the forces of one side to attempt the extermination, rather than merely the defeat, of the other."[53] This claim is statistically and historically inaccurate. The inconvenient truth is that

> [a]ttacks and atrocities against civilians are not a recent phenomenon. . . . Armies, armed groups, political and religious movements have been killing civilians since time immemorial. Some commentators speak today as if civilian suffering or the intentional killing of civilian populations is a novelty. But this is very far from the truth. There may have been lulls when certain wars were fought more cleanly than others but these blips are tiny exceptions in humanity's long and bloody history of conquest, group rivalry, religious fanaticism, empire building, and modern state formation.[54]

Does low-intensity internalized war among fighting units armed with light weapons build state capacity and coherence? Some scholars believe that such wars are necessary for the imposition and/or maintenance of a new political order and resemble the kinds of "primitive power accumulation" struggles that took place within the monarchies of early modern Europe.[55] Along these lines, Stathis Kalyvas has argued that internal wars of the contemporary world are not fundamentally different from civil wars of the past. For Kalyvas, warlords are never merely criminals or bandits. He says they are "primitive state builders" who levy taxes, administer justice, maintain order, and generally assume the burdens of government in the area they control.[56]

Other scholars argue that low-intensity internalized wars do not build state capacity. According to Christopher Cramer, internalized wars are "not repeating what European states underwent hundreds of years ago."[57] This is because, as Mark Duffield has argued, internalized wars in the current global order are *networked*; that is, they are fought through and around states. "Instead of conventional armies, the new [networked] wars typically oppose and ally the trans-border resource networks of state incumbents, social groups, diasporas, strongmen, and so on."[58] Thus, in many cases, internalized wars are kept alive by outside powers, remittances from diaspora communities, international aid projects, and even humanitarian intervention. In such wars "[t]he political and . . . economic support of the masses becomes superfluous; the resources vital to waging war can be requisitioned without mass support, resulting in an endless spiral of violence."[59]

Thus, history is not repeating itself. Even if warlords are "primitive state builders" as Kalyvas maintains, the current global threat trough prevents effective state formation by war. As Ann Hironaka has argued, the way that states were formed in the years after the Second World War is fundamentally different from the way they were formed before the war. She says:

> The population of states before 1945 was composed of strong battle-scarred states that had proven their capability to withstand both interstate and civil war. Since 1945, most colonies achieved independence and sovereign statehood not through victory in war but through the encouragement and support of the international system. Furthermore, international norms and laws increasingly discourage territorial reshuffling through wars of annexation or secession.[60]

Holsti concurs. He says that

> state-creation in the former colonial areas . . . has taken patterns and trajectories significantly different from those of Europe since the fifteenth century. In the latter, there was a lengthy historical project to give political meaning to the geographical expression called France, Germany, Sweden, and the like. . . . The original purpose of colonialism, in contrast, never included state-making. European overseas conquests after the fifteenth century had nothing in common with the state-consolidation projects of Louis XIV, Peter the Great, Frederick the Great, or Bismarck.[61]

European colonialism was not intentionally about state formation. Europeans never assumed that the people they colonized could create states of their own. If they did contemplate independence, it was to be in the very, very distant future. The boundaries of most colonies are artificial in that they were drawn by colonial administrators or international agreement without regard to local circumstances and, therefore, almost never corresponded to the pre-colonial boundaries of the colonized, if such boundaries existed, which they did not in most cases. In sum, "the territorial unit bore little or no relationship to any pre-colonial ethnic, religious, political, social, or religious communities, or political systems."[62]

   A related problem is that there were few whole peoples that coincided with the territorial boundaries of European colonies, or European states, for that matter. Most colonies, unlike the Vietnamese, Cambodian, and Laotian colonies of French Indochina, for example, did not reflect historically created nations. They often contained a multiplicity of ethnic groups with little emotional attachment among themselves to a broader national community. Hence, colonies were alien political fictions imposed by Europeans and "ruled by administrators who had little but contempt for the 'natives,' but who dressed up their more exploitive activities with paternalistic rhetoric of 'civilizing mission,' 'modernization,' and 'trusteeship' for the ultimate benefit of the subject populations."[63] A good example of this phenomenon is the boundaries of the state of Iraq, which, as will be shown below, were advocated by the British diplomat and explorer, Gertrude Bell (1868–1926), after the First World War, not by the so-called "Iraqi people."

When they arose after the Second World War, anti-colonial nationalist movements led by Western-educated, indigenous elites did not fundamentally challenge the alien colonial state itself, but who was in control of it. According to Holsti,

> for many colonies, this was not a case of a reasonably homogeneous historic, ethnic, language, and/or religious group claiming an upgrade of status from a "people" into a state, as happened in Europe in 1919. It was, rather, the literal creation of a nation out of dozens, and sometimes more, of "peoples" not unified sentimentally with anything resembling early twentieth century European nationalism.[64]

In other words, Western-educated indigenous elites rejected their own traditional political forms.[65]

The main reason for the failure of many former colonies' states is the fact that the Western-educated indigenous elites who took over the colonies at independence found their states to be in a *benign international environment*, which they made more benign by embracing the colonial boundaries given to them. Thus, they have been denied by the global state system and have denied themselves the main way that people governed by a state who are not already a nation become one; that is, by making war against other states. Instead, the elites in new states tend to face "internal threats in the form of attempted *coups d'état*, secession, ethnic, language, and religious violence, and subversion."[66] Therefore, as William Reno has argued, elites in the new states have "abjured state-building strategies" that would build up the extractive and regulative capacities of their states. Instead, rulers buy loyalty to themselves, not the state, by using state assets and patronage that diverts scarce resources away from state-forming projects into private bank accounts. Hence, warlords and strongmen are not "primitive state builders" as Kalyvas has argued. Moreover, because armies in these states are deprived of external enemies that they must prepare to fight, they tend to look inward and frequently become drawn into internal power struggles among contending groups. All too often, the army itself becomes one of the players involved in internal power struggles and seizes governing power. Military rule, warlordism, and predatory politics prevail within the state.[67]

For these reasons, the current global order contains a plethora of *weak* states.[68] Some of these are so weak that they are little more than "geographic expressions." No group within them has ever achieved a monopoly on the legitimate means of coercion, and, therefore, they do not exercise complete jurisdiction over their territories and people. Many states "do not really exercise effective control over all the territory that international agreements have allocated to them and therefore may not really merit the appellation of 'state' at all."[69] Moreover, many non-Western states lack a coherent sense of nationhood and to "varying degrees are fractured into more meaningful and effective political communities based on tribal, ethnic, and religious bases. State and nation do not coincide."[70] Some of these lesser communities do what governments do, but they lack recognized sovereignty over the territories they inhabit. One such "stateless government"[71] in the current global order is the former British-ruled northern portion of Somalia, which declared its independence in 1991 and called itself "Somaliland."

Attempts to transform weak states into strong states by Western states in the contemporary global order is called *"nation-building."*[72] This is a misnomer because the actions that these states take are essentially about *state formation*; that is, assisting non-Western states to build or restore "the state's monopoly over the means of coercion" by reestablishing its "political institutions (governments, ministries, local administration, national armies, police forces, judiciaries, etc.), the promotion of political participation (e.g., the holding of elections) and human rights, the provision of social services, and economic recovery."[73] Essentially, state formation in the contemporary world is *post-conflict construction and reconstruction of state institutions, not nation-building*. The implicit aim of this approach is to rebuild the non-Western state as a Western-style, liberal, secular state. According to Jabri,

> if the locals lack the capacity to achieve this for themselves, others, external agents, both state and non-state, can provide them with the means of doing so. This then is the late modern programme of state-building. It is distinctly modern, thoroughly rational, and international, or even cosmopolitan, involving as it does an international civil service provided by states, international institutions, and non-governmental organizations. It also comes, eventually, to involve local agents, but only as *reconstituted agents of liberal democracy*, fully trained in, for example, gender awareness, equal opportunities, human rights, civil society, and democracy. . . . [State-building] constitutes no less an ambition than the transformation of societies into full and able participants in democracy for the local population, legitimate and law-bound government, peaceful relations with neighbors, and exchange in the neo-liberal market place.[74]

In general, state formation in the contemporary global order is being attempted *without the kind of violence that led to the formation of the capable states of Europe*. In the words of one scholar:

> Humanitarian catastrophes like the French Revolution are to be avoided, and if they occur their participants may be prosecuted for crimes against humanity; civil wars like the U.S. Civil War are to be ended early by compromise settlements, and their participants perhaps prosecuted for war crimes; and little Bismarcks seeking to redraw territorial boundaries are not to be allowed.[75]

However, sometimes state formation is attempted by the force of arms from outside. According to Paul Miller, "Armed state building [such as in Sierra Leone, Liberia, and Afghanistan] is an exercise of military power by great powers to compel failed or collapsed states to govern more effectively."[76] Armed state formation is different from imperialism, he argues, in that it recognizes the sovereignty of the invaded state and seeks to compel non-Western states to abide by the globally accepted Westphalian norms of statehood, not territorial expansion and economic exploitation and dependence.

Essentially, state formation (armed or unarmed) in the contemporary global order involves *regulating and disciplining the sovereignty of the states* in the system that do not conform to prevalent European-constructed global norms about what constitutes legitimate rule. Non-European states are being compelled by outside intervention to adapt to the dominant logic in order to make the global system consist of similarly organized units. Sometimes this involves the violation of the sovereignty norm by powerful states that insinuate themselves into states that do not conform to their intersubjective understandings of what a sovereign state must be, as the United States did in 2003 when it invaded Iraq. Thus, powerful hegemonic states, such as the American state and certain European states, form a community of judgment, a kind of global management committee, that takes upon itself the task of reproducing and maintaining the territorial integrity of the states in the contemporary global order and the prevalent conception of legitimate political structures and governing practices, in this case neoliberal ones.

In sum, external state formation, armed or peaceful, is about constructing "some sort of institutional arrangement in [non-Western states] that will protect the interests of the powerful states, avoid conflicts among them, and not require the expense and conflict associated with direct [colonial?] rule."[77]

A major difference between the actions of hegemonic states today and hegemonic states in earlier epochs, however, is that weak states cannot be eliminated from the current system by wars of conquest because the sovereignty and territorial integrity norms are too deeply ingrained in the global order. Therefore, state formation from outside has not been a very successful strategy for strengthening the state and building a sense of nationhood. Outside powers can insinuate themselves between warring parties, enforce cease-fires, put in place institutions of liberal government, and build up the security forces of the state in order to gain some semblance of the monopoly over the means of coercion, but they cannot make the warring parties understand that they belong to a common people or nation, unless the outside power is seen by the great majority of the people in the state as an invader that threatens the sovereignty of the state and the way of life of the people within it. Moreover, aid from outside in the form of monetary and technical assistance (from the United Nations and donor states) does little to strengthen the idea of nationhood. All too often such assistance has been used by domestic elites, usually with the support of the intervening state, to strengthen their grip on power, and is used against internal enemies rather than to build a sense of national identity.

VARIETIES OF WEAK STATES

Although different from that of Europe, non-European state formation has not been identical for all non-European states. Two basic varieties can be discerned. First, in some places non-European peoples had been engaged in a war-driven process of state formation and constructed viable states *before* their encounter with Europeans. China, Japan, Iran, and Thailand, for example, are contemporary non-European states of this variety. Each has a long history of pre-European-contact, war-driven state formation. They were never directly colonized by Europeans. After their inclusion into the European-created Westphalian states system, their *indigenous war-driven state formation was curtailed*, however, and their sovereignty came to be *regulated and disciplined from outside* by more-powerful European states. Increasingly, these extant non-European states were pressured by powerful European states to *conform* to the Western idea of the state and incorporated into the Westphalian states system. At the same time, indigenous elites sought to reflexively remake their states in the European image by *emulating* the politico-military practices of European states.

Second, in other places there had been *little to no* history of indigenous war-driven state-building ongoing before the encounter with the West. In these places the people were stateless and easily defeated militarily, then colonized by Europeans. Essentially, *the state was imposed from outside in the form of a colony or a mandate under the League of Nations.* The imposition of the state from outside by Europeans created new politicized territorial spaces (colonies and mandates) in various places on the planet where they had not existed before. Within these spaces, new political, social, and economic hierarchies based on race, religion, and ethnicity generated relationships of domination and submission that had not existed previously among the indigenous peoples and generated an intense rivalry among them for control of these states, especially after they became independent.

In this section, two case studies of weak non-European states are presented: Afghanistan and Iraq. Afghanistan and Iraq offer contrasts with regard to the manner of their formation as states. Their contrasting histories of state formation explain why Afghanistan, despite much elite conflict and a long-running internal war, has maintained its territorial integrity, and Iraq, which has also had much elite conflict and an internal war, has completely collapsed as a state.

Afghanistan: From Monarchy to Presidential Republic

The history of the formation of the Afghan state and its transition from a monarchy to a presidential republic can be divided into three broad historical periods.[78] The first period is that of indigenous war-driven state-making, during which time the early Afghanistan monarchical state was produced by Pashtun military competition with neighboring peoples. The second period is that of reflexive state-making, during which time indigenous war-driven state-building was curtailed when the Afghan monarchy joined the Western state system in 1919 and Afghan rulers sought to "modernize" Afghanistan by emulating European politico-military practices. The third period is that of externally regulated and disciplined state-making, during which time the sovereignty and form of government of the Afghan state were increasingly regulated and disciplined first by Great Britain and imperial Russia, and later by the Soviet Union, Pakistan, Saudi Arabia, the United States, and the United Nations, as well as certain European states.

The first historical period of Afghanistan began around 1500 with the rise of the Pashtuns, a tribal people organized into clans, the most important of which were the Abdali and Ghilzai in the interstices between the Safavid (Persian), Mughal (Indian), and Uzbek empires. The chieftains of these clans were feudatories of their Safavid, Mughal, and Uzbek overlords. Gradually, the Pashtuns began to play an independent political and military role when the Safavid and Mughal empires went into a period of military decline at the end of the seventeenth century. The Ghilzai clan was the dominant force in the Safavid-controlled territory and remained loyal to the Safavid dynasty until an army sent by the shah to repel a Baluch invasion provoked a rebellion led by Mirwais (1673–1715), a wealthy chief of the Hotaki tribe who seized control of Qandahar. The Safavid shah sent any army to retake Qandahar. After his defeat, Mirwais was sent to the Safavid court in Isfahan as punishment and to stop him from leading additional rebellions. While at the Safavid court he learned how weak the Safavid empire had become, and, upon his return to Qandahar in 1709, organized a second, larger rebellion and was able to beat back a Safavid army sent by the shah in 1711 and retained control of Qandahar. Mirwais died in 1715 and was succeeded by his son, Mahmud. Realizing that Safavid rule was in decline, Mahmud Hotak (1697–1725) attacked and captured the Safavid capital of Isfahan in 1722, after which he proclaimed himself Shah of Persia. Mahmud was mentally unstable and an incapable ruler; consequently, within a year he was overthrown by his cousin Nader Afshar in 1725.

Nader Afshar (1688–1747), known to history as the "Napoleon of Persia," created a large empire, which collapsed when he was assassinated in 1747 by a group of dissident officers of his army. The leader of his elite Afghan cavalry, Ahmed Khan, who had participated in the assassination, rode southeastward with 4,000 cavalry and joined the chiefs of the Abdali tribes and clans near Qandahar where a *jirga* (council) was held to select a paramount chief. According to legend, Ahmed, the second son of the small but honored Sadozai lineage, was chosen when a holy man broke a deadlock within the *jirga* by declaring Ahmed the most deserving candidate, proclaiming him *Padshah, Durr-i-Durran* (Pearl of Pearls).[79] After being made leader he became known as Ahmed Durrani (1722–1772). Taking advantage of the decline of the Mughal power to the southeast and the Safavid dynasty in Persia to the west, Ahmed, a seasoned warrior, began to expand his realm. From his ascendancy until his death in 1772, he gained and maintained control over the region north of the Hindu Kush: the Punjab, Kashmir, and Lahore; he sacked Delhi in 1757 and, in 1761, defeated the Marathas at Panipat. Ahmed Durrani's empire was maintained with a large army of about 120,000 men divided into infantry, cavalry, and artillery. It was supported by a system of regular taxation. Ahmed Durrani is recognized as the founder of the Afghan monarchical state.

Ahmed Durrani was succeeded by his second son, Timur (1748–1793), who gained the throne by suppressing a revolt among his own clan in favor of his brother and executing the ringleaders. Timur moved the capital of Afghanistan from Qandahar to Kabul in 1776. During Timur Durrani's twenty-year reign, the empire that his father had built began to unravel and, by 1818, it had shrunk to an area within a one-hundred-mile-radius of Kabul. When Timur died he failed to designate an heir from among his many legitimate sons, all of whom claimed the throne. His fifth son, Zeman (1770–1844)—who gained the support of Painda Khan (1758–1844), Timur's vizier (high official), chief of the Muhammadzai lineage of the Barakzai clan, and the power behind the throne—became king at the age of twenty-three. After being placed on the throne, Zeman sought to reduce the power of Painda Khan's clan by stripping him of his office and executing him. One of Painda Khan's sons avenged his father's death by blinding Zeman and placing Mahmud Durrani (1769–1829) on the throne in 1800. Mahmud ruled only three years, after which he was overthrown and imprisoned by another of Timur's sons, Shuja. Shuja Durrani (1785–1842) ruled for six years before being deposed, with the help of the Barakzai clan, by his predecessor, Mahmud. Mahmud then attempted to curb the influence of the Barakzai clan by imprisoning Fatih Khan (?–?), chief of the Muhammadzai, and executing him. In 1818, Fatih's brothers avenged his death by seizing the crown from Mahmud and placing on it a series of puppet shahs.

It should be noted that the Durrani kingdom was not called Afghanistan, nor was it a coherent politico-military entity. It was a loose federation of tribes and principalities that insisted on autonomy and were willing to fight to maintain their independence from central authority. Tribal coalitions formed and reformed against the Durranis. Moreover, clans within the Durrani family fought over the issue of succession. Kabul was but one regional power center, even though it claimed a special status as the capital of the kingdom. The formative period of indigenous state-making did not produce a strong central government capable of monopolizing the means of physical coercion.

The Durrani kingdom remained weak and fragmented until the rise of Dost Mohammad Khan (1793–1863), another of Painda Kahn's sons, who declared himself amir, not shah, in 1826. Dost Mohammad spent the first ten years of his reign consolidating his power and extending it beyond Kabul. During this time he also had to defend the realm from external enemies, most notably the Sikhs who were expanding into the Hindu Kush. In 1836, Dost Mohammad's forces defeated those of Ranjit Singh (1780–1839), founder of the Sikh Empire, at Jamrud, then a frontier outpost of British India at the entrance to the Khyber Pass.

The victory of the Afghans at Jamrud put the kingdom in direct conflict with the British who were advancing from the east, and marks the beginning of the period of reflexive state-making. The British were interested in gaining influence over the Durrani kingdom because Britain was competing with imperial Russia for control of the region, a competition known as the "Great Game," during which Britain and Russia sought to subdue and subvert the small independent states that lay between them. Dost Muhammad was willing to come to terms with the British and sought an alliance. The British, who were seeking to dominate Afghanistan and make it a client state and buffer between themselves and the Russians, rejected his entreaties and invaded Afghanistan in 1838.

The British easily defeated Dost Muhammad in what is known to history as the First Anglo-Afghan War (1839–1842). After Dost Muhammad fled Kabul, the British re-enthroned his brother Shuja who had been living in British India. Opposition to Shuja, who was seen as a usurper, began immediately and the British had to remain in Afghanistan with troops to support his rule. After several failed attacks on the British and their protégé, Dost Muhammad surrendered and was allowed to go into exile in India. Even after the departure of Dost Muhammad, dual control by the British and Shuja was still unworkable because Shuja was unable to gain the support of Afghanistan's clan chieftains on his own and the British were unable to force his acceptance. By 1841, disaffected clans who wanted the British to leave the kingdom were flocking to the side of Dost Muhammad's favorite son, Mohammad Akbar. Faced with stiff resistance to their presence, the British decided to withdraw their army from Afghanistan in January 1842. Shuja was assassinated in April of the same year by a member of the Barakzai clan.

After months of chaos, Mohammad Akbar Khan (1816–1845) secured control and his father, Dost Muhammad, returned from India in April 1843. In the following twenty years, Dost Muhammad concentrated his efforts on the reconquest of his realm. At the end of his second reign, he had retaken control of almost all of present-day Afghanistan. He was helped in this effort by the British, because a strong Afghan ruler would help them meet challenges by a resurgent Iran and expanding Russia. The British made an alliance (the Treaty of Peshawar) with Dost Muhammad in 1855, an addendum to which, made in 1857, allowed a British military mission to be established in Qandahar. The British helped Dost Muhammad build a stronger state and a well-trained and properly equipped army under competent officers.

When Dost Muhammad died in 1863, a period of unrest ensued. The third son of his favorite wife, Sher Ali (1825–1879), assumed the throne. During the ten years of his reign, he built up the army, made administrative reforms, and reformed the tax system. Sher Ali Khan was the first to judge Afghanistan by Western standards and take actions to make it more progressive and modern; that is, Western. During Sher Ali's reign the Russians expanded into central Asia and reached Afghanistan's northern border in 1869. The Russians agreed that Afghanistan would fall within the British sphere of influence and willingly accepted it as a buffer state between the two empires. The Russians sent a delegation to Kabul in 1878, which initiated a British demand for the acceptance of a British mission. The Afghans did not reply and, as a result, the British invaded, occupied much of the monarchy, and began to rule it directly. In 1879, Sher Ali died and was followed on the throne by his son, Mohammad Yaqub. Mohammad Yaqub Khan signed the Treaty of Gandamark with the British, which gave them control over Afghanistan's foreign affairs in exchange for an annual subsidy and assurance of military assistance in case of foreign aggression as well as the extension of British control of the Khyber Pass. The imposition of direct foreign rule provoked regional revolts by Ghilzai Pashtuns and Kohistani Tajiks. Mohammad Yaqub abdicated and the British realized that they could defeat the Afghan tribes but could not govern them.

Unsure of the reliability of Sher Ali's sons, the British opened negotiations with Abdur Rahman Khan (1840–1901), an experienced field commander and a ruthless politician who was willing to accept the limitations on his power imposed by the British. Abdur Rahman wanted to subjugate the tribes, extend government control throughout the realm, and reinforce the power of the royal family. He set about doing this in three ways: first, he suppressed various rebellions, which he followed with harsh punishments and executions; second, he broke the power of many Pashtun tribes and transplanted the most troublesome of them from the south to non-Pashtun areas north of the Hindu Kush; and, third, he created a system of provinces that did not coincide with tribal boundaries. He gave the governors of these provinces great power to collect taxes directly and suppress dissent. He also created a regular army equipped with modern weapons, the monarchy's first bureaucracy, cabinet-like departments, and a *loya jirga* (grand assembly of tribal chiefs, local notables, and religious leaders). He also encouraged the technological development of the realm by importing European machinery and establishing small factories and improved transportation and irrigation. In 1893 he accepted a mission headed by the foreign secretary of British India, Mortimer Durand (1850–1924), to delineate the border between India and Afghanistan in Pashtun areas. He agreed to the so-called Durand Line in exchange for an increase in the British subsidy to his treasury. In effect, Abdur Rahman Khan made the Afghan state as currently constituted by centralizing its government and establishing its national territory.

When Abdur died in 1901, he was followed on the throne by his eldest son and heir, Habibullah Khan (1872–1919), without a succession struggle because he had groomed him for the throne. Habibullah was strongly influenced by a nationalist and modernist faction inspired by Mahmoud Beg Tarzi (1865–1933), a well-traveled poet and journalist, who advocated reform and full independence for Afghanistan. During Habibullah's nearly twenty-year reign, a military academy was founded; a new treaty was signed with the British in 1905; the border between Afghanistan and Iran, which heretofore was ambiguously delineated, was fixed, also in 1905; and, in 1907, the Anglo-Russian Convention was signed, which excluded Afghanistan from Russia's sphere of influence. Afghanistan remained neutral during the First World War, despite efforts of a pro-Turkish court faction to join the war on the side of the Ottoman Empire. Habibullah was assassinated in 1919 while on a hunting trip. He was followed on the throne by his third son, Amandullah Khan (1892–1960), who had seized control of the army and the national armory upon learning of his father's death.

Amandullah was the leader of the modernist faction at court and his reign was marked by dramatic changes in Afghanistan. In 1919, he achieved complete independence from Britain after his victory over the British in the Third Anglo-Afghan War (May 6, 1919–August 8, 1919). He established diplomatic relations with the Soviet Union, Iran, Britain, Turkey, Italy, and France; organized an air force, reformed the army, and instituted conscription; created schools for boys and girls; changed the constitution in 1923 to guarantee civil rights and establish a legislative assembly; created a system of secular penal and commercial law codes; abolished subsidies for tribal chiefs and the royal family; established a national tax system; and introduced a national currency, the Afghani. These and other reforms, which were designed to create a strong central government, sparked a rebellion of tribal and religious leaders, known to history as the Khost Rebellion (1923–1924), who saw their traditional way of life under threat.

In the late 1920s Amandullah's reign began to unravel. Shinwari tribesmen revolted and marched on the capital. Much of the king's army deserted to the rebels. Tajiks attacked from the north. In January 1929, Amandullah abdicated but attempted to regain power with a small armed force, failed, and went into exile. He was followed on the throne for nine months by a Tajik deserter from the army, a bandit and highwayman who called himself Habibullah Kalakani (1890–1929), but who was known to most as Bacha-i Saqqao (Son of the Water Carrier). With the help of the British, the eldest great-great nephew of Dost Mohammad Khan, Muhammad Nadir Khan (1883–1933), who had been the minister of war and a general in the Afghani army, led an army against the Tajik interloper, captured and executed him, and proclaimed himself amir. Muhammad Nadir Khan abolished most of his predecessor's reforms and promulgated a new constitution in 1931, which incorporated many traditional values of Afghani society and placated the religious authorities. He worked to slowly Westernize Afghanistan until he was assassinated by a young man whose family had been feuding with him since his accession to the throne.

He was followed on the throne by his nineteen-year-old son, Mohammed Zahir Khan (1914–2007), who ruled until 1973 with the help of his uncle, Muhammad Hashim (1885–1953), his father's prime minister. Hashim's policy until the outbreak of the Second World War was to strengthen the army and develop the economy. In 1935, the government invited German experts and businessmen, who were greatly admired because Germany had fought against both Russia and Britain as an ally with the Muslim Ottoman Empire, to set up factories and build hydroelectric projects. Afghanistan joined the League of Nations in 1934, and concluded treaties of friendship and nonaggression with Turkey and Iran in 1937. Afghanistan was neutral during the Second World War. After the war, in 1946, another of the king's uncles, Mahmud Khan (1890–1959), became prime minister. Influenced by young Western-educated elites, Mahmud began to liberalize political life. He allowed relatively free elections for the parliament, relaxed strict press censorship, and allowed opposition groups to form. When the *loya jirga* began to question the king's ministers; when political groups, such as the Kabul University Student Union, began to criticize the government; and when newspapers began to print articles critical of government policy, Mahmud reversed course and cracked down on political activity, which alienated the young reformers.

As a result, Mahmud Khan was replaced by Mohammed Daud Khan (1909–1978), the king's cousin and brother-in-law, in 1953. Mohammed Daud Khan was the first of the young educated members of the royal family to wield power. While not a liberalizer, Mahmud was a Westernizer. He took cautious steps to emancipate women; continued support for economic development projects, such as the giant Helmand Valley Project funded by the United States; and repressed a tribal war in the contentious Khost area near Pakistan. He also sought a closer relationship with the Soviet Union in order to balance what he regarded as an excessively pro-Western orientation in Afghanistan's foreign relations. During the Cold War he was able to obtain support from both the United States and the Soviet Union as they vied with one another for influence in Afghanistan. During these years, schooling was expanded; roads, airports, bridges, and other vital infrastructure were built; and the army was reequipped with modern weapons procured from the Soviet Union. Daud was forced to resign in 1963 because his obsession with the Pashtunistan issue[80] made normal diplomatic relations with Pakistan impossible. After Daud's resignation, the king took the reins of government into his own hands and ruled Afghanistan himself.

King Zahir Khan's greatest achievement was the 1964 constitution, which created a constitutional monarchy with a bicameral legislature. It barred the royal family from holding political office, championed individual rights over tribal rights, settled the succession issue within the royal family, used the word "Afghan" to denote all citizens, identified Islam as the religion of Afghanistan, and incorporated religious judges into the secular judicial system. Elections for the houses of parliament sparked the founding of political parties, such as the leftist People's Democratic Party of Afghanistan (DPA) in 1965. Zahir Khan's limited democracy was unstable, however, having five prime ministers in ten years, and in 1973, when abroad to receive medical treatment, Zahir was overthrown by the former prime minister, Daud Khan, who declared himself the first president of Afghanistan.

Daud's coup, known as the Saur Revolution (the Afghan name for the month in which it occurred), was supported by disaffected Soviet-trained military officers, who remembered his strong position on the Pashtunistan issue, and by the most-radical largely Pashtun elements within the DPA known as the Khalaqis, led by Nur Muhammad Taraki (1917–1979), one of the two founders of the party who became prime minister, and Hafizullah Amin (1929–1979). Declaring itself to be a revolutionary government, DPA instituted policies that were strongly pro-Soviet, and in favor of sweeping away of traditional society and replacing it with a socialist society. Consequently, the government launched a series of sweeping radical social and economic changes: land reform, equality for women, abolition of marriage payments, and the cancellation of many kinds of rural debts. It also changed the colors of the national flag from green to red. These and other changes sparked a series of small-scale insurrections in the countryside.

Daud was not a communist, however, and, in 1975 he began to purge leftist officers from the army and Islamists from his cabinet. He was an authoritarian and made it clear that he was not going to share power with the DPA. In 1977, he established his own political party, the National Revolutionary Party (NRP), and a secret police along the lines of SAVAK (Organization of Intelligence and Security) of Iran during the reign of Mohammad Reza Phalavi (1919–1980), shah of Iran. Resistance to the new government was suppressed. Daud moved away from Afghanistan's reliance on the Soviet Union for military and economic support. His movement toward the

West and his repressive government caused the army, supported by the DPA, to overthrow and murder him and his family in April 1978, thus ending the 231 years of rule of the Afghanistan state by Ahmed Shah and his Muhammadzai descendants. The DPA bound itself more tightly to the Soviet Union.

Increased Soviet involvement in Afghanistan sparked resistance among Afghans to the DPA government. Resistance was especially strong in eastern Afghanistan by groups later called the "mujahideen," supported by Pakistan with money, weapons, and fighters, while the United States, Saudi Arabia, and other Arab states contributed billions of dollars in financial aid. The Soviet Union sent military advisers to support the DPA government. Friction within the DPA between Khalqists (radicals) and the Parchams (moderates) resulted in the dismissal of Parcham cabinet ministers and the arrest of Parcham military officers. In 1979, Khalqist president Nur Muhammad Taraki (1917–1979) was murdered during a coup within the DPA orchestrated by a fellow Khalqist, Hafizullah Amin (1929–1979), who became president. Thinking that Hafizullah Amin was going to defect to the West, the Soviets assassinated Amin in 1979 and installed a Soviet-backed government led by the Parcham, Babrak Karmal (1929–1996), but inclusive of both factions, and invaded Afghanistan on December 27, 1979, to support the new government.

The invasion of Afghanistan by the Soviet Union marks the beginning of the period of direct, externally regulated and disciplined state-making in Afghanistan. The Soviet intervention was opposed by a wide coalition of Afghan groups—royalists, nationalists, non-DPA leftists, and Islamists. The Soviet strategy was to employ strong military force against those who resisted the government, believing they could pacify Afghanistan as they had done in their central Asian republics during the 1920s and 1930s. Despite air bombardment and aggressive search-and-destroy sweeps, the Soviets were unable to suppress the resistance, however. Gradually, the costs of the war, lack of success, and the coming to power of Mikhail Gorbachev (1931–) in 1985 caused the Soviets to seek a way out of Afghanistan. They installed Mohammad Najibullah (1947–1996) as president and accepted a United Nations offer to negotiate peace.

Despite having withdrawn from Afghanistan, the Soviets continued to support President Najibullah until the Soviet Union itself collapsed in 1991. With the common external enemy removed, the various Afghan militias and warlords supported by the United States, Saudi Arabia, and Pakistan began to fight each other over control of the Afghan state. Without Soviet support, the Najibullah government fell in 1992, and the United Nations brokered a power-sharing agreement, the Peshawar Accords, which created the Islamic State of Afghanistan and called for an interim government to be organized, followed by general elections.

The Islamic State of Afghanistan was riddled with mujahideen factions. One faction, the Hezb-e Islami led by Gulbuddin Hekmatyar (1947–) and supported by Pakistan, refused to recognize the interim government and attacked Kabul. In addition, Saudi Arabia and Iran supported Afghan militias hostile to one another, Iran the Shia Hazara Hezb-i Wahdat forces of Abdul Ali Mazari (1947–1995), and the Saudis the Ittihad-i Islami faction led by the Wahhabite Abdul Rasul Sayyaf (1949–). A full-scale internal war ensued, which the interim government was unable to suppress. The capital city, Kabul, fell into chaos and lawlessness. An estimated 25,000 Afghans, mostly civilians, died and about 500,000 fled to neighboring states.

In 1994, the factions fighting for control of Kabul were defeated by the minister of defense, Ahmad Shah Massoud (1953–2001) and steps were taken to impose government control throughout Afghanistan. Massoud invited all factions to join in a national unity government and prepare for democratic elections, but one faction refused, the Taliban. The Taliban (meaning "religious students") was a cross-border movement of Pashtuns from Kandahar that had arisen in madrasas (religious schools) in Pakistan, which sought to create a pure Islamic state along Salafist (ultra-conservative Sunni Islam) lines. The following year, the Taliban attacked Kabul but were repulsed by Massoud's forces. In 1996, with Pakistani military support and financial support from Saudi Arabia, the Taliban again besieged Kabul. The siege was successful. Massoud retreated from Kabul and the Taliban, led by the Islamist Mullah Mohammed Omar (1959–), formed the Islamic Amirate of Afghanistan. The Taliban sought to impose a mixture of Salafi Islam and Pashtunwali, the cultural code of the Pashtuns, on Afghanistan. They were hostile to Sufism, banned all forms of entertainment, and attempted to eliminate all images of living things. They drove women from public spaces, enforced a strict code of veiling and seclusion, created a religious police, and applied harsh Islamic punishment (amputation of hands for thieves, public executions for murderers, etc.). The Taliban government allied itself with other Islamist groups, such as al-Qaeda.

After retreating from Kabul, Massoud and Abdul Rashid Dostum (1954–) formed a coalition against the Taliban called the Northern Alliance. In addition to the Tajik forces of Massoud and the Uzbek forces of Dostum, the Northern Alliance included Hazaras under Haji Mohammad Mohaqiq (1955–) and Pashtuns led by Abdul Haq (1958–2001) and Haji Abdul Qadir (1951–2002). Dostum's forces were defeated in 1998. During this period, the Taliban, supported clandestinely by Pakistan, made war against Massoud and civilians, especially Shiites and Hazaras. Many thousands were killed and tortured.

Between 1996 and 2001, al-Qaeda established itself in Afghanistan and joined the Taliban in its fight against the Northern Alliance. Only about 25 percent of those fighting against the Northern Alliance were actually Afghans. Massoud was assassinated on September 9, 2001. Two days later, about 3,000 people were killed by al-Qaeda operatives who hijacked four commercial aircraft, took over the controls, and flew two of them into the identical World Trade Center towers in New York City and one into the Pentagon in Washington, DC. The third hijacked plane, which was supposed to hit the White House, was prevented from doing so by its passengers and crashed in a field in Pennsylvania. The United States identified the organizer of the attacks, now known collectively as 9/11, as al-Qaeda and demanded that al-Qaeda leader Osama bin Laden be given up to stand trial in the United States. The Taliban refused to give up bin Laden and disband al-Qaeda.

In October 2001 the United States, supported by Great Britain, sent special operations forces to work with the Northern Alliance to overthrow the Taliban government and disband al-Qaeda. They called in precision air strikes with Cruise missiles and laser-guided bombs on Taliban and al-Qaeda positions, which forced them to flee across the porous border with Pakistan and caused their disintegration. The United States expelled al-Qaeda from Afghanistan, toppled the Taliban government, and installed a new government under Hamid Karzai (1957–) from an impeccable Afghan lineage, the Popalzai of the Durrani clan. Karzai was the compromise choice of the leaders of the Northern Alliance (also known as the United Front) at a meeting held in Bonn, Germany, who wanted to bring the internal war to a close and were willing to accept a president from the Durrani clan, which had produced Afghanistan's first king and whose descendants ruled until 1818. Karzai revived the aura of Durrani royal leadership.

Karzai assembled an emergency *loya jirga* in 2002 to ratify the decisions made at Bonn. It was asked to accept his provisional government for two years until a constitution could be written and elections held. A constitutional *loya jirga* met in 2003 to decide the nature of the new government, unitary or federal, presidential or parliamentary. Those favoring a unitary state and a strong president won the day on the grounds that Afghanistan needed a strong, centralized state. Karzai was elected president in 2004. The Taliban, and other opponents of the new regime, refused to participate in the *loya jirga* and the writing of a new constitution. They continued, and continue at this writing, to wage war against the new government from Qandahar and Helmand provinces in the south, legitimizing their claim to rule in religion.

Despite the continuation of the war and much corruption within government ministries, Karzai made some progress establishing democratic institutions and improving the economy. Parliamentary elections were held in 2005, which resulted in a legislative body composed of former mujahideen fighters, Islamic fundamentalists, local warlords, former communists, reformers, and Taliban members. The parliament became the focus of political opposition to the Karzai government, and Karzai's popularity declined significantly. Nonetheless, he was reelected for a second term in 2005 when his opponent,

Karzai's former minister of foreign affairs, Abdullah Abdullah (1960–), did not participate in the runoff election owing to massive and obvious electoral fraud.

During Karzai's presidency, the United Nations Assistance Mission in Afghanistan (UNAMA), and the United States pushed him to establish a centralized governmental system. Karzai favored decentralization; followed the Afghan style of leadership; and built patronage networks of personal clients bound to him. Non-Pashtuns agreed to his approach, if they gained local autonomy in exchange. Until the end of his second term, which expired in 2014, Karzai was dependent upon American support, which could be seen in his relationship with Zalmay Khalilzad (1951–) an Afghan-American and President Bush's special envoy to Afghanistan in 2001 and ambassador in 2003.[81]

In 2014, Abdullah Abdullah ran for president a second time against Ashraf Ghani (1949–), a former employee of the World Bank and Afghanistan's finance minister from 2002 to 2004. Neither candidate received 50 percent of the vote, forcing a runoff. Each accused the other of electoral fraud and refused to participate in a runoff election. Under pressure from the United States, they agreed to form a national unity government with Abdullah becoming prime minister and Ghani becoming president.

In sum, Afghanistan's indigenous war-driven state-formation process was curtailed in 1919 by the integration of Afghanistan into the emerging European-dominated global system of states. Subsequently, indigenous rulers at the national level sought to "modernize" Afghanistan by emulating institutions and practices from the West, which were resisted by local tribal and religious leaders. This ushered in a long period of internal war among various elite factions and clans seeking to gain control of the Afghan state. This internal struggle has been complicated and fueled by the involvement of foreign states (especially the Soviet Union and the United States) in order to regulate and discipline Afghanistan's sovereignty for their own strategic ends. Owing to the fact that it has its own lengthy history of indigenous state formation, and strong sense of national unity forged during the war against the Soviets, the internal struggles within Afghanistan never threatened the territorial integrity of the Afghan state. All Afghan factions have wished to maintain a unified Afghanistan, and never pushed to divide it along ethnic lines.[82]

It remains today weak but unified.

Iraq: From League of Nations Mandate to Collapsed and Dismembered State

Iraq's history of state formation and deformation can be divided into four broad periods.[83] The first period begins with the British mandate after the

First World War, during which time Iraq's sovereignty was directly regulated and disciplined by the British. The second begins with the overthrow of the monarchy established by the British and the formation of a republic. During this period an intense internal struggle for indigenous control of the state began among elites representing Iraq's competing ethnic and sectarian groups. The third period began in 1990, after which Iraq's sovereignty was again directly regulated and disciplined by an outside power, in this case the United States. The fourth period begins with the return of sovereignty to Iraq and its subsequent collapse and dismemberment by its warring factions and groups allied with outside forces.

Iraq's first broad historical period began during the First World War when the British occupied the Fao peninsula in Basra in 1914, Baghdad in 1917, and Mosul in 1918, and the Ottoman Empire surrendered to British forces. The Treaty of Sèvres (1920) abolished the Ottoman Empire and forced the Turks to renounce rights over the Arab Middle East and North Africa. The treaty laid the groundwork for the partition of the Ottoman Empire's territories outside of the Arabian Peninsula between Britain and France in accordance with the spheres of influence defined by the secret Sykes-Picot Agreement (1916). Accordingly, the administrative regions (*vilayets*) of Basra, Baghdad, and Mosul were placed under British authority as the British Mandate of Mesopotamia in 1921. The mandate encompassed four major ethnic groups: Arabs, Kurds, Assyrians, and Turkmen; three religious groups: Muslims, Christians, and Jews; and two major sectarian groups: Shiites and Sunnis. Fifty-six percent of the population were Shiites, who resided in the region to the south of Baghdad; 36 percent were Sunnis, who resided to the north of Baghdad up to Mosul; and about 25 percent of the population were Kurds, who lived in the landlocked mountainous regions in the north and northeast.[84]

Gertrude Bell, a British writer, traveler, political officer, administrator, spy, and archaeologist, and T. E. Lawrence (1888–1935), the liaison officer between the British army and the Arab tribes during the Arab Revolt (1916–1918) against Ottoman rule, were instrumental in shaping the government and selecting the leadership of the new Iraqi state. At a conference held in Cairo in 1921, Bell and Lawrence recommended that Faisal bin-Hussein (1883–1933), the son of the Hashemite ruler of Mecca, Hussein bin-Ali (1854–1931), be made the first king of the new state of Iraq because he had sufficient nationalist and Islamic credentials to be respected by the Sunnis, Shias, and Kurds to keep these three groups united and controlled, which was essential to British imperial interests in the Middle East. They argued that the Shiites would respect him because he was a direct descendant of the Prophet Muhammad. Sunnis and Kurds would follow him because he was a Sunni from the Hashemite dynasty.

Faisal was crowned king in August 1921 and Bell advised him on local matters involving tribal geography and local politics during the early 1920s. Relations between the British and the new Iraqi monarchy were formalized by the Anglo-Iraqi Treaty of 1922, which guaranteed British military and administrative control over the new kingdom. An indigenous Iraqi army officered by Sunnis who had served under the Ottomans with ranks filled by Shiite tribal elements was established with the advice and assistance of British officers. British advisers were placed in government ministries. Because Iraq's political institutions were created by a foreign power and because there was no tradition of democratic governance, the parliament lacked legitimacy and its members never developed territorial constituencies. Political life actually revolved around important personalities and cliques representing the emerging landowning Shiite Arab tribal sheikhs, the wealthy and prestigious urban-based Sunni families, and the Ottoman-trained army officers and bureaucrats.

In 1929 negotiations between the Iraqi and British governments produced the second Anglo-Iraq Treaty (1930), which granted full Iraqi independence from the date of Iraq's admission to the League of Nations. The treaty called for a close alliance between Britain and Iraq for a period of twenty-five years after independence, during which time the British were to provide military assistance to the Iraqis, if attacked; maintain close cooperation in foreign affairs; be allowed to maintain two air force bases at Basra and al Habbaniyah and move troops across the country; and to continue training and equipping the Iraqi armed forces. Iraq became a member of the League of Nations on October 3, 1932. On that date the British mandate ended and Iraq became officially an independent state. Immediately after independence, the Iraqi government declared that Kuwait, which had been severed from the *vilayet* of Basra by the British, was rightfully part of Iraq's national territory.

In 1933, King Faisal died and was succeeded on the throne by his only son, Ghazi (1912–1939). During Ghazi bin Faisal's brief reign (he died in a motor car accident in 1939) Iraqi nationalists and pan-Arab nationalists began to agitate against the continued British presence in Iraq. This split the Iraqi political class into pro- and anti-British politicians and resulted in the rising and falling of numerous governments. During this period there were also several revolts and uprisings that were brutally suppressed by the Iraqi army commanded by General Bakr Sidqi (1890–1937), who was of Kurdish origins but an Arab nationalist. In 1933, the Iraqi army under his command massacred hundreds of Assyrians at Simele and, in 1935–1936, brutally suppressed Shiite uprisings in the mid-Euphrates region, as well as Kurdish anti-conscription uprisings and a Yazidi revolt in Jabal Sinjar.

The indigenous Sunni officer corps of the army, which had become the site of Iraqi nationalism, pushed for the departure of the British. High-ranking nationalist officers jockeyed for power with pro-British civilian governments. In 1936, the acting commander of the Iraqi army, General Sidiq, who had been strongly influenced by European fascism and favored the creation of a strong state capable of reversing British domination, seized power in a military coup d'état, the first military overthrow of a government in the Middle East. General Sidiq ruled Iraq until he was himself assassinated in a counter-coup in 1937 by a small group of Sunni officers (the "circle of seven"), who shared a pan-Arab vision for Iraq. There followed four additional coups carried out by high-ranking officers of the army seeking to pressure the government to concede to army demands.

The last of this series of coups was carried out in 1941 when a group of nationalist and pro-fascist army officers seized power and removed the pro-British prime minister Nuri al-Said (1888–1958) and replaced him with Rashid Ali al-Gaylani (1892–1965). Al-Gaylani attempted to restrict the rights of the British under the 1930 treaty and asked for assistance in this endeavor from Fascist Italy and Nazi Germany. Al-Gaylani also sent the Iraqi army to the British Royal Air Force base at Habbaniya to demand that the British leave Iraq. The British refused and demanded that the Iraqi army depart. When it did not comply, the British began bombing Iraqi positions. The war between Britain and Iraq lasted about a month and resulted in defeat for the Iraqis. In 1947 a third treaty with the British was signed that returned the two air force bases to Iraq, but continued the arming and training of the army by the British. Widespread demonstrations against the treaty led to the declaration of martial law and return of Nuri al-Said as prime minister. He pursued a pro-British, pro-Western policy and dominated Iraqi politics until he was assassinated in 1958. During this period, nationalist and communist ideas spread within the army, especially among younger officers from poor social backgrounds. Opposition to al-Said's government became a secret movement modeled on the Egyptian Free Officers Movement led by Colonel Gamal Abdel Nasser (1918–1970), which had overthrown the Egyptian monarchy in 1952.

The second broad period of Iraq's political history began on July 14, 1958, when the Iraqi "Free Officers," led by Abd al-Karim Qasim (1914–1963) and Abdul Salam Arif (1921–1966) seized power. The 1958 coup was a major turning point in Iraq's political history because it overthrew the monarchy, ended British involvement in Iraq, and changed the internal dynamic among Iraq's competing ethnic and sectarian groups. Iraq became a republic governed by the Revolutionary Command Council (RCC) with Qasim as prime minister and Arif as deputy prime minister. The king and members of the royal family were executed.

Nonetheless, the Free Officers Movement was plagued by internal dissension. It lacked a clear ideology and organizational structure. Consequently, a power struggle developed between Qasim and Arif. Qasim, who was of mixed Sunni and Shia parentage, favored and promoted a civic Arabo-Kurdish nationalism that recognized Kurds and Arabs as equal partners in the Iraqi state. The Kurdish language was legally permitted and became the medium of instruction in educational institutions in the Kurdish areas and as a second language in the Arab territories. His government encouraged the idea of a Kurdistan annexed to Iraq in order to coopt Iranian Kurds to support unifying with Iraq. The Kurdish leader, Mustafa Barzani (1903–1979), who had been exiled by the monarchy, was allowed to return to Iraq. The Qasim government also resurrected Iraq's irredentist claims to Kuwait. His position was supported by the Communist Party of Iraq (CPI), which had been legalized after the coup.

Arif, on the other hand, was a pan-Arab nationalist who supported unification with Nasser's United Arab Republic (UAR), which consisted of Egypt and Syria, and opposed Qasim's focus on Iraqi nationalism and legalization of the CPI. Eventually, Arif was removed as deputy prime minister and minister of the interior and was forced to become Iraq's ambassador to Germany. After a short time, he returned to Iraq and, amid rumors of an attempted coup, was arrested, brought to trial for treason, and condemned to death. His death sentence was commuted to life in prison in 1962. Despite the removal of Arif, pan-Arab opposition to Qasim continued and, in 1963, he was overthrown by a group of pan-Arab officers, who disliked his focus on Iraqi nationalism, and members of the Ba'ath Party of Iraq, which saw him as being too close to the CPI. In the wake of the coup, Qasim was executed and about 3,000 members of the CPI and its sympathizers were hunted down and murdered.[85] Arif was released from prison and returned to power as president and Ahmed Hassan al-Bakr (1914–1982), the head of the military bureau of the Ba'ath party, became prime minister. The RCC was disbanded and replaced by the National Council of the Revolutionary Command (NCRC).

Like its predecessor, the NCRC was fraught with divisions. Arif and pan-Arab officers wanted to join the UAR. Al-Bakr and the Ba'athists were opposed. In 1966 Arif died in a helicopter crash and was succeeded by his older brother, Abdul Rahman Arif (1916–2007). Arif the elder's government was weak and, in 1968, al-Bakr, supported by Abd ar-Razzaq al-Naif (1934–1978) the deputy head of military intelligence, and Ibrahim Daud (?–?), the commander of the Republican Guard, led a coup against the older Arif. For his part in the coup, Naif became prime minister. Al-Bakr, who was elected to the NCRC, retained his post as the Iraqi regional secretary of the Ba'ath Party. He appointed his cousin, Saddam Hussein (1937–2006), to the post of chief of the party's intelligence services. Al-Bakr, who was a cunning and well-organized operator, ousted Naif and Daud in July 1968, the so-called July 17 Revolution. Together, he and Hussein strengthened Ba'ath party control over the government and renamed the NCRC the Revolutionary Command Council (RCC).

A-Bakr and Hussein sought to neutralize the army, which had, up to that time, played a determining political role in Iraq. This was done by transforming military elites into civilians and creating parallel coercive agencies linked to departments of the Ba'ath party to balance the army. In 1969, al-Bakr appointed civilians to the RCC, which had been up to that point composed exclusively of military officers, and purged its non-Ba'athist members. Hussein was made deputy secretary of the Regional Leadership section of the Ba'ath party and deputy secretary of the RCC. Ba'athist elements were also installed in key commands within the military, and the military academy became restricted to Ba'ath party members.

From the mid- to late 1970s, Hussein's power within the Ba'athist government grew and he became de facto leader of Iraq, although al-Bakr remained as president. Eventually, he assumed the leadership of the Ba'ath party, the presidency of the republic, and chairmanship of the Revolutionary Command Council after waging a successful campaign against the Iraqi communist party and suppressing a revolt against the Sunni-led government by Shiites emboldened by the Iranian Islamic revolution of 1979. Hussein assumed absolute power by presenting himself as the father of the nation and taking control of Iraq's formal institutions of government by appointing kinsmen from his hometown, Tikrit, and exploiting friendships built up since he joined the Ba'ath party in 1957.

Border clashes between Iraq and Iran in 1980 were the precursors to a full-scale war between the two states. Thinking that Iran could be quickly defeated and hoping thus to regain control over all of the Shatt al-Arab area, which had been lost to Iran in 1975, Iraq invaded Iran in September 1980. The Iranian regime proved to be too strong and was able to push the Iraqi army back into Iraq in 1982. In 1988, after a series of Iraq victories, a cease-fire was arranged between Iran and Iraq and the war ended in a stalemate.

The third broad period of Iraq's history as a state began when Kuwait decided to increase its oil output, which led to a big drop in the price of oil per barrel on the international market. As the price decrease reduced Iraq's oil revenues, Hussein accused Kuwait of siphoning oil from the ar-Rumaylah oil field located on the border between the two states, and threatened to invade if Kuwait did not comply with its demands. In July 1990, Hussein demanded that Kuwait repay Iraq for the oil that it had "stolen" from Iraq and nullify Iraq's $50 billion debt to Kuwait. The Kuwaiti government failed to meet Hussein's demand. The Kuwait failure to comply, coupled with Iraq's long-standing irredentist claim to Kuwait, brought the invasion of Kuwait on August 2. The invasion was condemned by the international community, which demanded the immediate withdrawal of Iraqi troops. Hussein responded by annexing Kuwait to Iraq. His defiance led to a decision of the United Nations Security Council to authorize the formation of a military coalition to force Iraq's withdrawal from Kuwait. After a forty-two-day aerial and naval bombardment, led by the United States, the largest military coalition since the Second World War made a ground assault on Kuwait and pushed Iraq's army out of the territory one hundred hours after the attack began. In retreat, the Iraqi army sabotaged Kuwaiti oil wells, causing massive fires and much environmental damage. A cease-fire was arranged and took effect on February 28. Iraq was forced to accept Kuwaiti sovereignty and to cease its program to develop weapons of mass destruction.

A few days after the cease-fire, the Saudi Arabia–based radio station Voice of Free Iraq, which was funded by the United States Central Intelligence Agency (CIA), broadcast a message encouraging the Iraqi people to rise up against the "criminal tyrant of Iraq." This message led many Iraqis to believe that the United States would support a national uprising. In March 1990 an uprising of Shiites began, which was quickly crushed by forces loyal to Hussein. In 1991, the United Nations Security Council passed Resolution 688, which established a no-fly zone over the Kurdish-inhabited area north of the 36th parallel to protect Kurds. In 1992, a second no-fly zone was established south of the 32nd parallel to protect Shiites. The Iraqi air force was prohibited from flying within these zones, which were patrolled by air forces from the United States, Britain, and France.

After the terrorist attacks on the World Trade Center towers in New York City in 2001, President George W. Bush and his government decided to reorder the Middle East by invading Iraq and deposing Saddam Hussein. The invasion in March 2003 was made under the pretext of Iraq's having weapons of mass destruction (WMDs) and having connections to al-Qaeda, the perpetrator of the 2001 attacks. On March 19, a combined military force composed of units from the United States, Britain, Australia, and Poland invaded Iraq. Baghdad was taken on April 19. Hussein and the leaders of his government went into hiding. Iraq was occupied by coalition forces and governed by the Coalition Provisional Authority (CPA), headed by L. Paul Bremmer (1941–), until June 2004. Hussein's regime having been seen as an intolerable threat to regional and world peace, the CPA began to establish a democratic regime friendly to the United States and its allies that "would not threaten its neighbors." Bremmer dissolved the Ba'ath party, prohibited its members from participating in the new government, and dissolved the army and security apparatus of the old regime. He allied the United States with the Shiite Dawa Party, the Kurdistan Democratic Party (KDP), and the Popular Union of Kurdistan (PUK). Opposition to the occupation came primarily from Ba'athist Sunnis who were ousted from their positions of power in the military and bureaucracy by the United States' de-Ba'athification program.

The fourth broad period in the history of the Iraqi state began when elections were held for a constituent assembly and Iraq became self-governing once again, albeit with much disciplining and regulating by the United States. Of the 275 seats, the United Iraqi Alliance (UIA), a coalition of Shiite parties, including the Dawa Party led by Nuri al-Maliki (1950–), won 140 seats; a coalition of Kurdish parties, essentially the KDP and the PUK, called the Democratic Alliance of Kurdistan (DAK), won 75 seats; and a secular list led by Ayad Allawi (1944–), a Shiite who had lived in exile for thirty years before returning to Iraq after the invasion, won 40 seats. Positions within the interim government were allocated according to the new correlation of political forces produced by the election. The presidency went to a Kurd, Jalal Talabani (1933–), with two vice-presidents, one Shiite and one Sunni; the speaker of the legislature to a Sunni Arab; and the prime ministership to a Shiite, al-Maliki. The various government ministries became fiefdoms of the parties. The Sunni community, about 20 percent of the population, was unrepresented, marginalized, and opposed to the new regime.

Although some Sunnis decided to participate in the regime by participating in the second election held in December 2005, the chair of the Council of Muslim Scholars, Harith Sulyman al-Darih (1941–2015) which was linked to deposed military officers and radical Islamic parties, such as the Jamaat Ansar al Sunnah, the Islamic Army in Iraq, and al-Qaeda, supported resistance and insurgency.[86] In February 2006 Sunni militants blew up the Shiite shrine in Samara. In retaliation Sunni mosques were attacked by Shia militants. Further violence ensued and the populations of Iraq's ethnically mixed cities divided themselves into sectarian neighborhoods. More than one hundred Iraqis were killed every day by suicide bombers and assassins. The United States sought to reintegrate Sunnis and regain their trust during the surge of 2007, but Nuri al-Maliki's government alienated them after the United States withdrawal by imprisoning Sunni leaders and disbanding their militias. The United States forced al-Maliki to resign in August 2014. He was replaced by another Dawa Party member, Haider al-Abadi (1952–), who, it was hoped, could bring an end to the sectarian violence. Meanwhile, the Kurdish region of Iraq, which had been untouched by internal war because the PUK and the KDP made peace in 1998 (the Washington Peace Accord), gradually established a unified regional government. Massoud Barzani (1946–), the son of Mustafa Barzani, is the current head of the KDP and the president of the regional government.

In sum, the struggle among Iraq's ethnic and sectarian groups, which has been aided and abetted by outside states and groups, has become a full-blown, internal war and has dismembered the Iraqi state along the lines of its sectarian and ethnic divisions. The so-called "Iraqi government" in Baghdad under Shiite control has not even the semblance of a monopoly of the means of coercion over the national territory. The Iraq army is forbidden by law from entering the autonomous Kurdish region, which has its own army, the Peshmerga. In the west, the Islamic State of Iraq and the Levant (ISIL), which is led by and mainly composed of Sunni Arabs from Iraq and Syria, has successfully erased the borders between Syria and Iraq and begun to carve out a new state, its so-called "caliphate," that transcends them.

ISIL began as Jama'at al-Tawhid wal-Jihad, one of the insurgent groups that came into being after the invasion of Iraq by the United States–led international coalition. It joined with other Sunni insurgent groups to form the Mujahideen Shura Council, which claimed the formation of the Islamic State of Iraq (ISI) in October 2003 in the western part of Iraq where the population is mostly Sunni. It has made war on Iraqi government security forces, Kurdish Peshmerga forces, American troops, foreign diplomats, and civilians from various smaller Iraqi religious groups, such as the Yazidis. About one-third of its leadership are former Ba'athist government officials and military officers who served during Saddam Hussein's rule and spent time imprisoned by United States forces after the invasion. In 2011, ISI established cells in Syria, recruited fighters, joined with the al-Nursa Front, and made war against the government of Bashar al-Assad (1965–). After joining with the al-Nursa Front, ISI renamed itself the Islamic State of Iraq and the Levant (ISIL).

ISIL has defeated Iraqi security forces and successfully established its presence in central and northern Syria and western Iraq where it has proclaimed a caliphate. In June 2014 it captured Mosul, Iraq's second-largest city. An estimated eight million Iraqis and Syrians live in ISIL's caliphate, within which it has established a working government that provides them with order and security. Corrupt officials have been ousted and uncorrupt officials have been kept in their jobs after pledging support for ISIL. ISIL's caliphate provides modern welfare services, collects taxes from the wealthy, repairs roads, and keeps the electricity on and the water flowing. It has also maintained food production. Many "Sunnis in Iraq and Syria now feel that [ISIL] is the only defense against brutal retribution from the Damascus and Baghdad governments."[87]

In sum, ISIL has established a nascent, alternative form of the state that transcends the Sykes-Picot border between Syria and Iraq. Moreover, it claims a worldwide caliphate and has attracted support from radical Islamists from Algeria, Afghanistan, Yemen, Libya, Nigeria (Boko Haram), Niger, Chad, Cameroon, Chechnya, and the Philippines, as well as thousands of individuals from Western Europe and the United States.

ISIL has been classified as a "terrorist organization" by the United Nations, the European Union (EU), and sixteen states because of its human rights abuses, war crimes, persecution of religious groups (Shias; Alawites; Assyrians; Chaldean, Syriac, and Armenian Christians; Yazidis; Druze; Shabaks; and Mandeans), the military use of children, the use of chemical weapons, the destruction of cultural and religious sites, sexual violence against women, the beheading of captives, and the mass execution of captured soldiers. For these and other violations of the norms and practices of the current

Westphalian global order, a large number of states and groups are at war with ISIL, and the United States is leading a global coalition to defeat it. At this writing, it remains to be seen if ISIL will be defeated and the territorial integrity of Iraq and Syria reestablished.

CONCLUSION

Weak states are states that do not have a monopoly on the means of coercion, are not institutionalized, and have not pacified their populations and territories. They are wracked by low-intensity, internalized wars among ethnic, regional, and religious factions competing for control or dismemberment of the state. The anti-belligerency norms of the contemporary global order make bringing such groups together into a single nation very difficult, if not impossible. As there are no threats to their sovereignty by predatory neighbors, the elites of many non-Western states have not had to fight wars against other states, and therefore have abjured state- and nation-building strategies. Moreover, in many cases state elites benefit and profit from state weakness. The internalized low-intensity wars that wrack these states will not build state capacity and a sense of nationhood. Efforts to build/rebuild them from outside are bound to fail.

The basic problem for weak non-Western states is that their sovereignty has been heavily regulated and strongly disciplined by the powerful correcting states of the European-created Westphalian states system. Moreover, the territorial integrity norm forbids the dismemberment of an extant state and the formation of new states by contending groups, unless it is done without violence through negotiations and/or referenda.

There are significant differences among weak states especially with regard to the maintenance of their territorial integrity. Owing to its long history of indigenous, war-driven state-making, the Afghan state has deep enough roots to survive intact, despite endemic succession struggles for the throne in its early history and elite/clan struggles for control of the state in recent history. In other words, a direct line can be drawn between the establishment of the Afghan monarchy in the eighteenth century and the contemporary Afghan state. Iraq, on the other hand, has no history of indigenous state-making. It was the brainchild of Gertrude Bell and T. E. Lawrence. It has almost no sense of nationhood and has not been able to survive the overthrow of Saddam Hussein and his Ba'athist government, which held it together. Iraq has been ripped asunder by its warring factions and has collapsed into three warring proto-states: the Shiite rump of the original state in the south, the Kurdish autonomous region in the north, and the caliphate of ISIL in the west.

Thus, many, but not all, non-Western states are weak politico-military entities within which many groups contend with the force of arms to gain control of the state or break it apart to form new states. Western states take it upon themselves to intervene on the side of one faction against the others for their own strategic reasons. This means that internal wars are not state-building wars because there is no incentive for contending groups to come together against an outside foe that is seeking to conquer the state and include it within a new, larger state. Internal wars go on and on seemingly without end. Low-intensity internalized wars within weak non-European states being waged with AK-47s, IEDs, and RPGs are intertwined with the global policing wars waged with UAVs and "smart" munitions by advanced, mostly Western, neoliberal states to maintain the global order and discipline the sovereignty of non-Western states. How these modes of war are intertwined and how they affect the relationship between the state, the army, and the people is the subject of the concluding chapter.

NOTES

1. Steven Pinker, *The Better Angels of Our Nature: Why Violence Has Declined* (New York: Viking, 2011), p. 305.
2. R. Harrison Wagner, *War and the State: The Theory of International Politics* (Ann Arbor, MI: University of Michigan Press, 2007), p. 76.
3. Aaron Ralby, *Atlas of Military History* (Bath, UK: Parragon, 2012), *passim*, and Jeremy Black, *War and the World: Military Power and the Fate of Continents, 1450–2000* (New Haven, CT: Yale University Press, 1998), *passim*. See also, Doyne Dawson, *The First Armies* (London: Cassell & Co., 2001).
4. Yale H. Ferguson and Richard W. Mansbach, *Polities: Authority, Identities, and Change* (Columbia: South Carolina University Press, 1996), pp. 80–81, 175–78, 121–22.
5. Victor Davis Hanson, *Carnage and Culture: Landmark Battles and the Rise of Western Power* (New York: Anchor Books, 2002), pp. 1–24.
6. Tonio Andrade, *The Gunpowder Age: China, Military Innovation, and the Rise of the West in World History* (Princeton, NJ, and Oxford: Princeton University Press, 2016), p. 10.
7. Daniel R. Headrick, *The Tools of Empire: Technology and European Imperialism in the Nineteenth Century* (New York: Oxford University Press, 1981), p. 115.
8. Philip T. Hoffman, *Why Did Europe Conquer the World?* (Princeton, NJ, and Oxford: Princeton University Press, 2015), p. 14.
9. Headrick, *op. cit.*, p. 85. See also, John Ellis, *The Social History of the Machine Gun* (Baltimore, MD: The Johns Hopkins University Press, 1975), chapter 4.
10. Andrade, *op. cit.*, p. 237.
11. Black, *op. cit.*, p. 116.
12. *Ibid.*, p. 12.
13. *Ibid.*, p. 224.
14. Miguel Angel Centeno, "Limited War and Limited States," in Diane E. Davis and Anthony W. Pereira, eds., *Irregular Armed Forces and Their Role in Politics and State Formation* (Cambridge: Cambridge University Press, 2003), p. 94. The website www.andrewclem.com/LatinAmerica/LatAmer_wars.html lists nine wars in Latin America between 1835 and 1982: Texas War (Texas vs. Mexico, 1835–1836); Chilean War (Chile vs. Peru-Bolivia Confederation, 1838); Mexican-American War (U.S. vs. Mexico, 1846–1848); War of the Triple Alliance (Paraguay vs. Argentina, Uruguay, and Brazil, 1864–1870); War of the Pacific (Chile vs. Peru and Bolivia, 1879–1883); Chaco War (Bolivia vs. Paraguay, 1832–1835); Peru-Ecua-

dor War (1941); Soccer War (El Salvador vs. Honduras, 1969); and the Falklands/Malvinas War (Britain vs. Argentina, 1982).

15. Cameron G. Thies, "War, Rivalry, and State Building in Latin America," *American Journal of Political Science,* 49 (No. 3), July 2005, pp. 451–65.

16. The exceptions to this rule were the Portuguese colonies—Angola, Mozambique, and Guinea-Bissau—which had to fight for their independence.

17. Jeffrey Herbst, *States and Power in Africa: Comparative Lessons in Authority and Control* (Princeton, NJ: Princeton University Press, 2000). See also, Jeffrey Herbst, "War and the State in Africa," *International Security,* 14 (No. 4), Spring 1990, pp. 117–39.

18. Stein S. Eriksen, "The Congo War and the Prospects for State Formation: Rwanda and Uganda Compared," *Third World Quarterly,* 26 (No. 7), 2005, pp. 1,097–113.

19. Brian D. Taylor and Roxana Botea, "Tilly-Tally: War-Making and State-Making in the Contemporary Third World," *International Studies Review,* 10 (No. 1), March 2008, pp. 27–56.

20. Adham Saouli, *The Arab State: Dilemmas of Late Formation* (London/New York: Routledge, 2012).

21. Ian S. Lustick, "The Absence of Middle Eastern Great Powers: Political 'Backwardness' in Historical Perspective," *International Organization,* 51 (No. 4), Autumn 1997.

22. Lingyu Lu and Cameron G. Thies, "War, Rivalry, and State Building in the Middle East," *Political Research Quarterly,* 66 (No. 2), 2013, pp. 239–53.

23. Syed Ali Raza Zaidi, et al., "War Making and State Making in Pakistan," *South Asian Studies,* 29 (No. 2), July–December, 2014, pp. 379–94.

24. Michael N. Barnett, *Confronting the Costs of War: Military Power, State, and Society in Egypt and Israel* (Princeton, NJ: Princeton University Press, 1992).

25. Vicken Cheterian, "The August War in Georgia: From Ethnic Conflict to Border Wars," *Central Asian Survey,* 28 (No. 2), 2009, pp. 155–70.

26. Joel S. Migdal, *Strong Societies and Weak States: State Society Relations and State Capabilities in the Third World* (Princeton, NJ: Princeton University Press, 1988).

27. Kalevi J. Holsti, "Reversing Rousseau: The Medieval and Modern in Contemporary Wars," in William Bain (ed.), *The Empire of Security and the Safety of the People* (New York: Routledge, 2006), p. 43.

28. Evan Luard, *The Blunted Sword: The Erosion of Military Power in Modern World Politics* (New York: New Amsterdam Books, 1989), p. 9.

29. Holsti, *op. cit.,* pp. 40–41.

30. Cédric Gouverneur, "Country Without a Port," *Le Monde Diplomatique,* September 2015.

31. Kalevi J. Holsti, "The Decline of Interstate War: Pondering Systematic Explanations," in Raimo Väyrynen, *The Waning of Major War: Theories and Debates* (London/New York: Routledge, 2013), pp. 139–40.

32. Martin Shaw, *The New Western Way of War: Risk-Transfer War and Its Crisis in Iraq* (Cambridge, MA: Polity Press, 2005), p. 72.

33. Wagner, *op. cit.,* p. 125.

34. Jane Burbank and Frederick Cooper, *Empires in World History: Power and the Politics of Difference* (Princeton, NJ: Princeton University Press, 2010).

35. Kalevi J. Holsti, *Peace and War: Armed Conflicts and International Order 1648–1989* (Cambridge: Cambridge University Press, 1991), p. 323.

36. Brian Schmidt, *The Political Discourse of Anarchy: A Disciplinary History of International Relations* (Albany, NY: State University of New York Press, 1998), p. 194.

37. Holsti, *Peace and War,* p. 323.

38. Robert Latham, *The Liberal Moment: Modernity, Security, and the Making of the Post-War International Order* (New York: Columbia University Press, 1997), p. 10.

39. *Ibid.,* p. 47.

40. Hendrik Spruyt, "Normative Transformations in International Relations and the Waning of Major War," in Väyrynen, *op. cit.,* pp. 185–206.

41. On the evolution of the territorial norm see Mark W. Zacher, "The Territorial Integrity Norm: International Boundaries and the Use of Force," *International Organization,* 55, 2, Spring 2001, pp. 215–50.

42. Michael C. Desch, "War and Strong States, Peace and Weak States?" *International Organization,* 50 (No. 2), Spring 1996, p. 237.

43. Boaz Atzili, "When Good Fences Make Bad Neighbors: Fixed Borders, State Weakness, and International Conflict," *International Security,* 31 (No. 3), Winter 2006/2007, p. 149.

44. Shaw, *op. cit.,* p. 50.

45. John Mueller, *Retreat from Doomsday: The Obsolescence of Major War* (New York: Basic Books, 1989), p. 227. The evidence of the waning of major war is very strong. See Martin Shaw, *Post-Military Society* (Philadelphia, PA: Temple University Press, 1991), Table 2.1, p. 59. See also Steven Pinker, *The Better Angels of Our Nature: Why Violence Has Declined* (New York: Viking, 2011), esp. chapter 5.

46. Cited in Raimo Väyrynen, "Introduction: Contending Views," in Väyrynen, *op. cit.,* p. 1.

47. John Mueller, "Accounting for the Waning of Major War," in Väyrynen, *op. cit.,* p. 74.

48. Mary Kaldor, *New and Old Wars: Organized Violence in a Global Era,* 2nd Edition (Stanford, CA: Stanford University Press, 2007), p. 98.

49. *Ibid.,* pp. 98–99.

50. Larry Kahner, *AK-47: The Weapon That Changed the World* (New York: John Wiley & Son, 2007), pp. 6–7.

51. https://en.wikipedia.org/wiki/improvised_explosive_device.

52. https://en.wikipedia.org/wiki/Rocket-propelled_grenade.

53. Geoffrey Parker (ed.), *The Cambridge Illustrated History of Warfare: The Triumph of the West* (Cambridge: Cambridge University Press, 1995), p. 369.

54. Hugo Slim, *Killing Civilians: Method, Madness, and Morality* (London: Hurst, 2008), p. 5.

55. Youssef Cohen, Brian R. Brown, A. F. K. Organski, "The Paradoxical Nature of State Making: The Violent Creation of Order," *American Political Science Review,* 75 (No. 4), December 1981.

56. Stathis N. Kalyvas, "'New' and 'Old' Civil Wars: A Valid Distinction?" *World Politics,* 54 (No.1), October 2001, p. 105.

57. Christopher Cramer, *Violence in Developing Countries: War, Memory, Progress* (Bloomington: Indiana University Press, 2006), pp. 199–200. John Mueller writes in *The Remnants of War* (Ithaca, NY: Cornell University Press, 2004) that today's civil wars in failed states are the same as the wars among criminals, brigands, thugs, rogues, and vagabonds in early modern Europe.

58. Mark Duffield, *Global Governance and the New Wars: The Merging of Development and Security* (London/New York: Zed Books, 2014), p. 14.

59. Hans Joas and Wolfgang Knöbl, *War in Social Thought: Hobbes to the Present,* trans. Alex Skinner (Princeton, NJ: Princeton University Press, 2013), p. 232.

60. Ann Hironaka, *Neverending Wars: The International Community, Weak States, and the Perpetuation of Civil War* (Cambridge, MA: Harvard University Press, 2005), p. 7.

61. Holsti, *The State, War, and the State of War,* p. 61.

62. *Ibid.,* p. 64.

63. *Ibid.,* p. 66.

64. *Ibid.,* p. 70.

65. Basil Davidson, *Black Man's Burden: Africa and the Curse of the Nation-State* (New York: Random House, 1992).

66. Holsti, *Peace and War,* p. 283.

67. William Reno, *Warlord Politics and African States* (Boulder/London: Lynne Rienner, 1998).

68. Robert I. Rotberg (ed.), *When States Fail: Causes and Consequences* (Princeton, NJ: Princeton University Press, 2004).

69. Wagner, *op. cit.,* p. 205.

70. Holsti, *Peace and War,* p. 324.

71. Wagner, *op. cit.,* p. 222.

72. Francis Fukuyama (ed.), *Nation-Building: Beyond Afghanistan and Iraq* (Baltimore: The Johns Hopkins University Press, 2006), p. 2. Emphasis added.

73. Pierre Englebert and Denis M. Tull, "Post conflict Reconstruction in Africa: Flawed Ideas about Failed States," *International Security,* 32 (No. 4), Spring 2008, p. 106.

74. Vivienne Jabri, *War and the Transformation of Global Politics* (New York: Palgrave Macmillan, 2010), p. 158. Emphasis added.

75. Wagner, *op. cit.,* p. 224.

76. Paul D. Miller, *Armed State Building: Confronting State Failure, 1898–2012* (Ithaca, NY: Cornell University Press, 2013), p. 4.

77. Wagner, *op. cit.,* p. 224.

78. The historical details in this section are from Thomas Barfield, *Afghanistan: A Cultural and Political History* (Princeton, NJ: Princeton University Press, 2010), *passim,* unless otherwise noted.

79. *Ibid.,* p. 98.

80. The Pashtunistan issue was the demand that arose in Afghanistan in 1947 when British India was partitioned and the new state of Pakistan created that Pashtuns living in Pakistan should be granted a state of their own, autonomy within Pakistan, or the right to join Afghanistan.

81. Barfield, *op. cit.,* pp. 309–10.

82. *Ibid.,* p. 278.

83. The historical details in this section are from Phebe Marr, *The Modern History of Iraq,* Second Edition (Boulder, CO: Westview Press, 2004), *passim,* unless otherwise noted.

84. Adham Saouli, *The Arab State: Dilemmas of Late Formation* (New York: Routledge, 2012), pp. 108–9.

85. *Ibid.,* p. 117.

86. *Ibid.,* p. 131.

87. Anonymous, "The Mystery of ISIS," *New York Review of Books,* August 13, 2015, p. 28.

Chapter 9

Conclusion: War and State Deformation

It is impossible to say with absolute confidence that the threat trough that exists in the current Westphalian global order is a permanent condition. Major inter-state war may be cyclical, its frequency waxing and waning rather than gradually declining and eventually disappearing.[1] All that can be said at this point in time is the frequency of inter-state war has declined significantly in all regions of the world but remains a distinct possibility in a few places on the planet where states still directly oppose one another with conventional armed force, such as between North and South Korea; between India and Pakistan over Kashmir; between Georgia and Russia over Abkhazia and South Ossetia; between Moldova and Russia over Transnistria; between Ukraine and Russia over the Donbass; and between Armenia and Azerbaijan over Nagorno-Karabakh. Nonetheless, in general, contemporary war is quite different from war in the pre-1945 period. Low-tech internal wars among the people and high-tech global policing wars have replaced full-blown, conventional inter-state war in the contemporary global order.

Unmanned policing wars waged by advanced neoliberal states are not about defending the national territory, despite the rhetorical language used to legitimate them by their political elites who say that they are. Rather, they are about managing the Westphalian global order by (1) upholding the sovereignty of states (e.g., the First Persian Gulf War to restore Kuwaiti sovereignty), (2) imposing liberal government within the states that comprise it (e.g., the Second Persian Gulf War to overthrow Saddam Hussein, and the American war in Afghanistan against the Taliban), (3) upholding global norms (e.g., the proposed air strike on Syria at the beginning of its civil war for violating the international convention on the use of chemical weapons), (4) defending universal human rights (e.g., the war in Bosnia-Herzegovina from 1992 to 1995 to stop "ethnic cleansing"), and (5) preventing non-Westphalian state forms from coming into being (e.g., the present air campaign against the Islamic State of Iraq and the Levant [ISIL]).

According to Vivienne Jabri, unmanned post-modern policing wars have reconstituted war so that it is no longer fought against enemy states, but rather against concepts, such as the "war on terrorism," and against particular individuals, so-called "bad guys," such as Osama bin Laden. Essentially, "it is no longer possible to distinguish war from policing activity conducted in the name of humanity as a whole and legitimised in the name of human rights."[2]

The transformation of state-centric, Clausewitzian, conventional modern war to unmanned postmodern policing war has been made possible by the development of information technology, nanotechnologies, the biological and psychological enhancement of combatants, the development of nonlethal weapons, and the advent of cyber war.[3] Therefore, in the age of unmanned postmodern policing war there are no enemy states to be defeated decisively, only "bad guys" (terrorists, rapists, robbers, drug dealers, pirates, brigands, thugs, rogues, vagabonds, torturers, tyrants, etc.), who are to be found and executed by so-called "smart" weapons.

In order to wage unmanned postmodern policing war, the coercive apparatus of the neoliberal state has been reconfigured and outsourced in such a way as to *fuse law enforcement with national security*. Increasingly, law enforcement issues have become prominent in national security discourse, military hardware and technology have been increasingly converted for policing missions, the overlap between law enforcement and intelligence communities has increased, and the military has been increasingly deployed for internal and external policing operations. Twenty-first-century armies increasingly resemble paramilitary national police forces such as the Italian Carabinieri, the French Gendarmerie, the Spanish Guardia Civil, and the Portuguese Guarda Nacional Republicana. A consequence of this reconfiguration has brought the *civilianization of soldiering* and the *militarization of policing*.[4] In the age of perpetual unmanned postmodern policing war, the distinction between "peacetime" and "wartime" that was hitherto made has disappeared. As Mary Dudziak has written: "Wartime has become the only kind of time we have."[5]

According to Jabri and others, unmanned postmodern policing wars are also a new form of imperialism. For her, they

> function as an element, a tool, or a technology in the government of populations, and specifically their disciplining into societies more amenable to management [by] the [states] of the liberal democratic West. [They are] twenty-first century forms of colonial war now expressed in terms of state building and peace building.[6]

In sum, as Christopher Cramer has written, the purpose of unmanned post-modern policing war is to "rebuild a nation-state in the self-image of the Western liberal state. [This involves] transplanting Western models of social, political, and economic organization into war shattered states in order to control civil conflict: In other words, pacification through political and economic liberalization."[7]

Unmanned postmodern policing wars and internal wars in non-Western states occupy a "single frame."[8] Increasingly, policing wars waged by advanced European states and internal wars among the people within non-European states connect and intersect within and across state borders in what David Keen has called "*resource wars*." According to Keen, internal wars create large financial opportunities fueled by international economic and military assistance programs for the various groups fighting within non-European states. Policing wars of the neoliberal state create financial opportunities for the various entities of their military-industrial-research complexes. Therefore, both benefit financially from resource war. Keen suggests that the financial incentives are so strong that many on both sides favor the *prolongation* of the war rather than its end. Keen believes that the object of resource war is *not to win but keep the war from ending.*[9] Therefore, war in the contemporary world is unintelligible in the classical Clausewitzian sense: "War is no longer a continuation of politics by other means, but an end in itself."[10]

The arms industries of the neoliberal states and the various groups fighting within weak states are brought together by the "globalized war economy."[11] The non-state fighting forces within weak states procure the arms, ammunition, and military equipment they need on the private international arms market or from arms transfers from advanced states. According to Mary Kaldor, non-state fighting forces pay for their arms and matériel in two ways: (1) from internal asset transfers or (2) from external sources. With regard to the first method, she says that in internal wars

> [r]ich people are killed and their gold and valuables stolen; property is transferred in the aftermath of ethnic cleansing; cattle and livestock are raided by militiamen; shops and factories are looted when towns are taken. Hostages are captured and exchanged for food, weapons or other hostages, prisoners of war or dead bodies. . . . More sophisticated income-generating activities include "war taxes" or "protection money" from the production of primary commodities and various forms of illegal trading.[12]

With the regard to the second method of generating income, she says that financial assistance comes from (1) remittances from abroad to individuals and families; (2) direct assistance from diaspora communities; (3) assistance from foreign governments; and (4) humanitarian assistance.[13]

The transformation of warfare from classical inter-state war to resourced postmodern war has profoundly changed the relationship between war, the state, and the people across the globe. First, in the neoliberal states that wage unmanned postmodern policing war, the tight relationship between the people and the military is loosening with every passing year. The military forces of the neoliberal states are increasingly becoming detached, decoupled, and insulated from the general population among whom the obligation to serve in the armed forces as a duty of citizenship has all but disappeared.[14] The people have, in effect, become "spectators" of unmanned policing war conducted by all-volunteer military forces and private military companies (PMCs) that, more and more, resemble police forces. Rather than being asked to enlist and sacrifice for the war effort, the people of the neoliberal states are encouraged to go about their daily lives and leave the fighting to those who either prefer military work or are forced to do it by poverty. Those who do not wish to serve, for whatever reason, are expected to do no more than thank those who do for their service. In the neoliberal state, war is being fought by a small sliver of the people; therefore, it can be said that the tight connection between the state, the army, and the people that came into being over the last two centuries of Clausewitzian inter-state war has completely broken apart. Michael Ignatieff sums up these changes thusly:

> War . . . is no longer a struggle for national survival; with the end of conscription, it no longer requires the actual participation of citizens; because of the bypassing of representative institutions, it no longer requires democratic consent; and as a result of the exceptional growth of the modern economy, it no longer draws on the entire economic system. These conditions transform war into something like a spectator sport.[15]

Second, the relationship between the state, armed forces, and the people in weak non-European states with no history of indigenous, war-driven state formation was never strong in the first place. The armed forces of such states, like the all-volunteer armed forces of the advanced neoliberal states, are decoupled and detached from the people because they lack the external threats to their sovereignty and territorial integrity necessary to bring them together into something akin to Clausewitz's "remarkable trinity." In some cases, the state's armed forces, or units of its armed forces, form one of the fighting groups inside the state contending for control of its governmental apparatus. Thus, internal wars in the weak non-European states experiencing them are essentially power struggles among groups inside the state, aided and abetted by outside forces (other states, diasporas, arms dealers, non-governmental organizations [NGOs], private military companies [PMCs], etc.), for control of the state, usually for private gain or ethnic advantage, and even for their survival.

Internal wars in weak states are often "no-win contests" because the purpose of the war is not to win but to continue the war. This is the case because the groups fighting often lack central control, are highly fragmented, and develop highly local power centers. It is also because their political power can be best maintained by continuing the fighting, and because there is no central authority capable of stopping the fighting. Finally, the presence of humanitarian organizations that deal with civilian casualties, provide food for the famine-stricken victims of the fighting, and rehabilitate child soldiers, unwittingly prolong the war by giving the society the capacity to continue to destroy itself.[16]

Unlike unmanned postmodern policing wars, which have almost no direct physical consequences for the people of the neoliberal states that wage them (except, of course, the few who volunteer to serve in the military and actually see combat), the physical consequences of internal war for the people of non-Western states are direct and often horrific. The people in these states are not only ignored; they are abused, exploited, and often murdered by the warring groups as they struggle against one another to gain or retain control of the state or make war on one another. Ninety percent of the casualties in internal wars since 1945 have been civilians, mostly women and children. Five million civilians have died in them since the end of the Second World War.[17] In addition, vast numbers of the weak state's people flee the fighting to neighboring states where they become impoverished refugees living in camps supported by the host government, the United Nations High Commission for Refugees (UNHCR), and non-governmental international humanitarian organizations.[18] Thus, internal wars do not build up weak states by binding the state, the army, and the people together. Instead, they deepen and widen the chasm that already exists between the people, armed forces, and the state.

Essentially, *both* unmanned postmodern policing wars and internal wars in weak states break the linkage between the people, the army and the state. Unmanned postmodern policing war is no longer the concern of the people in neoliberal states who are required to do no more than tacitly support the war. Such wars are conducted by national security elites behind a veil of secrecy. In weak states war is the concern of para-military groups; militias; warlords; capos of drug cartels; professional racketeers; and gangs of thugs who extort, loot, pillage, blackmail, steal humanitarian aid, and illegally extract natural resources, not the people of the state in which the war is being waged. In the advanced neoliberal states the people, in general, are no longer direct participants in war but are *spectators* of war. In weak states the people are not participants in war but are the *victims* of war.[19] Therefore, it can be argued that the all-volunteer, occupational military in Western states and non-state fighting groups in weak states are increasingly disconnected *from the people and operate according to their own networked logic*, not unlike transnational corporations (TNCs) in the global economy. Resource war does nothing to strengthen weak non-European states and deforms strong Western neoliberal states by disconnecting the people from the army and the state.

The disconnect between the state, the armed forces, and the people is here to stay. There is no going back to classical Clausewitzian inter-state war and the trinitarian relationship between the people, armed force, and the state. The technological imperative applied to military technology guarantees the continued development of weapons that require less and less human intervention to operate and, therefore, a smaller and smaller, more technologically sophisticated, armed force dependent upon civilian technology and interwoven into civilian society. It also guarantees that unmanned robotic military technologies will become increasingly accessible to non-state actors.

On the disconnect between the people, armed force, and the state, one scholar of war has written that the twenty-first century is "perhaps the first time in the history of the modern military, [that] the military machine—a state-owned and run apparatus—is explicitly thinking of and, in some cases, even operating outside of the orbit of the state."[20] Essentially, war-making in the contemporary global order has taken on a life of its own and is increasingly fought independently of states and their people by increasingly private entities. This "heralds a shift in [the] world order, from the state-centric Westphalian system back to the status quo ante of the Middle Ages,"[21] when war-making was not bracketed and regulated by states. This does not mean that states are disappearing. They will continue to exist but in competition with other global actors, such as the United Nations, NGOs, TNCs, politicized religious groups, terrorist groups, and transnational criminal organizations (TCOs). Essentially, the world is returning to a pre-Westphalian system where "no single type of political actor dominates the world stage, as states have done in recent centuries. Historically, sovereignty [has been] generally fragmented among different actors, as it was in the Middle Ages, and . . . the past four centuries of Westphalian supremacy by states is anomalous."[22] In the post-Westphalian age armed conflict will more and more resemble medieval warfare. There will be neither clear victory nor defeat, only perpetual policing war and perpetual internal wars in which, from the perspective of the Western states, each "death—friendly and enemy—is enormously magnified. Ours is a numerically anomalous tragedy; theirs an exaggerated and over-magnified victory."[23]

NOTES

1. Raimo Väyrynen, "Introduction: Contending Views," in Raimo Väyrynen, *The Waning of Major War: Theories and Debates* (London and New York: Routledge, 2006), p. 2.

2. Vivienne Jabri, *War and the Transformation of Global Politics* (New York: Palgrave Macmillan, 2007), p. 53.

3. George R. Lucas, "Postmodern War," *Journal of Military Ethics*, 9 (No. 4), 2010, pp. 289–98.

4. Peter Andreas and Richard Price, "From War Fighting to Crime Fighting: Transforming the American National Security State," *International Studies Review*, 3 (No. 3), 2001, pp. 31–52.

5. Mary L. Dudziak, *War Time: An Idea, Its History, Its Consequences* (Oxford: Oxford University Press, 2012), p. 8.

6. Jabri, *op. cit.*, pp. viii and xi.

7. Christopher Cramer, *Violence in Developing Countries: War, Memory and Progress* (Bloomington: Indiana University Press, 2006), p. 257.

8. Martin Shaw, *The New Western Way of War: Risk-Transfer War and Its Crisis in Iraq* (Cambridge: Polity Press, 2005), p. 47.

9. David Keen, *Useful Enemies: When Waging War Is More Important than Winning Them* (New Haven, CT: Yale University Press, 2012), chapter 2.

10. K. J. Holsti, "Reversing Rousseau: The Medieval and Modern in Contemporary Wars," in William Bain (ed.), *The Empire of Security and the Safety of the People* (London: Routledge, 2006), p. 47.

11. Mary Kaldor, *New & Old Wars: Organized Violence in a Global Era*, 2nd Edition (Stanford, CA: Stanford University Press, 2007), pp. 95–118.

12. *Ibid.*, pp. 108–9.

13. *Ibid.*, pp. 109–10.

14. Thomas E. Ricks, "A Widening Gap between the Military and Society," *Atlantic Monthly*, July 1977, pp. 66–78; Ole R. Holsti, "Widening Gap between the U.S. Military and Civilian Society, Some Evidence," *International Security*, 23 (No. 3), Winter 1998, pp. 5–42; and Peter D. Feaver and Richard H. Kohn (eds.), *Soldiers and Civilians: The Civil-Military Gap and American National Security* (Cambridge, MA: M.I.T. Press, 2001). See also Andrew J. Bacevich, *Breach of Trust: How Americans Failed Their Soldiers and Their Country* (New York: Henry Holt, 2013), esp. chapter 2, and Rachel Maddow, *Drift: The Unmooring of American Military Power* (New York: Crown Publishers, 2012), esp. chapter 8.

15. Michael Ignatieff, *Virtual War: Kosovo and Beyond* (New York: Viking Books, 2000), p. 191.

16. K. J. Holsti, *op. cit.*, pp. 47–49.

17. *Ibid.*, p. 47 and p. 52.

18. For example, the UNHCR website (www.unhcr.org) reports that the Syrian civil war has produced 4,016,227 refugees or about 22 percent of Syria's total population. Accessed August 15, 2015. Nearly one million have made their way to Europe.

19. Benjamin Ginsberg in *The Worth of War* (Amherst, NY: Prometheus Books, 2014, pp. 216–17) suggests that America's superfluous war-making potential has been turned inward and redefined American citizens as victims or potential victims of criminal violence.

20. Manabrata Guha, *Reimagining War in the 21st Century: From Clausewitz to Network-Centric Warfare* (London: Routledge, 2010), p. 1.

21. Sean McFate, *The Modern Mercenary: Private Armies and What They Mean for World Order* (Oxford/New York: Oxford University Press, 2014), p. 165.

22. *Ibid.*, pp. 167–68.

23. William M. Arkin, *Unmanned: Drones, Data, and the Illusion of Perfect War* (New York/Boston/London: Little, Brown, 2015), p. 18.

Bibliography

Afghanistan, A Country Study. Washington, DC: U.S. Government Printing Office, 1986.

Allinson, Gary D. *Japan's Postwar History*. Ithaca, NY: Cornell University Press, 1997.

Almond, Gabriel A. *A Discipline Divided: Schools and Sects in Political Science*. Newbury Park/London/New Delhi: Sage Publications, 1990.

Alvarez, David. *The Pope's Soldiers: A Military History of the Modern Vatican*. Lawrence: Kansas University Press, 2011.

Aly, Götz. *Why the Germans? Why the Jews? Envy, Race Hatred, and the Prehistory of the Holocaust*. New York: Metropolitan, 2014.

Andrade, Tonio. *The Gunpowder Age: China, Military Innovation, and the Rise of the West in World History*. Princeton, NJ, and Oxford: Princeton University Press, 2016.

Andreas, Peter, and Richard Price. "From War Fighting to Crime Fighting: Transforming the American National Security State." *International Studies Review*, 3 (No. 3), Fall 2001, pp. 31–52.

Arkin, William M. *Unmanned: Drones, Data, and the Illusion of Perfect War*. New York/Boston/London: Little, Brown, 2015.

Atzili, Boaz, "When Good Fences Make Bad Neighbors: Fixed Borders, State Weakness, and International Conflict." *International Security*, 31 (No. 3) Winter 2006/2007, pp. 139–73.

Ayoob, Mohammed. *The Third World Security Predicament: State Making, Regional Conflict, and the International System*. Boulder, CO: Lynne Rienner, 1995.

Bacevich, Andrew J. (ed.). *The Long War: A New History of U.S. National Security Policy since World War II*. New York: Columbia University Press, 2007.

_____. *Breach of Trust: How Americans Failed Their Soldiers and Their Country*. New York: Henry Holt, 2013.

Balthasar, Dominik. "Somaliland's Best Kept Secret: Shrewd Politics and War Projects as a Means of State-Making." *Journal of Eastern African Studies*, 7 (No. 2), 2013, pp. 218–38.

Barfield, Thomas. *Afghanistan: A Cultural and Political History*. Princeton, NJ: Princeton University Press, 2010.

Barkawi, Tarak. *Globalization and War*. Lanham, MD: Rowman & Littlefield, 2006.

Barkawi, Tarak, and Shane Brighton. "Powers of War: Fighting, Knowledge, and Critique," *International Political Sociology*, 5 (No. 2) June 2011, pp. 127–31.

Barker, Ernest. *The Development of Public Services in Western Europe, 1600–1930*. Hamden, CT: Archon Books, 1966.

Barnett, Michael N. *Confronting the Costs of War: Military Power, State, and Society in Egypt and Israel*. Princeton, NJ: Princeton University Press, 1992.

Bartlett, Robert. *The Making of Europe: Conquest, Colonization, and Culture Change, 950–1350*. Princeton, NJ: Princeton University Press, 1993.

Bates, Robert H. *Prosperity and Violence*. New York: W. W. Norton & Co., 2001.

Bayart, Jean-François. *The State in Africa: The Politics of the Belly*, 2nd Edition. Cambridge, MA: Polity Press, 2009.

Bell, David A. *The First Total War: Napoleon's Europe and the Birth of Warfare as We Know It*. Boston/New York: Houghton Mifflin, 2007.

Bendix, Reinhard. *Kings or People: Power and the Mandate to Rule*. Berkeley: University of California Press, 1980.

Binder, Leonard. *Crises and Sequences in Political Development*. Princeton, NJ: Princeton University Press, 1971.

Black, Jeremy. *Why Wars Happen*. New York: New York University Press, 1998.

_____. *War and the World: Military Power and the Fate of Continents, 1450–2000*. New Haven, CT: Yale University Press, 1998.

_____. *Western Warfare: 1775–1882*. Bloomington: Indiana University Press, 2001.

_____. *Rethinking Military History*. London and New York: Routledge, 2004.

_____. *The Age of Total War, 1860–1945*. Lanham, MD: Rowman & Littlefield, 2006.

_____. *European Warfare in a Global Context, 1660–1815*. London and New York: Routledge, 2007.

_____. *War and Technology*. Bloomington: Indiana University Press, 2013.

Blainey, Geoffrey. *The Causes of War*. 3rd Edition. New York: Free Press, 1988.

Boix, Charles, Bruno Codenotti, and Giovanni Resta. "War, Wealth, and the Formation of States." In *Political Economy of Institutions, Democracy and Voting*. Berlin: Springer-Verlag, 2011, pp. 45–74.

Bobbitt, Philip. *The Shield of Achilles: War, Peace, and the Course of History*. New York: Anchor Books, 2003.

Boot, Max. *War Made New: Technology, Warfare, and the Course of History*. New York: Gotham Books, 2006.

Borton, Hugh. *Japan since 1931: Its Political and Social Developments*. Westport, CT: Greenwood Press, 1940.

Bousquet, Antoine. *The Scientific Way of Warfare: Order and Chaos on the Battlefields of Modernity*. New York: Columbia University Press, 2009.

Bowden, Mark. "Drone Warrior: Has It Become Too Easy for the President to Kill?" *Atlantic Magazine*, September 2013.

Brock, Lothar, *et al. Fragile States: War and Conflict in the Modern World*. Cambridge: Polity Press, 2012.

Brubaker, Rogers. *Nationalism Reframed: Nationhood and the National Question in the New Europe*. Cambridge: Cambridge University Press, 1996.

Burbank, Jane, and Frederick Cooper. *Empires in World History: Power and the Politics of Difference*. Princeton, NJ: Princeton University Press, 2010.

Carneiro, Robert L. "A Theory of the Origin of the State." *Studies in Social Theory No. 3*. Menlo Park, CA: Institute for Humane Studies, 1977.

Caryl, Christian. "Predators and Robots at War." *New York Review of Books*, September 29, 2011.

Centeno, Miguel, and Fernando López-Alves. *Blood and Debt: War and the Nation-State in Latin America*. University Park: The Pennsylvania State University Press, 2002.

Cerny, Philip G. *The Changing Architecture of Politics: Structure, Agency, and the Future of the State*. London/Newbury Park/New Delhi: Sage, 1990.

Chabal, Patrick and Jean-Pascal Daloz. *Africa Works: Disorder as a Political Instrument*. Oxford: James Curry/Bloomington: Indiana University Press, 1999.

Cheterian, Vicken. "The August 2008 War in Georgia: From Ethnic Conflict to Border Wars." *Central Asian Survey*, 28 (No. 2), 2009, pp. 155–70.

Cipolla, Carlo M. *The Economic Decline of Empires*. London: Methuen, 1970.

Cohen, Benjamin J. *The Question of Imperialism*. New York: Basic Books, 1973.

Cohen, Youssef, Brian R. Brown, and A. F. K. Organski. "The Paradoxical Nature of State Making: The Violent Creation of Order." *American Political Science Review*, 75 (No. 4), December 1981, pp. 901–10.

Coker, Christopher. "Outsourcing War." *Cambridge Review of International Affairs*, 13 (No. 1), 1999, pp. 95–113.

_____. *Humane Warfare*. London and New York: Routledge, 2001.

_____. *Waging War without Warriors: The Changing Culture of Military Conflict*. Boulder and London: Lynne Rienner Publishers, 2002.

_____. *The Future of War: The Re-enchantment of War in the Twenty-First Century*. Oxford: Blackwell Publishers, 2004.

_____. *The Warrior Ethos: Military Culture and the War on Terror*. London and New York: Routledge, 2007.

_____. *War in an Age of Risk*. Cambridge: Polity Press, 2009.

_____. *Warrior Geeks: How 21st-Century Technology Is Changing the Way We Fight and Think about War*. London: Hurst, 2013.

Coleman, James S. *Education and Political Development*. Princeton, NJ: Princeton University Press, 1965.

Colley, Linda. *Britons: Forging the Nation, 1707–1837*. New Haven, CT: Yale University Press, 1992.

Contamine, Philippe. *War in the Middle Ages*. Oxford: Basil Blackwell, 1980.

Corvisier, André (ed.). *Dictionary of Military History and the Art of War*. Trans by Chris Turner. Oxford: Basil Blackwell, 1994.

Cramer, Christopher. *Violence in Developing Countries: War, Memory, Progress*. Bloomington: Indiana University Press, 2006.

Davidson, Basil. *Black Man's Burden: Africa and the Curse of the Nation-State*. New York: Random House, 1992.

Davies, Norman. *Europe: A History*. Oxford: Oxford University Press, 1996.

_____. *Vanished Kingdoms: The Rise and Fall of States and Nations*. New York: Viking, 2012.

Davis, Diane E., and Anthony W. Pereira (eds.). *Irregular Armed Forces and Their Role in Politics and State Formation*. Cambridge: Cambridge University Press, 2003.

Dawson, Doyne. *The Origins of Western Warfare: Militarism and Morality in the Ancient World*. Boulder, CO: Westview Press, 1996.

_____. *The First Armies*. London: Cassell & Co., 2001.

Der Derian, James. *Virtuous War: Mapping the Military-Industrial-Media-Entertainment Network*. Boulder, CO: Westview Press, 2001.

Desch, Michael C. "War and Strong States, Peace and Weak States." *International Organization*, 50 (No. 2) Spring 1996, pp. 237–68.

Diamond, Jared. "Vengeance Is Ours." *New Yorker*, April 21, 2008, pp. 74–86.

Dörries, Herman. *Constantine the Great*. Trans. by Roland H. Bainton. New York: Harper Torch Books, 1972.

Downing, Brian M. *The Military Revolution and Political Change: Origins of Democracy and Autocracy in Early Modern Europe*. Princeton, NJ: Princeton University Press, 1992.

Duby, Georges. *The Three Orders: Feudal Society Imagined*. Chicago: University of Chicago Press, 1978.

Dudziak, Mary L. *War.Time: An Idea, Its History, Its Consequences*. Oxford: Oxford University Press, 2012.

Duffield, Mark. *Global Governance and the New Wars: The Merging of Development and Security*. London/New York: Zed Books, 2014.

Durant, Will. *Caesar and Christ: A History of Roman Civilization and of Christianity from Their Beginnings to AD 325*. New York: Simon & Schuster, 1944.

Duyvesteyn, Isabella, and Jan Angstrom (eds.). *Rethinking the Nature of War*. London and New York: Frank Cass, 2005.

Easton, David. *The Political System: An Inquiry into the State of Political Science*. New York: Knopf, 1953.

Easton, Stewart C. *The Western Heritage: From the Earliest Times to the Present*. New York: Holt, Rinehart & Winston, 1970.

Ellis, John. *The Social History of the Machine Gun*. Baltimore, MD: Johns Hopkins University Press, 1975.

Ellul, Jacques. *The Technological Society*. Trans. John Wilkinson (New York: Vintage Press, 1964).

Elshtain, Jean Bethke. *Women and War*. Chicago: Chicago University Press, 1987.

Englebert, Pierre. *Africa: Unity, Sovereignty & Sorrow*. Boulder, CO: Lynne Rienner, 1999.

Englebert, Pierre and Denis M. Tull. "Post-Conflict Reconstruction in Africa: Flawed Ideas About State Failure." *International Security*, 32 (No. 4), Spring 2008, pp. 106–39.

Eriksen, S. S. "The Congo War and the Prospects for State Formation: Rwanda and Uganda." *Third World Quarterly*, 26 (No. 7), 2005, pp. 1097–1113.

Ertman, Thomas. *Birth of the Leviathan: Building States and Regimes in Medieval and Early Modern Europe*. Cambridge: Cambridge University Press, 1997.

Evans, Peter B., Dietrich Rueschemeyer, and Theda Skocpol (eds.). *Bringing the State Back In*. Cambridge: Cambridge University Press, 1985.

Eviatar, Daphne. "Contract With America." *Harper's Magazine*, October, 2007.

Faust, Drew Gilpin. *This Republic of Suffering: Death and the American Civil War*. Waterville, ME: Thorndike Press, 2008.

Favret, Mary A. *War at a Distance: Romanticism and the Making of Modern Wartime*. Princeton, NJ: Princeton University Press, 2010.

Fay, Sidney Bradshaw. *The Rise of Brandenburg-Prussia*. New York: Henry Holt, 1937.

Feaver, Peter D., and Richard H. Kohn (eds.). *Soldiers and Civilians: The Civil-Military Gap and American National Security*. Cambridge, MA: M.I.T. Press, 2001.

Ferguson, Niall. *Civilization: The West and the Rest*. New York: Penguin, 2011.

Ferguson, Yale H., and Richard W. Mansbach. *Polities: Authority, Identities, and Change*. Columbia: University of South Carolina Press, 1996.

France, John. *Western Warfare in the Age of the Crusades, 1000–1300*. Ithaca, NY: Cornell University Press, 1999.

Friedrich, Carl J., and Charles Blitzer. *The Age of Power*. Ithaca, NY: Cornell University Press, 1957.

Fukuyama, Francis (ed.). *Nation-Building: Beyond Afghanistan and Iraq*. Baltimore: Johns Hopkins University Press, 2006.

Gat, Azar. *War in Human Civilization*. Oxford: Oxford University Press, 2006.

Garon, Sheldon. *Making Japanese Minds: The State in Everyday Life*. Princeton, NJ: Princeton University Press, 1997.

Gee, Alastair. "The Dark Art of Cyberwar." *Foreign Policy*, November 12, 2008. Accessed from http://foreignpolicy.com/2008/11/12/the-dark-art-of-cyberwar/.

Geis, Joseph, and Francis Geis. *Life in a Medieval Castle*. New York: Harper and Row, 1979.

Giddens, Anthony. *The Nation-State and Violence*. Berkeley: University of California Press, 1985.

Ginsberg, Benjamin. *The Worth of War*. Amherst, NY: Prometheus Books, 2014.

Glass, Charles. "The Warrior Class." *Harper's Magazine*, April 2012.

Goldhagen, Daniel Jonah. *Worse than War: Genocide, Eliminationism, and the Ongoing Assault on Humanity*. New York: Public Affairs, 2009.

Gongora, Thierry. "War Making and State Power in the Contemporary Middle East." *International Journal of Middle East Studies*, 29 (No. 3) 1997, pp. 323–40.

Gopal, Anand. *No Good Men among the Living: America, the Taliban, and the War through Afghan Eyes*. New York: Metropolitan, 2014.

Gorman, Siobhan, and Julian E. Barnes. "Cyber Combat: Act of War?" *Wall Street Journal*, May 31, 2011.

Gray, Chris H. "Posthuman Soldiers and Postmodern War." *Body & Society*, 9 (No. 4), 2003, pp. 215–26.

Greenfeld, Liah. *Nationalism: Five Roads to Modernity*. Cambridge, MA: Harvard University Press, 1997.

Grew, Raymond (ed.). *Crises of Political Development in Europe and the United States*. Princeton, NJ: Princeton University Press, 1978.

Guha, Manabrata. *Reimagining War in the 21st Century: From Clausewitz to Network-Centric Warfare*. London: Routledge, 2010.

Haas, Ernst B. *Nationalism, Liberalism, and Progress: The Rise and Decline of Nationalism Vol . I.* Ithaca, NY: Cornell University Press, 1997.

Hall, Rodney Bruce. *National Collective Identity: Social Constructs and International Systems.* New York: Columbia University Press, 1995.

Hanson, Victor Davis. *Carnage and Culture: Landmark Battles in the Rise of Western Power.* New York: Anchor Books, 2001.

Headrick, Daniel R. *The Tools of Empire: Technology and European Imperialism in the Nineteenth Century.* New York: Oxford University Press, 1981.

Heer, Friedrich. *The Medieval World, 1100–1350.* trans. Janet Sondheimer. New York: New American Library, 1961.

Helman, Gerald B. and Steven R. Ratner. "Saving Failed States." *Foreign Policy,* Winter 1992–1993, pp. 3–20.

Herbst, Jeffery. *States and Power in Africa: Comparative Lessons in Authority and Control.* Princeton, NJ: Princeton University Press, 2000.

_____. "War and the State in Africa." *International Security,* 14 (No. 4) 1990, pp. 117–39.

Hersh, Seymour M. "The Online Threat." *New Yorker,* November 1, 2010.

Hindley, Geoffrey. *Medieval Sieges and Siegecraft.* New York: Skyhorse Publishing, 2014.

Hinton, Harold C., *et al.* (eds). *Major Governments of Asia.* Ithaca, NY: Cornell University Press, 1958.

Hironaka, Ann. *Neverending Wars: The International Community, Weak States, and the Perpetuation of Civil War.* Cambridge, MA: Harvard University Press, 2005.

Hoffman, Philip T. *Why Did Europe Conquer the World?* Princeton and Oxford: Princeton University Press, 2015.

Holsti, K. J. "Reversing Rousseau: The Medieval and the Modern in Contemporary Wars." In William Bain (ed.), *The Empire of Security and the Safety of the People.* London: Routledge, 2006, pp. 37–59.

Holsti, Kalevi. *Peace and War: Armed Conflicts and the International Order, 1648–1989.* Cambridge: Cambridge University Press, 1991.

_____. *The State, War, and the State of War.* Cambridge: Cambridge University Press, 1996.

Holsti, Ole R. "Widening Gap between the U.S. Military and Civilian Society: Some Evidence." *International Security,* 23 (No. 3) Winter 1998, pp. 5–42.

Holtman, Robert E. *The Napoleonic Revolution.* Philadelphia: J. B. Lippencott, 1967.

Hopkins, Andrea. *Knights.* New York: Artabras, 1990.

Howard, Michael. *The Causes of Wars and Other Essays.* 2nd Edition, Enlarged. Cambridge, MA: Harvard University Press, 1984.

_____. *War in European History.* Updated Edition. Oxford: Oxford University Press, 2009.

Hui, Victoria Tin-bor. *War and State Formation in Ancient China and Early Modern Europe.* Cambridge and New York: Cambridge University Press, 2005.

Huntington, Samuel P. *The Soldier and the State: The Theory and Politics of Civil-Military Relations.* Cambridge, MA: Harvard University Press, 1957.

_____. *Political Order in Changing Societies.* New Haven, CT: Yale University Press, 1968.

Ignatieff, Michael. *Virtual War: Kosovo and Beyond.* New York: Viking, 2000.

Jabri, Vivienne. *War and the Transformation of Global Politics.* New York: Palgrave Macmillan, 2007.

Jackson, Robert H. *Quasi-States: Sovereignty, International Relations and the Third World.* Cambridge: Cambridge University Press, 1993.

Jackson, Robert H., and Carl G. Rosberg. "Why Africa's Weak States Persist: The Empirical and the Juridical in Statehood." *World Politics,* 35 (No. 1) October 1982, pp. 1–24.

Janowitz, Morris. *The Professional Soldier: A Social and Political Portrait.* New York: Free Press, 1960.

Japan: A Country Study. Washington, DC: U.S. Government Printing Office, 1992.

Jenks, Edward. *History of Politics.* London: Macmillan, 1900.

Joas, Hans, and Wolfgang Knöbl. *War in Social Thought: Hobbes to the Present.* Trans. Alex Skinner. Princeton, NJ: Princeton University Press, 2013.

Jones, Eric. *The European Miracle.* 3rd Edition. Cambridge: Cambridge University Press, 2003.

Judge, David. *The Parliamentary State*. London: Sage, 1993.

Judt, Tony. *Postwar: A History of Europe since 1945*. New York: Penguin, 2005.

Kahner, Larry. *AK-47: The Weapon That Changed the World*. New York: John Wiley & Son, 2007.

Kaiser, David. *Politics and War: European Conflict from Philip II to Hitler*. Cambridge, MA: Harvard University Press, 1990.

Kaldor, Mary. *New and Old Wars: Organized Violence in the Global Era*. 2nd Edition. Stanford, CA: Stanford University Press, 2007.

Kalyvas, Stathis N. "'New' and 'Old' Civil Wars: A Valid Distinction?" *World Politics*, 54 (No. 1), October 2001, pp. 99–118.

Kaplan, Edward. *To Kill Nations: American Strategy in the Air-Atomic Age and the Rise of Mutually Assured Destruction*. Ithaca, NY: Cornell University Press, 2015.

Keegan, John. *A History of Warfare*. New York: Vintage Books, 1994.

Keen, David. *Useful Enemies: When Waging War Is More Important than Winning Them*. New Haven, CT: Yale University Press, 2012.

Keen, Maurice. *Medieval Warfare: A History*. Oxford: Oxford University Press, 1999.

Kelly, Jack. *Gunpowder, Alchemy, Bombards, and Pyrotechnics: The History of Explosives that Changed the World*. New York: Basic Books, 2004.

Kennedy, Paul. *The Rise and Fall of the Great Powers: Economic Change and Military Conflict from 1500 to 2000*. New York: Random House, 1987.

Kershaw, Ian. "Europe's Second Thirty Years' War." *History Today*, September 2010, pp. 10–17.

Kesselman, Mark, *et al. European Politics in Transition*. Fifth Edition. Boston: Houghton Mifflin, 2006.

Knox, MacGregor, and Williamson Murray (eds.). *The Dynamics of Military Revolution, 1300–2050*. Cambridge: Cambridge University Press, 2001.

Kohn, Hans. *The Idea of Nationalism: A Study in Its Origins and Background*. New York: Macmillan, 1944.

Krause, Keith. *Arms and the State: Patterns of Military Production and Trade*. Cambridge: Cambridge University Press, 1992.

Langer, William L. (ed.). *Western Civilization: Paleolithic Man to the Emergence of the European Powers*. New York: Harper & Row, 1968.

_____. *Western Civilization: The Struggle for Empire to Europe in the Modern World*. New York: Harper & Row, 1968.

LaPalombara, Joseph, and Myron Weiner (eds.). *Political Parties and Political Development*. Princeton, NJ: Princeton University Press, 1966.

Latham, Robert. *The Liberal Moment: Modernity, Security, and the Making of the Post-War International Order*. New York: Columbia University Press, 1997.

Leander, Anna. "Wars and the Unmaking of States: Taking Tilly Seriously in the Contemporary World." In Stefano Guizzini and Dietrich Jung (eds.), *Contemporary Security Analysis and Copenhagen Peace Research*. London and New York: Routledge, 2004, pp. 60-80.

Levi, Margaret. *Of Rule and Revenue*. Berkeley, Los Angeles, London: University of California Press, 1998.

Levy, Jack S. *War and the Great Power System, 1495–1975*. Lexington: University of Kentucky Press, 1983.

Levy, Jack S., and William R. Thompson. *Causes of War*. New York: John Wiley & Sons, 2010.

Lewis, Martin W. and Kären E. Wigen. *The Myth of Continents: A Critique of Metageography*. Berkeley: University of California Press, 1997.

Lichtblau, Eric. "Questions Raised Anew About Religion in the Military." *The New York Times*, March 1, 2009.

Livermore, H. V. *A New History of Portugal*. Cambridge: Cambridge University Press, 1969.

López-Alves, Fernando. *State Formation and Democracy in Latin America, 1810–1900*. Durham, NC: Duke University Press, 2000.

Luard, Evan. *The Blunted Sword: The Erosion of Military Power in Modern World Politics*. New York: New Amsterdam Books, 1988.

Lubasz, Heinz (ed.). *The Development of the Modern State*. New York: Macmillan, 1964.

Lucas, George R. "Postmodern War." *Journal of Military Ethics*, 9 (No. 4), 2010, pp. 289–98.

Lustick, Ian S. "The Absence of Middle Eastern Great Powers: Political 'Backwardness' in Historical Perspective." *International Organization* 51, (No. 4), Autumn 1997, pp. 653–83.

Maccartney, C. A. *National States and National Minorities*. New York: Russell & Russell, 1934.

Maddow, Rachel. *Drift: The Unmooring of American Military Power*. New York: Crown Publishers, 2012.

Marques, A. H. de Oliveira. *A History of Portugal, Vol 1*. New York: Columbia University Press, 1972.

Marr, Phebe. *The Modern History of Iraq*, 2nd Edition. Boulder, CO: Westview Press, 2004.

Marriot, J. A. R. and Charles Grant Robertson. *The Evolution of the Prussian State*. Oxford: Clarendon Press, 1946.

Massing, Michael. "The Volunteer Army: Who Fights and Why?" *New York Review of Books*, April 3, 2008.

Mazower, Mark. *Dark Continent: Europe's Twentieth Century*. New York: Knopf, 1999.

McChrystal, General Stanley. *Team of Teams: New Rules of Engagement for a Complex World*. New York: Penguin Random House, 2015.

McFate, Sean. *The Modern Mercenary: Private Armies and What They Mean for World Order*. Oxford: Oxford University Press, 2014.

McNeill, William H. *The Rise of the West: A History of the Human Condition*. Chicago: University of Chicago Press, 1963.

_____. *The Pursuit of Power: Technology, Armed Force, and Society since A.D. 1000*. Chicago: University of Chicago Press, 1984.

_____. *Keeping Together in Time: Dance and Drill in Human History*. Cambridge, MA: Harvard University Press, 1995.

McPherson, James M. *The War That Forged a Nation: Why the Civil War Still Matters*. New York: Oxford University Press, 2015.

Migdal, Joel S. *Strong Societies and Weak States: State Society Relations and State Capabilities in the Third World*. Princeton, NJ: Princeton University Press, 1988.

Miller, Paul D. *Armed State Building: Confronting State Failure, 1898–2012*. Ithaca, NY: Cornell University Press, 2013.

Morris, Ian. *War! What Is It Good For? Conflict and the Progress of Civilization from Primates to Robots*. New York: Farrar, Straus & Giroux, 2014.

Moskos, Charles C., John Allen Williams, and David R. Segal (eds.). *The Post-Modern Military: Armed Forces after the Cold War*. Oxford/New York: Oxford University Press, 2000.

Mosse, George L. *Fallen Soldiers: Reshaping the Memory of the World Wars*. Oxford: Oxford University Press, 1990.

Mueller, John. *Retreat from Doomsday: The Obsolescence of Major War*. New York: Basic Books, 1989.

_____. *The Remnants of War*. Ithaca, NY: Cornell University Press, 2004.

_____. *War and Ideas*. London and New York: Routledge, 2011.

Nieman, Michael. "War Making and State Making in Central Africa." *Africa Today*, 53 (No. 3), 2007, pp. 20–39.

Nowell, Charles E. *A History of Portugal*. New York: Van Nostrand, 1952.

Opello, Walter C., Jr., and Stephen J. Rosow. *The Nation-State and Global Order: A Historical Introduction to Contemporary Politics*. Boulder, CO: Lynne Rienner, 2004.

Oppenheimer, Franz. *The State: Its History and Development Viewed Historically*. Indianapolis, IN: Bobbs-Merrill, Co., 1914.

Osiander, Andreas. *The States System of Europe, 1640–1990: Peacemaking and the Internal Conditions of Society*. Oxford: Clarendon Press, 1994.

Painter, Sidney. *The Rise of the Feudal Monarchies*. Ithaca, NY: Cornell University Press, 1951.

Panda, Ankit. "Article 9 of Japan's Constitution: Nobel Peace Prize Laurate Material?" *The Diplomat*, April 25, 2014. Accessed from http:// www. thediplomat.com//2014/04 article-9-of-japan's-constitution-nobel-peace-prize-laurate-material/

Parker, Geoffrey. *The Military Revolution*. Cambridge: Cambridge University Press, 1989.

_____. (ed.) *The Cambridge Illustrated History of Warfare: The Triumph of the West*. Cambridge: Cambridge University Press, 1995.

Payne, James L. *A History of Force*. Sandpoint, ID: Lyntton Publishing, 2004.

Payne, Stanley G. *A History of Spain and Portugal Vol. 1*. Madison, WI: University of Wisconsin Press, 1973.

Peters, B. Guy. *European Politics Reconsidered*. New York: Holmes & Meier, 1991.

Pincus, Steven C. A. *1688: The First Modern Revolution*. New Haven, CT: Yale University Press, 2009.

Pinker, Steven. *The Better Angels of Our Nature: Why Violence Has Declined*. New York: Viking, 2011.

Poggi, Gianfranco. *The Development of the Modern State: A Sociological Introduction*. Stanford, CA: Stanford University Press, 1978.

Porter, Bruce D. *War and the Rise of the State: The Military Foundations of Modern Politics*. New York: Free Press, 1994.

Press, Eyal. "Israel's Holy Warriors." *New York Review of Books*, April 29, 2010.

Pye, Lucian W., *Communications and Political Development*. Princeton, NJ: Princeton University Press, 1963.

Pye, Lucian W. and Sidney Verba (eds.). *Political Culture and Political Development*. Princeton, NJ: Princeton University Press, 1965.

Reno, William. "War, Markets, and the Reconfiguration of West Africa's Weak States." *Comparative Politics*, 29 (No. 4), 1997, pp. 493–510.

_____. *Warlord Politics and African States*. Boulder, CO: Lynne Rienner, 1998.

Ricks, Thomas E. "A Widening Gap between the Military and Society." *Atlantic Monthly*, July 1997, pp. 66–68.

_____. *The Generals: American Military Command from World War II to Today*. New York: Penguin, 2012.

Riley-Smith, Jonathan (ed.). *The Oxford Illustrated History of the Crusades*. Oxford: Oxford University Press, 1997.

Roberts, J. M. *A History of the World*. New York: Viking Penguin, 1983.

Rodgers, Clifford J. (ed.). *The Military Revolution Debate: Readings on the Military Transformation of Early Modern Europe*. Boulder, CO: Westview Press, 1995.

Rosow, Stephen J. and Jim George. *Globalization and Democracy*. Lanham, MD: Rowman & Littlefield, 2015.

Rotberg, Robert I. (ed.). *State Failure and State Weakness in a Time of Terror*. Washington, DC: Brookings Institution Press, 2003.

_____. (ed.). *When States Fail: Causes and Consequences*. Princeton, NJ: Princeton University Press, 2004.

Roth, Kenneth. "What Rules Should Govern US Drone Attacks?" *The New York Review of Books*, April 4, 2013.

Rothman, Stanley. *European Society and Politics*. Indianapolis: Bobbs-Merrill, 1970.

Rowen, Herbert H. *The King's State: Proprietary Dynasticism in Early Modern France*. New Brunswick, NJ: Rutgers University Press, 1980.

Russell, Jeffery Burton. *Medieval Civilization*. New York: John Wiley, 1968.

Saouli, Adham. *The Arab State: Dilemmas of Late Formation*. London/New York: Routledge, 2013.

Scarry, Elaine. *Thermonuclear Monarchy: Choosing between Democracy and Doom*. New York/London: W. W. Norton, 2014.

Schevill, Ferdinand. *A History of Europe from the Reformation to the Present Day*. New York: Harcourt, Brace, 1930.

Schmidt, Brian C. *The Political Discourse of Anarchy: A Disciplinary History of International Relations*. Albany: State University of New York Press, 1998.

Schmitt, Carl. *The Concept of the Political*. Expanded Edition. Chicago: University of Chicago Press, 1996.

Schwarz, Rolf. *War and State Building in the Middle East*. Gainesville: University Press of Florida, 2011.

Seward, Desmond. *The Monks of War: The Military-Religious Orders*. London: Archon Books, 1972.

Sharlet, Jeff. "Jesus Killed Mohammed." *Harper's Magazine*, May 2009.

Shaw, Martin. *Dialectics of War: An Essay in the Social Theory of Total War and Peace*. London: Pluto, 1988.

_____. *Post-Military Society: Militarism, Demilitarization and War at the End of the Twentieth Century*. Philadelphia: Temple University Press, 1991.

_____. *The New Western Way of War: Risk-Transfer War and Its Crisis in Iraq*. Cambridge: Polity Press, 2005.

Sheehan, James J. *Where Have All the Soldiers Gone? The Transformation of Modern Europe*. Boston/New York: Houghton Mifflin, 2008.

Simms, Brendan. *Europe: The Struggle for Supremacy from 1453 to the Present*. New York: Basic Books, 2013.

Singer, Peter J. *Wired for War: The Robotics Revolution and Conflict in the Twenty-First Century*. New York: Penguin, 2011.

Sire, H. J. A. *The Knights of Malta*. New Haven, CT: Yale University Press, 1994.

Skocpol, Theda. *Protecting Soldiers and Mothers: The Political Origins of Social Policy in the United States*. Cambridge, MA: Harvard University Press, 1992.

Slim, Hugo. *Killing Civilians: Method, Madness, and Morality*. London: Hurst, 2008.

Smith, Rupert. *The Utility of Force: The Art of War in the Modern World*. New York: Random House, 2008.

Snyder, Timothy. *Bloodlands: Europe between Hitler and Stalin*. New York: Basic Books, 2010.

Sobeck, David. *The Causes of War*. Cambridge: Polity Press, 2009.

Sorensen, Georg. "War and State-Making: Why Doesn't It Work in the Third World?" *Security Dialog* 32 (No. 3), September 2001, pp. 341–54.

Spruyt, Hendrik. *The Sovereign State and Its Competitors: An Analysis of Systems Change*. Princeton, NJ: Princeton University Press, 1994.

Stahl, Roger. "Have You Played the War on Terror?" *Critical Studies in Media and Communication*, 23 (No. 2), June 2006, pp. 112–30.

Stillman, Sarah. "The Invisible Army." *New Yorker*, June 6, 2011.

Stoessinger, John G. *Why Nations Go to War*. Tenth Edition. Belmont, CA: Thompson-Wadsworth, 2008.

Strachan, Hew, and Sibylle Scheipers (eds.). *The Changing Character of War*. Oxford: Oxford University Press, 2011.

Strayer, Joseph R. *Feudalism*. New Bruswick, NJ: Krieger Publishing, 1965.

_____. *On the Medieval Origins of the Modern State*. Princeton, NJ: Princeton University Press, 1970.

Swedburg, Richard (ed.). *The Economics and Sociology of Capitalism*. Princeton, NJ: Princeton University Press, 1991.

Tarrow, Sidney. *War, States, and Contention: A Comparative Historical Study*. Ithaca, NY: Cornell University Press, 2015.

Taylor, Brian D., and Roxana Botea. "Tilly-Tally: War-Making and State-Making in the Contemporary World." *International Studies Review*, 10 (No. 1), March 2008, pp. 27–56.

Thies, Cameron G. "War, Rivalry, and State Building in Latin America." *American Journal of Political Science*, 49 (No. 3), July 2005, pp. 451–65.

_____. "Public Violence and State Building in Central America." *Comparative Political Studies* 39, (No. 10), 2006, pp. 1,263–82.

_____. "The Political Economy of State-Making in Sub-Saharan Africa." *The Journal of Politics*, 69 (No. 3), August 2007, pp. 716–31.

Thompson, W. R., and K. Rasler. "War, the Military Revolution(s) Controversy, and Army Expansion: A Test of Two Explanations of Historical Influence on European State Making." *Comparative Political Studies*, 32 (No. 1), 1999, pp. 3–31.

Thomson, David. *Europe since Napoleon*. 2nd Edition. New York: Knopf, 1962.

Thomson, Janice E. *Mercenaries, Pirates, and Sovereigns: State Building and Extraterritorial Violence in Early Modern Europe*. Princeton, NJ: Princeton University Press, 1994.

Tilly, Charles. *The Formation of National States in Western Europe*. Princeton, NJ: Princeton University Press, 1975.

_____. *Coercion, Capital, and European States, AD 990–1990*. Cambridge, MA: Basil Blackwell, 1990.

Tilly, Charles, and Wim P. Blockmans (eds.). *Cities and the Rise of States in Europe: AD 1000 to 1800*. Boulder, CO: Westview Press, 1994.

Titmuss, Richard M. *Essays on the Welfare State*. 2nd Edition. Boston: Beacon Press, 1963.

Treitschke, Heinrich von. *Origins of Prussianism*. London: George Allen and Unwin, 1942.

Young, Crawford. *The African Colonial State in Comparative Perspective*. New Haven, CT: Yale University Press, 1994.

Young, Crawford, and Thomas Turner. *The Rise and Decline of the Zairian State*. Madison: University of Wisconsin Press, 1985.

Vasquez, John A. *The War Puzzle Revisited*. Cambridge: Cambridge University Press, 2009.

van Creveld, Martin. *Technology and War*. New York: Free Press, 1989.

_____. *The Rise and Decline of the State*. Cambridge: Cambridge University Press, 1999.

_____. *The Changing Face of War: Lessons in Combat from the Marne to Iraq*. New York: Ballantine Books, 2006.

Väyrynen, Raimo. *The Waning of Major War: Theories and Debates*. London/New York: Routledge, 2013.

Vincent, Andrew. *Theories of the State*. Oxford: Basil Blackwell, 1987.

Vu, Tong. "Studying the State through State Formation." *World Politics* 62 (No. 1), January 2010, pp. 148–75.

Wagner, R. Harrison. *War and the State: The Theory of International Politics*. Ann Arbor: University of Michigan Press, 2007.

Waltz, Kenneth N. *Man, the State and War: A Theoretical Analysis*. New York: Columbia University Press, 1954.

Weber, Cynthia. *Simulating Sovereignty: Intervention, the State and Symbolic Exchange*. Cambridge: Cambridge University Press, 1995.

Webster, Graham. *The Roman Imperial Army*. 3rd Edition. Totowa, NJ: Barnes and Noble, 1985.

Weiss, L. "War, the State, and the Origins of the Japanese Employment System." *Politics and Society*, 21 (No. 3), 1993, pp. 323–54.

Weltman, John D. *World Politics and the Evolution of War*. Baltimore, MD: Johns Hopkins University Press, 1994.

Westney, Eleanor. *Imitation and Innovation: The Transfer of Western Organizational Patterns in Meiji Japan*. Cambridge, MA: Harvard University Press, 2000.

White, Lynn, Jr. *Medieval Technology and Social Change*. Oxford: Oxford University Press, 1962.

Wright, Quincy. *A Study of War*. Abridged. Chicago/London: University of Chicago Press, 1964.

Wills, Gary. *Bomb Power: The Modern Presidency and the National Security State*. New York: Penguin, 2010.

Zacher, Mark W. "The Territorial Integrity Norm: International Boundaries and the Use of Force." *International Organization*, 55, (No. 2), Spring 2001, pp. 215–50.

Zaidi, Syed Ali Raza, *et al*. "War Making and State Making in Pakistan." *South Asian Studies* 29 (No. 2), July–December 2014, pp. 379–94.

Zartman, I. William. *Collapsed States*. Boulder, CO: Lynne Rienner, 1995.

Zeitlin, Maurice (ed.). *Political Power and Social Theory: A Research Annual* Vol 1. Greenwich, CT: JAI Press, 1980.

Zieger, Robert H. *America's Great War: World War I and the American Experience*. Lanham, MD: Rowman & Littlefield, 2000.

Index

About the Author

Walter C. Opello Jr. was born on July 13, 1941, in Aguadilla, Puerto Rico, where his father, then serving in the United States Army Air Corps, was stationed. After graduating from Newburgh Free Academy (New York) in 1959, he attended the University of Colorado, Boulder, receiving his BA in 1963 with a major in anthropology. Upon graduation he was commissioned a second lieutenant in the United States Marine Corps. He completed the active-duty portion of his military obligation in 1966 with the rank of captain and returned to his alma mater to do graduate work in political science. After earning his PhD in 1973, he was a research associate at the Comparative Development Studies Center, the State University of New York at Albany, until 1976, when he joined the Department of Political Science at the University of Mississippi. During his eleven years at Ole Miss, he attained the rank of professor, was twice a Fulbright scholar to Portugal, and published numerous articles and several books on the liberation movements in the Portuguese colonies and on Portugal's transition to democratic government. In 1987 he left Ole Miss to become the chair of the Department of Political Science at the State University of New York at Oswego, where he remained until his retirement in 2015.

While at Oswego, he began to work on historical studies of the state and the role of war in its formation and transformation. During his years at Oswego, he authored (with Stephen J. Rosow) *The Nation-State and Global Order: A Historical Introduction to Contemporary Politics* (1999, 2004), and with his daughter, Katherine A. R. Opello-Giblet, *European Politics: The Making of Democratic States* (2009). While at Oswego, he also served as the associate provost for international programs from 2002 until 2007 and directed the global and international studies major from 2008 until 2014.

Since retiring, he and his wife, Olivia, divide their time between their home in Fayetteville, New York, and their apartment in Louvain-la-Neuve, Belgium, where their daughter, and his co-author, lives and teaches at the Université Catholique de Louvain (UCL). He is currently an associated researcher at UCL's Centre d'étude des crises et des conflits internationaux (CECRI).

CPSIA information can be obtained at www.ICGtesting.com
Printed in the USA
BVOW08s1203141016

465076BV00001B/1/P